D1118910

KIALOA
US-1

DARE TO WIN
IN BUSINESS | IN SAILING | IN LIFE

JIM KILROY

SEAPOINT BOOKS

AN IMPRINT OF SMITH/KERR ASSOCIATES LLC

KITTERY, MAINE

WWW.SMITHKERR.COM

Distributed to the trade by National Book Network
Generous quantity discounts are available through Smith/Kerr Associates LLC,
One Government Street, Suite 1, Kittery, Maine 03904 (207) 703-2314
or www.SmithKerr.com

Copyright © 2012 by John B. (Jim) Kilroy

All rights are reserved. No part of this book may be reproduced or transmitted
in any form by any means, electronic or mechanical, including photocopying and
recording, or by any information storage or retrieval system, without written
permission from the publisher. Request for permission should be directed
to Smith/Kerr Associates LLC, One Government Street, Suite 1, Kittery,
Maine 03904 USA.

Cataloging-in-publication data is on file at the Library of Congress.

ISBN-10 0-9830622-5-0
ISBN-13 978-0-9830622-5-7

Cover and book design by Claire MacMaster | Barefoot Art Graphic Design
Printed in China through Printworks International

Contents

A Daring Life, Fully Lived

by Herb McCormick

To declare that Jim Kilroy has lived a full, challenging, interesting and accomplished life is to traffic in understatement. It's like saying Alaska is a large state, or the Pacific a wide ocean. It diminishes the adjectives. It's also inaccurate.

For Jim Kilroy has actually experienced a wide range of different but equally successful existences: family man, veteran, developer, businessman, athlete, civic leader, political insider, adventurer, yachtsman. For most men, what Kilroy has achieved in any one of those many pursuits might be considered a singular highlight in a life well lived. For Jim, they are but the sum parts of a mighty whole.

My own first encounter with Jim Kilroy wasn't exactly with the man himself but with a group of select fellows who would—and did—follow him to some of the farthest and most remote places on the planet, the watery parts of the world and the distant islands and shorelines that dotted them. I'm speaking, of course, of the crews of a series of the most respected and triumphant ocean racers in the history of competitive yacht racing, all of which were called *KIALOA*.

The *KIALOA* sailors that I encountered at Antigua Sailing Week in 1982 were, quite frankly, some of the coolest characters one could ever hope to meet. Tanned, salty, grinning, assured—and all bedecked in the red *KIALOA* t-shirts that they wore proudly, like a badge of honor—they laughed heartily and spoke in all sorts of regional twangs from South Auckland, South Sydney, Southern California and so on. That is, they were a happy presence at yacht club bars and regatta parties every time they were ashore. At sea, though they still enjoyed a good joke amongst themselves, they were no jokers. They were skilled, nononsense mariners who sailed not for money but because they loved to sail. And they were winners. Man, were they winners.

In sailing circles, the best sailors are often referred to as "rock stars." I think the first real rock stars, the origins of the species, if you will, were the crews of *KIALOA*. I've also spent a good part of my life at sea, and while I've fulfilled many of many sailing goals, I do have one major regret: I never wore one of those faded red *KIALOA* t-shirts.

In fact, it wasn't until many years after Jim had retired from competitive offshore racing that we did meet, near his winter home in Punta del Este, Uruguay, while I was in the midst of a long voyage of my own. We naturally shared a love of the sea but as it turned out, we also both enjoyed writing and telling stories. As Jim would surely say, it's part of the Irish in us.

In any event, one thing led to another, and Jim asked my advice in looking over the book, "Dare to Win", that you now hold in your hands. It's been a pleasure, and an honor. It's also been a surprise. I knew I'd learn a good deal about the fascinating world of high-stakes, Grand Prix yachting. I didn't realize I'd receive so many important lessons about life.

"Dare to Win" is a lot of things: a coming-of-age story, a sailing yarn, a biography. It's also an in-depth analysis of the boom in Southern California real estate and development; a back-room tale about the fall of one sometimes misunderstood American politician, Barry Goldwater, and the rise of two other Republicans who went on to rewrite history, Richard Nixon and Ronald Reagan; and a memoir of a self-made man who served his country and community in countless ways, and how and why he did it.

It's also about Alaska and Ireland and Hawaii and the Mediterranean and the South Seas. In other words, it's a pretty darn good travel book.

Finally, however, Jim Kilroy's remarkable journey, as related in "Dare to Win", is both an object lesson on how to succeed and a window on a remarkable era. Through it all, there's a common thread, even a philosophy, about how to approach our days and years, and also how to maximize and enjoy them. As it turns out—as Jim explains while recounting his own remarkable journey in these pages—sailing is a pretty good metaphor for life itself.

Turn the page. You'll see.

A sixth-generation native of Newport, Rhode Island, Herb McCormick has been racing and cruising from above the Arctic Circle to Antarctica—and chronicling his adventures and travels in magazines, newspapers, and on the Internet—for over three decades. The former editor-in-chief of Cruising World *magazine and yachting correspondent for* The New York Times, *McCormick has notched over 75,000 offshore miles in his sailing career, including the historic 2009-2010 Around the Americas expedition that circumnavigated North and South America via the Northwest Passage and Cape Horn. An award-winning journalist, his stories and articles have earned numerous First Place prizes in Boating Writers International's annual writing contest. He is also the author of three books, including an anthology,* Gone to the Sea, *and* One Island, One Ocean, *about the voyage Around the Americas.*

Preface

The chapters of this book will present the outstanding sailboat racing records of the five *KIALOA*s against the world's most competitive yachts and crews. These results were the foundation for the award of sail number US-1 by US Sailing, the nation's sailboat racing authority, to the *KIALOA*s and their owner-racing skipper.

The first three *KIALOA*s were also great cruising yachts, visiting the oceans of the world. *KIALOA IV* and *KIALOA V* were not required to have cruising capabilities.

KIALOA II and *KIALOA III* were also fairly close in their high percentage of victories; however, *KIALOA III* sailed in more international competitions and could be more closely analyzed for racing results.

KIALOA III is recognized throughout the world for winning many major races and is said by international sailors to be the winningest yacht in yachting history. As you read this book, consider the challenges and the results: The first to finish victories, the record setting victories, and the handicap corrected time victories against smaller and larger yachts. We who raced *KIALOA III*—our all-amateur crew, and me, their captain and primary helmsman—were thrilled with her results and recognized throughout the world.

KIALOA II, III, IV and *V* were crowned as world champions both in day and longer distance races, winning almost all the most challenging races in the world. I say "almost" because we never did win the Fastnet Race, the 605-mile race to Fastnet Rock in the Irish Sea, having several "almosts." However, an "almost" doesn't count.

The formation of the International Class "A" Yachting Association (ICAYA) for maxi yachts—the purpose of which was so we could race together for better defined competition, particularly for handicap results, as we all sailed in the same conditions—was another great series for the *KIALOA*s, especially *KIALOA III, IV* and *V*. *KIALOA III* only sailed in one ICAYA year as our racing was being turned over to our new *KIALOA IV*, which had been rigorously test sailed against *KIALOA III*, and would now become our cruising boat.

During the active years of racing *KIALOAs*, I was frequently asked, "What was your favorite race?" or "What was the most important race?" My quick answer was always, "The next race," and this was a sincere response. It was essential to consider how we would prepare for each succeeding race as they were always new challenges, frequently with new competitors, and all the variables that go with Grand Prix sailing. As always, time was short with family activities, business activities and community activities, which I have tried to set forth in this account of my life.

When we did look back, it was mainly to review our mistakes, or what I would call "winning failures," focusing on how or why the mistake was made. In essence, the idea was to turn yesterday's failure into a future success. Now that time has gone by and I look back at the *KIALOA* racing days, I can see opportunities that were missed, and mistakes that were not capitalized on, at least not fully. I do wish to emphasize that we all learn from our failures, which are the foundation of success.

Even now, today, when I am asked, "What was your favorite race?" or "What was the most important race?", I still cannot provide a true answer. I enjoyed them all: the frustrating light-air races (a tremendous challenge of concentration), the ones conducted in heavy-air and seas (again a tremendous challenge of concentration), and all the races in between (always a tremendous challenge of leadership).

Leadership is not being obviously dominant. It is not being hard on your crew. It is a show of strength in maximizing the talent and participation of all of those aboard, with a common focus on the primary objective, sailing hard and fast, and managing the variable weather and sea conditions.

As I now look back at the prior years of racing and crew participation, I am satisfied and amazed at what the series of *KIALOAs* have accomplished, the high percentage of overall races won, the many 2nd and 3rd positions, and all the class victories in addition to the overall victories.

Perhaps I should clarify class victories in comparison to overall race victories. Overall race victories mean the lowest corrected time after handicap allowances are adjusted between all larger and smaller yachts. Larger yachts sail faster than smaller yachts (at least that's the practical theory) and smaller yachts are given time allowance credits. A further anomaly is that in races of more than just a few miles, large and small yachts may be sailing in different wind, sea and tidal conditions due to speed differentials. All of these features make victories more complicated. We'll delve into more detail on these matters as the book progresses.

I now look back and ask myself, "How did the *KIALOA*s do? How successful were our yachts, our all-amateur crews, our personal performance, our skills and strategy?" Authoritative sources have stated that *KIALOA III* and the *KIALOA* campaigns in general have been the most successful ocean racing yachts in history.

But *KIALOA III* is probably the standard by which all the others were measured, especially in the year 1977: Four major international race victories, record-setting performances and the award as the World's Ocean Racing Championship (which we all won in '75 and '76). You will read about our challenges, and our victories, in the following pages.

As you read this book, however, you'll discover that it is not just about yachting. It is about living. It is about accepting responsibility and participating in issues of great importance to your community, to your children and those of the future.

The beauty of sailboat racing is that you never have all of the answers. You continue to learn new ideas and different techniques, to challenge the variables of the sea and the winds of life.

It's difficult to describe how a few inches of sail trim, or a small adjustment of sail pressure, tuned to the rhythm of the sea, even in stormy conditions, may increase your yacht's speed. But it's true.

In much the same way, with equally small adjustments, opportunity always exists. Even in nasty, stormy seas there is rhythm and counter rhythm before you…just as in life. Take my advice and find the rhythm of the seas with your fellow sailors, the sailors of your life. To be successful, one must adjust to the variables of life and the sea, always trying new ideas, a new rhythm or a counter rhythm. I frequently sing for the rhythm—and focus—it brings me in heavy-weather conditions.

As is life, sailing is a sport of skill, of planning, navigation, technology, patience, and participation, fully joined by those who are with you: your crew, your partners.

The success we enjoyed on our *KIALOA*s was founded upon the spirit of motivation, the will to learn from each other, the acceptance and correction of mistakes, and the full challenge of the Seas of Life! This is our story:

A STORY OF TEAMWORK

A STORY OF PARTICIPATION

A STORY OF MOTIVATION

And, of course, A STORY OF POSITIVE LEADERSHIP

We invite you to join us.

 # From the Author

To Our Crew and Friends of *KIALOA*,

In writing these chapters about the five *KIALOA*s, we have tried to be exceedingly careful about the accuracy of all data and race results. When one considers that racing results and comments go back to the early 1950s, there must be some margin of error. If there are errors, they are not intentional errors.

I have been amazed at the total amount of data, newspaper and magazine articles, race instructions, crew lists, photographs, letters and other technical data in our files.

I have also tried to be most careful in the use of names of crew for each race or event. I could have used many more names in my commentary on each race, and each event. My reluctance to use more names has been the fear of excluding those who contributed equally to each event or chapter.

The *KIALOA* crew have all been part of the world-wide *KIALOA* family, teamwork and continuing friendship. I am humbled by their accomplishments.

We thank you all, *KIALOA* 1956–2005 and Memories

and all Crews

KIALOA Colors
The Red "T" Shirt

I have always been interested in self motivation, the small nuances of colors, of words, of sound, of the whistle of the train as it moves towards you, the red colors of the stars that move towards you, the motivation of music or the soothing of an Irish lullaby, the challenge and fun of attack as compared to that of defense.

KIALOA, in the Maxi fleet, intentionally had a slightly lower speed rating than our key competition, requiring *KIALOA* and crew to be in attack mode instead of defense mode. When first entering sailing competition our crew shirts were red, white or blue, our national colors—peaceful and non-challenging. A few of us talked and a question was raised: "Which shirts are the winning shirts?" To nobody's surprise it was the red shirts, the highly noticeable challenging shirts—a picture of power. We emphasized the ship's name *KIALOA* on one arm and the *KIALOA* logo on the back, highly identified on the dock or ashore—dynamic identification aboard.

This was motivation by the extension of the laws of physics—red means speed!

KV *Tom Whidden, Dennis Conner, Jim Kilroy. Covering from ahead, Sardinia.*

The "red-shirted" crew" aboard KIALOA V sharing a victory at Yacht Club Costa Smeralda, Porto Cervo, Sardinia.

1

I ask the reader to recognize the strength, the will,
and the love of my mother, willing to face all challenges
for her children and always in good humor.

And my father, his weakness overwhelmed his wonderful strengths,
my mother diluted the passage of such weakness to their children
and we cannot help but remember the beautiful singing of
Irish lullabies as we were placed in our beds by our father.

We had leadership, we had the strength of family love, we had
classical music and wonderful literature, with supplemental
home teaching, we were being prepared to meet the world,
and were taught creativity, all in good humor, with an optimistic view.

Growing Up
From Alaska, by Dogsled, to California

My given name is John Beresford Kilroy. As a young boy, my older brother and sister could not say "John Beresford Kilroy" or even "John Kilroy." I think the "Beresford" scared them. But they could say Jim Kilroy, which my mother accepted. In retrospect, like much of my life, "It just happened."

It has been suggested by friends who know me well that I start this book by recalling the horrors of a vicious storm at sea, such as experienced in the 1975 Transatlantic Race, the 1977 Sydney to Hobart Race or the 1979 Fastnet Race. Yes, these races were contested in severe conditions; in some instances lives were lost and many boats suffered damage, including the version of *KIALOA* that we were campaigning at the time. But all of these situations are typical of the many problems we face in everyday living. Based upon each individual's lifetime experiences, the thresholds or perceptions between what constitutes a "good" or a "bad" condition are very different in much of life.

And for that reason, I would like to begin by telling you a little about mine.

My father, George Fredrick Kilroy, was a talented Irishman, educated at Trinity College in Dublin, who possessed great skills in literacy, poetry and the telling of wonderful Irish tales. He was a strong advocate for a free Irish Republic. The Kilroy family, from Schull in County Cork, Ireland, eventually moved en masse to South Africa in opposition to the English control of Ireland. Overcome by emotional foolishness, they decided to fight with the Boers against the English.

After the Boers' defeat at the hands of the Brits, the men of the family left South Africa for the United States, and my father ended up in Alaska as a principal in the ownership and operation of a gold-mining dredge. He became a very successful gold miner. He soon met and married my mother, Rowena Lewis Kilroy, who had moved to Nome, Alaska, at a young age with her mother and brothers after her father died in South Dakota.

Despite his successes, my father had three basic problems: 1. He was Irish. 2. He couldn't drink alcohol. 3. He couldn't gamble when he was drunk. He lost the entire family fortune three times before my mother finally said, "Out of Alaska!" The year was 1925, and I was almost three-and-a-half years old, living with my family in Ruby, an Athabascan Indian village along the Yukon River.

The "out of Alaska" decree was easier said than done. To meet my father in Fairbanks, about 180 miles to the east, my mother had to set forth from Ruby on two dogsleds, traveling along the Yukon River with three children. One sled contained my older brother and sister, and was "mushed" by an Indian guide. I was on the other dogsled, which also carried our food and the dogs' food. This sled was "mushed" by my mother. I still have a photograph of her with the loaded dogsleds before she left Ruby, a very strong and determined woman moving her brood to a better future on an epic journey in the middle of an Alaskan winter.

Having left Alaska at such an early age, I have no remembrance of the place. My first memory is of being in Berkeley, California; then watching a cattle drive in Arizona; and finally, relocating to the strong blue-collar Los Angeles neighborhood of Walnut Park, between South Gate and Huntington Park, and attending the third grade.

In 1930, after several years working as a journalist and writer, my father decided that he couldn't stand civilization and left, deserting his family purportedly to work in New York. Actually, he ended up back in Alaska and the Northwest. We saw him a few times over the years. He never financially supported his family, and we later learned that his departure signaled the beginning of a long-term depression.

To make ends meet, my mother found a job working at night as a telephone operator at the *Los Angeles Daily News*, which was a rival to *The Los Angeles Times* in 1930. We would see her briefly during the day and on weekends. I was eight, my brother, Walter, almost 12 and my sister, Shirley, 10. My brother and I found jobs doing many things and contributed our small earnings to the household.

We became quite ingenious at finding and creating jobs. We mowed lawns and sold subscriptions to *Liberty* magazine and other periodicals and newspapers. We stuffed and delivered papers, as did so many children, for the *Huntington Park Signal*. We worked in bicycle shops repairing and building bicycles. During Christmas, at the Famous Department Store, I would spoke the bicycle wheels, building them on a piecework basis. I loved this arrangement, because I could make more money than working at a fixed hourly rate.

We worked in stores and restaurants because they not only paid a wage; they had food that supplemented our diet. When we needed clothes, we would find some way to work at a clothing store in exchange for clothing.

We were all avid readers of science, historical novels, non-fiction history and exploration, and we received strong support and guidance from our teachers. I'll always be grateful for that. They gave me extra books to read, extra work to do, extra papers to write, all of which I enjoyed. When I was in third grade, I was accelerated to the fourth grade, which ultimately allowed me to graduate from high school one month after my seventeenth birthday. Fortunately, I was a pretty big kid and able to handle the guff given to me by older students.

The desire to work, to read and to push ourselves was instilled in us by our mother, who challenged us on our individual responsibilities with the following thought:

"There is a God-given purpose in your creation. You have the obligation to fulfill this purpose by doing all that you can to succeed, to be successful and to be considerate of others, for if you do, you take others with you."

When I recall that photograph of my mother in command of a dogsled in a harsh Alaskan winter, the question was obvious, "How could we fail to meet this challenge?"

As to the thresholds of challenge, I have always remembered one challenge that I failed, even though I was well prepared. It was my junior year in high school, and I was asked to give a speech in the main auditorium before the entire student body. I spoke so rapidly that most of the students could not understand me. It was a great lesson: slow down, speak slowly and clearly, watch the eyes of your audience, try to command their attention. Yes, I did get teased, but I took it with a smile because of what I learned. After this gaffe, I felt much more comfortable speaking to a group.

Sports were also important, and we were also fortunate to compete in high school and college athletics. In track, I ran the high and low hurdles, and on the basketball team I played power forward. For many years I held our league records. In slightly different words, but with the same meaning, the head coach of South Gate High School, Barkham Garner, preached the same philosophy as our mother. He did this not just for us but for lots of young men that he coached, and he became a surrogate father to many of us. We treasured him dearly.

(As an aside, shortly after World War II, many of Coach Garner's former athletes, including me, became involved in a foundation named after him to provide scholarship funds to needy South Gate High School students, an institution that still exists over 70 years after our high school graduation. My speech to the Barkham Garner Foundation in the 1990s is included on the website KIALOA-US1.com.)

Coach Garner wasn't the only person who helped guide and shape us, and as I look back at my early years, I have a debt of gratitude to so many people and places: Santa Barbara State College, Douglas Aircraft, The U.S. Army Air Corps, and those who assisted me in building my own business. They all helped show me the way.

As I left high school, I narrowed college down to two choices: The University of Southern California or Santa Barbara State College. Both offered a scholarship, and each had a good engineering school. This was a tough choice, particularly as I had worked out and practiced track and field at USC during my junior and senior years in high school, and they treated me very well.

USC was big and in the city. Santa Barbara State was small and in the beautiful city of Santa Barbara, with its wonderful beaches and the Pacific Ocean. I had done a little surfing and sailed a few times, and I liked the idea of a small school. So, I selected Santa Barbara State College. It turned out to be a good choice.

Due to the lingering aftermath of the Depression, the scholarship to Santa Barbara State really meant jobs, and mine included working in restaurants as a "pearl diver" (dishwasher), and for the school in a job program called "NYA"—the National Youth Administration—where I graded test papers, proficiency tests and other tests. Since I knew many of the people whose tests I was grading, everything was confidential. However, it gave me great insight into measuring people and their approach to meeting challenges, as well as my own personal makeup and ability to meet such challenges.

It was now 1940; the war was upon us, or would be shortly. I had read Hitler's *Mein Kampf* and believed that he intended to do what he said. I was also mindful of the problems in Asia and China and was familiar with Japan's "Greater Asia Co-Prosperity Sphere." Japan, an emerging industrial giant, had no meaningful natural supply of energy, oil or minerals to fuel its ambitions. In essence, "The Greater Asia Co-Prosperity Sphere" meant that China and other Asian nations must subjugate themselves to Japan, or Japan would take them over militarily.

While still in high school, and later in college, I observed forces that were aligned against our American freedom and our Federated Republic. "Technocracy" was one word for it, "communism" another. At South Gate High and Santa Barbara State, I was exposed to teachers and professors supporting and advocating these concepts when they should have been teaching. In some cases, they convinced students I knew to become card-carrying members of the Communist Party.

Clearly, many divisive forces were challenging our nation. Again, it was the crucial and historic year of 1940; I was all of 18 years old and had completed my first year of college. And it was at that fateful intersection of time and history that I was offered a job at Douglas Aircraft, which included additional engineering training while on the job.

I was introduced to Donald Douglas, Sr., the company's founder and chairman, with whom I became better acquainted as time went by. "Doug," by the way, was an avid sailor. I was assigned to Douglas El Segundo—where the SBD Dauntless Navy Dive Bomber was designed and being built—first as the lead inspector in the receiving department, which also involved some outside manufacturing inspection, including the inspection of assembled materials and inspection control as they moved into production. I was told to introduce new ideas and possible production solutions to our chief inspector, Earl Luff; to our material controls manager, Denny Thorne; and to the renowned Douglas engineer, Ed Heineman. I did so, and fortunately for me, my suggestions worked and improved the inspection, material control and manufacturing process. Looking back, perhaps I was more of a conveyor of their ideas, and I was just the spark that ignited their solution. But I learned how to be a very good listener and ask a lot of questions. What an education!

While at Douglas, I rapidly moved up the corporate ladder and soon became the Assistant Chief Inspector/Special Projects, which meant I was assigned to many different activities. The SBD Dauntless Dive Bomber was the Navy's attack backbone; its capability was demonstrated in the Battle of Midway, where it was instrumental in destroying much of the Japanese aircraft-carrier attack fleet. The El Segundo plant had high production capacity along with a high remodel rate to address the needs for better, tougher, more capable battle aircraft.

Our team would have frequent meetings with Naval officers about performance and the need to make changes to strengthen certain components. On one occasion we had over 500 aircraft on the flight line that needed to be completed with a fly out over a weekend. I headed up the inspection team in coordination with the engineers to inspect and approve the airplanes for flight departure. In so many ways, it was a great challenge and opportunity.

Along with the officers, I met several engineers from Naval Procurement and many others who were visiting our beautiful state of California for the first time, who all commented on our excellent production capability and acknowledged that Southern California was the aerospace capital of the U.S. with unique concepts of design and manufacturing.

I also had occasion to visit many of our outside manufacturers and to understand their tooling and facility needs, and to observe that our outside manufacturers' facilities were fairly primitive and were in need of replacement. During this period, I met many individuals who became friends for years and lent me great help and advice. One was D.W. "Bud" Gardiner, who went on to become senior vice president of manufacturing for Douglas and remained a close friend as well as one of our *KIALOA* crew. He was also a co-partner in the company formed to build *KIALOA II* in the early 1960s. The other partners were Don Douglas, Jr., the president of Douglas Aircraft (and son of the chairman), and Kenny Watts, the talented and innovative sail maker.

As time passed, I was given other assignments and was named as the Douglas Aircraft Inspection Representative to the National Aircraft War Production Council. As a result, I met many of the stars of aircraft design and construction, and became better acquainted with Don Douglas, Sr.; Ski Kleinhaus, the great aerospace aerodynamics engineer; Lee Atwood, chief engineer and president of North American Aviation and designer of the P-51 Mustang; Jack Northrop, president of Northrop Aircraft; Ed "Hot Rod" Heinemen, chief designer of the AD series airplanes; and many, many others.

These friends and experiences became the foundation of my later life. So too did my ongoing education in manufacturing processes, the practicality and nuances of engineering and design, and an expanding understanding of Bernoulli's Theory of Fluid Dynamics. All of this strengthened my belief that California had become the center of the high-tech world and would need modern facilities and infrastructure to accommodate this new order.

I decided that I should experience the other side of the aircraft-manufacturing arena to further my overall knowledge as to how to proceed after the war. Confidential movies screened to the company by the military to lend us a better understanding of the "in field," combat flying application of the product convinced me that I needed a broader perspective, and so I decided to go active. So in 1944, I began active duty in the US Army Air Corps Reserve, which gave me additional, first-hand experience in flying and training. I was stationed in the Western Flying Training Command until the end of 1945, and my tour of duty ended, officially, in early 1946.

Once again, the subject of individual thresholds that limited the performance of some, but not others, was very interesting. I was particularly cognitive of this as we were training pilots for the Chinese Air Force, as well as for our own Air Corps. We are all individuals, for which we can thank our Lord and Creator, with different reactions, thresholds, thought processes and desires. How fortunate we are.

Regarding my future, I had made my decision. All of my experiences and self-searching questions told me that Southern California was the place to take the next step. It was the acknowledged center of the emerging high-tech and aerospace industries, and it was obvious to me that it would grow tremendously. Even though, historically speaking, California seemed remote, with punitive long-distance freight rates and other unfair charges, this fact is now recognized throughout the nation. But new, modern facilities were essential. The pros of the state's favorable climate; moderate temperatures; and productive, knowledgeable workers offset the cons of pulling up roots for businesses that had been ensconced on the Eastern seaboard. I had all the right ingredients and motivations to become involved: $165 in cash, a car, a wife and a child. And so, after the war, I went into the real estate business with an established firm, Sentinel Realty, in Inglewood, near both the Los Angeles International Airport (LAX) and the aircraft industry.

I kept in contact with my aerospace and manufacturing friends. I sold a few houses. I worked with banks that had taken over manufacturing plants and sold these facilities. In addition to making a commission, I was frequently involved with remodeling and modernizing the assets so the properties could be sold at favorable prices.

I joined a service club, the Kiwanis, and a young executive group, the 20-30 Club. I played golf to become acquainted with local businessmen and broaden my base of recognition. I became involved in the Los Angeles Chamber of Commerce and other community organizations, as well as a strong supporter of economically oriented political causes. Having studied the production process through the war, I expressed ideas on improving facilities and productivity based upon the fundamental manufacturing modules.

I worked with a builder and an architectural engineering organization to develop different facility concepts and to come up with a modular plan for different sizes of buildings. The idea was to have fewer columns and increased ceiling heights using standardized steel production lengths while refining cost controls. I took copies of these plans to my friends in the aerospace world and my acquaintances at banks and insurance company lenders and asked for their ideas as to how the designs should be modified. I received wonderful ideas for changes, which were incorporated into the plans, and I operated under the philosophy that there is nothing like being a "little pregnant." As these friends in the industry had a pre-existing need, they had "pre-designs" of buildings, which included their personal ideas and which could fit their requirements with only slight modifications. I had to include a site as well as obtain the funds to sell or lease the facility. All of this had been previously discussed with the potential lender and the most likely landowner. With a few negotiations and touch-ups, I could quickly put the lease or purchase package together, obtain the financing and provide rapid occupancy at favorable costs for a high-quality, productive asset.

After several successful projects, I bought 87% of the construction company I'd worked with, Coordinated Construction, for virtually no cash, as I already was their biggest client. Our team became ingenious at adapting new ideas, engineering solutions and planning procedures. Together, we developed land for projects with high restrictions on landscaping, design, architecture and so on, commonly called CC&R, which stands for Covenants, Conditions and Restrictions. Los Angeles County, the city of Los Angeles and many other communities accepted the concepts we established as their template for basic planning provisions.

Our clients became many of our old friends: North American Aviation, Douglas Aircraft, Northrop Aircraft, Electronic Industries, Curtiss Wright, Philco Ford Aeroneutronics, Hughes Aircraft and many, many others, particularly the emerging electronics businesses and other high-tech concerns.

By the early 1950s, now with substantial construction and development experience, I felt that I had a reliable team and business foundation and that I could responsibly delegate more details and become involved in additional activities. I eased back on the time-consuming game of golf and took up sailing.

I had surfed, both body surfing and board surfing, before World War II, and had learned to fly during and after the war. Surfing, flying and sailing had something in common: All three pursuits involved fluid dynamics, aerodynamics and hydrodynamics. I was enchanted by the combination, absolutely hooked. And Bernoulli's theorem and its relation to fluid dynamics at sea fascinated the engineer in me.

Sailing has the combination of three atmospheres: the high density of water, the low density of air, and the interface between the two, the waves atop the sea. A combination of three of the extreme forces! In sailing, we introduce the variables of designing and adjusting your own aerodynamic shapes – the sails – to fit the wind and the sea. It's much more complicated than flying…and as I was to learn, much more rewarding.

Actually, my first exposure to the sport had come many years before. When I was about 11, I was one of the winners in a contest to sell newspaper subscriptions for the *Huntington Park Signal* and earned a ride on the "old red car"—the Pacific Electric Railway—to Balboa Island off Newport Beach. We were given very brief instructions, put in a 12-foot Snowbird and allowed to sail for two hours. Incredible! I still cannot believe I didn't turn the boat upside down. This was my start in sailing, a sport that would begin to become my passion in the early 1950s. I never realized what a challenge it would be.

My Parents

My Mother: Rowena Lewis Kilroy (1887–1975)

A rock of love and foundation for her children's growth. Set guidelines with expressions and actions. Loved opera, music and poetry with all their expression of life's love and feelings. Emphasized the value of literature, history and communications as an essential to family growth and relationships. Simplified family communication through partnership in life, love and governance. Resourceful, with mutual respect and loving requirement for performance by her children, emphasized by her own positive actions. A great poker player, never for money or personal gain. Played her hands beautifully, observing personal actions and response. A wonderful training technique for her children, for response to the games of life and to consider the reactions of others. Firm, always loving. The guardian and leader of her flock. Yet, so tender, so sensitive, so loving. My soul, my life, is based upon this wonderful caring mother, her guidance and her challenges:

"There is a God-given purpose in your creation. You have a God-given obligation to fulfill this purpose. If successful, you carry others with you for the benefit of mankind."

Mother, I have tried. I am your child who loves his mother.

My Father: George Fredrick Kilroy (1875–1972)

Always a dreamer. Intelligent. Poetic. A great communicator. A life of fantasy. Irresponsible. An explorer; a boxer; a creative, technical thinker. Accomplished much —irresponsibly lost. Sang his children to sleep with Irish lullabies and loving words. Communicated with heart-warming poetry. Lost his way through alcohol. Lost his assets and dignity through alcohol and gambling…more than once and forever. Lost his family, also forever…except for the underlying love of children for a father.

My father, you gave me many things. By showing me your losses, you provided me with great choices. My father until I was eight. My father in dreams forever. I love my father.

2

The early 1950s provided a wonderful entry in the development
and ownership of high tech facilities. We commenced, constructed
and sold or leased 1,300,000 square feet of outstanding buildings
in less then fifteen months. We constructed and leased
272,000 square feet of high technology building adjacent to
LAX and completed phase 1 of the Airport Imperial office buildings
leasing to long term aerospace tenants. We identified our capabilities
in building, ownership and operating high tech facilities,
which set a path for future years.

Building a Business
Adjusting Thresholds:
1950–1960 and Beyond

In 1950, I attempted to buy, for development, sixty acres of well-located industrial land on a major corner near Northrop Aircraft and Los Angeles International Airport. My plan was to subdivide the property to a planned building development program and lease or sell the buildings. I offered the owner 25 percent cash and 75 percent as a mortgage to be repaid over five years as each parcel was developed. With the architects and engineers, we had prepared a fairly comprehensive development plan, and I thought we had a deal.

Suddenly, the property owner called and said he had an all-cash offer, the parties had agreed upon terms and they were now in escrow. I was shocked. I thought the owner and I had a fairly detailed understanding of my plans, and the final contract and escrow instructions were being drafted.

So, I pondered how to proceed. I discovered who the buyer was and his familiarity with land development. He had been involved in other projects as an investor where the land was bought, subdivided and then resold. His name was George Page, and he was the owner of a large fruit basket packing and sales organization called Mission Pak, a company that enjoyed very large sales at Christmas time and other holidays.

I called George Page, introduced myself and gave him the names of banks and other references to check on me. I told him that I was trying to buy and develop the property in question, to then lease or sell the buildings. I had design concepts and had drafted a financial analysis, and suggested that since he was in the process of buying the property, we should talk to see if we could find a common interest.

We did, and decided that we could work together under an arrangement where I would be the developer, the contractor and the broker, plus have an interest in the project.

My plan came together and was a huge success; in fact, it worked out better than I anticipated. There were many reasons it was so successful, one of which was that the land was unencumbered—no loan—and that we had preplanned the lot sizes and had preliminary plans for buildings to be developed. Also, the property was located in the County of Los Angeles, with no city jurisdiction. That meant we received instant approvals and cooperation, as we were well known and respected for the quality of our projects. Previously, Los Angeles County had incorporated into their planning ordinance the covenants, conditions and restrictions we imposed upon all of our projects—it was a large step forward in architectural, landscaping and parking requirements, and imposed restrictions upon unsuitable, noisy or otherwise dirty industries.

Additionally, several months earlier, I had been asked to attend a meeting with the president of Northrop Aircraft, an Air Force general in charge of procurement, and other aerospace executives to discuss lease terms and conditions for new buildings which could be acceptable to the Air Force, aerospace industry and to the real estate investment community. I was the sole representative for the real-estate interests. We negotiated terms for leases that were mutually acceptable to all parties, and drafted lease provisions to address how lease obligations would be charged in U.S. Air Force procurement contracts.

We had immediate demands to lease buildings in our project—the Crenshaw-El Segundo Industrial Park—which was designed in accordance with our latest, previously mentioned covenants, conditions and restrictions for architecture, landscaping, high-ratio parking and other value-enhancing details. We then acquired another 20 acres, and in 13 months we built and leased a series of high-quality buildings, containing over one million square-feet of floor area, to the aerospace industry as well as a diverse group of high-quality tenants.

This development was a great project and a tremendous success for all concerned. We developed an outstanding team, set forth a game plan, delegated authority and responsibility, and compensated our people accordingly.

As I look back at this project, it again brings up the issue of fixed or moving thresholds. My initial offer and proposed deal for the purchase of the land had been suddenly and even improperly rejected. Should my threshold have been to say, "Too bad, lost the deal," or become angry and commence legal action? No: too much time and too much expense. My response, instead, was, "Move the threshold. Make a deal with the new owner." And, it worked.

The lesson? Be positive. Adjust your threshold.

By then we were an active, integrated and highly efficient organization for development, construction, marketing and ownership, either on our own or performing these functions for others. Indeed, our construction company, Coordinated Construction, Inc., was now performing general contract work for other projects and developers, as well as for our own deals.

The philosophy was straightforward. We were actively involved in changing pre-existing ideas about engineering and design, and resolved that our buildings would maximize efficiency and incorporate the latest technology in structural and construction techniques, but also remain flexible enough to integrate top-quality electric and mechanical installations.

To that end, we soon became a leader in concrete, pre-cast, "tilt up" construction, with higher, wider panels in the floor plans that allowed more favorable column spacing.

For example, Northrop needed a new facility of about 72,000 square-feet near LAX and then another facility of 200,000 square-feet also near the airport, which we ultimately designed, built and leased to them. The smaller building was a basic, "high bay" warehouse. The larger facility was an exceedingly functional high bay, wide-column spacing, steel-girder concrete roof design with much more flexibility. It also included a two-story engineering office building. In view of the fact that it was used as a U.S. Air Force contract facility, we made the apparent architecture very "plain Jane" in appearance. However, it could readily be converted into an attractive office or high-tech facility, which we ultimately did. At the time of this writing in 2012, this facility has been continuously leased, with no vacancy, for over 50 years with only three major credit tenants. It is currently the design center for Mattel Toys, and they have extended their lease for another 15 years.

Time and again, we found that the LAX location was highly attractive and beneficial for local, national and international tenants. The south side of LAX bordered the city of El Segundo, with favorable tax rates and services, and only about 12,000 residents. El Segundo became the home for North American Aviation, Douglas-El Segundo's missile division, the Space and Communication Division of Hughes Aircraft, the Thompson Ramo Wooldridge Aerospace Corporation and many others. In 2012, the Kilroy Realty Corporation, a NYSE Corporation (KRC), still owned major office and high-tech facilities in El Segundo, along with many, many additional holdings in other locations.

As the business grew, we looked for new opportunities and growth areas. The key to expansion in the Los Angeles Central Basin and other areas was the emerging plan for freeway construction. Naturally, freeways had a great impact upon the San Fernando Valley, which was not part of the Central Basin and was primarily accessible by two passes: through the Santa Monica Mountains using smaller roadways, or via the Hollywood Freeway as the primary route through the Cahuenga Pass.

The Central Basin is the area from Santa Monica to Newport Beach along the Pacific Ocean, from Newport Beach to the mountains to the northwest, and back to Santa Monica. Downtown Los Angeles, at that time, was the hub for all of this original development.

The Santa Ana Freeway, emerging from downtown Los Angeles, was slowly being built to the southeast toward Anaheim and Santa Ana. The Harbor Freeway, to the south of the city, was being built and extended to the Hollywood Freeway. To get a better grasp on the geography, we obtained a plastic topographical map on which we painted the freeways and the mountains so we could better understand the ramifications and explain the benefits of certain areas to our prospective clients. I would fly the region in our Cessna-172, which we used to inspect locales, review traffic flows and assess the many variables of places we might want to develop.

As we were very close to the high-tech world—and the housing of their engineers, which were generally located within close proximity to the ocean—this factor became an important element in our marketing strategy. It was also obvious that housing growth would follow the Santa Ana Freeway and access to the freeway. This was where we centralized our land purchases, consistent with local roadways, utilities, drainage and other matters. We considered all locations as sub-market areas of larger, general markets, and kept on the lookout for "boutique" areas.

There were, of course, other factors to be considered: utilities, drainage and the cost of bringing subdivided site locations on stream were exceedingly important. Sewage and drainage always had to be considered; this applied to the invert of sewer systems and surface drainage of rainwater. We employed our own surveying and engineering group that would consider all of these issues before deciding how to proceed.

One unique situation was a parcel of 100-plus acres we considered acquiring in south Santa Ana; however, it had serious drainage problems, as did several hundreds of additional acres owned by others. The big issue was that the flow line, the invert, of the nearby San Gabriel River was too high, and although they were going to grade the flow line to a lower level, it would be still too high to drain this specific property.

We analyzed the small cost of lowering the invert of the river flow line compared to the savings in the overall development of the area and the economic benefits from these several hundred acres, which convinced the U.S. Corps of Engineers to agree to lower the river flow line. This saved us well over $500,000, while substantially enhancing the value of our property and the entire tract.

In the 1950s, we built and leased several buildings at the Santa Ana location, which were very well received. Within two or three years, we had increased the developed land value from a low cost to over $30,000 per acre. But then, in sudden, shocking fashion, the value plunged.

Our chief competitor in the area was the Irvine Company, which owned roughly 100,000 acres about two miles to the east of us. They were actively developing and selling homes and had just brought in a new president, Charles Thomas, the retired U.S. Secretary of the Navy. Irvine's real estate brokers convinced Charlie that they could sell more homes if they attracted more industry to the area, particularly on their property. So they reduced their industrial land price by 50 percent, to $15,000 per acre. As a further incentive, if a building were to be promptly constructed, they would give an option on an adjacent similar-sized property for five years at a price of $15,000 per acre (1950s prices).

It was an economic tragedy! I asked Charlie Thomas why he lowered the price since industrial or high-tech personnel who leased our buildings or purchased our property could buy Irvine homes equally, as well as those occupying Irvine property. Charlie's response was, "Since Irvine was an Old Spanish land grant, it had little or no-cost basis for their property," and they wanted to maximize income and growth now. There was nothing to do but accept this serious loss of value to our property and move our efforts elsewhere. Over the next few years, however, we did manage to make satisfactory lease deals and sales of this property.

A few years later, we made a tax shelter deal with a well-known singer/actor on the remaining property with a substantial amount of prepaid interest and occasional payments of principal over 10 years. Fortunately for the buyer, the values increased substantially.

Our Orange County emphasis now shifted to Anaheim, a highly productive blue-collar manufacturing area. Closer to downtown Los Angeles and the industrial hub, we secured a number of major tenants, including North American Aviation, Ford Motor Company Aeroneutronics (Philco Ford), Thompson Products, the Fluor Corporation and many other companies in the Anaheim area. Orange County was alive, active and well. The freeways were extended. Disneyland was up and operating. We received great cooperation from the City of Anaheim. Business was very good.

Before Disneyland moved into Anaheim, Disney commissioned the Stanford Research Institute (SRI) to do an economic feasibility study to analyze the probability of a successful theme park. We carefully read this report and then contacted an old friend, Buzzy Price at SRI, and contracted with them to write a new Orange County Economic Report, which we gave to all of our prospects.

This was a real winner for us. One of the features that the report highlighted was that a homeowner in Los Angeles, if they were to be employed in Orange County, could sell their older Los Angeles home for a higher price than the purchase of a new home in Orange County. The cash down payment would be small and the mortgage payments lower, leaving the new buyer with more available cash for other purposes, lower loan payments, as well as a new home in an area with new schools and parks, and less traffic. It was a huge windfall for many families and a wonderful value for scores of new Orange County industries and their employees. From a marketing standpoint, our Orange County Economic Report reaped great benefits.

Life in the 1950's was also challenging. I was working hard, reinvesting as much money as possible, developing favorable credit lines with banks and insurance companies and building a great team with my headquarters in the Stock Exchange Building in Downtown Los Angeles, as well as offices in El Segundo, Glendale and Anaheim. Aside from the everyday work, there was a lot of travel, many appearances before city councils and planning commissions, family obligations to fulfill, and a reasonable amount of sailing and sailboat racing. I was also actively involved in the Republican Party and candidate fundraising.

In 1950, I built a lovely home on the side of a hill in Palos Verdes Estates overlooking the South

Bay, with views of the ocean and beaches to Malibu, and north to the Hollywood Hills and downtown Los Angeles. We also rented a home on Lido Island in Newport Beach to accommodate the time required in our Orange County development operations in Santa Ana and in Anaheim, as well as later activities in Fullerton.

Then a family issue arrived. My first wife, Grace, felt that beautiful Palos Verdes was too remote from her parents and friends, about 12 miles away, yet she liked the Newport Beach area where we had the rental home on Lido Island.

We sold the Palos Verdes home, moved to the rental home, and had our architect design a new home on two large parcels along the Balboa beach waterfront, about two blocks from the Balboa Bay entry channel. It was a striking home with a large garden near a great beach and surf, and a quiet area where you could listen to the sound of the waves, the occasional foghorn on the jetty, the frequent songs of the birds and the cry of the seals.

Our five children were all small but able to swim, and we had a great, large Labrador dog named Flash. Flash was the babysitter for our kids and the neighbors' kids, and he wouldn't allow anyone near but the parents and family members of the children. Sometimes, with loose supervision, the kids and Flash would go to the waterline (by "loose supervision" I mean that a nearby adult was carefully monitoring the scene). If Flash thought the waves were safe, the kids could go into the water. If he did not like the waves, he would pull the kids out by their pants and surf himself.

On many a morning, we would awaken to find that Flash had brought a friend home to our garden. This friend would be a seal of equal size, and they'd be having a great time. We would call the lifeguard to pick up the seal and take it back to the water or to the jetty about two blocks away.

Early each morning, I took great delight in walking along the sand and water, playing games with my five children and swimming and surfing as we walked. It was a great home for relaxing and entertaining, for quiet reading and for Friday office work at home.

However, issues do repeat themselves. Summer traffic on Balboa Boulevard, the single and central street of Balboa Peninsula, was jammed with traffic during the summer and over Easter. We kept a small outboard-motor boat at a friend's house to move around Balboa Bay, which we used for both fun and when traffic was heavy. And once again my wife complained, "Too much traffic!" As the old saying goes, it was déjà vu all over again.

And so, we sold this house and built a new one on the small lots of the Lido Island waterfront with a dock in front for my first ocean racer, *KIALOA I* (it was also large enough to later accommodate *KIALOA II*). It was a great location, right on the bay, but it wasn't right along a beach like Balboa. The morning walks and the joys of the children playing on the beach were over. And as an aside, having a yacht in front of your house may sound interesting, but it wasn't to me. Maintaining the yacht, the miscellaneous repairs, the arrival of the racing crews, and so on, all took away from the privacy of the home.

As one might surmise, there were difficulties in my marriage: drifting apart, my demanding business schedule and what I considered a lack of resolve to commitments. The marriage to Grace terminated a few years later.

So living in Newport Beach on Lido Island with developments in Santa Ana, Anaheim, Glendale, Los Angeles and the Los Angeles International Airport areas, as well as some more remote locations, made for a tough day. Additionally, our construction company, Coordinated Construction, was doing more general contract work in Los Angeles and Orange Counties, which made the schedule more demanding.

With two social lives—Newport Beach and Orange County on one hand, and the City of Los Angeles and the Los Angeles County area on the other—we kept an apartment in L.A. for business and social affairs. It was also handy as I was becoming more involved in the Republican Party, community activities, college boards and other organizations. They all took time and effort, as well as deep study and thought. I was not involved for social gratification; I wanted to improve and protect our system, a concept we'll return to in subsequent chapters.

With our expanding business and social obligations, life was more than a little stressful. Developing the Grand Central Industrial Park in Glendale for owner Major Moseley did not reduce the strain. Negotiations with the city of Glendale and the local utility companies for this project were all very time consuming. But we did obtain the necessary approvals for the park and commenced building and leasing. Since the property had formerly been the Grand Central Airport, used for small aircraft, as well as an Air Force primary training field during World War II, we encountered "interesting" soil conditions. At one location, we discovered a 40-foot-long bomb shelter about four-feet underground; we had fun using it as a partial foundation for a large warehouse building.

Major Mosley, an old-time pilot, was a great guy; however, there were problems with the project. Major would let his people sign checks, but only for a maximum of $50, and most of the time he was out of town. About halfway through the job, we decided the project and the payments were too complicated, so we parted company. Mosley's men followed our plan and continued with their own personnel. Ultimately, it was a successful development.

While we were still on the project, we met an unusual set of clients: two men in a rental car who wanted to see a 50,000 square-foot building under construction. They provided their names but not the name of their company. They asked us what it would take to design a new building with some different criteria. We said that we would prepare some preliminary plans, which they asked to be sent to a legal office back east. We discussed, in detail, the design concepts, and they said they would be in touch with us ten days after receipt of the plans. So we selected a site in the area they requested, prepared the plans and sent them to their attorney.

Unbeknownst to them, during our first meeting, one of our people checked out their car and found it was from the Hertz office at LAX. Since we knew when they were leaving L.A., we dispatched someone to the Hertz counter and discovered that the car was rented to a couple of major aircraft engine company executives. This gave us further insight in how to design the building, as they did tell us that the facility would be used for maintenance on heavy-machinery.

After the plans were delivered, out of nowhere, I received a check in my name by registered mail for the full cost of the project, over $3 million. The accompanying instructions were simple: "Buy the land, build the building, and give us the title when the building is complete with an approximate date." There was nothing to sign; just acquire the land and perform the work, and when all is complete, give them the title. I was amazed; what a way to do business. So, we built them a tremendous building, took care to control the costs, and when it was finished, discovered that we had saved money from the original estimate. When we gave them the deed, we also gave them a check for the unspent balance. All we could say was, "Wow! Where do we get more customers like this?"

By that time, the Korean War was underway. It soon became apparent that the Russian MiG-15 fighter was probably a better airplane than our F-86 airplane, designed and built by North American Aviation. But North American had in the works a new and much better fighter-bomber, the F-100, which was superior to the MiG-15. Obviously, the F-100 was urgently needed. North American required a new, final assembly plant at Los Angeles International Airport, and quickly. They asked us to help.

We contracted the manager at LAX, a friend, and were able to lease a substantial area at the southeast corner of the airport, but it required new supplemental roadways and utilities on a 15-acre site. We negotiated and expedited the lease and building contract and rapidly constructed a new 150,000-square-foot high bay, wide column spacing, all concrete structure to accommodate their needs for the final assembly of the new, exceptional F-100 fighter. For such a serious technical operation, a highly sophisticated building was required, one that included parking and service ramps as necessary.

We had fun designing and building the three individual 65-foot hangar doorways to accommodate the F-100 and future airplanes. We tried to pre-cast them in concrete as single units, one of which exploded in the air in the grasp of two heavy-duty cranes because a rigger made a silly mistake and chained one leg to the floor. When the chain tightened, it sent a shock wave into a beam and the doorway exploded in midair—a good experiment and lessoned learned.

It's always something, however, and this time a union problem occurred. Coordinated Construction had no union contracts; we normally paid above union wages for performance and overtime when we could expedite construction under a specific formula.

Each construction job has what we called a daily burden rate, based upon non-specific construction costs. At the overtime rate, however, whenever we could spend 50 percent of the daily burden rate to gain a day of construction by using overtime labor, we would do so. Our construction crews loved and understood this concept, and we expedited completion of all of our buildings. We had outstanding construction worker relations.

LAX is a high-traffic area and the construction superintendent asked if we could work around it. Specifically, he wanted to start two hours earlier, at 6:00 a.m. so as to avoid the morning rush, and leave two hours earlier in the afternoon. We said yes, with one condition; this would be considered a normal, non-overtime rate workday. About two months later, our superintendent called and said that the union had been advised of this two-hour earlier start, and technically, under union work rules, the two hours between six and eight in the morning could be considered overtime. We reluctantly wrote checks to all of our employees for this additional "overtime pay." Every employee voluntarily endorsed the check and returned it to us, and asked that the two-hour early start be continued. Under this arrangement, they would continue to endorse the checks to Kilroy Industries.

Our crew in the field subsequently discovered that an electrical contractor foreman, who was a union job representative, raised the technical overtime complaint and pursued it with the union. After a visit from some of our workers who heard about this matter, the electrician departed the jobsite very suddenly and was never to be seen again on any of our jobs.

Apparently, during or after the discussion between our guys and the electrician, his lunch box and toolbox were unfortunately run over by a skip loader, and his car apparently ran over some loose nails, which required a tow truck. We reminded our crew that all job sites should be policed and cleaned to prevent damage or injury. They responded that this was exactly what they always did.

The assembly plant was a complicated affair on multiple fronts—ownership, design, financing—and a major challenge with a short time frame. To complete it, to get those F-100 fighter planes to the pilots who needed them, we overcame many obstacles by again challenging and widening the thresholds. The construction crew had a great celebration party upon completion of this crucial defense and security project…without the union, or the electrician.

An Interest in Everything

Many years after the events described in this chapter, just before the start of the 2005 Transpacific race to Honolulu, I met Eric D. Chowanski, a young man sailing as the bowman with John McClaren's yacht, *Pendragon*. John's crewmembers were top sailors, and we began talking about this book and personal history. A few days later, I received the following e-mail from "Chewy."

Jim,

It was nice to meet you. I'm sorry – boat/social commitments meant I missed your offer of a cold beer. But perhaps we can do that soon. I'm interested in your thoughts on motivation. But it struck me that your interests likely span a range wider than even many of your friends know.

Those who are interested in everything represent fewer than 5% of the population, so it was no surprise that I had not met anyone similar until about eight years ago. I now know perhaps seven people who share an interest in everything, deep understanding in diverse domains, a vision of the connections between domains, and an openness to explore everything around them. So when you linked sailing, life and business through motivation, I was fairly certain you think in a similar way – with wonder, curiosity and creativity.

A while back, I wrote a friend:

"The people who do share this wonder are tiny lights in a large void of twilight. In their presence there's this rush of truth, as if the light, now closer, has illuminated everything. But it's really nothing more than shared joy in wonder. Wonder at things. Wonder at complexity. Wonder at everything. It's wonder at the same, everyday things that everyone else has grown accustomed to. Time with those people is brief but the effects endure."

Maybe we can have that beer.

Chewy

(Eric Chowanski)

I responded with the following e-mail. My response was a challenge: "Play the game of life as best you can."

To: Eric,

My thoughts go to many different factors of life. Life is a fleeting thing which can be meaningful or just a passage. We are put here for a purpose and we should try to make a difference. However, it all starts from a great quotation of Shakespeare, "This above all, to thine ownself be true, for thou cans't not then be false to any man." In substance, do not believe your own press or BS.

Life is a game, a game of effort, of learning and of contribution. As you proceed to help yourself, you help others. And so, they help you and join in a contribution to the critical mass of intelligence, beneficial to all.

My mother set the basic criteria. This is not a complicated concept! I have been involved in many things: developing a successful business, being involved in community affairs, commissions, public policy, political affairs, national, state and city educational institutions, charities, and above all, helping others, as a means of helping myself. Cocktail talk means nothing! Performance means everything!

I could go on and on, life is a great game. Live it, make your contribution, it is a great reward. I speak, not only for myself, but also for my wife, Nelly, who has contributed so much to the Southern California community. We make a great team.

Jim

3

KIALOA I, a victorious finish of the 1430 mile San Diego Acapulco Race in 1962 and its outstanding crew.

From left to right: Jim Kilroy, Warwick Tomkins, Gene Bricker, Ken Watts, Burke Sawyer, Verne Ruppert

KIALOA I
and the First Transpacs
Our Introduction to Grand Prix Sailing

Newport Beach, California was a great place to learn to sail. Years before, while in high school, I'd had the opportunity to go sailing a few times, and I found it a fascinating experience. Sailing was a practical combination of fluid dynamics and the romance of world discovery. Under sail, I could imagine that I was Columbus, Sir Francis Drake, Magellan, a Phoenician or one of the other great explorers of our world. Sailing enhanced my already great fascination for history, exploration and discovery.

My first sailboat was a 12-foot Snowbird, which was soon taken over by my children, who had such a natural response to the technique of sailing.

In the early-1950s, I felt that I could venture to Catalina or the local islands with my family, so I bought *Serena*, a 46-foot Island Clipper sloop, from an old friend. It was fine for cruising but only so-so for racing, but proved to be a good learner boat.

Milt Wegeforth of San Diego, a former International Star Class world champion (he won the 1935 worlds and the 1937 International Star Championships), also had an Island Clipper sister ship, and we would race one another. By simply beating me, he was a great help, as I could ask how he did it. Slowly, I began to put the practical together with the theoretical. After a while, based upon Milt's instructions, we became fairly even on the racecourse, and my enthusiasm level increased.

Milt had a great sense of humor. He bought a powerboat and named it *Dumpling*, which I thought was an odd handle for a boat. So, I asked him why he'd done it. Milt's response was perfect. He said, "Jim, you're fairly new to yachting, so you should understand that I named my new powerboat *Dumpling* because it is logical. A "dumpling" is made by pouring a lot of dough into hot water, hence my boat's name." Not only was Milt both humorous and practical, he also taught me a lot about preparation, organization and sailboat racing. Most importantly, he had taught me how to make a "dumpling."

About this time, Ed Grant, a Douglas engineer and sailor who developed the reaching strut and many other items of sailing hardware, had also written a manual on yacht measurement and tactics that he sold to me for $75. In the long run, this was probably the most expensive purchase in my sailing life as it led to my great interest in sailing, racing and cruising.

A few years later, in 1956, as I was beginning to broaden my threshold and learn what I was doing, my friend Freddy Schenck, a yacht broker and former Snipe class world champion, called and said, "Have I got a deal for you!" Tom Shorts' *Tasco II*, a 50-foot sailboat designed by Sparkman & Stephens, was for sale. *Tasco II* was a fractional-rigged yawl, about eight-years-old, which exhibited substantial speeds but lacked consistency.

Tom Short was a San Francisco-based sailor, a yachting ship chandler, who loved to sail and cruise. He enjoyed the biennial race from Los Angeles to Honolulu called the Transpac; however, he also felt that carrying a spinnaker at night was an imposition upon enjoyable sailing and cruising. With so much power from the downwind sail, you can go much faster, but you can also lose control. Tom also loved to display his latest chandlery store items aboard the yacht, adding tremendous weight to an already heavy yacht. Fred Schenck, some friends and I all sailed the yacht and felt there was strong potential for improvement. I bought the boat for a favorable price.

We immediately commenced surgery on the new yacht, which I renamed *KIALOA*. I'd heard the name before, liked the sound of it and did some research. Roughly translated, in native Hawaiian it meant "long, white canoe." There would be many other long, white canoes to follow.

On the first *KIALOA*, we began by removing hundreds of pounds of equipment and unnecessary weight from the boat. A great surprise was that much of the electrical cable was lead-shielded cable, including tremendous lead-cable weight in the mast. A large, heavy Loran Alpha navigation device, a heavy lead-gimbaled table, a 75-pound ladder and other heavy, miscellaneous objects were all removed. I do not know the total amount of weight we removed; however, *KIALOA*, later known as *KIALOA I*, now floated well over two inches higher in the water.

We also worked on re-cutting and replacing sails, and continued eliminating weighty running rigging and other items, anything that seemed unnecessary or unusually heavy. Kenny Watts, an ex-lifeguard, great California sail maker and crewmember, was instrumental in redesigning and building new sails, which helped bring *KIALOA* to life.

As *KIALOA* was transformed, we practiced our skills and tried to become more qualified sailors. My crew, all amateurs with the love for sailing, and I were all on a steep learning curve, asking questions and making modifications. In our quest for sailing victories, all of our crew expressed their opinions about what we might do to better the performance of the boat and ourselves, and increase our own personal skills.

In the evolution of her racing career, *KIALOA I*—originally a fractional-rigged yawl—would eventually become a masthead yawl with a taller mizzen mast before closing her career as a modified masthead sloop. We toyed with different sail plans, ballast, flotation, rating certificates and other concepts that would affect the performance of *KIALOA I*. The idea was to leave no stone unturned.

By the middle of 1957, it was time to try to aggressively compete. Along with a few shorter contests, the 120-mile offshore race from Newport Beach, California to Ensenada, Mexico was our first major test. We sailed against over 150 other yachts and placed only moderately in the fleet. In a dying breeze near the end of the race, we learned much about the yacht's potential while keeping a close tab on the currents en route for reference in future races.

In the next race, the Huntington Tidelands race, a shorter event about 20 miles long along the coast of Southern California, we were first to finish and second in our class. We were learning; we were enthused.

The next test was a big one: our first trans-oceanic race, the Transpac, some 2,225 nautical miles from Los Angeles Harbor to Diamond Head Light on the Hawaiian island of Oahu. For a boatload of newly developing ocean racers, it was a challenging and ambitious goal. Our preparations were parallel and twofold: 1) readying the boat, sails and rigging, and 2) preparing our tactics and strategy on how to sail the race.

The latter was, of course, a key factor, as it is for all Transpac crews. Due to the high-pressure cell that's stationed in the center of the North Pacific, it's impractical to sail a great circle, straight-line course to the finish line. A yacht must "guesstimate" the most successful route around the high via the pressure gradients, or isobars, that circle around high-pressure systems in a clockwise pattern. It's a delicate balance. Successful Transpac yachts make the most of the wind in the pressure gradients while still sailing the shortest, most efficient course to Honolulu.

The core of the high cell has a pressure gradient of about 1035 isobars, which varies from month to month and year to year, as does the overall location of the high itself, primarily from north to south. In general terms, the winning yachts found the 1020 isobar gradient to be optimal in terms of wind and distance sailed; however, this is always subject to change. Modern sailors must remember that from the 1950s through the 1970s, we did not have today's electronic capability or satellite imagery, and that a lot of the weather information was substantially less accurate than it is for contemporary racers.

We knew that we needed practical advice. Prent Fulmore, the owner of *Staghound*, a yacht that won multiple Transpacs, was a friend, and I asked Prent and his navigator for tactical help. They advised that after rounding Catalina Island we should first sail a slightly lower course to a position of about 30°N, 125°W, which would give us a fast headsail reach for the first stretch of the course. Once we hit those coordinates, we'd pick up the 1020 isobar and the wind would both increase and move slightly aft. From there, the idea would be to sail a course, dependent on the wind, to a position around 25°N, 140°W, again adjusting our strategy en route according to the wind angle, barometric pressure and wave directions. The last part was important to get right, as waves coming from the right direction can provide surfing acceleration to the boat.

Our navigation lessons continued. For the final stretch of the race, Prent suggested that we sail as fast as possible to Kalapaupa Light on the Isle of Molokai and then jibe to a starboard tack, maneuvering as necessary to clear Makapu Point and Coco Head, to the finish line off Diamond Head, just east of the beaches along Waikiki. Handicapping—the mathematical rating system in yacht racing that allows boats of different sizes to compete on a level playing field—was not discussed in detail at these meetings. However, it was clear to our lead crew, or afterguard, that the handicap formula in this traditionally downwind race, favored the smaller yachts such as *Staghound* as there was little of the upwind sailing that benefits bigger yachts with their longer waterlines. In the Transpac, the upwind stretch amounted to only about one percent of the distance of the entire race; the currents were also beneficial to the smaller boats because of the longer time they spent at sea.

Another interesting facet of the Transpac, one that was essential for safety but again useful to the smaller yachts, was the daily roll call transmitted over the high-seas radio. Every Transpac yacht had to provide their noon position and localized weather information. As a mid-sized yacht, we could use this information to analyze the conditions astern, determine where our wind was coming from, and try to sail to the most favorable position. We could also interpret what was happening ahead of us and determine how or if we should vary our course, also dependent upon the wind coming from astern. However, there was no such guarantee of a static condition. Again, I should remind today's reader, there was little or no such thing as reliable electronic navigation. Celestial navigation was essential.

Once underway, we had some great sailing and some significant problems during our first Transpac race, as well as lighter and more variable wind conditions than expected. One 50-footer, Charlie Ullman's *Legend*, decided to go farther south than the fleet, which provided more spinnaker reaching than usual. By employing this substantially different tactic—a radical departure from the conventional, traditional Transpac wisdom and technique—*Legend* found stronger breeze and a more favorable sailing angle than her competition. At an early roll call, when the rest of the yachts heard of Charlie's tactics, we all thought they'd dug their own grave; it sounded like a losing proposition. Aboard *KIALOA I*, we were reluctant to experiment and stuck with our game plan, which brought some good sailing conditions and some very light conditions.

We had a great start, perhaps first or second on the starting line when the gun sounded. We enjoyed an outstanding sail toward the west end of Catalina on a windward beat. We maintained a heading slightly up the California mainland coast above Point Fermin before sailing the longer leg

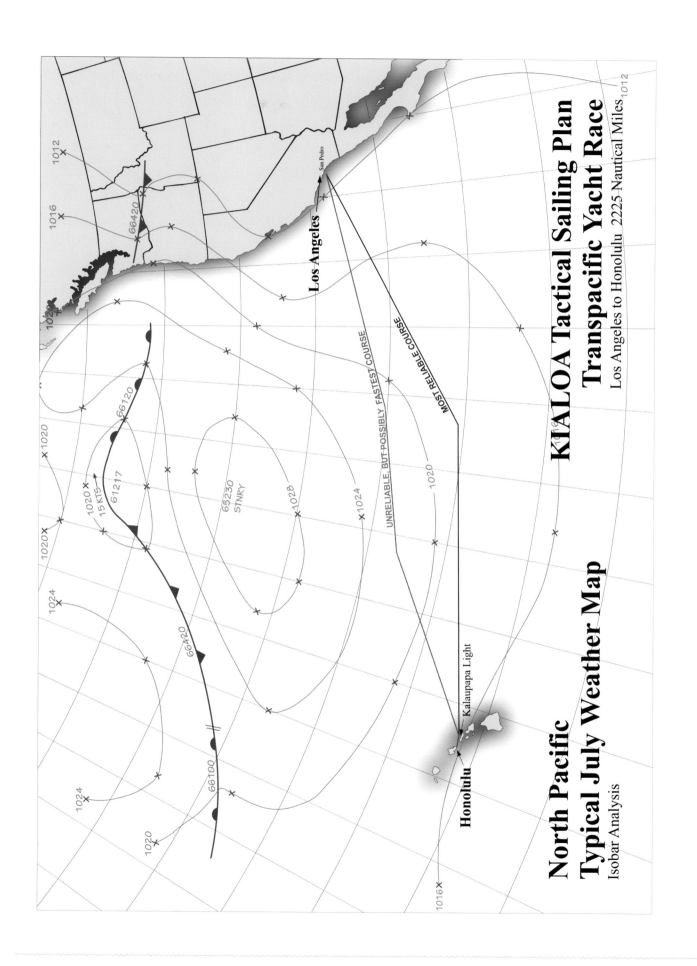

KIALOA Tactical Sailing Plan
Transpacific Yacht Race
Los Angeles to Honolulu 2225 Nautical Miles

North Pacific
Typical July Weather Map
Isobar Analysis

MOST RELIABLE COURSE

UNRELIABLE, BUT POSSIBLY FASTEST COURSE

Los Angeles

San Pedro

Honolulu

Kalaupapa Light

15 KTS

65230 STNRY

1012
1016
1020
1024
1028

toward the west end of Catalina, an outstanding sail to weather. Tactically, it seemed like a good choice at the time; only later did we realize it was a mistake that cost us time and distance. We rounded the west end of Catalina in good shape and then sailed a close reach on a course of about 240 degrees magnetic, slightly off the wind, to our first waypoint, 30°N by 125°W. As we sailed further along this course, the wind continued to shift aft, toward our beam, and we soon set a spinnaker.

All was more or less going according to plan. After the close-hauled windward sail in west southwest breeze to Catalina, the wind slowly shifted to the northwest, and then continued shifting until we hit the northeast trade winds. Yachts would sail the first two to three days on headsails, change over to reaching headsails, and then switch to spinnakers on the third day.

On the fourth day of that first Transpac, we were in an excellent position, calculated to be 3rd overall in fleet with many miles and changing wind conditions yet to sail. The *KIALOA* crew set the big blue spinnaker and a mizzen staysail and morale soared. None of the crew had sailed such a long ocean race, and we'd only logged a few miles together before this race. In fact, I'd only sailed a few "offshore" races and none more than 125 miles. I too had much to learn.

But Day 4 was a pleasant spinnaker reach almost exactly on the desired course, with all sails flying: a spinnaker, staysail, full main, mizzen staysail and full mizzen in 15 to 18 knots of breeze. It was a beautiful sail in warm weather, and everyone took advantage of the pleasant conditions to have a "shower" with buckets of salt water that we also used to clean up the boat.

On the 5th and 6th day, however, trouble began to occur. A few minor sail repairs weren't too bothersome, but we discovered a major issue with our electrical system. After a few hours of studying the system, which had just been reworked by an electrician before we left, we found numerous problems including several unconnected wires, all of which we tried to rebuild while KIALOA was surfing and rolling down the waves.

A major electrical relay blew up with a little smoke and sparks. But the main problem was the voltage regulator. We had to "jury rig" the wiring to minimally charge our batteries for radio transmissions and other shipboard electrical use. During this fire drill of trying to fix the electrical system, the motor, with the alternator as an appendage, was switched on and off many times, and crewmembers were involved in trying to make a fix.

Aboard *KIALOA*, the thru-hull fitting for the engine's exhaust system always had to be in the off position when the engine was not running, and then manually opened to start and run the engine. Perhaps it was because people were tired or just confused, but the engine was kicked over while the thru hull was in the off position and a huge explosion occurred that blew out the side of the exhaust muffler: a new problem to solve. We had to encase the muffler with tin cans so that exhaust fumes would not fill the cabin and asphyxiate the crew. More sleep was lost while this was accomplished.

Of course, this assortment of little issues triggered our collective sense of humor, which thankfully we didn't lose. Even our high-seas radio, which we needed for roll call and safety purposes, had a few problems. Each time we switched it on the light on the top of the mizzenmast would blink on and off with every transmission. We all agreed that our shoreside electrician had unusual wiring concepts.

But we were learning, and our Transpac setbacks underscored the fundamental and cardinal rules that must be addressed before going to sea:

Don't make too many system changes before going on a long sea voyage, unless they are tested over a period of several days.

Complete all mechanical/electrical changes well before your departure date.

Doublecheck all electrical, plumbing and fuel flow drawings and schematics well before departure.

And, remember, there are no warranty fixes at sea.

All of this is equally true with the management of your crew. Specific duties must be well defined before the race, and the responsibility for managing and testing each system and the yacht's equipment and gear must be specifically delegated.

On the 7th and 8th day out, the North Pacific high was in bad humor and quite pacific. A series of low-pressure cells were invading from the south, causing the trade winds to shift more to the east and drop to about 5 to 8 knots, which forced us to steer *KIALOA I* well above course to keep moving. We jibed in light conditions to the south, which appeared to be an equally bad option and also induced nasty rolling conditions in the leftover seaway and light air. It wasn't until the 10th day out that the wind filled in to about 15 knots, and we jibed back to the starboard tack to put us back on track.

Because of the battle between the lows and the trades, we now had confused seas, not the usual tradewind surfing conditions. The effect, again, was a rolling boat. As we rolled from side to side, the boom would drag in the water while the spinnaker pole nearly dipped in the waves. It was a miserable ride.

The fractional rigs of this period—with their smaller spinnakers and bigger mainsails—could be beasts when running in rough downwind conditions. A partial blanketing of the spinnaker from the boat's roll as the wave trains came through would cause dangerous and uncomfortable control problems. Under the then existing CCA Rule, masthead spinnakers that could "breathe" over the main were much more controllable and suitable for the sea conditions *KIALOA* was encountering; however, in a Catch 22 loophole, masthead spinnakers could not be used on a fractional rig.

On the 11th day of the race, we jibed back to port with good wind and rough seas but a better ride. At about 7:30 p.m. on the 12th day out, *KIALOA I* was having a fast but rough spinnaker ride on a starboard jibe in 20 knots of breeze and surfing seas. I was at the helm when the wheel lost its load on the rudder, and with it, my ability to steer. A rudder cable had broken.

I hollered for all hands on deck, ran forward of the helm and cut the tack line of the mizzen staysail. It flew free, unloading leverage on the after section of *KIALOA I*, and I called for the spinnaker to be immediately doused. I did not want the mizzen or the mizzen staysail to drive the boat to a 90-degree angle to the sea and cause *KIALOA I* to ride on her beam with the sails almost in the water. We set a small staysail and doused all sails but the main. We then trimmed the main hard to hold a course about 50 degrees north of where we wanted to go, on a heading away from Hawaii. It then took us over two hours in the lazarette, a small area under the cockpit where the rudder cables are attached to the large rudder quadrant, to make the repair. It was a serious loss of time and distance.

The problem had been elemental. The new wire cable—which attaches to a bicycle-type chain from the wheel, and then connects to each side of the quadrant and is fastened to the rudder—simply failed. The shipyard installed an improper type of cable. Instead of a braided-steel cable, they rigged a new, stainless, braided cable with a fabric core. After a proper connection with the wrong wire cable, swaged fittings were compressed on the cables; however, the load on these cables allowed the fabric core to shrink, and the cables failed right at the fittings. It was a totally irresponsible mistake by the shipyard, which could have led to a sunken boat.

Fortunately, we kept the original, replaced cables as a backup, which we installed, tested and then sailed for the rest of the race. Our time loss was well over two hours, which seriously impacted our finish results.

But the final miles were fantastic. We sailed toward Kalaupapa Lighthouse on Molokai on a port jibe and then jibed back to starboard. We had a great surfing spinnaker sail to the finish off Diamond Head light on the island of Oahu. On all of the *KIALOA*s, I have always enjoyed the last leg of this race, which rarely fails to bring powerful, off-the-wind surfing under the biggest spinnaker. It's a thrilling sail.

Looking back at the first Transpac, yes, we did have several problems. They could have been serious, but they were all addressed and overcome. Luckily, no one was hurt, and we had an important, but poorly timed, education.

Next time, I knew, we'd be better prepared.

We had a wonderful time in Honolulu. Upon arrival, there was an outstanding reception, and we had a fine place to stay at the Royal Hawaiian Hotel. This was the old Waikiki: the hotel's garden and grounds were beautiful, there was the typically charming South Seas atmosphere and music, with the moon shimmering on the ocean. Plus, we were coming off a reasonably challenging inaugural long-distance ocean sail. So the '57 Transpac was an educational introduction into the world of Grand Prix ocean racing. I was hooked.

The Colonial-style Royal Hawaiian was the "Grand Dame" of the local hotels, and the awards presentation there was magnificent. The ceremony and dinner were conducted in a beautiful garden fringing the beach under a beautiful starlit sky. The full moon was shining and reflecting off the sea and the waves glistened with phosphorescence as they rolled onto the beach. All the yachts had arrived and the romance of the islands was in the air…this was Old Hawaii, before the high-rises, and you really felt that you were far, far away from the rest of the world. Did I mention I was hooked?

With all our problems—many of them self-made—our results weren't as bad as one might think. We were the seventeenth yacht to finish, third in our Class C on corrected handicap time, and the seventeenth overall on corrected time in a fleet of 34 boats. If not for the failure of the rudder cables and the time lost to repair them, we could have been close to second place in our class, with a substantially improved placing overall.

I was satisfied, but not content with the lapses in our overall performance, which included organization and preparation. It was a tremendous learning exercise as to the capability of both *KIALOA* and our new crew. It also showed me I needed to improve not only my leadership, but also my management capabilities, not only during the race, but also in the areas of planning, preparation, organization and implementation. We were beginners, but we'd passed a new threshold and performed well based upon our experience. Still, we needed a better understanding of *KIALOA*'s strengths and weaknesses, in both racing and mechanical terms, as well as a broader understanding and execution of ocean-racing tactics. As captain, it was my responsibility to address all these matters; it was clear we could make changes to the boat's and crew's performance. To do so, I'd need to step up my game.

After the Transpac awards ceremony, *KIALOA I* then sailed in the inter-island race to Kauai, a spinnaker run and headsail reach to the smaller island west and north of Oahu, ending off Lihue on the isle's east coast, a course of about 100 miles. We were the first yacht to finish and I believe the overall winner in a fleet of perhaps a dozen boats. As we sailed past the breakwater at the harbor entrance, we were reminded that a tsunami had struck the port a few months before, flooding the Lihue area and grounding all the yachts in the harbor for a short time. Fortunately, we had no problems.

The island of Kauai is notable for its beautiful "Grand Canyon" open from the sea on the far westerly side of the island. *KIALOA*'s crew enjoyed the beautiful anchorage on the north side of the island, Hanalei Bay.

With regard to the boat, we'd discovered on the race that a fractionally rigged spinnaker was not powerful enough and could be blanketed by the mainsail when running and surfing before the wind on a deep downwind angle. To address that deficiency, we believed that we could manage a full masthead spinnaker and masthead headsails. That raised another thought: Why not fly a small spinnaker on the mizzen when off the wind, instead of just a triangular mizzen staysail? As we discussed the idea, we also decided to raise the height of the mizzenmast and pay the penalty for an even bigger masthead spinnaker, increasing the area by lengthening the spinnaker poles.

We checked the legality of all of these changes, working with our sailmaker, Kenny Watts, and Ed Grant, an aeronautical engineer from Douglas Aircraft, a sailor and a good friend. Together, we went forward and made many changes to the rig, along with building a new sail inventory. *KIALOA I* was an excellent yacht, and getting better.

The learning process continued in the 1959 Transpac. We all know that we learn from our mistakes, and that one can never get an answer without first posing a question. After the 1957 Transpac, we asked a lot of questions about our boat and our crew, after which we tried and practiced many new techniques, and made significant modifications and improvements to *KIALOA I*. The '59 Transpac would show us how much progress we made.

With good wind, good speed, and good crew work, we arrived off Kalaupapa Light, about 50 miles from the finish, in very good shape, and it appeared that we might make the winners circle. Our closest competitor, *Nalu II,* was well behind us, and we were under spinnakers, sailing downwind in about 30 knots of wind with optimal surfing waves.

Our other main competitor, *Chubasco*, skippered by Don Haskell, had already finished and was moored in Ala Wai Yacht Harbor. We received a radio call and it was none other than Don, who asked, "Where are you?"

"Off Kalaupapa Light," I replied.

"Thank you," said Don, "and you have *Chubasco*'s congratulations as the probable winner of this great race." I thanked Don for his comments and courtesy but suggested that they were premature, that many things could still happen.

Unfortunately, I was right.

Almost immediately, the wind velocity dropped from 30 knots to about 3 knots. The aftermath of the blow left big waves but *KIALOA I* had almost no helm control, and the boat rolled and bucked like a cowboy's horse at the rodeo, tearing sails, breaking the sheets and guys controlling our sails, and generally creating havoc aboard. On top of that, we made no progress for hours.

Worse still, we kept checking on the progress of *Nalu II* and the other yachts behind us, all of which were having a wonderful sail and closing the gap rapidly. The closer they got, the more perilous our hopes for victory, or even for beating *Chubasco*.

Finally, we got the breeze the other boats had carried from behind to catch up with us. But it was too late. Even though we had a fine, fast sail to the finish line, *Nalu II*, accompanied by another trio of smaller yachts, held the following wind all the way to the finish. For *Nalu*, it was a fair wind indeed. Once the corrected times were applied, she finished first in class and first overall. *KIALOA*

STARTS

•**Los Angeles**

•**San Diego**

•Ensenada

UNITED STATES
MEXICO

San Benito Light
Isla Cedros
Bahia Tortuga

Baja

Gulf of California

•Puerto Magdalena

•La Paz

Cabo San Lucas

Mazatlan
•*FINISH*

Acapulco •

Bahia de Acapulco
FINISH

Punta Pilares

Punta Lorenz

Boca Chica
entry at Acapulco

Boca Chica

Punta Coyuca   Isla Roqueta   El Morro

Pacific Ocean

Punta Mita
•**Puerto Vallarta**
Cabocorrientes

•Chamela
•Tenacatita
• Navidad
• Manzanillo

N
W   E
S

Ixtapa
• Zihuatanejo

Los Angeles - Mazatlan Race
——• 1032 Nautical Miles

San Diego - Acapulco Race
——• 1430 Nautical Miles

Acapulco
FINISH

I was the fourteenth yacht to finish, fifth overall on corrected time, and second in class.

The July 17, 1959 edition of *The Honolulu Advertiser* had a great photo of *Nalu II* crossing the Diamond Head finish line under the headline, "Winning Yacht." The accompanying story explained that three yachts crossed the line within five minutes of each other. *KIALOA I* was the first of the three, followed by *Robon* and the ketch, *Marilyn*, both of which were bigger yachts. The story also pointed out that *KIALOA* was at one time a top contender for overall fleet honors.

We took two things from that Transpac, the first one a reminder that in all sailboat races, the wind and waves ultimately control the results. But it also confirmed that we had strong possibilities for the future.

In the 1961 Transpac, we learned that when it comes to navigation and "conventional wisdom," the status quo doesn't always hold true. That year, Bob Robbs, the skipper of the Class A yacht, *Nam Sang*, won the race by taking a short cut and bypassing the 1020 isobar of the North Pacific high, forgoing the southerly arc boats usually take for the optimal wind conditions and pointing the boat almost exactly for the finish line. The shortest distance between two points is a straight line, and *Nam Sang* won the race by sailing almost a direct course between California and Hawaii, adding only 44 miles to the base course distance of 2,225 miles.

Was it a gamble or was it a brilliant tactic that took advantage of an abnormal, confused North Pacific High Cell? Whatever it was, it propelled *Nam Sang* into the winner's circle, the first Class A yacht to score an overall victory in 27 years. George Sturgis's Class B contender, *Ichiban*, finished second, only 43 minutes in arrears on corrected time. (George was a frequent *KIALOA* crew.) *Nalu II* and *KIALOA* were eighth and ninth, respectively.

As *KIALOA* closed in on the islands, the bigger Class A and B yachts were either far ahead, or finished and comfortably anchored in Ala Wai Yacht Harbor. All the competitors in Class C and D prayed for wind and our prayers were finally answered…and them some. *Yachting* magazine columnist Al Lockabey later wrote a piece entitled, "All Yachts Make Port in a Rough Race," and reported that *KIALOA I* lost five spinnakers in the last two days of the race. Al was right on target, but at least we had excess wind saved up from the lack of breeze in the early part of the race. The eventful 1961 Transpac was the last Honolulu Race for *KIALOA I*, a boat that taught us so much about sailing, yacht design and how to make a slow boat go very fast.

In addition to the Transpacs, *KIALOA I* raced in many Southern California contests, including the Whitney Circuit, the Ahmanson Circuit, the Ensenada Race, the San Francisco series and the 1,430 nautical mile Acapulco race, which was one of my personal favorites. This 1,430 nautical mile offshore event had many challenges and winning boats had to employ decisive tactics. Adverse currents were one problem, as was rounding the tip of Baja California and sailing into the open ocean after 830 miles of shifty, coastal downwind sailing, and negotiating Cabo Corrientes at the southern tip of Banderas Bay before making way to Acapulco.

Our first Acapulco race was in 1958, after our first Transpac, but before we switched from a fractional rig to a masthead rig (in fact, that inaugural Acapulco race played a major role in making the change). As with all those early ocean races, we learned a great deal and finished eighth in a fleet of 35 yachts, placing 11th on corrected time. We carefully watched our key rival, Ash Brown's 40-footer, *Carousel*. We analyzed his course, where he made gains on *KIALOA I*, and where he lost ground, an infrequent occurrence. Afterwards, we went ahead and revised *KIALOA I*'s sail plan, converting her to a masthead yawl.

Our second Acapulco Race was in 1960. Again, we took the lessons learned in the earlier event, continued our efforts to upgrade our tactics and crew work, and formed a game plan based on our experiences and a personal theory we'd developed on nocturnal wind shifts and tidal and current data based on talks with local fishermen. Ultimately, our plan was largely successful, and we went on to record a first in class and third overall on corrected time after finishing fifth on a boat-to-boat basis in the 37-boat fleet.

All this was in spite of the fact that we incurred major rudder damage about 500 miles from the finish. It happened at about 11 p.m. on a dark night, at a change of watch. We were several miles to sea from Cabo Corrientes at the southeast end of Banderas Bay.

I was swinging into my bunk when I was suddenly thrown against a bulkhead and *KIALOA I* came to a sudden stop. We all rushed on deck and then carefully checked the bilge for water and damage, but everything looked fine. I checked with the helmsman who said the rudder struck something twice, violently, jerking the wheel from his hands and stopping the boat cold.

KIALOA I still had steerage, but all the sensitivity and "feeling" of the helm was gone. It was like driving a truck instead of a sports car. As the breeze was dying and the water was fairly smooth, we decided to sail as best we could for the rest of the night, keep a careful eye on everything, and make an underwater inspection at first light. The next morning, two of us went in the water and discovered that our wood rudder, attached to the trailing edge of the keel, was badly damaged and that pieces of fractured wood were barely held in place by a stainless steel frame around the outer edges of the rudder.

The fractures in the rudder left a very rough and jagged surface of about 1-inch thick horizontal sections, which were previously glued together and further secured by the stainless steel frame along the trailing edge. At impact—with whatever we'd hit—the glued joints had failed and some sections were laterally displaced by over two inches. The now very inefficient rudder was a good way to slow the boat. We could still steer *KIALOA I*, but not with its former precision. We also had minor damage to our propeller.

We soon discovered that we were sailing in an area of basking whales and we surmised that we'd hit one who hit us back! It was, literally and figuratively, a shocking surprise! Clearly, our rudder damage would hamper our progress for the several hundred miles ahead of us; however, we kept pressing *KIALOA I* to her maximum ability. Given all that, we were quite pleased with the results in the 1960 race.

Two years later, in 1962, our tactics and strategy were confirmed when *KIALOA I* was fourth boat to finish in a 21-boat fleet; first in class; and first overall on corrected time, setting a new record in the process. We absolutely followed our game plane and enjoyed a fantastic spinnaker ride for the last hundred miles. The Wind Gods were with us.

Before the race, because the winds radically shift up and down, we made one very significant change to *KIALOA I*'s configuration. By removing the mizzenmast, we lightened the stern and eliminated the weight of the mizzen staysails. The alterations worked and *KIALOA I* won its first race as a sloop. The awards ceremony was outstanding.

Looking back, *KIALOA I* was the platform aboard which our ability to race sailboats was founded and confirmed. Many modifications were made, many techniques of sailing were tested; over time, *KIALOA I* and her crew became winners. We take great pride in saluting her results.

We sold *KIALOA I* to a Seattle banker who subsequently resold the boat, and she set forth into the South Pacific. A few years later she was sailed back to Lahaina, Maui and poorly anchored too close to the beach. Heavy southwesterly winds set in, and *KIALOA I* was blown ashore and destroyed. It was a tragic, careless end for a magnificent yacht.

KIALOA I
Damaged Rudder

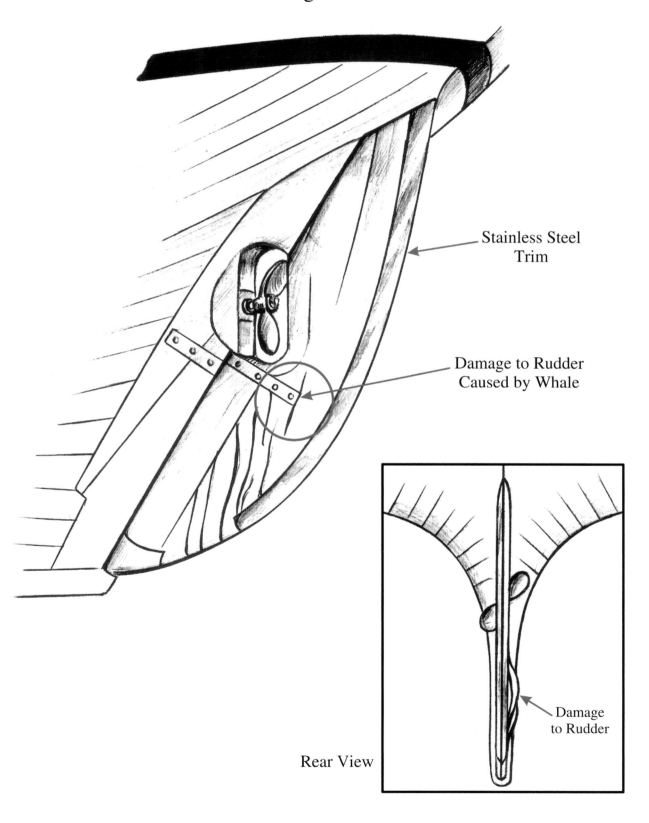

Stainless Steel Trim

Damage to Rudder Caused by Whale

Rear View

Damage to Rudder

Finish
1962 Acapulco
Race

1st Overall
1st Class B

New Corrected
Time Record

Crew:
Ken Watts
Burke Sawyer
"Commodore" Tompkins
Gene Brickan
Verne Ruppert
Jim Kilroy

KIALOA I
Many Changes Brought Results 1957-1962

KIALOA I (as purchased)
Fractional Rig

What a wonderful record for our first learning yacht. There have been many changes over 6 years of aggressive racing and cruising with much technical input from our amateur crew and friends. KIALOA I taught us a lot. Keep allowing the good in the yachts design to expand. Each yacht has a personality. Find it, improve it.

OVERALL VICTORIES		
1st	11 of 33	33.33%
2nd	2 of 33	6.06%
3rd	3 of 33	6.09%
first 3		48.48%

CLASS	
16 of 38	42.11%
11 of 38	28.95%
6 of 38	15.79%
	86.85%

KIALOA I
Mast Head Rig
Taller Mizzen

KIALOA I
Sloop Rig

Prideful Memories

Racing Proud to Acapulco Comments by Carleton Mitchell

In the March 3, 1962 edition of *Sports Illustrated*, my good friend, Carleton Mitchell, who wrote for the magazine and was the only skipper to ever win three consecutive Newport to Bermuda races, analyzed our winning tactics and strategy in the 1962 Acapulco Race.

In the minds of most West Coast ocean racers, the 1,430-mile run from San Diego to Acapulco has a pattern, a traditional formula: you play the beaches, stay close in and work the sea breezes by day and the offshore zephyrs at night, or you haven't got a chance. But this year John (Jim) Kilroy, standing seaward aboard the 50-foot sloop KIALOA in calculated defiance of the formula, not only won the overall prize, but set a new corrected-time record in what was, for almost everybody else, a fairly slow race.

On two previous occasions, Jim Kilroy had raced KIALOA down the California and Mexican coasts. In 1958, he finished 11th in fleet—as he remembers it, "sitting becalmed everywhere you could get becalmed." Two years later, KIALOA moved up to third in fleet, winning her class. After each race, Jim Kilroy carefully analyzed performances of the fleets, noting who had benefited by going where. On post race cruises back home to Newport Beach, he studied wind and current patterns. On the evidence, Kilroy decided a break with the traditional formula seemed logical.

In preparation for this year's race, KIALOA was first altered to a masthead rig, and then converted from a yawl to a sloop by removing the mizzenmast. The sails were subsequently re-cut to make them draftier for the downwind slide. The net effect of the conversion and refinements with a lower handicap rating, with only a slight loss in efficiency.

By bearing seaward this year, KIALOA's crew not only was breaking with tradition, but also, as any West Coast veteran will acknowledge, sacrificing some of the pleasure of the race…

Part of Kilroy's strategy was to avoid a foul countercurrent that runs along the coast between Corrientes and Point Telmo. "We learned about it the hard way. Two years ago, Ash Brown in Carousel gained 34 miles on us overnight by staying offshore." This time it was KIALOA that profited, moving up to fourth position overall in a fleet of 21 boats, a Class B vessel ahead of six of the nine in Class A. At the end of the night, she was only 65 miles astern of Sirius, with an allowance of 44 hours over the scratch boat.

4

The identity gained *by the KIALOAs* success in the highly technical
and physical sport of worldwide yachting has been exceedingly
beneficial to my success and the success of the Kilroy companies.
This recognition provided identity, respect, and introduction
to the world of business and finance as well as many personal
and continuing friendships.

Over the years, I have been asked to lecture before business schools,
financial organizations and other entities on the similarities
of yachting and business success.
Many of the wonderful friendships still continue.

A Growing Business
Expansion and Concepts: 1960 Onward

In the early 1960's, we added to our portfolio the development and ownership of a series of "moderate rise" office buildings, up to 13 stories. Our first buildings were located in an area with which we had extensive knowledge and experience: the south side of Los Angeles International Airport (LAX) in the city of El Segundo, overlooking the airport with views of the city of Los Angeles, the mountains to the north, and the beaches and oceans from Palos Verdes to Malibu.

By providing substantial tax benefits to all tenants as compared to the city of Los Angeles, El Segundo continued to be an attractive option for business and development. With no tax on gross receipts—a material benefit to our tenants—our buildings were rapidly occupied. There was great diversity in our tenants and clients. While the nature of their businesses were substantially from the high tech and aerospace worlds, our tenants weren't only from the southwest Los Angeles basin, but also from Chicago, New York, Boston and elsewhere in the eastern states. Business executives could fly to LAX and quickly be in their offices. Following our basic criteria and business philosophy, these were once again high quality, low cost maintenance facilities with highly functional electrical and mechanical systems. High-density parking was another key feature that proved appealing. The market was good in the 1960's and remains good in the 2000's.

In the early 1960's, we sold our construction company to the employees. Our initial purpose had been fulfilled: We learned the business in detail. During the tenure of our ownership, we'd conjured and introduced new concepts of construction efficiency and engineering management skills, while reducing "burden," or non-construction, costs and expediting the speed in which we built and completed projects.

The purpose behind our sale of Coordinated Construction was to gain new ideas from other contractors in the realm of design techniques and overall construction organization. We would select two or three contractors to provide bids on new preliminary designs and maximum cost bids, and each contractor would propose their concepts to our construction management team.

We would then make our choice, and the building would be designed to meet our joint criteria within the cost budget and under the supervision of the contractor-owner team. The contractor-owner team would make every effort to reduce cost, while improving construction, quality and completion time.

Making instant decisions on the job site was essential. No set of plans or specifications is really complete, nor do they restrict opportunities to make improvement changes or cost reduction changes underway, consistent with design intent. Each construction project had a daily burden rate. Daily burden rate simply means that expediting construction can reduce overhead, equipment rental and many other costs. An earlier rental date may also come into play.

We had a daily schedule and our construction supervisors could authorize overtime or address other expenses equal to 50 percent of the daily burden rate if we could expedite construction completion by this simple formula and criteria. This system worked well and provided better quality and economics from each building. The contractor would be paid his agreed upon fee and the cost savings would reduce our construction cost. For this system to work well in terms of cost and quality control, making immediate decisions on the job site is essential.

We became involved in development projects in Silicon Valley and were successful there, too. However, rentals and demand in the area were like an amusement park rollercoaster ride: up and down. Since we are primarily builders/investors/developers, we ultimately decided to sell our Silicon Valley projects and concentrate on Southern California, where we were highly recognized and very successful. However, in the 1960's and 1970's, we did make two exceptions: We built about 550,000 square feet of office space across the highway at the main entrance to Seattle's Sea-Tac Airport, which we sold in 2008 after many years as a profitable, going concern. We also established an office in Chicago, partnering with a Chicago-based architect, builder, broker and a few other investors, as well as an office in New York.

These were also successful endeavors, though our key purpose in both was to identify and liaise with lenders and tenants who wished to come to California. The concept worked and introduced many new clients. After a few years, we sold both operations to again concentrate in Southern California, where we expanded our business in Los Angeles County, Orange County, San Diego County and a few other areas.

Facilities continued to be built and leased to the aerospace and high tech industries. For the most part, the leases were net rental agreements where the tenants would pay taxes, as well as operation and maintenance costs, in compliance with the specific terms of our net lease agreements. We would regularly inspect the quality of the maintenance program and general upkeep and they were obligated to comply with the rigorous but equitable provisions of our lease agreements and the expressed conditions for how the facility would be returned to the landlord. Most of our tenants were in for the long term and most of their leases were renewed.

We have always discussed with our clients the design and operational efficiency of our facilities. A good example was back in the late 1950's when we designed, built and leased three facilities, totaling 450,000 square feet, to a single major client. Their specifications called for only about a third of the area to be air-conditioned. The rest of the area was to be heated and ventilated. They intended to run a three-shift, 24-hour-a-day operation. We suggested that there would be substantial productivity savings if the entire facility were properly air conditioned with a high quality HVAC system. The test would be the cost of the total HVAC system—both capital cost and operating cost on a one shift basis—versus their analysis of a productivity benefit from HVAC on a one shift basis. Using their analysis, the HVAC system would pay for itself in 15 months. We proceeded with the installation of a full HVAC system in each building.

The mathematical analysis is very simple. Our client's overall company facility costs were about 3.5 percent of gross products sold while labor costs were about 62.5 percent. Quality facilities must be considered in the same light as machine tools and have a great effect upon labor costs. The leverage in this case was about 18:1, a tremendous savings potential. Improvement in the working environment is an essential ingredient to success. Simply put, highly productive, quality facilities reduce cost.

This was the central tenet of our development strategy and philosophy. The relationship between higher productivity and better, more efficient, high quality building standards and working spaces must be considered as a central component in any business's facility requirements. Over the years, we have had many such discussions and I cannot recall where any of our recommended upgrades were less efficient. This discussion takes me to a very sensitive issue with which many facility engineers will agree: Facility engineers are asked to keep costs down, which generally means a lack of functionality.

Breakdowns and repairs incur not only the cost of fixing things or replacing them; they also incur the cost of wasted labor and the loss of productivity. In general, I feel that a highly qualified owner under a management fee basis outside of the lease agreement could much better maintain leased facilities. This is debatable to some, perhaps because of a lack of confidence in the owner.

We have a provision in many leases whereby we can install, at the tenant's expense, any necessary equipment that will pay for itself over three years of operation. And why not? It saves them money. Smart development in selected locations, efficient buildings and operations, quality tenants, a reliance upon the quality of our services, favorable rentals, affordable operating costs: All have been a tremendous benefit to our operation and our growth.

5

1962 Acapulco Victory
As Ever, It's the Details That Count

The Sailor and the Sea
True Wind, Apparent Wind, Sailing Angles

How can one understand oneself without facing the vagaries of nature? For sailors, the elemental forces of their sport are the sea and the wind, both of which are driven by the sun's solar rays and the rotation and wobbling of the earth, a phenomenon known as Coriolis force. One moves slowly—the sea—and the other—the wind—moves rapidly. The lighter air is wispy and twitchy: quick to warm, to cool or shift, sometimes with damaging consequences. The heavier sea, fluid and substantial, is greatly affected by the breeze, which can accelerate across the surface and command the waters to grow into towering heights, to be sculpted into rough, devastating waves that crash and roar, with potentially overwhelming consequences. Yet, while both can display the harshness of nature, both also can be the source of beauty and delight. For a sailor, they always present tremendous challenges.

In fact, there is nothing more challenging in the art of sailing than chasing every little "cat's-paw" of wind on the water in the early glow of the morning to keep a large racing yacht moving toward the finish line. It reminds me of flying an airplane on low fuel: monitoring the fuel flow, keeping a light touch on the controls, trimming the foils with each lifting thermal to maintain or gain altitude. Like a pilot, a helmsman is absolutely focused on the task at hand, is sensitive to every nuance of trim and weight.

Our *KIALOA*s have been in such situations time and time again, after vigorous nights or days of sailing, trying to finish a race at dawn's first light, crossing an invisible line that signals the end of the contest. These early morning conditions can happen anywhere, and even if you've sailed a brilliant race almost to its conclusion, the loss of wind on a fateful early morning can greatly change a yacht's handicap position with the finish line literally in sight.

Sailors must be optimistic and believe that they will always finish in a breeze, or through sheer will and talent will be able to manage and conquer such light-weather conditions, keeping their yacht moving to a rapid and successful finish. An adage that must be followed is to keep your light sails and gear readily available as you approach land and the finish line. We, and many others, after long and short races, have approached the finish line with much optimism and then spent hours trying to cross it because of light, shifty winds and adverse tides. Along with the skill and resourcefulness of the skipper and the crew, it often comes down to the luck of the game.

That doesn't mean you don't do the best to prepare for the challenge. That's the reason builders and designers of new racing yachts ask a lot of questions. What are the plans for the boat? Will it race inshore or offshore? Where will it be campaigned? Boats like KIALOA that race in so many different areas around the world—Australia, New Zealand, the Tasman Sea, the China Sea, California, Mexico, Florida, the Caribbean, the East Coast, the Atlantic, the Pacific, Hawaii, England, Ireland, the Mediterranean, the Baltic Sea, —present huge challenges because of the different sea states, currents, and wind and sea interactions. Ideally, to race in any given area with the greatest chance of success, one would design a racing yacht for that specific area to fit the local conditions.

All of the KIALOA's were designed to sail in many sea states and wind conditions. None were optimized for a given area and have thus lost potential speed benefits for certain locales. That said, we always did our best to fine-tune the boat and its sails everywhere we competed.

Except for KIALOA I, a boat which we purchased and then modified, in designing the other four KIALOA yachts that followed, we had to consider the average wind and sea conditions in all of the areas where we would race, and then design to what we thought would be the best universal strengths to competitively fit all those distinct areas. As we move through this chapter, we will discuss sailing angles in terms that are second nature to sailors: upwind, reaching, downwind and so on. We'll also discuss what's known as "apparent wind," which is the true wind modified by the boat speed; the wind we feel and see on our instruments.

Don't be confused by apparent wind. Instead, think of your car. The wind speed flowing over your car will increase or decrease as you drive faster or slower. If you drive directly into the wind, the apparent wind over the car is the true wind plus the car speed. For instance, if you're driving 35 miles per hour directly into a 10-mile per hour breeze, your apparent wind will be 45 m.p.h. If you turn around and drive directly away from the wind, the true wind is subtracted from the car speed. In this case, the apparent wind on your return trip will be 25 m.p.h. (The only difference is that boat speed is registered in knots, or nautical miles per hour, as a nautical mile is about 1.15 the length of a statute mile.)

Unlike a car, however, a yacht sailing upwind—toward the breeze—cannot sail directly into the wind. On average, most modern racing boats sail on an angle about 35° to 45° off the direction of the true wind; this angle may sometimes be a little less or a little more dependent upon the wind velocity and sea state.

Upwind sailing increases the wind velocity over the deck, just like "upwind" driving increases the flow of air over the car. Downwind sailing decreases the velocity over the deck because you are literally sailing away from the wind. Changes of sailing angles and yacht speed can increase or decrease the apparent wind velocity and the effective power of the wind over the decks.

A yacht cannot sail effectively "dead" downwind, which is also potentially dangerous as well as inefficient, because the boom on which the mainsail is set is more difficult to control when it is eased out when sailing before the breeze. So a yacht must maintain a safe angle to the apparent wind based upon sea and performance conditions. But yachts do like breeze. In higher apparent wind velocities, yachts can sail a deeper angle to "dead" downwind. In lower velocities, the yacht must sail an angle closer to the breeze. Again, since downwind sailing is away from the wind, the apparent wind force is a lower figure than upwind sailing in the same amount of breeze.

The apparent wind is always a key and driving factor in the sailing techniques employed by a yacht's helmsman, who can effectively increase or decrease the speed and angle of the apparent wind with skillful steering and planning and by working in tandem with a skilled crew. A good example was *KIALOA II*'s first race on the East Coast. We were sailing in a short distance race, about 22 miles, during the New York Yacht Club's annual cruise in Long Island Sound. In a highly competitive fleet of about thirty yachts, *KIALOA II* was lined up against a strong boat about the same size and length.

Our upwind sailing was excellent, and we were now spinnaker reaching about 5° higher than our optimal course in a light breeze. Two outstanding local sailors were in the cockpit, and I was driving. One of them, a former America's Cup helmsman, said, "We have a wind shift, let's trim back the pole and come to course." I had been playing "leading the wind" games with the apparent wind and sail trim for speed, and we had moved exceedingly well on our competition.

With the goal of learning something new, a lifelong pursuit, I suggested that he take the helm, and as he did he called for the spinnaker pole to come back and the mainsail to be re-trimmed while he sailed the 5° lower course. The speed dropped one knot, and he commented that there was a drop in the wind and a wind shift. Yes, there was an apparent wind shift and a drop in velocity because of our changed sail angles and the loss of apparent wind speed.

I told my friend that this was an issue of technique and suggested that my son, John, drive while we discussed what he was doing. John was about 16 at the time.

John called for a re-trim of the pole and sails to our prior setting. He then reached up towards the wind, whereby our boat speed began to increase. Very tenderly, while maintaining our boat speed and sailing the spinnaker right on its edge, he eased *KIALOA II* back to our former heading about 5° above the actual course. The boat was again a knot faster than when our friend was in command. It may not sound like a lot, but over a 10- or 20-mile course, it's a significant difference.

Sailing a "hotter," faster angle was a new technique for East Coast sailors. I do not say this to criticize. Their racing conditions did not have as many off the wind and downwind legs as we did on the West Coast; the Transpac registered 2,225 miles, the Acapulco Race 1,430 miles, and there were many other events contested in primarily off the wind in light conditions.

We learned more about apparent wind the day *KIALOA III* was launched and christened at Pat Haggerty's Palmer Johnson boatyard in Wisconsin. Pat, a noted electronics scientist, owned an Admiral's Cup yacht called *Bay Bea.* On her first sail that day, *KIALOA III*'s upwind performance was excellent, even though the boat wasn't fully tuned for racing. Sparkman & Stephens naval architect David Pedrick, a key member of the design team, was onboard with several other S&S designers, and everyone was impressed with the new boat's speed on multiple sailing angles. Her upwind tacking angles were very close and impressive.

The next day, the famous naval architect, and the head of S&S, Olin Stephens, was scheduled to arrive. Before he did, by phone, he heard about the sail test and said our tacking angles were too close and that the instruments onboard needed to be tuned and calibrated. I replied that we weren't taking the numbers off the instruments, but referring to the angles recorded by the compass.

After Olin arrived, we took *KIALOA III* back out and then moved the boat to Long Island Sound for more detailed and thorough sail testing, and tuning the rig, main mast, mizzen mast and shrouds in light and heavy winds. Through all of this, the design team from Sparkman & Stephens remained perplexed about the instrument readout of our tacking angles and well as the true wind readout.

Sailing Angles, Distance Sailed and Jibes

The following charts and pictures define and depict commonly described sailing angles and issues to be considered.

Yachts must tack in upwind sailing and jibe in downwind sailing. They must sail a longer distance than actual course distance. Chart 1 shows different sailing angles. Chart 2 calculates the added distance sailed based upon average assumptions.

Sailing Angles
UPWIND - REACHING - DOWNWIND

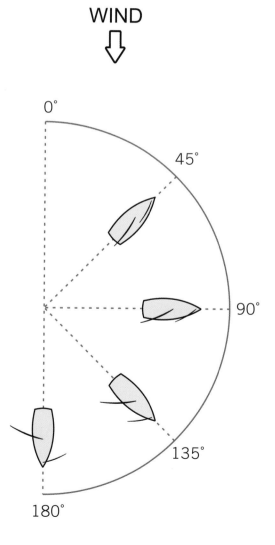

UPWIND
A Yacht can not sail directly upwind. The general definition of a 45° angle to the wind, a 90° tack is sailing upwind.

REACHING
The general definition for reaching would be 45° to 135° off the wind.

DOWNWIND
Running the general definition would be 135° to 180° off the wind.

Course Distance vs. Distance Sailed

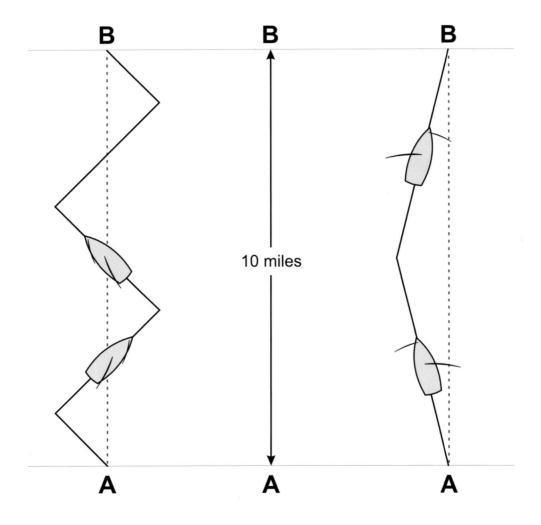

Upwind	Distance	Downwind
90° Tacking Angle	Sailed	30° Jibing Angle
14.0± miles	**A-B**	11.1± miles

KIALOA III *sailing upwind on a port tack in the Irish Sea, Fastnet Rock Race*

PORT JIBE **STARBOARD JIBE**

The two pictures show *KIALOA III* surfing downwind on a port and starboard jibe in the 1975 record setting 635-mile Sydney Hobart Race in the Tasman Sea, along the coasts of Australia and Tasmania.

This record, in one of the most challenging sailboat races of the world, was held for 21 years and then broken by only 29 minutes by *Morning Glory*, sailed by New Zealand's Russell Coutts and his winning America's Cup crew.

In view of all of the technological changes in design, weight, use of carbon fibers and other highly advanced lightweight materials, we consider this an even greater elapsed time victory for *KIALOA III*, 21 years earlier.

In this race, as well as many other victorious races in downwind sailing, such as the overall victory in the 1977 Transpacific Yacht Race from Los Angeles to Honolulu, enroute to Australia, we considered the five sail ketch rig a most powerful downwind sail plan, maximizing sail area for downwind surfing.

We would like to explain to the reader why we used five sails, as well as the steps taken to jibe *KIALOA III* in sailing the fastest speed over our tactical course to the finish.

The reader must understand that it is impractical and dangerous to try to sail a racing yacht directly downwind. We must sail at an angle to the wind, coming from astern.

In this case, we were sailing an angle of about 15° to the actual wind, surfing on every wave we could catch, and with the surge in velocity, we would be able to sail a little closer to the actual course.

KIALOA III is shown on a port jibe and on its mirrored image a starboard jibe with a total angle between the two courses of perhaps 30°, 15° on each side of the wind. At least, that is our assumption for this discussion. As discussed above, the added speed of surfing would move the apparent wind forward, and we might move from 15° off the wind to 10° and sometimes even lower for the free ride on the wave.

We believe it might be of interest to explain the series of events and complication of an actual jibe from a port jibe to a starboard jibe.

All crew necessary in the jibe are well trained and familiar with the precision required and the potential of danger if mistakes are made. In some jibes, it may be necessary to have the entire crew on deck instead of just the "watch" on deck.

Starting from the bow, the five sails are:

The spinnaker, tacked to the spinnaker pole, to weather, extending over the open water on the port side of *KIALOA III*.

The "shooter", a very sensitive sail tacked on the foredeck to leeward of the spinnaker.

The mainsail on the mast, and the boom trimmed to leeward.

The mizzen spinnaker tacked to the weather deck and flying high to leeward.

The mizzen on the mizzen mast trimmed for balance and steering control.

With five sails and several control lines to each sail, one must make certain that each line or braided wire guy is properly coiled to run, in or out for the maneuver to be performed and that all crew are in the correct position.

The helmsman must call for the jibe, "Prepare to jibe."

The bow man, holding the new 165-foot long starboard braided wire afterguy, prepared to insert the afterguy in the spinnaker pole, will view the crew positions and will call "ok to jibe" when all are ready. The bowman must also observe that the spinnaker pole has been eased forward about 3', that the shooter has been "doused," dropped to deck and that the mizzen spinnaker has been doused." The helmsman will watch the waves, and respond "jibing" when all are ready, hopefully riding the new wave.

The helmsman steers *KIALOA III* 30° to starboard in rhythm with the performance of the crew and the surfing of *KIALOA*.

The port topping lift crew pulls the release of the port afterguy from the spinnaker pole and then drops the pole to a specific mark while the foreguy to the pole pulls the pole forward to the bowman.

The mainsail crew have released the preventer and vang and are cranking the main to the deck center line and then ease to leeward. The bowman, holding the loose starboard afterguy inserts the wire in the pole, the foreguy is eased and the topping lift is hoisted while the afterguy and pole are trimmed to about 3' short of its final trim position, horizontal to the water. The leeward spinnaker sheet is trimmed through the jibe to keep the spinnaker properly set.

The spinnaker and main are now powering *KIALOA III* as the mizzen spinnaker is hoisted to leeward, tacked off the weather deck while all sails are properly trimmed and *KIALOA III* is steering its new course.

The mizzen is now being properly trimmed or taken down as appropriate. The mizzen is not a powerful sail in these conditions and is being used more for balance.

The helmsman and crew now decide on the shooter. Should it be set? Probably, yes. If set and *KIALOA III* is properly balanced, the spinnaker pole can be trimmed further aft to a balanced helm.

A great advantage of a shooter is that *KIALOA III* can be sailed a little wider, perhaps 10° off the wind or even less with steering control, particularly in a surf. However, if the shooter collapses and the spinnaker pole is not eased forward, the leeward pull of the shooter may induce an unfavorable weather role from leeward pulling force on the bow. An excellent helmsman is required, and yes, *KIALOA III* did have outstanding helmsmen.

The outstanding crew of *KIALOA III* or the other *KIALOAs* performed magical jibes—with mutual compliments to all.

Overall Corrected Time Winner
Class Corrected Time Winner

Many sports have handicap formulas to determine the overall winner, which may not be the first participant to finish, while others install some form of mechanical or weight penalty to slow a faster competitor.

A classic example would be horse racing, where a horse that frequently wins must carry more weight to slow down excessive speed capabilities as they race at major horse racing tracks around the world. It's a way to "fix" the competition.

Yacht racing is exceedingly hard to handicap because the course for an ocean race is the dynamic, fluid sea with tides and currents moving in different directions and with counter currents that are caused by weather and shoreline formations. And of course the shifting winds add another factor to this dynamic equation.

These handicap complications are further enhanced by the difference in speed between the bigger, faster yachts and the smaller, slower yachts. A difference in speed of 1 knot between two yachts could mean that the bigger yacht may be 24 miles ahead at the end of the first day and 48 miles ahead at the end of the second day, sailing in entirely different wind and sea conditions.

There are further variables that commonly occur, including seas and storms. Furthermore, a yacht sailing hard on the wind close hauled must tack back and forth, an angle on average of about 80° from a port tack to a starboard tack or vice versa, which causes an added sailing distance of about 40%.

One yacht well separated from other large or smaller yachts may be helped or hurt by upwind sailing conditions. In theory, such disparate conditions may average out in a longer race. I will make comments about such conditions in given races, which I will try to minimize; however, they are important to understanding the results.

Aboard the *KIALOA*s, we have continuously studied the probability of such adverse conditions, avoiding them where possible and capitalizing on them when they proved to be an advantage.

We must always remember the current, which can be a free ride or a tremendous liability. The benefits and losses of the Gulf Stream are explained in the chapters about the SORC, Southern Ocean Racing Circuit, and the benefits of Pacific currents are touched upon in the chapters on the 2,225-mile Transpac Race.

These are facts of life which sailors face. It's all part of the wonderful game, the challenge of the great sport of sailing.

6

Masterful Political Stroke!!!

Should any President sacrifice any component
of our security for his own personal gain?

Daisy Girl

The Daisy Girl
Nixon, Reagan, Goldwater and the '64 Elections

My first brush with Richard Nixon was in 1946, when he was running for Congress and came to our offices looking for support. We became friends, and to this day, I remain a strong supporter of President Nixon in consideration of all the facts and issues of his career. Many years later, well after Watergate, he was living in Oceanside and one evening he gave a talk there. He spoke for an hour without notes and held the audience in rapt attention. There was complete silence; people were hanging on every word. That's how good and clear he was at discussing things. In my own discussions with him over the years, I was equally impressed. He was always quite open, a man who wanted to learn and learn and learn.

As time went on, I became quite involved in community and political affairs, and with the Republican Party. During the 1964 Presidential election, I had a ringside seat for the proceedings.

My interest in politics goes back to my mother, and to my education and upbringing. Like my mother, I was a voracious reader, and I devoured books about history. Like many Alaskans, my mother used the long months of winter to study and read. If you stop and think about it, you see a bit of a renaissance woman—like my mother—in Sarah Palin.

By the time I was ten, we were no longer living in Alaska, but I recall seeing a photograph taken around that time of White Russian Army soldiers who were executed by Communists near the Bering Sea. This image struck home, as my mother's brothers were fishing in the Bering Straits between Alaska and Russia and were driven to the Russian shore by a serious storm. It was explained to me, at the time, that the White Russian Army had merged with the Communists to overthrow the Czar. But later, the White Russians were double-crossed and liquidated by those very same Communists, who distrusted them.

All of this piqued my interest and left a lasting impression. And as I grew older and read historical accounts about Europe and Russia, including Marx's *Communist Manifesto*; Hitler's *Mein Kampf*, and the account of his March on Munich; and the growth and power of those two primary dictators, I always thought back to those executed soldiers. I was unalterably opposed to Communism and Fascism and the terrible and insidious false representations of what I call the Dictatorship Religion.

Well after the war, through various sources, I met several ex-Communist agents who were now working with our FBI. One of them was Karl Prussian, who was featured on the television program, *I Was A Russian Spy*. Others had equally interesting stories.

Two friends and entrepreneurs introduced me to a retired FBI official, Cleon Skousen, who had structured a group called the Anti-Communism Crusade. I introduced these ex-Russian spies to personal and business friends, and we all made contributions to his organization and also made new contacts. We were all concerned about the intrusion of Communism into the mass-media and the riots in our colleges.

Our circle of like-minded individuals continued to expand. Next, I met a well-known television director named Doc Livingston and a TV executive, Bob Raisbeck, who was a producer of *Queen for a Day*. We talked about the need to make the Republican Party a more active and enthusiastic group. The year was 1964, toward the end of President Johnson's short term following the assassination of President John Kennedy.

I was a delegate at that year's Republican Convention, where Barry Goldwater faced Nelson Rockefeller for the nomination as the party's presidential candidate. After a nasty battle, Goldwater was selected and Rockefeller withdrew from the Convention.

An ex-Air Force general, Goldwater was a fine, forthright man and candidate. He told everyone what he thought—and was usually right on target—which made him very popular to Republicans. But he was a lightning rod, and he also stirred up serious political and Left Wing opposition. Unfortunately, because he believed it should be a more forthright and improved piece of legislation, he voted against the 1964 Civil Rights Bill. It passed, and he was recorded as a no-vote. Politically, this was very damaging. It was also incredibly amateurish.

Henry Salvatori (who chaired Goldwater's campaign in California), Doc Livingston, Bob Raisbeck and I thought that Barry needed help and that Ronald Reagan—the actor who was already making outstanding speeches on fundamental issues set forth by the Republican Party—would be an excellent choice to speak for the principles advocated by Barry Goldwater. We asked Ron Reagan, and he agreed to do so. I then went to Washington and discussed the matter of a Reagan television program with Dean Burch, Goldwater's national campaign manager, and Ralph Cordiner, the Republican Party finance chairman, who was also the chairman of General Electric Corporation.

Both Ralph and Dean bought into the concept, and we formed a separate "Barry Goldwater Television Committee," for which I was chairman. Our funding plan was simple: Henry Salvatori and I would put up "seed money" for the filming, editing and airtime for the first show. During the program, after Reagan's speech, we'd ask for contributions that could be put towards future shows.

The money pitch was straightforward: "If you agree with the words of Ron Reagan and Barry Goldwater, the Republican Candidate for President, please send your contribution to P.O. Lock Box 80, Los Angeles, California." We went ahead and made this commercial, and money began pouring in to Lock Box 80, which was actually an account at Security Pacific National Bank in Los Angeles. The bank charged only 50-cents per contribution and provided not only "Thank You" letters to each contributor, but financial reports to the Congressional Oversight Group, the Republican Party and our Committee. The entire scheme was a great success and the Ron Reagan speech was broadcast nationally on numerous occasions. It gave him incredible visibility.

Just before the election, however, Lyndon Johnson and the Democratic Party turned the tables and proved how important a role the emerging medium would play in national affairs. The Democrats countered with their own commercial, just 30-seconds long, which continues to be known as the most dynamic political television spot in history. I certainly agree. It was called "The Daisy Girl."

A bit of background: Prior to the commercial, in a press conference during his campaign, Goldwater stated that we should consider using a "light nuclear" bomb against the North Vietnamese, and that such a tactic would quickly end the war.

Johnson's simple, powerful response was the "Daisy Girl."

It featured a young, pretty girl, about 6 or 7 years old, gathering daisies in a green field. She picked a daisy and counted, "One." She picked another and counted, "Two." On it went until she reached number nine, at which time the cloud of a light nuclear bomb appeared, and the pretty girl was gone…

And so was Barry!

Daisy Girl

Even so, good things occurred. Most notably, everyone involved with the campaign believed that our Republican Party had benefited greatly from the Ron Reagan speeches.

Henry Salvatori held an election night party at the Ambassador Hotel in Los Angeles to hear the Goldwater vs. Johnson election results, and of course, we were all saddened by Barry's loss.

Ron and Nancy Reagan were there, but they left early after Goldwater's defeat was confirmed. But a few of us stayed on and talked further into the night. Suddenly Holmes Tuttle—a local businessman who was also involved in the party—said to three of us, "Let's talk outside." And we did. Tuttle said, "Why don't we run Ron Reagan for Governor? With all the political exposure and his great speeches, he'd be an excellent, well-recognized candidate and Governor." We agreed, and not long after Ronald Reagan began his ascent to the presidency and his rightful place in the history of our great country.

At the next Republican National Convention in 1965, I was asked to chair a new Republican Party Television Committee. I accepted this position, knowing that we'd need a successful fundraising program and commercial, much like Reagan's speech in 1964, which raised millions of dollars. As I considered the obligations of the Television Committee, it became clear that it provided an opportunity to effectively set the goals and standards for the Republican Party. I also realized I couldn't individually assume that position and would need a major party leader as co-chairman.

We presented storyboards on well-researched key issues to the Republican National Committee, and, upon my recommendations, it was agreed that the television programs must have the support of the Republican House and Senate leaders. I called Barry Goldwater, outlined the game plan and concepts, and he thought they were great; however, he declined to be co-chairman, saying that he had just finished an exhausting Presidential campaign and it was someone else's turn.

I then began what turned into several ongoing discussions with my old friend Richard Nixon. While he wholly bought into the concept, Dick felt that his active participation on the committee might have certain undefined conflicts in connection with his future objectives and declined.

Next, we talked to the new national chairman of the Republican Party, who expressed his personal lack of interest in such a program. He suggested instead that we give the $350,000 cash remaining in our individual committee coffers to the Republican National Committee. This time it was our turn to decline, and as a separate committee, we had the right to do so.

On we went. We met with Jerry Ford, then head of the Republican Congressional Committee, who perhaps not surprisingly suggested we use the existing funds to finance the speeches of Congressmen, and raise other money with another commercial as we'd done in 1964. Our next meeting was with Senator John Tower, the chairman of the Senatorial Committee, whose position was the same as Jerry Ford's.

By now, my tentative committee, composed of Doc Livingston, Bob Raisbeck and other advisors, felt that we were getting nowhere, and that we needed dynamic TV presentations to fund a continuance of effective programs. But after considerable discussion with many Republican leaders, we advised the National Committee that our proposed committee, under my leadership, would withdraw, pursuant to the understanding that my initial acceptance was conditional as previously stated. We returned the $350,000 in the bank to public-spirited Republicans who had loaned additional money to our committee for the Ronald Reagan speech and were willing to help continue with our program if it was decided to do so.

We regretted our decision. However, as the committee's chairman, I understood that without full cooperation and an acceptable game plan from leading Republicans, my associates and I could not take on the responsibility of effectively being the spokesmen for the Party.

In subsequent years, Republican leaders have approached me to become involved in similar committees. My answer's always been the same. I'd be happy to help organize such a committee but am too involved in other activities to take a leadership role.

Do I still think the idea could work as a great fundraiser for the Republican Party? Absolutely, but solely based upon the program content, and above all its honesty, research and simplicity.

And in retrospect, it was great to work with Barry Goldwater—a most fundamental, honest and decent man with a great and broad sense of humor. As a former member of the U.S. Army Air Corps, I salute my General Barry Goldwater.

7

KIALOA I "Our Learner's Yacht" Became a Winner

We had acquired *KIALOA I*, raced it in the Pacific to Honolulu, Hawaii,
in Mexico to Acapulco, in the major races in San Francisco and Southern
California, with reasonably successful results and some overall victories.
We made many changes to *KIALOA I*, improving her performance
with the help of friends in the aerospace world and friendly competition
with Ash Brown from San Diego and his yacht *Carousel*.

We now felt that we could compete elsewhere, to race and cruise
on the US East Coast and perhaps Europe in a new *KIALOA II*.
For a new *KIALOA II* we decided that the hull should be aluminum,
computer roll formed to reduce weight and improve hull form.

With an ever-growing process of design ideas,
manufacturing ideas and the expertise of friends and sailors,
KIALOA II became a wonderfully successful yacht in
worldwide competition and we learned so much from this competition.

The Birth of *KIALOA II*
New Challenges Aboard a New and Bigger Yacht

K IALOA I had raced in the Pacific Ocean to Hawaii, along the Mexico Coast to Acapulco and in most of the races in California. We'd competed against yachts from the South Pacific, Australia and New Zealand, and versus East Coast sailors who'd ventured west to test themselves in the excellent sailing and racing conditions. Through it all, *KIALOA I* became a very successful yacht.

We now wanted to expand our activities to race and cruise on the east coast of Florida and the Caribbean, the major sailing centers in the Northeast—New York and Long Island Sound, Newport, R.I., and Marblehead, Massachusetts—as well as across the Atlantic to Ireland, England and the Mediterranean. From business and personal visits, we were generally familiar with these areas from the shore-side vantage point. But now we wished to view them from the sea, which is always a different and unique perspective.

The centerpiece of all these plans was a new yacht, *KIALOA II*. The famed Newport-Bermuda Race was on our agenda, so we decided the new boat should be the maximum size allowable under the then-existing "Bermuda Rule," which was 72 feet.

The New York-based naval architects, Sparkman & Stephens, had designed *KIALOA I* and were widely considered to be the leading yacht designers of the era, so I met with them to talk about ideas for the new *KIALOA II*. Olin prepared a preliminary set of plans for discussion purposes. I also asked a group of friends in the aerospace world to offer their comments and ideas. We all agreed that *KIALOA II* should be an aluminum hull, which was not only a departure from the typical wooden hull, but probably the biggest aluminum hull of that time.

After much back and forth discussion and input from our team—an all-star line-up that included Don Douglas Sr., Ski Kleinhaus, Don Douglas Jr., Bud Gardiner and Ed Grant, all from Douglas Aircraft; Kenny Watts, the great sailmaker; and Allen Puckett, the president of Hughes Aircraft—we agreed to proceed to the final design stage and on to construction. Next, Olin finalized the design and a new company, called Yacht Dynamics, was formed by three members of the design team (Douglas, Jr., Gardiner and Watts) to build *KIALOA II* in San Pedro, California.

Many of those employed by this new shipbuilding concern, Yacht Dynamics, were from Douglas Aircraft and were familiar with techniques for shaping and building large aluminum structures. The hull form and all frames and plates were computer lofted and roll formed at Douglas's facilities in Long Beach. It was a great advance in yacht construction, employing the latest welding techniques and technicians.

Leading members of the marine and materials industries joined the aerospace industry to work on the final rig design, sail plans, deck equipment, winches and other essential equipment. As with the hull, the idea was always to take advantage of the latest technologies. And building *KIALOA II* in San Pedro, about 12 miles from my home in Newport Beach and also close to Douglas's Long Beach operation, proved to be a tremendous advantage over building on the East Coast. *KIALOA II* was rapidly, but carefully, constructed following aircraft inspection and test rules; all questions or issues were immediately addressed, as were all changes or modifications.

KIALOA II was launched on time, meeting an exacting schedule, and after initial sail testing in light to medium wind conditions in Southern California, we took the boat north for "real-world" trials on San Francisco Bay. The St. Francis Yacht Club's Perpetual Series would be the first regatta, and the competition was strong with two other 73-footers on the starting line: Jim Michaels' *Baruna* and Tim Mosely's *Orient*.

Michaels and Mosely were the co-owners of Barient Winches (you can see how they came up with the name), a new company that designed and built *KIALOA II*'s four-speed, linked pedestal winches used to trim our headsails and spinnakers. We'd been sold on Barient over a year earlier while *KIALOA II* was still being built. A meeting with the Barient group and the *KIALOA II* team was held aboard *Baruna* at the St. Francis Yacht Club Stag Cruise, up the Sacramento River on Tinsley Island. A number of noted sailors and yachtsmen from across the country attended this event to review plans and specifications and make some final decisions about *KIALOA II*. In attendance were Olin Stephens, Kenny Watts, Jim Michael, Tim Mosely, Bob Keefe and Jim Kilroy.

At the end of the meeting, the decision was made to go with Barient winches. And Tim Mosely, a great engineer as well as a gear manufacturer, offered ideas about Barient providing titanium-based blocks and rigging components for *KIALOA II*. With their new, high-speed, cross-connected pedestal winches—as well as all the other primary and secondary winches for the boat—"the new kids on the block" landed the largest order ever, in terms of dollars, for a winch package on a single sailboat.

It was essential to test the newly designed winch system in heavy air, which is why the San Francisco venue was so important. And in our early tests we were pleased to discover that *KIALOA II*'s straight-line performance on all points of sail was excellent. But the stiff winds did reveal a weakness in the winch package when shifting gears. Specifically, we couldn't shift to lower gears for the extra "grunt" needed to sheet home the sails, which meant we had a terrible time completing tacks and trimming sails with precision.

The temporary solution was to bring aboard Barient's chief engineer, Juan Guarena, to manually shift the gears from down below, which meant we had to remove the cosmetic ceiling for access to the linkage gear in the shifting mechanism. As the crew cranked on the winches from above, they'd call down to Juan in the main saloon to pull the proper string to shift into the appropriate gear to trim the sails. This was obviously frustrating to the crew and our maneuvers suffered. Down below, we'd sometimes hear Juan, who hailed from Cuba, cursing in Spanish. After this series, Juan adjusted and redesigned minor components, and we had a great set of winches.

With the San Francisco trials behind us, *KIALOA II* was ready for its first offshore contest, the 1,430-mile San Diego to Acapulco Race, starting on February 2, 1964. We had much to learn about the best techniques for sailing *KIALOA II*; however, from those first trials, it was apparent that *KII* had great speed potential. The racecourse would provide the final answers.

Our first Acapulco Race in 1958 aboard *KIALOA I* hadn't been a success: an eleventh out of 35 boats. Afterwards, I flew our twin-engine Aero Commander along the coast of Baja, paying close attention to the valleys and canyons lining the mountainous shores. The flight convinced me that wind pressure from the Gulf of California played a key role in the local conditions by shifting the breeze along the west coast based upon differential pressures. By using what I'd learned and referencing the latest Air Force charts, we developed a new plan for the next races in 1960 and 1962, which worked well. *KIALOA I* finished third on corrected time in '60 and first overall in '62. So we knew the course well and felt we could quickly adapt to different conditions as they arose.

As it turned out, in *KIALOA II*'s inaugural Acapulco Race in 1964, we were second to finish and second in Class A, behind Howard Ahmanson's *Sirius II*, but only eighth overall. (The overall corrected-time winner in the 33-boat fleet was Ash Brown's 40-footer, *Carousel*.) *Sirius II*, a yacht nine-feet longer than *KIALOA II*, got ahead of us by sailing well offshore the first night out (which we were reluctant to do so early) in a heavy offshore breeze. *Sirius II* consolidated their lead by taking advantage of a new northwesterly breeze and beat us by three-and-a-half hours on corrected time. After that first night, conditions became light and fluky; *Sirius II*'s average speed over the eight days and 15 hours it took to finish the race was only 6.9 knots. Still, the 1964 Acapulco Race was encouraging in that it confirmed *KII*'s speed potential and left us confident that with more sailing time we could do even better, particularly in light air.

The *Sirius II* crew borrowed a small power boat, found a local guitar player and met *KIALOA II* as we were trying to sail, in a very light breeze, through Boca Chica—Spanish for "Small Mouth"—

one of the two entrances to Acapulco Bay (the other is Boca Grande, or "Big Mouth") near the finish line. The *Sirius* crew serenaded us with "modified" Mexican songs of greeting. It was a fun finish to the event.

We had a great time in Acapulco, which was a much quieter place than it is today. From our quarters at the Boca Chica Hotel on a high bluff overlooking the bay, we had a fine place to watch the smaller yachts finish.

After the trophy presentation at the Acapulco Yacht Club, *KIALOA II* cruised up the Mexican Coast, stopping first at Zihuatanejo, a lovely, small fishing and resort village; and then on to Manzanillo and Tenacatita Bay, where we watched the mating of the Manta Rays. Their leaps from the ocean in the moonlit, phosphorescent waters against a backdrop of rippling waves and the golden, sandy beach were a most unusual and beautiful sight.

At a dinner at the home of Mexico's president, Miguel Alemán, I teased him about the various discrepancies in the prices of fuel at the small fuel docks dotted along the coast, and he immediately provided me with a signed picture which said, "El Yate *KIALOA*, Mi Amigo, Jim Kilroy, El Presidente Miguel Alemán." He said to show this to the attendants at the fuel docks and we'd get a discount. He was right.

We carried on around Cabo Corrientes to beautiful Puerto Vallarta, a relatively undeveloped area in 1964 with only two or three small hotels. *KIALOA II* anchored along the beach called Los Muertos—which means "the dead," and is not a good anchorage if there are any large waves.

After Puerto Vallarta, *KIALOA II* sailed west about 200 miles across the Gulf of California to La Paz, the fishing center on the east coast of Baja, California, to spend a few days before flying home from their small but busy airport. On other occasions we went to Cabo San Lucas and stayed at the beautiful Hotel Cabo San Lucas, constructed by Bud Parr. We always enjoyed Mexico and have wonderful, romantic memories of our time there. Aside from picking up a few new racing ideas, on the voyage north we positively learned that *KIALOA II* was an exceedingly comfortable and powerful dual-purpose racing/cruising yacht, which we would enjoy in both capacities over the next several years.

Upon *KIALOA II*'s return to Newport Beach, it was time to prepare for the Southern California racing season. The first test would be the 1964 Los Angeles Yacht Club Whitney Series, consisting of six races, five of which would count toward an overall series winner. *KIALOA II* participated in four races of distances from sixty to 147 miles, registering a clean sweep—first to finish, first in class and first overall on corrected time—and setting a new elapsed-time record in the 147-mile San Nicolas Race. The courses played to the boat's versatility and strengths, with long beats to weather and fine spinnaker runs returning home. These were her elements for victory.

The Newport Harbor Ahmanson Series was the next event, a series of six races ranging from

25 to 80 miles, the best five results of which would determine the winner. Due to business commitments and my involvement with Barry Goldwater's campaign and the Reagan commercials, we could only make three of the races, winning two overall and recording a fourth overall in the third.

Next up was the "fun" Ensenada Race, 142 miles from Newport Beach to Ensenada, Mexico. Over 400 sailboats participated—some old, some new, in a fleet that was full of surprises—in the downwind, reaching race. For *KIALOA II*, which recorded yet another clean sweep while winning overall honors, it was especially fun.

Clearly, the first few months of racing were going well. Now it was off to San Francisco for the St. Francis Yacht Club Big Boat Series, a four-race regatta consisting of closed-course racing in the Bay. With only a reasonable knowledge of the currents, which play such a huge role on the Bay, we faired not too badly. There were eight boats in our class and we scored second overall.

During our second visit to San Francisco aboard *KIALOA II*, we were intrigued by some comments from a very experienced sailor, Bob Keefe, the sales manager for Barient and the staff commodore at the St. Francis Yacht Club. Bob was a frequent sailor on *Baruna* and he also spent some time crewing on *KIALOA II*.

Bob was surprised that *KIALOA II*, at 72 feet long, was such a giant yacht compared to *Baruna*, which also measured 72 feet. With *KIALOA II*, it was easy to see where the rating rules were taking yachting. In comparison, *Baruna* had a small, fractional rig with a much smaller sail area and a very low rating number.

In concept and execution, *KIALOA II* was just the opposite. For example, she sported an enormous masthead foretriangle; clearly, her owner and designers had no fear of a much higher rating figure and a lower handicap allowance. But the boat begged several questions: Could *KIALOA II* sail to such a high rating and be a winner? Could her crew shorten sail in heavy weather conditions and still maintain the performance to win? The week of racing provided no real answer except for those who professionally made a study of yacht racing.

Bob states: "In light to moderate conditions, *KIALOA II* could get so far ahead of *Baruna* that *Baruna* could barely see *KIALOA II*. However, in a typical San Francisco breeze in the Bay's protected, smoother waters (which you find in the lee of the shoreline and islands), *Baruna*'s excellent windward capability made her very competitive with *KII*."

In summation, Bob said, "The handwriting was on the wall. The day of the low-rating 'Big Boat' was over." The new concept was to be big and fast. *KIALOA II* had the horsepower to sail exceedingly well in light to moderate conditions, and could shorten sail in heavy weather and still be highly competitive.

Like every event thus far, the round the buoys racing in San Francisco was encouraging. It was now time to again head offshore.

After the Big Boat Series, *KIALOA* II returned home for the Los Angeles Yacht Club's 930-mile Mazatlan Invitational race. The first half of the course was much like the first leg of the Acapulco Race, from Southern California to Cabo San Lucas. The second leg, across the Gulf of California to Mazatlan, included what was basically a left-hand turn at Cabo to sail east under the lee of the Baja's southerly tip, a notoriously fickle area.

For the 1964 Mazatlan Race, we were once again matched up against our rival, Howard Ahmanson's "M" boat, *Sirius II*, which beat us in the 1964 Acapulco Race. Once again, *Sirius II* was first to finish, only 35 minutes ahead of us on elapsed time. But this time we got the better of them on corrected time by two hours, 48 minutes, finishing first in class and fourth overall. The race was once again a slow, light affair; our average speed was only 6.59 knots. But we were pleased with the victory, as slow races often favor smaller yachts, which is always a danger when racing in Mexican waters.

After the awards ceremony, where the *Sirius II* crew received their "first to finish" prize and the *KIALOA* II team picked up the Class A trophy, both crews went to dinner at a great second-story Mexican café overlooking the moonlit bay with mariachis singing beautiful Mexican music. There were many mutual margarita toasts between the sailors. A noted West Coast banker, Howard Ahmanson elected to show us his big silver platter, the coveted first to finish hardware. Ahmanson carried this beautiful trophy tray like a waiter starting to clear tables. You can guess what the *KIALOA* sailors did. All of our crew deposited their dirty dishes on Howard's trophy.

Howard was usually quite serious, and this was a dilemma. But surprisingly, he broke into a loud laugh and said, "You got me!" Another round of margaritas followed in a mutual toast of respect.

We ended our first year of racing with a pleasant cruise to the Hotel Cabo San Lucas and a bit of scuba diving at Chileno, a small bay west of Cabo, before flying back to Los Angeles. We were proud of the first year's performance, of our crew and our friendships... building, racing and cruising *KIALOA* II had been a total team effort. Looking ahead, we also knew we couldn't be complacent. Together, we knew we'd have more competition in 1965. It all raised a central question: "How could we further improve *KIALOA* II?"

Almost immediately, we set forth searching for answers.

After returning from Cabo, we began preparing for Year Two of the *KIALOA* II campaign. First up, in February of 1965, was the three-race Southern California Yachting Association Regatta, where we faced the America's Cup 12-Meter, Columbia. They took all three races and the experience was summed up succinctly in our log book: "Columbia kicked the hell out of us."

For the 1965 Whitney High Point Series, we again had good results. In five races, *KIALOA* II registered three clean sweeps and overall victories, as well as a corrected time record in the San Nicolas Island Race. In the Ahmanson Trophy Races, we were first to finish, second in Class and second overall. And in the San Clemente Island Race, we were first to finish and third in Class but

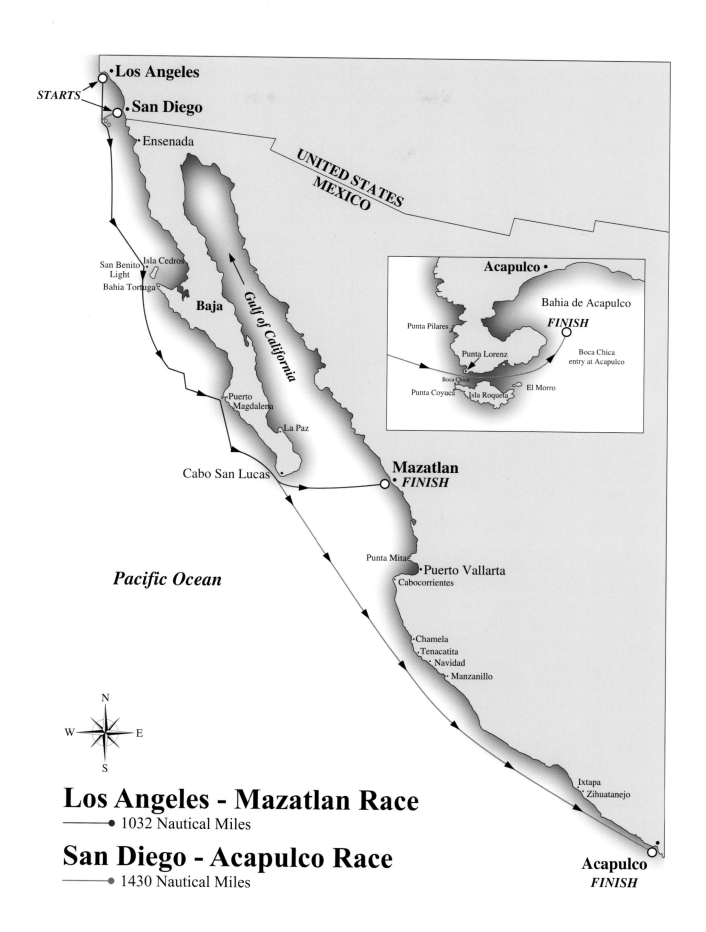

Los Angeles - Mazatlan Race
—●— 1032 Nautical Miles

San Diego - Acapulco Race
—●— 1430 Nautical Miles

a disappointing twentieth overall, due to our silly experimental tactics.

Let me explain. Dennis Conner, an up-and-coming sailor from San Diego who had yet to make his mark as a legendary America's Cup skipper, had sailed with me in 1964 and was again sailing on *KIALOA II* in 1965, when we decided to experiment in the San Clemente Island Race. The conventional tactics for the event were to first round Catalina Island to port; sail south along the backside of Catalina; and continue around San Clemente, keeping the island to port. No one in the race's history had sailed directly to San Clemente without rounding Catalina, and we thought, with the existing wind conditions, that we might pull it off. If the ploy was successful, we imagined we could set a fantastic, perhaps unbeatable record.

In essence, we effectively abandoned the race to see if our crazy scheme would work. It didn't. It was awful. Stupid. Later, we could only laugh at the folly of our personal egos. We battled through a terrible lee under Catalina, reconvened with the fleet at the end of the pack, and, as mentioned, worked our way up to first to finish and third in class, but a distant twentieth in the fleet. This blunder cost us the overall series victory, though we did manage a second. Still, this was a valuable learning experience. We took a chance for glory, also took our eyes off the grander prize...winning the race and the overall series.

DEAR MR KILROY

I AM WRITING YOU THIS NOTE TO THANK YOU FOR THE WONDERFUL THINGS I HAVE ENJOYED ABOARD KIALOA IN THE LAST 4 MONTHS. IT WAS AN EXPERIENCE WHICH WILL BE INVALUEABLE TO ME IN LATER LIFE.

I WANT YOU TO KNOW THAT I HAVE REALLY APPRECIATED THE OPPORTUNITY TO BE ABOARD YOUR BOAT AND IT WAS A REAL HONOR TO SAIL WITH SUCH A TALANTED SKIPPER AND CREW.

I KNOW I SHALL NEVER FORGET THE FANTASTIC TRIP TO HONOLULU OR THE RIDE HOME FROM SAN NICHLOS ISLAND.

IF EVER YOU OR JOHN WOULD LIKE TO SAIL IN SAN DIEGO AND ARE IN NEED OF A BOAT IT WOULD BE MY PLEASURE TO ACCOMADATE YOU. IN ANY CASE PLEASE CALL IF YOU HAVE THE CHANCE.

I WANT TO WISH YOU ALL THE LUCK IN THE WORLD IN YOUR FUTURE SAILING AND I AM LOOKING FORWARD TO SEEING YOUR NAME APPEAR WHERE IT BELONGS .... IN FIRST PLACE. THANK YOU AGAIN FOR EVERY-THING.

YOUR FRIEND,

Dennis Conner

That wasn't the only lesson learned early that year. In the midst of breaking the elapsed time record in the San Nicolas Island Race, we had a potentially serious accident. A well-known surgeon and friend who sailed with us asked if he could bring his 13-year-old son along, a request to which we agreed.

Once into the race, we were making a spinnaker change, in heavy breeze, to our reaching chute. During the takedown, the sheet for the old spinnaker did a full wrap around the boy's body, and the foot of the chute fell in the water. Dragging hundreds of pounds of pressure, the immersed sail reduced the size of the young boy's waist by almost half, while the force of the wind against the flapping chute tried to fling him overboard into the water. We quickly put a forward guy on the boom, sailed by the lee, and barely avoided a serious problem. So that was the second lesson: With strangers aboard, have a buddy system in place.

As I was exceedingly busy in my business at this stage, we only competed in two of the races in the Newport Harbor Yacht Club Ahmanson Series. With forty to sixty boats in the fleet, we scored a first to finish, second in class and second overall in one race, and first to finish, third in class and ninth overall in the other, a very light race. This was followed by another light, very slow Ensenada Race; in a fleet of 162 yachts, *KIALOA II* scored a 5-4-7: wrong place, wrong time. We did a little better in the next Newport Harbor non-Class races: first to finish and second in Class.

In the subsequent best-of-three match racing California Cup, *KIALOA II* again dueled with the former America's Cup winner, the 12-meter *Columbia*, owned by Briggs Cunningham. *Columbia* won the first race and *KIALOA II* took the second, setting up a winner-take-all rubber match. It was a tight finish, with *Columbia* barely ahead. However, during the last leg of this final race, *Columbia* fouled *KIALOA II* as we attempted to pass her on the way to the finish line. Our ensuing protest was upheld, making *KIALOA II* the series victor.

As we were all good friends, this was a bit interesting. *Columbia*'s helmsman and captain, Jerry Driscoll, had supervised the construction of *KIALOA II*. It all worked out in the end. In those days, yachtsmen were fierce rivals on the racecourse but remained jovial friends when not in competition.

With the California Cup behind us, it was now time for *KIALOA II*'s first crack at the West Coast's premier event, the 2,225-mile Transpac. These days, of course, we have satellite pictures of the entire racecourse, and particularly the position of the North Pacific high-pressure cell.

(To refresh reader's memories, the course consists of about 25 miles of windward work from San Pedro to Catalina Island; a beat up the island to the West End; a headsail reach for a couple of days; a spinnaker reach for one day; and then a spinnaker run and surf for about 1,800 miles in the North Pacific high to Honolulu.)

As previously mentioned, history has shown that most winners succeed by following the 1020 isobar. In 1965 and into the late 1970's, you had to guess where the 1020 isobar might be situated, and as explained in Chapter 3, we tried to follow the lead of Prent Filmore's *Staghound*, a consistent winner in the 1950s.

In the 1965 Transpac, which drew 56 yachts, *KIALOA II*—which was quite successful under the North American Yacht Racing Union's (NAYRU) Measurement Rule and time-allowance handicap tables, which were used for the race—again employed *Staghound*'s overall tactics, augmented with the weather reports and position updates for our competition issued by the committee boat accompanying the fleet. Upon reaching Honolulu, *KIALOA II* was the first yacht to finish, first overall in class A and fourth overall on corrected time.

However, the NAYRU time allowance table was developed for handicapping a race sailed around an equilateral triangle, where each leg of the triangle is the same linear length; but in this scenario, one leg of the triangle requires sailing a much longer distance, about 1.39 times the distance of each of the other two legs. The longer distance is a reflection of the fact that sailboats cannot sail directly upwind, but must tack back and forth when sailing to weather. On the Transpac course, this formula equates to 289 miles of added distance, making the (theoretical) third leg about 1,031 miles long. So, when added to the actual 2,225-mile handicap course distance—the actual mileage from Los Angeles to Honolulu—the total mileage on which the race was scored under the NAYRU time allowance formula was multiplied by a factor of 1.13 (1.13 x 2,225 miles = 2,514, not 2,225).

I have suggested over the years that the organizers of such an off-wind race, with only 30 miles of upwind sailing, should adjust the handicap course distance accordingly (but still take into account the fact that all yachts customarily sail a slightly longer, arcing course to the south to round the North Pacific high in favorable breeze). My final suggestion was that a 6% to 7% reduction of the 2,225-mile course distance would be a fair and equitable solution. Transpac officials responded that other international ocean races make no such modification to address the lack of windward sailing, and therefore, neither will they.

However, our series of *KIALOA*s have sailed many major ocean races besides the Transpac, including Transatlantic events, the Fastnet, the Sydney-Hobart, the Tasman Sea Race, the races to Acapulco and Mazatlan, and I can remember none that have as little as 2.5% to 3% of windward sailing on a consistent basis; actually, most have substantial sailing to weather. Still, my protests have fallen on deaf ears.

In any event, with the Transpac behind us, we returned to the West Coast to get ready for the next big event on the schedule, the Acapulco Race. The 1966 race proved to be a challenge and a bit of a mixed bag, with some good sailing days and some very light and fluky days. It seemed like we went through our entire sail inventory: Heavy spinnakers, light spinnakers, drifters and various headsails. After the first three days (with runs of 213, 218 and 182 nautical miles, respectively), we made continuous sail changes but still couldn't match the early pace. The next five days brought daily mileage runs as follows: 150, 156, 170, 124 and 137. For the last 100 miles, we averaged only 5.74 knots. All together, the race took 8 days, 17 hours and 36 minutes.

But there were some highlights. Near Cabo San Lucas, the winds were light and the seas sloppy, but we enjoyed a beautiful moon, phosphorescent water, warm weather, and we had the opportunity to work on our light-air spinnaker techniques. And after those first three days, in the handicap standings *KIALOA II* didn't look very good, holding 13th place. Yet in a way it was fine, as 13 is our lucky number.

KIALOA II would again race to Acapulco in 1968.

8

The 1960 Bermuda Race
"A learners race in a borrowed boat"

The first New York Yacht Club Cruise
The short successful version

Wonderful success in results and lessons learned
in six races to Acapulco

Community participation
"All part of our happy world"

East and West
Meeting the Challenge of East Coast Yachting

My first real taste of East Coast racing came not aboard *KIALOA II*, but in the 1960 Newport-Bermuda Race, aboard a chartered Block Island 40 called *Tia Maria*. I wanted to challenge my good friend Carleton Mitchell, who'd won the legendary 635-mile ocean race in 1956 and again in 1958 aboard his 38-foot yawl, *Finisterre*. *Tia Maria* seemed like a logical choice; the 40-foot centerboard yawl was reputedly a quick boat and in good shape, as she was owned by the builders of the Block Island line of boats.

We had a strong beginning. *Tia Maria* was indeed fast, especially when sailing hard on the breeze in moderate conditions, which is what we encountered in the first two days of the race. We'd started in Class D, and by the next morning, we'd caught up to the boats in the rear of the Class A fleet. We were cautiously optimistic. At that juncture we were slammed by the tail end of a tropical storm and miscellaneous gear aboard *Tia Maria* began to fail. What had begun in moderate weather turned out to be a stormy race, with many yachts "heaving to" to wait out the blow with sails dropped and a long line and drogue streaming from the bow to try and hold their position.

Although we thought we made a full inspection of the chartered boat before the race, we missed something important—a weak toggle connecting the head stay and the bow fitting. When the storm came it blew up, and all of a sudden we had a free-swinging head stay. Fortunately, we also had a strong mast. We initially eased the traveler and rapidly dropped the mainsail and the flogging headsail.

We had brought with us a small forestaysail that we were able to rig, without a stay, to help support the mast and control the boat. We then attempted to replace the head stay toggle with a spare that was aboard. What a task. The helmsman tried to hold the bow directly into the head seas while three of us, layered on top of one another and secured to the yacht with life harnesses, tried to affect the repair.

I was on the bottom of the layer cake. Two other crewmen kept me pinned down which freed up both of my hands to work. The guys, in turn, were holding on one arm and pointing a flashlight or passing me tools with the other. All of the above makes little sense; however, it seemed all we could do. We did manage to re-rig the spare toggle and head stay but we couldn't gain enough leverage to set a headsail, a problem that was compounded due to a fouled halyard aloft. Like many other boats, *Tia Maria,* was now "hove to" on a long line attached at the outboard end to a sail bag with miscellaneous gear stored inside. This went on until morning. We endured a few very sloppy hours, incurred a bit more damage to miscellaneous gear and wound up with a lot of water in the bilge. At daylight we were able to retrieve the halyard, slightly tune the mast, and sail back on the course to Bermuda.

We finished sixteenth out of approximately 100 boats in the 1960 race; if I recall correctly, we were one of the top boats in our class. Even so, I felt very stupid when I learned that Carleton Mitchell and *Finisterre* had again won the Bermuda Race for a record-setting third straight time. It was a testament to a great sailor, crew and boat, with tactical intelligence being the key to their success. Mitchell chose a course more to the southwest, around the backside of the storm.

For the 1966 Bermuda Race, we'd be aboard our own *KIALOA II*. But first we had to get there.

Following our second in the '66 Acapulco Race, *KIALOA II* continued along the west coast of Mexico and Central America to Panama, for her first trip through the Panama Canal. After a short visit, *KIALOA II* continued east along the shores of Colombia and Venezuela and called at several islands en route to Port-au-Spain in Trinidad. My wife Kathy and I could not make the sail from Acapulco to Trinidad due to business commitments, so we planned to spend a few days in Port-au-Spain prior to *KIALOA II*'s arrival.

We were staying at the Hilton Hotel, an unusual "upside down" lodge built on the side of a hill overlooking a large grass and palm tree park. The first floor of the hotel was on the top of the hill and all of the rooms were flanked down the slope to the park, providing beautiful views from every room. At sundown on our first night there, the steel bands began to play classical music and even a few Beatles songs, including "Yesterday." With Trinidadian rum and cokes in hand, we took in the red sky sunset and the lovely reflection on the waters. The Hilton marketing team in Port-au-Spain knew what they were doing. After a few days our guests arrived and we cruised Grenada and a few of the neighboring islands. It was all most enjoyable.

Another highlight of the Caribbean trip was that our son, John, was racing, cruising and going to school on *KIALOA II* with a capable tutor aboard. After several days of cruising, our guests and we departed and the boat continued sailing on to New York in preparation for a string of major races in Long Island Sound and the '66 Bermuda Race.

Our first challenge would be the 21st running of the annual Block Island Race, a 227-mile event that started off the Larchmont Yacht Club, sailed east out of Long Island Sound and around Block Island, and finished off the coast of Connecticut at the Stamford Yacht Club. A hundred and sixty eight of the East Coast's best yachts were also on the starting line.

According to a John Rendel story in *The New York Times*, the 1966 Block Island Race was a light and variable affair with heavy fog enveloping the course for long stretches, though the leaders had fair winds most of the time. But aboard *KIALOA II*, our ship's log clearly states that for over seven hours we averaged an over-the-bottom speed of only 4 knots; coupled with the standing fog, it wasn't exactly a formula for success. In hindsight, we also felt that we might have been too cautious in the heavy fog. We'd originally planned on sailing somewhat close to the Connecticut shore on our return course; however, as we didn't know the area very well, we moved offshore into variable winds…according to the locals, not the best place to be.

Still, *KIALOA II* was first to finish, some 46 minutes ahead of our major competitor, the 72-foot S&S design, *Bolero*. However, we owed *Bolero* about 50 minutes of handicap credit. It appeared this would be her race, a four-minute victory on corrected time. But the title of Rendel's piece in the *Times* told the story: "Yacht Race Ends in Protest." Yes, *Bolero* had fouled another yacht while starting and was duly penalized, thus opening the door for *KIALOA II* to take first overall in this inaugural East Coast race, surely an auspicious debut.

The next day, Kathy and our friends George and Lari Bissell, decided to have lunch at one of the sponsoring yacht clubs. As we entered the club, we advised the desk that we were from the yacht *KIALOA II* that had won their fine Block Island Race the day before, and we'd like to join the club for their Sunday morning brunch. I gave the clerk our names and yacht club affiliation back home in California and waited to be promptly ushered in for the Sunday brunch. Not so fast: I was asked if I had the name of a member sponsor and their telephone number? I gave the clerk names but had no telephone numbers. She found the numbers and placed some calls but no one was home. I asked for the manager; he was not there. We thanked her for her efforts and left.

As I stepped off the last step of the entry way a passing seagull let fly a prodigious squirt of guano…and hit me right on the nose! We all laughed and said that's what a West Coast yacht gets for winning their major race on a protest. (We did feel sorry for the poor girl at the front desk, a "temp" filling in for the regular clerk.) Still, it somehow seemed appropriate. We looked at each other, still laughing, and agreed that we now had earned our official entry to East Coast sailing.

And better yet, we offered our own pointed response in our next race on Long Island Sound, a clean sweep—first to finish, first in class and first overall corrected time—in the Indian Harbor Yacht Club's Whitmore Race.

Now that we'd made our "official" foray into East Coast yachting circles, it was time to hoist *KIALOA II*'s sails for the 1966 Bermuda Race, the region's most prestigious event. On one hand, we believed *KIALOA II* had the potential for victory. But we were also concerned about the meandering reverse currents in the Gulf Stream, the racecourse's major feature and obstacle. And we were mindful of Carleton Mitchell's "end run" around the back of the storm in his victorious 1960 Bermuda Race, which we'd sailed aboard *Tia Maria*.

Indeed, we remembered all this in the 1966 Bermuda Race…to no avail. To summarize, there was no storm, little wind and the small boats won. Though *KIALOA II* was the first boat to finish and scored second in Class A, the final overall result was a "horrible"—I must use the world twice: "horrible"—fiftieth place in the 170-boat fleet.

While in Bermuda, Nick Schaus—a sailing friend and the executive of a major insurance company—and I began talking about racing *KIALOA II* in the New York Yacht Club cruise. There was one caveat: Only members could skipper yachts racing during this annual event, a series of several short destination races that sail to the next overnight spot. But Nick was a member, so we made a deal. We would charter *KIALOA II* to him and sail it with our crew. The terms were simple ones I'd heard about elsewhere. Nick would pay a "due consideration" fee of one dollar and serve as our nominal skipper.

It turned out that this was "not the year" for such an arrangement as the NYYC Commodore had chartered *Bolero* at a considerably higher rate, the not insignificant cost of a new headsail for the 72-footer. Once he'd heard about our deal with Nick, the commodore took great objection and we were only allowed to sail one race, The Queen's Cup Race.

Our racing friends in the Club were quite incensed at the commodore's stance, but he was not swayed by their reaction. Since we were cut out of the cruise, we decided to make a good show out of the Queens Cup, a twenty-two mile race out of Newport, Rhode Island. We had a good crew: a combination of Californians and New York Yacht Club members, including Olin Stephens and Arthur Knapp. Artie had previously won the America's Cup, as had several of Olin's designs.

We left the dock early to look at the race start area and to plan our strategy. We decided to match up with our closest rival, *Bolero*, which of course was chartered to and skippered by the NYYC commodore.

The breeze was moderate, about 9 knots. At a minute and 30 seconds before the start, we had control of *Bolero* and the commodore, who was trying to close-reach to the committee boat-end of the starting line. *KIALOA II* was ideally situated a boat length to leeward and a half boat length ahead. By the rules of yacht racing, we had every right to sail hard on the wind, which would have blocked *Bolero* from the line. *Bolero* would then be forced to either foul us, or make the quick decision to tack away from the line and maneuver for a restart.

Obviously, we wanted to win the race and beat *Bolero* in the process; we were still annoyed that they would not allow us to race and sail in their cruise under arrangements that had previously been allowed.

We suggested that the commodore "come up" to put *Bolero* hard on the wind, which he refused to do. Someone then called attention to the commodore's natty sailing attire: navy-blue blazer, white pants, tie and white yachting cap. On *KIALOA II* we were attired in our "fighting red" T-shirts, and we decided we couldn't ruin his day with a protest. Plus, we would have more fun racing against *Bolero* than not. At that point, the race became the West Coast vs. the East Coast.

The first leg was a beat to windward along the shore, dodging fishermen and their nets, before bearing off on a spinnaker reach. *KIALOA II* was moving ahead very well, and after the second mark, we set our light spinnaker on a course about 130 degrees to 140 degrees off-the-wind.

We sailed a "leading-the-wind" spinnaker angle of about 90-degrees apparent, which allowed us, as we gained speed, to move the apparent wind substantially forward from the true wind. We were then able to steer a compass course very close to the desired heading on the racecourse, at a speed well above what could be obtained by trying to sail a normal spinnaker reach without the benefit of the extra acceleration we enjoyed by initially sailing closer to the wind.

We were now well ahead of the fleet and some of the Easterners aboard said we had some lucky wind shifts. I suggested that they take the helm and drive the boat with their technique, and we would see what happened. They did, and *KIALOA II* lost substantial speed on a course only a few degrees lower than sailed before. We then agreed to compare techniques. I asked my son, John, to take the helm (this is the episode briefly described in Chapter 5). He rolled the boat up to windward; as we re-trimmed the spinnaker, pole and sheet, the boat accelerated. He tenderly brought *KIALOA II* to a course only 5 degrees above the course sailed by the locals and was over one-and-a-half knots faster in speed through this technique. However, this technique requires careful attention to sail trim and quick jibes when appropriate, but the result is more crew work and more fun.

We finished the race in winning fashion, a little more than two hours ahead of the next finisher, gaining over 5.6 minutes per mile on our closest competitor over the course of the 22-mile event. The crew work had been excellent and we were happy with the results of the East vs. West showdown.

We appreciated the kind comments from the several participants who came by *KIALOA II* that evening, as well as at the dinner party that night. Unfortunately, we could not continue with the cruise, so it was time for *KIALOA II* to pack up and return to California for a refit and another series of West Coast events before returning for the 1968 Bermuda Race. But we'd had a good run and were pleased with our success in our first competition against the leading crews and yachts from the East Coast; we'd read about them and their challenging races, but we'd put together a consistent performance in all three of *KIALOA*'s contests (the Indian Harbor Whitmore Race, the Queen's Cup and the Block Island Race): first to finish, first in class and first overall.

What a year it was turning into. I was exceedingly busy with our companies and all their related activities: building, development, leasing and management. I was also co-chairman of the campaign to re-elect the outstanding Mayor of Los Angeles, Sam Yorty, and I was chairman of our campaign to bring the 1976 Olympic Games to the city of Los Angeles; we were hopeful that the Olympics would come to the U.S. in the bicentennial year of our nation's founding in 1776. The key to my participation in these various programs was my ability to delegate organizational duties and responsibilities to my excellent staff. They were so good that they permitted me to wear many hats.

On top of all that, we were in the midst of planning a major refit and remodeling of *KIALOA II*. In the meantime, in the first five months of 1967, we raced in the following Southern California series with good results:

The Whitney Series: Though *KIALOA II* missed some of the individual events, we were first overall in three races, second overall in another, and a distant seventeenth in a third. Still, our cumulative scores were good enough to take overall honors for the Whitney Series.

The Ahmanson Series: In this best five out of six race series, *KIALOA II* only made two races, scoring first overall in one and fourth overall in the other.

Later in the year, immediately after the work on the boat was completed, we faced the higher rated, lightweight South African yacht *Stormvogel* in a match-race regatta. We won one race but lost the series. Clearly, the *KIALOA II* crew had much to learn about the revised yacht.

In the 1965 Transpac, *KIALOA II* had been quite successful, for a maxi, placing fourth overall in the fleet on corrected time and first in class on corrected time, just 23 minutes ahead of our key rival, *Windward Passage*, which placed fifth overall and second in class. For the '67 Transpac, due to the previously discussed time-allowance tables, which did not take into account the lack of windward sailing, everyone on the boat knew it was highly unlikely that a big boat could aspire to the overall victory. Still, the '67 Transpac was a nightmare, and probably the worst in race history for the Maxi-boat fleet. *KIALOA II* earned a second in Class A, but when the handicap allowance was factored in, we were a terrible 32nd on corrected time, even though we'd finished third on elapsed time. That's how it goes in some Transpacs. Bob Allen, in his Cal 40, *Holiday Too*, corrected out as the overall winner.

Following the 1967 Transpac, *KIALOA II* sailed back to the mainland to San Francisco to compete in the 1967 St. Francis Perpetual Series. There was a lot of good windward sailing to weather and after four excellent races, *KIALOA II* wound up in a first place tie with *Baruna* for first place overall. However, St. Francis Yacht Club's tie-breaking rule opted in favor of *Baruna* and *KIALOA II* was awarded second place.

The San Francisco regatta concluded the 1967 season. Our next major race would be an old favorite, the 1,430-mile Acapulco Race along the west coast of Baja and the Mexico mainland. We had now proven that the 1967 modifications were excellent; however, we still had more to learn to maximize performance.

We concentrated on miscellaneous small items to improve the yawl rig, and replaced or reworked much of our sail inventory, in the process adding some larger headsails, and going to 170% LP Genoas spinnakers, spinnaker poles, etc. Our measurement rating was increased from 63.4 to 63.9 under the formula for the CCA rating rule. We had a great crew, who were all familiar with *KIALOA II*, and at the start of the race at the crack of noon on February 4th, 1968, had a pleasant breeze to get underway.

KIALOA II was first off the starting line under spinnaker and rapidly sailed ahead of the fleet… but only for an hour and a half. At that point the wind died, then went light and shifty for the next 22 hours. Our first day's 24-hour run was only 51 miles, and the second day's just 110 miles.

To some, this may sound like easy racing. It most certainly is not. These conditions call for continuous sail trim and sail changes, plus plenty of tacking and jibing to maintain headway. The frustration limit is very high; keeping the boat moving takes a great deal of concentration and management. Great dinners by the cook, and a one-drink Happy Hour, were also a great help. We do find it remarkable how many Happy Hour drinks get spilled when half full in light weather when there's no rhythm to the boat. Anything under half full, however, does not get replaced.

In this 1968 race of 10 days and 20 hours, we had one great 203-mile day, and good days of 170 and 164 miles, but the remainder were all under 155 miles. We did have wind off Cabo San Lucas— which is unusual—a big, long-lasting puff of a few hours' duration with high seas that required quick sail douses. But that was about the only breeze of any consequence.

Still, our patience was rewarded with another clean sweep: first to finish, first in class and first overall on corrected time. Counting this victory, here are our cumulative results for the six Acapulco races sailed by *KIALOA I* and *KIALOA II*.

2-1st overall
1-2nd overall
1-3rd overall
1-4th overall
1-11th overall

Acapulco victory trophy

The 1968 event was our last race to Acapulco, which we always enjoyed for the challenging mixture of light and occasional heavy weather upwind and downwind sailing conditions that required continuous focus and many sail changes, and a great reception at the finish.

We were also proud of the many friendships we made with business and government leaders of Mexico through our participation and success in races to Acapulco. Thanks to these friendships, I was able to review Mexico City's planning and construction of facilities for the 1968 Olympic Games in my capacity as chairman of the Los Angeles committee bidding for the 1976 Summer Olympics.

With *KIALOA II*'s refit completed and the West Coast sailing schedule behind us, it was time to retrace our steps back through the Panama Canal and the Caribbean en route to New York for a full slate of competition: the Storm Trysail Club's Block Island Race, the Newport-Bermuda Race and the Transatlantic Race from Bermuda to Travemunde, Germany.

Following that final Acapulco Race, we met *KIALOA II* in St. George's, Grenada, after Roy Bream,

Jim Woller and a great crew wrapped up their 30-day delivery via Colombia, Venezuela, Curacao and several other stops. Everyone was relaxed and sporting suntans; they'd picked up a few new Spanish phrases along the way as well the ability to make excellent margaritas.

Kenny and Polly Watts, Al and Virginia Lockabey, and Kathy and I joined the boat in St. George's for a three-week cruise through the Leeward Islands, with calls at Carriacou, the Tobago Cays, Bequia, St. Vincent's, St. Lucia and Martinique. Our guests then left and Lari and George Bissell, along with other members of our family, stayed for a continuing cruise of Martinique, Dominique, Isles de Saints and onto English Harbour, Antigua. Once our family left, we were next joined by world champion Star sailor and good friend, Malin Burnham and his wife, as well as Ash Brown, another Star world champ and owner/skipper of the great yacht *Carousel*, and his wife. We all enjoyed a dinner at the Admiral's Inn before flying to Los Angeles a few days later.

Looking back to those days almost 40 years later, having visited the islands intermittently over the years and again fairly recently, it's unbelievable on one hand how much they've changed with the influx of so many tourists and development, yet also how much they've stayed the same.

From Antigua, *KIALOA II* sailed on to Puerto Rico, Bermuda and New York, ultimately bound for a shipyard in City Island, to prepare for our second Block Island Race, which necessitated a re-measurement of the boat under the Storm Trysail Rule (the rating was 40.7). It turned into a very slow race that didn't favor the big boats; *KIALOA II* averaged only 5.33 knots. The results were very close: Out of 143 yachts, *KIALOA II* was first to finish, third in class and eleventh overall on corrected time, some 57 minutes out of first based on the Storm Trysail Club's handicap formula.

The light wind and speeds were spawned by Tropical Storm "Brenda," situated off Bermuda, the mid-Atlantic island to which *KIALOA II* and many other boats would be racing in three weeks.

The 1968 Bermuda Race aboard *KIALOA II* was not a heavy weather race. In fact, it was a race with hardly any weather. In the first 24 hours, our speed over the bottom was only about 5 knots, as we registered a run of 125 miles. The second day was a little better—182 miles—and the third was quite good, as we knocked off 213 miles. The final thirteen hours into Bermuda were also reasonable: 118 miles. But that first "killer slow" day was the undoing of our aspirations. Not only were the winds light, but the seas were bumpy as we engaged the Gulf Stream sailing under our big, double headsail rig, which we carried most of the way.

KIALOA II was the third yacht in the 151-boat fleet to finish the race, which corrected out to eighteenth overall and third in our class. The results weren't necessarily bad, but not what the *KIALOA* crew could accept as a good finish, either. Given the conditions for the '68 race, the logical assumption was that one of the smallest boats, if well sailed, would be the winner. The logic held. Ted Hood's new *Robin* was the right boat in the right race. *Robin*'s formula was simple: a good crew with lots of experience.

The Bermuda Race is always full of surprises, particularly between larger and smaller yachts; the weather and the Gulf Stream, both so variable, constantly changes the equation amongst a fleet full of differently-sized boats. One thing that never changes is the exciting finish and hospitality in Bermuda. And it was especially exhilarating in 1968, because the Transatlantic Race to Travemunde, Germany, in the Baltic Sea, would start just a few days after the Bermuda Race celebrations were over. *KIALOA II* was entered and ready to go. New adventures were right on the horizon.

Modifications to *KIALOA II*

The latter years of the 1960s brought many changes to the CCA measurement rule. These changes had an impact upon the entire sport of yacht racing. The evolution in rating rules came about as international racing authorities began moving towards a new way of handicapping race boats: the new IOR (International Ocean Racing) rule. Some of the many changes in rating rules were good; some weren't. But it was a complicated time for sailors who wanted to keep their boats competitive for handicap racing. One of the broader issues was how the rules would affect older yachts. Old-age allowances reduced the measurement (speed) number for older boats, providing greater time allowances, or credits, to many vintage yachts.

We carefully reviewed *KIALOA II* and decided that the latest generation of racing yachts, the changes in measurement rules, and greater international competition necessitated modifications to *KIALOA II*. Over the first five months of 1967, our design group considered and proposed a range of modifications. Ultimately, we came up with this list for the yacht's refit:

- Improve steering—install a spade rudder with trim tab.
- Convert to a yawl rig—install a mizzen mast, with the added benefit of a mizzen staysail for reaching and running conditions.
- Revise ballast and flotation.
- Increase headsail areas to improve light-weather sailing.
- Increase spinnaker size with wider foot dimensions and penalty poles to improve spinnaker reaching and running.
- Miscellaneous other changes.

Most of the changes are set forth on the following sketch.

From our very first sail trials aboard *KIALOA II*, we'd begun compiling a list of modifications to increase performance. One feature that bothered me from the beginning was the length and weight of the mainsail boom due to the low aspect rig requirements of the CCA rule. Even though we designed the rig so we'd have the ability to effectively reef the mainsail and hoist the mainsail boom, we still had a continuous problem of the boom dragging in the water in heavy seas when reaching and running downwind. By shortening the boom and converting to a yawl rig with a tall mizzen mast, we enjoyed much more peaceful and faster sailing in heavier air.

KIALOA II

As Built

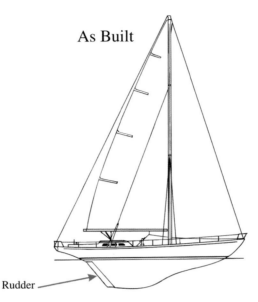

Rudder

As Modified

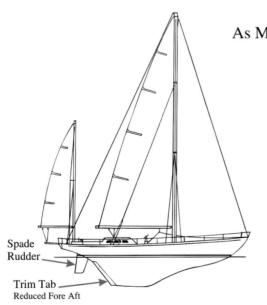

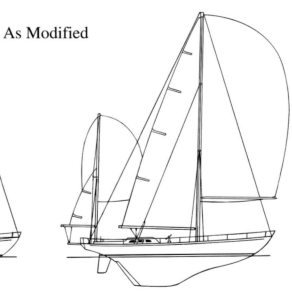

Spade
Rudder

Trim Tab
Reduced Fore Aft

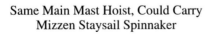

Same Main Mast Hoist, Could Carry
Mizzen Staysail Spinnaker

Carrying Spinnaker, Main,
Mizzen Spinnaker, 50% Mizzen

As we will discuss later, mainsail aspect ratios were quite an issue between the RORC's handicap rule, in effect for racing in Europe, and the CCA formula, which was used in the United States. The RORC favored high aspect mainsails, which are much more efficient than low aspect mainsails. High aspect sail plans translate to a taller mainmast and sail, and a shorter, lighter mainsail foot and boom. On *KIALOA II*, we increased the aspect ratio by shortening the boom.

One other note about the refit: Work was proceeding at Jerry Driscoll's shipyard when the cradle supporting *KIALOA II* collapsed, inflicting serious damage to the hull, which also had to be repaired. The deadline to complete the new work and repair the damages was tight, but Jerry and his technicians did an amazing job. Fortunately, Jerry knew *KIALOA II* well, as he was the construction coordinator for me when Yacht Dynamics built *KIALOA II*.

9

A long 3534-mile race across the Atlantic and into the Baltic

Adrift in the English Channel

A race within a race

"Business and Thoughts at Sea"

The First Transatlantic
From Bermuda to Germany on KIALOA II

By the middle of 1968, during four years of campaigning *KIALOA II*, we'd successfully raced on the East and West Coasts of the United States, to Hawaii, and down the coast of Mexico. Now it was time to spread our wings yet again, on a Transatlantic Race from Bermuda to Travemünde, Germany on the south coast of the Baltic Sea, a distance of some 3,534 miles. We debated about the amount of time the race would take away from my business and other activities. Ultimately, the destination worked in my favor.

At the time, I was chairman of the committee to bring the 1976 Summer Olympics to the United States, and participating in a major international yacht race to Germany could provide additional opportunities to meet European members of the International Olympic Committee's Board of Directors as well as members of the European Sports Federation (FISA). In short, as an international sportsman making new friends with related interests, the Transatlantic Race could be useful to the objectives of our committee.

The Travemünde Race started from Bermuda a few days after the finish of the annual Bermuda Race. The course took the fleet north-northeast to "Point Alpha," the mark established by the U.S. Coast Guard to keep south of the iceberg fields, and then onward to the north of Ireland and Scotland and across the English Channel. From there, competitors rounded Skagen at the tip of the Skagen Peninsula, and then went south between the Fynn and Zealand Islands. The finish line was off the lightship at Fehmarn Island, to the north of Travemünde.

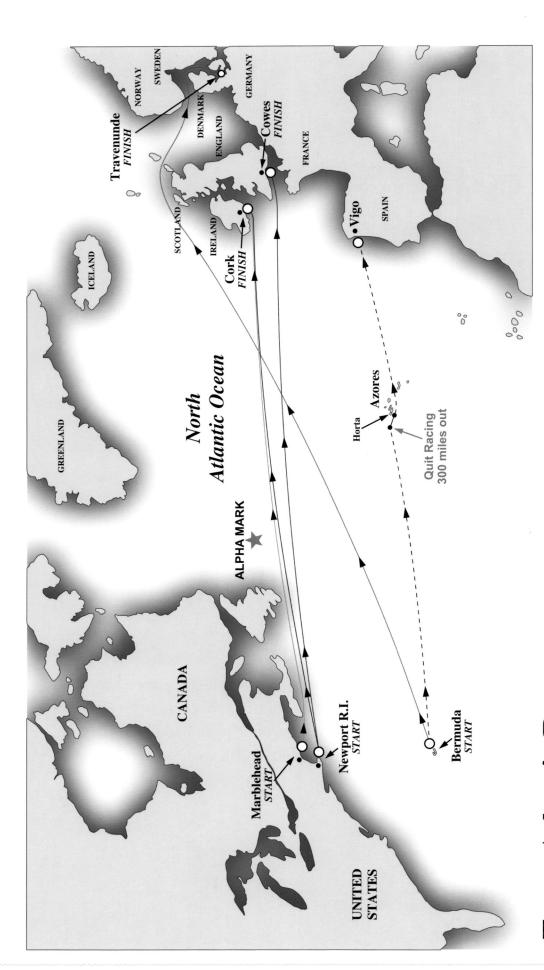

Trans Atlantic Races

- KIALOA II - 1968 Bermuda over Scotland to Travemunde
- KIALOA II - 1969 Newport R.I. to Cork Ireland
- KIALOA II - 1972 Bermuda to Vigo Spain
- KIALOA III - 1975 Newport R.I. to Cowes England
- KIALOA III - 1979 Marblehead to Cork Ireland

★ Alpha Mark - Notice of Location given day before Start of Race (moves with Iceberg Flow)

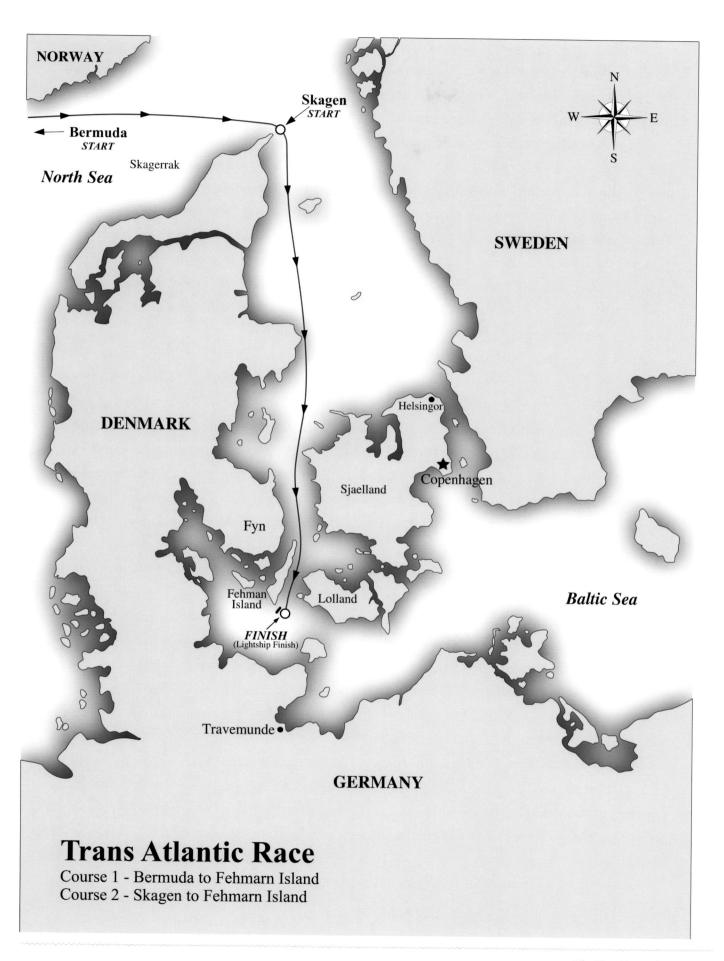

Trans Atlantic Race

Course 1 - Bermuda to Fehmarn Island
Course 2 - Skagen to Fehmarn Island

Our primary competition were two aluminum boats like *KIALOA II*—Huey Long's *Ondine* and Dr. Herr Krupp's *Germania*—and Kess Bruynzeel's light, off-wind flyer *Stormvogel,* built of Bruynzeel plywood at the owner's plywood plant in South Africa.

Because of the handicap formula used for the race, all of us aboard the maxis knew that an intermediate-sized yacht would probably win the race. But I wasn't sailing just for the competition and the contacts. For me, an important additional benefit was to understand more about the tragedy of World War II, and in that regard I had long discussions with Herr Krupp once we reached Travemünde. My son, John, a member of our crew, was also involved in these discussions.

Once underway, for several days *KIALOA II* held the lead. But the racing was close, with *Ondine* and *Stormvogel* within visible range. Conditions were mostly routine—moderate and even light winds—with the exception of a rather startling invasion of several waterspouts that could have caused severe problems.

After passing Point Alpha, *Ondine* and *Stormvogel* decided to sail more to the northeast, which was a decided departure from our tactical plan. We decided not to "cover" and follow, even though we were still slightly in the lead. Perhaps their strategy was correct. But we'll never know as we had a severe wind shift that forced us to sail up the Irish West Coast to round Ireland and Scotland, ultimately sailing into a fogbank with virtually no wind off the northeast corner of Scotland.

The fog lifted, though the wind didn't fill, and we found our two competitors, *Ondine* and *Stormvogel*, about three miles to the north of our position. The day passed with little wind before the fog returned in the late afternoon and through the night. When it lifted the morning, we discovered that many smaller yachts had joined us.

A 50-footer called *Rage* was the closest boat to *KIALOA II*, and we played a game of "catch," throwing oranges back and forth between the two boats.

The new wind finally came in from the north-northwest, and *Ondine* and *Stormvogel* made way for the Baltic and Skagen. *KIALOA II* was next, and we enjoyed a fairly fast sail to Skagen and an even faster sail to the south between Fynn and Zealand Islands and on toward the finish line off Fehmarn Island. Even though it was part of the Transatlantic course, the fast 195-mile stretch from Skagen to Fehmarn was scored as a separate "race within the race." Pat Haggerty's *Bay Bea* was the winner of this sprint, with *KIALOA II* second in fleet on corrected time.

In the grander scheme of things, unfortunately, but as expected, the maxis were at the tail of the pack. *Ondine* finished 2 hours ahead of *KIALOA II* and *Stormvogel* an hour ahead; on handicap, however, we finished slightly ahead of our maxi competitors, taking 31st on corrected time. No it definitely wasn't a race for big boats, but the sailing was interesting, particularly through the Danish Islands.

And when all was said and done, it was indeed a pleasure to meet many people in the European sailing world as well as sportsmen and sportswomen involved in other European sports. Kathy and I made many contacts with European IOC and FISA leaders and formed friendships that continued over the years. We also spent time in Munich visiting with the leaders of their Olympics' organizing committee, which we'll address in upcoming chapters.

Business and Thoughts at Sea

The foundation of my sailboat-racing career was based on my experience managing a successful business and building a management team with a clearly defined game plan and delegation of responsibility. It's no coincidence that there was a corollary between my vocation and my avocation.

Racing meant that I would be away from the office for lengthy periods. In my absence, it was imperative that my organization continued to run effectively. This meant not only fulfilling all of our obligations, but creating new business activities and opportunities.

The key was developing functional game plans and allowing for creative ideas to flourish. Areas of responsibility were clearly drawn. Executives and project managers were given the flexibility to make independent decisions. My executive team was given authority to do what was necessary to meet the high quality of our projects and to fulfill the needs of our clients.

I found that our clients were exceedingly interested in following and even participating in the sport of sailing and other projects in which I was involved. I would take them sailing and some clients would even join us as racing crew. They became enthusiastic about the decisions and teamwork required in racing and cruising. Lifetime relationships were established along with mutual confidence.

At sea, in a racing sailboat, the character and interdependence of all the crew and all those aboard are clearly identified. Your clients can see who you are and you can truly see who they are.

I am always mindful of one of the first major financing deals we obtained for a fairly large project. I had arranged a schedule to meet the senior executives of our proposed partnership in Boston, at their convenience. When I arrived, I was immediately taken to a rather large meeting and to my surprise, found that it was a regularly scheduled meeting of their Board of Directors, most of whom were sailors, some of whom I knew and had raced against. I was introduced; they knew about my credibility; and after some casual talk about sailing, we discussed the financing for my project, which was approved. The project was very successful, and we all enjoyed a long and lasting relationship.

Character and leadership count. They are essential ingredients to successful sailing and successful business. While at sea, at scheduled intervals, I would talk to my team ashore over high seas radio. Looking back, some of the conversations seem rather laughable; the topics were serious but the discussions often took place when the sailing conditions were exceedingly rough, requiring intense concentration, with spicy sailor's humor in the background. Of course, upon reaching land, clearer, more concise conversations could be easily conducted. But the groundwork had already been established. While at sea, there is much time for reflective thought about life, about family, about business, about the future and about your true objectives. It's an environment that cultivates fresh ideas about how to approach problems and issues, and above all, to sort out which are the important matters and which are the non-issues.

One cannot enjoy the sea aboard a racing sailboat without being a participant. It is not a spectator sport for those onboard. And one cannot be at sea on a racing sailboat without understanding the essential mutual interdependence of your fellow sailors.

At sea, life becomes elemental. You become one with the simple beauty of the sky, of moonlit clouds, of the ocean's rhythm, of reflections on the water, of phosphorescent waves. You also realize that you're not in charge. You are part of that beauty, and yes, you are sometimes engaged in the violence of nature, as well. In coping with extreme conditions, two things are essential: teamwork, and facing reality. Sailing is like life. It teaches the essential necessity for humility in mankind.

10

The Ted Turner, Bob Johnson, and Jim Kilroy challenges commenced in 1969, and continued for many years. Ted Turner in *American Eagle* and *Tenacious,* Bob Johnson in *Windward Passage* with its multiple speed increasing revisions and old age allowances, and Jim Kilroy in *KIALOA II* and *KIALOA III.*

Outstanding competition set forth in many chapters, sharpening the skills of the skippers and crews.

Southern Comforts
The Gulf Stream, Ted Turner and the SORC
1969 Jamaica Race

In the 1960s and 1970s, the biggest ocean racing series in the United States was the annual winter ritual known as the Southern Ocean Racing Conference, or SORC. To achieve success in the SORC required a fundamental understanding of the high velocity Gulf Stream, which flows northbound through the Straits of Florida between the east coast of Florida and the west coast of the Bahamas at a speed up to 3.9 knots. The Stream also comes into play when sailing along the Gulf Coast of Florida in the St. Petersburg area and south to the Florida Keys.

A manual entitled "Hints for Sailors and Winds and Currents for the Southern Ocean Racing Conference and Other Races," published in November, 1968, was essential reading for any sailor competing in the SORC. Even so, there were many variables and counter currents that weren't covered in the guide. It's important to factor in "local knowledge" at any racing venue. But things happen on every racecourse beyond the scope of conventional wisdom and the best how-to manuals.

If all yachts were the same size and speed, you could assume they'd usually be close together, which is generally the case with one-design fleets. However, with different sized yachts that have substantial speed differences, even during the same race they may be sailing in entirely different current and wind conditions. A careful analysis of the fundamental current and wind conditions will show that smaller yachts, based upon the courses sailed, will gain substantial advantages from the normal Gulf Stream current.

For example, take a larger yacht with a basic upwind speed of 9 knots and a smaller vessel with a basic upwind speed of 6 knots. Both are sailing north course for a distance of 36 miles; the speed of the current is 3 knots.

If there were no current, the smaller yacht would cover the 36-miles in six hours. But with the boost of that 3-knot current, the smaller yacht's speed over the bottom—nine knots—will allow it to cover that distance in four hours. Thus, the 3-knot current provides a 50% increase in speed, saving 2 hours.

The larger yacht, sailing upwind, will take four hours to cover 36-miles. With the benefit of the current, however, it will make 12-knots over the bottom and cover the course in three hours, for a 33% increase in boat speed. In other words, the smaller yacht saves two hours of time while the larger boat saves an hour. The smaller yacht gains one hour in elapsed time over the bigger yacht.

Sailing east or west in normal wind conditions across the Straits, again, the Gulf Stream can provide substantial benefits to smaller boats. And that's before taking into account the shifting counter currents that also occur over SORC racecourses; if used properly, these too can offer significant gains. Of course, we must always realize that currents are a force of nature that can significantly vary from what is forecast or expected. Once again, local knowledge is an essential factor for success.

In 1969, *KIALOA II* entered its first SORC. Everyone aboard realized that we had much to learn, that there were handicap issues, and that we'd be sailing against strong competition, particularly a 72-footer named *Windward Passage*, a light-displacement craft with a hull that was said to be based on a Thistle sailing dinghy. With a substantial beam almost 30% wider than the average maxi, the ketch-rigged *Windward Passage* was a radical design. Along with the two-masted, split rig, she carried a bowsprit that extended her foretriangle significantly and allowed her to carry bigger headsails and spinnakers.

On top of her lightweight construction and wide beam, she had minimal interior accommodations. That translated to added stability, which would be important with the long stretches of upwind sailing that were prevalent in SORC racecourses. *Windward Passage*'s rating, 79.1 feet, was quite high compared to *KIALOA II*'s (63.1) and Ted Turner's *American Eagle* (60.5). We debated on how we should proceed to compete with *Windward Passage*. My decision was that we should sail *KIALOA II* "as is" for the '69 SORC, in the configuration we knew very well. In fact, we even decided to forgo new sails, and to sail with the well-used inventory from the 1968 Travemünde Transatlantic Race, which had been back and forth to Europe. How else, I reasoned, could we compare the two yachts and learn what we must do to improve and compete against *Windward Passage* over the next two or three years?

Of course, *Windward Passage* wasn't our only formidable competition. We knew that Ted Turner's *American Eagle*, the converted 12-Meter, would be very well sailed and display truly outstanding performance at certain wind angles. The accompanying sketch shows the primary SORC waters, including the Gulf Stream. It provides a good reference point when discussing the "Grand Dame" of Grand Prix racing in the U.S. during this exciting era.

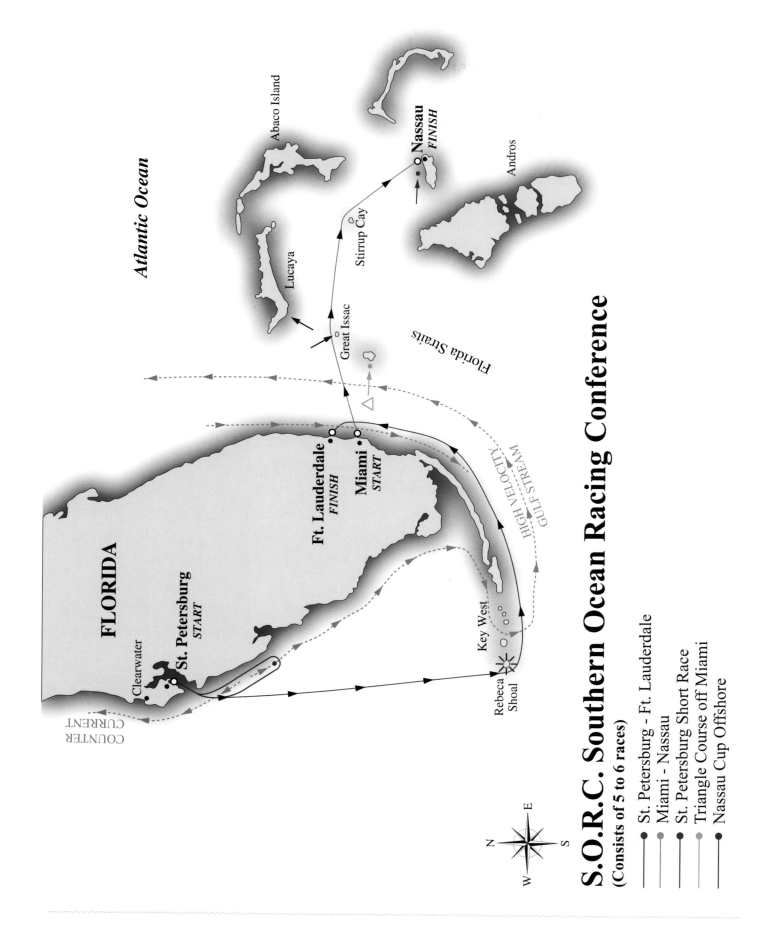

S.O.R.C. Southern Ocean Racing Conference
(Consists of 5 to 6 races)

- St. Petersburg - Ft. Lauderdale
- Miami - Nassau
- St. Petersburg Short Race
- Triangle Course off Miami
- Nassau Cup Offshore

To get an idea of the ratings discrepancy, in the inaugural event of the series, the 105-mile St. Petersburg-Venice Race, *Windward Passage* would owe *KIALOA II* a total time allowance of 41 minutes, 54 seconds, or 23.94 seconds a mile. It wasn't much, especially considering *Passage*'s substantially longer waterline length, her 31,000 pounds less displacement, and her increased stability, which again meant the ability to carry more sail area in heavier air. It seemed that *Windward Passage* held an overwhelming advantage.

There's no question that *Windward Passage* was a tremendous step forward towards the new IOR rule, which would be put into effect in 1971. The six-race SORC series in 1969 would go a long way toward determining the future of *KIALOA II* and many other yachts. Here's how the regatta unfolded.

1969 SORC

Race 1—St. Petersburg-Venice (105 nautical miles):

It didn't take long for *Windward Passage* to show her outstanding capabilities. In a slow, light and shifty race, *Windward Passage* was first to finish and first on corrected time, some three hours and 56 minutes ahead of *KIALOA II*. After the application of a time allowance of 41 minutes 54 seconds from the higher rated *Windward Passage*, *KIALOA II*, the 2nd yacht to Finish, was 2nd in Class and 2nd in the fleet on corrected time – 3 hours 14 minutes behind *Windward Passage* on corrected time. As Red Marston, the noted yachting writer, said, "It was a drifter that was a classic for the sun seekers on shore." Perhaps, but certainly not for the sailors.

In this first race, *Windward Passage* took a risk and sailed farther offshore, probably in more current, effectively sailing a farther course, but in the end receiving more benefits. We thought the offshore option was too risky and sailed a more direct course. In hindsight, perhaps *KIALOA II* was the one that averted risk by not sailing with *Windward Passage*. It brought to mind the old cliché: No risk, no reward.

Race 2—St. Petersburg-Ft. Lauderdale (370 miles):

The course took the fleet from St. Petersburg, on the west coast of Florida, south around Rebecca Shoals along the Florida Keys, and then north of Miami to Fort Lauderdale, seeking the benefit of the Gulf Stream current.

It was a traditional windward start in nine knots of wind that soon escalated to 22 knots with gusts to thirty. In addition to the tough sailing to weather, there was the matter of finding and locking into the Gulf Stream, not a foregone conclusion. Because of the gains in boat speed, and the greater benefit that small boats obtained from the Stream's "free ride," the bigger boats sailed more of a direct course inshore and along the keys. The idea was to keep out of the counter current while remaining in the western portion of the Stream.

To our surprise, *Windward Passage* did not win our class. No, the overall corrected-time winner, and first in Class A—finishing three hours behind *Windward Passage* on elapsed time, and an hour ahead of *KIALOA II*—was *American Eagle*.

Windward Passage (fourth overall on corrected time) beat *KIALOA II* (fifteenth overall on corrected time) by 1 hour, 32 minutes.

In this race, *Windward Passage* played to her strengths, displaying her stiffness, long water-line and light displacement. And *Passage's* navigator, Ben Mitchell, who later sailed in a winning Sydney-Hobart effort and other victories, knew the Gulf Stream well and called a tremendous race.

Race 3—Miami-Lucaya (100 miles):

The third race in the series, an even hundred miler, started off Miami and then took the fleet twenty miles north to windward to round the entry buoy off Fort Lauderdale (the goal was to stay in the Stream and avoiding a southerly flowing inshore countercurrent along the beach). From there, it was a close reach across the Gulf Stream to Lucaya on the south coast of Grand Bahamas in the Providence Channel.

One hundred yachts participated in this race, which was forecast to be a heavy air affair in equally heavy seas. The wind actually moderated to about 15 knots, but the seas remained bumpy. *Windward Passage* dropped out due to an equipment problem. Throughout the race, there was close reaching and occasional windward sailing. That left *KIALOA II* and *American Eagle* in what was mostly a close-reaching duel, with a bit of windward work as well.

American Eagle was first to finish, a mere seven minutes ahead of *KIALOA II*, correcting out to first in class and second in fleet. On corrected time, *KIALOA II* was second in class and third in fleet. The overall winner was the Class B yacht *Touché*, fourteen minutes ahead of *American Eagle* on corrected time.

Race 4—The Lipton Cup (28 miles):

Theoretically, the 28-mile course, an equilateral triangle, should have provided a windward leg, a reaching leg and a running leg of equal distance—nine-and-one-third miles per leg. Of course, in a yacht race with a windward leg, the actual distance sailed should be about 30 or 31 miles, taking into account the extra mileage necessitated by tacking back and forth to weather.

At the start, the wind was out of the south and the course was situated so that part of the triangle was in the Gulf Stream and part of it was in the counter-current along the shore. This gave yachts a minor boost in both directions, inshore and offshore, further shortening the sailed distance.

The first and second legs were ideal for the fast reaching and running capabilities of *Windward*

Passage, which ended up first to finish, second overall and first in class. *American Eagle* took second in class and fifth overall. *KIALOA II* had a poor race: seventh in class and twenty-second overall, some 23 minutes behind *Windward Passage* and seven minutes behind *American Eagle*. During the race, a late wind shift meant little windward sailing on the last leg. In other words, it wasn't a *KIALOA II* day.

Race 5—Miami-Nassau (184 miles):

This is always a favorite race of the small yachts, which benefit greatly from the Gulf Stream and usually win. The race starts off the Miami entry buoy, heads east and then northeast to Great Isaacs, enters the Northwest Providence Channel, and then carries around the Berry Islands and onto Nassau.

In this race, on elapsed time, *Windward Passage* was again first to finish, sailing the course in 15 hours, 54 minutes, 17 seconds. *KIALOA II* was the second boat across the finish line, an hour and 22 minutes behind *Passage*. *American Eagle* was the third finisher. Once the corrections were applied, *Windward Passage* placed thirteenth in class and fifty-third overall, with *KIALOA II* placed fifteenth in class and sixty-first overall (only 8 minutes behind *Windward Passage*).

The results for the top Class A yachts were not unusual for this race. A few years later, the distance was shortened to a realistic 174 miles; however, it remained a small-boat race, with the Gulf Stream being the key.

Another fundamental bias in fleet scoring for the overall SORC results was ultimately corrected. In the cumulative scoring of the six races to determine the overall winner, the Miami-Nassau Race had a factor of 35%, the same as the regatta's major race from St. Pete to Ft. Lauderdale. But the Miami-Nassau contest was just 184 miles, with a major boost from the Gulf Stream, while the St. Petersburg-Ft. Lauderdale course was 370 miles, and was not as strongly influenced by the Stream. Rightfully, the 35% factor for the Miami-Nassau Race was ultimately reduced.

Race 6—Governor's Cup Race (30 miles):

This was a fun race along the north shore of Paradise Island, Bahamas (formerly called Hog Island), usually over a windward/leeward course, with only tidal current to address. (Later, the race was moved to a bay at the east end of Nassau.) Many of the local yachts would be on the water to watch the race along with spectators on the beach of Paradise Island. In relatively short order, *Windward Passage* was first to finish, first in class and first overall. *KIALOA II* was right behind her: second to finish, second in class and second overall. It was a great way to finish our first challenging series with *Windward Passage*, a rivalry that continued for years.

When all was said and done, our results in the 1969 SORC were better than anticipated. We finished second overall in a pair of races, and third overall in another. In the races where we had to contend with the unfavorable impact of the Gulf Stream, we recorded a fifteenth, twenty-second and sixty-first, respectively. Furthermore, we identified some improvements that could be made prior to our next Transatlantic Race, to Cork, Ireland, later that year.

1969 Miami-Montego Bay, Jamaica Race

The 1969 SORC was over, but not the competition between *KIALOA II*, *Windward Passage* and *American Eagle*. The next race was truly an offshore contest: the 811-mile classic from Miami to Montego Bay.

It was a fine, picturesque, warm-weather course that began through the Bahamian islands of the Spanish Main. From Miami, the first leg took the fleet on a windward passage to Eleuthera. Once north of the island, sheets were eased to a close reach, and soon spinnakers were hoisted in shifty winds as the yachts maneuvered into the open sea. Approaching the coast of Cuba (boats had to stay at least three miles off), the course then cuts through the Windward Passage between Haiti and Cuba. Surprisingly, as we entered the Windward Passage, a Cuban patrol boat chased us but could not keep up the pace.

The wind conditions were ideal for *Windward Passage*, and she took an early lead well ahead of *KIALOA II*. It wasn't a fast sail for us, but we maintained steady speeds in spite of changing wind velocities. Despite the lack of any special preparations for either the recently concluded SORC or the Jamaica Race, we made good progress for the first four days, with daily runs of 175, 170, 176 and then 200 miles, respectively.

Once through the Windward Passage, but in the lee of Cuba, winds went very light and variable, and sometimes disappeared altogether. The last 110 miles took *KIALOA II* twenty-two hours, dashing our hopes for one of the top places. *Windward Passage* finished 11 hours ahead of *KIALOA II*, but they owed us 5.5 hours of handicap time. Even so, *Windward Passage* won Class A, with *KIALOA II* in fourth, and both boats broke the elapsed time record for the race. The corrected time winner was *Flyaway*, a Class C yacht.

Well in the back, Ted Turner's *American Eagle* took a flyer—what Ted mistakenly thought was a shortcut—around the east end of Crooked Island. It didn't work. Ted was dead last, which made him a little more sympathetic than usual.

Once Ted was finally ashore, he decided he needed sympathy and selected a piglet as his pet, and proceeded to tour the island with his new pet. Have Ted tell the story.

1970 SORC – The Challenge Continues
A Maxi Race – First Three Places

KIALOA II, Windward Passage, and *American Eagle* meet again, fully prepared for the 1970 SORC.

Following the 1969 SORC, *KIALOA II* and *American Eagle* raced in the 1969 Transatlantic Race to Cork, Ireland, in Cowes Week and the Fastnet Rock Race in the Irish Sea, with reasonable victorious results. *Windward Passage* raced in the 2,225-mile Transpac race, a downwind race to a new elapsed time record and what appeared to be a victory. However, that victory was taken away by the loss of a starting line foul.

The challenge in the 1970 SORC would be slightly different—six races, with each challenger selecting the best five races for the total point score. This worked out well because both Ted Turner and I had business commitments the day of the Lucaya Race.

The net product of our mutual three best challenges for the 1970 SORC Series was very close, a first three overall fleet-corrected time placement for the threes Maxis:

1st	*American Eagle*	1975.5 points
2nd	*Windward Passage*	1952.7 points
3rd	*KIALOA II*	1948.7 points

Could we have placed better if we had raced the Lucaya Race? We will never know. However, an odd penalty happened to *KIALOA II*, diminishing our point score—a propeller handicap penalty.

For the entire life of the boat, *KIALOA II* had sailed with a fairly conventional propeller, with a flattened tip as opposed to a radius tip, much like that of a P-51 fighter airplane. Though we were now into the boat's seventh year of racing, our propeller was suddenly ruled illegal and our rating was increased by 1.1 foot, a material reduction in time-allowance credits. We had been rated several times and were in full compliance with all prior measurements. This was the last year of racing under the CCA rule, and in 1971 we would be competing under the new IOR MKIII rule.

Remarkably, our propeller was not penalized under the implementation of the IOR rule. A 1.1 foot rating was a huge penalty. I still ask, "How did this happen?" I've never received a satisfactory answer.

11

Our Irish Homeland

Winning this race was a must. We privately willed it before the start.
At least it would have the ultimate concentration of skills.
Even our Irish jokes were set aside. However, at happy hour,
one drink of Irish whiskey was allowed.

We knew we had to be the victor, and we had to beat our
key rival Ted Turner in *American Eagle.* Our Irish dream came true
and there was a fantastic Irish celebration. Being truly Irish,
the Prime Minister presented the magnificent, one of a kind,
Waterford Global Trophy, to my wife Kathy.

An outstanding tour of Ireland followed.

Our Irish Homeland

A Historic Return to Ireland in the '69 Transatlantic Race
2,750 miles

On Sunday, June 22, 1969, *KIALOA II* set sail bound for Cork, Ireland, in the 2,750 nautical mile Transatlantic Race sponsored by the Cruising Club of America and the Royal Cork Yacht Club. The Royal Cork, according to the Irish, was the oldest such club in the New World, and 1969 was its 250th Anniversary. To say that we were excited about this event would be a huge understatement. In many ways, for so many of us, the passage was more than just a sailboat race. It addressed a fundamental and historic desire to return to our heritage.

More than 50% of our crew were of Irish descent and each crewmember had an interesting story of how his family left Ireland…either voluntarily or involuntarily. We were a boatload of Irish Americans, Irish New Zealanders and Irish Australians. The Aussies and Kiwis had particularly amazing family histories. As children, we'd all become familiar with Irish lullabies, Irish literature and, of course, the many Irish folk stories. All of our Irish crew wanted to visit the counties and cities of their family's origin. A love of Ireland was ingrained in almost all of us.

My family was from County Cork, where my father and uncle and their family were active in many things, with a probable emphasis on a Free Ireland. Somehow, even though they were Catholics, my father and uncle—who were also involved in forming the ongoing rugby team in County Cork—were able to attend Trinity College, where they received a wonderful education. Reading, writing and literature became a way of life.

Pat Reynolds—our outstanding navigator, who would prove to have a sixth sense on which were the quickest sailing angles to Ireland—was our newest Irish crewmember. Based in New England, his "day job" was senior navigator for Pan Am airlines. He became a great asset to *KIALOA II* in this race and many others.

Pat also introduced us to an old German navigation system from World War II called "consol," that had been enhanced by our U.S. Navy after the war. The system employed a series of dots and dashes transmitted at extremely low frequency from radio antennas in Alaska, Norway and Spain. Consol was somewhat similar to the aircraft omni "radio-approach" navigation units on aircraft (though omni was broadcast at a much higher short-range frequency). It worked well and was used as a supplemental system to our standard navigation systems.

While many of us aboard were reasonably qualified navigators, with Pat we always seemed to be in the right place at the right time. Like many others navigators who learned the craft before the advent of GPS, I still treasure my sextant and other basic navigation tools, some of which are antiques dating back centuries to the magnificent era of history and exploration of Persia and the Middle East.

As we prepared for the race to Ireland, we also discussed the country's ongoing transition since gaining their freedom from England, specifically their defined plan for economic growth. A key element to this plan was the foundation of the Irish Development Authority (IDA). The IDA engaged successful Irish businessmen and entrepreneurs in the United States and elsewhere and asked them to become members of the organization and to provide recommendations as to how Ireland should grow their economy.

Needless to say, along with recommendations, the IDA also asked for funding. I became a member of the group and offered suggestions and a moderate contribution. The United States and California were rapidly expanding their leading roles in the electronics and high-tech worlds, and many IDA members suggested that Ireland, as a member of the European community, would be a great location for tax-free outsourcing and marketing into Europe.

A highly literate nation with a strong background and history in education, Ireland was making inroads into the fields of science, electronics and physics, and realized they'd need to expand their educational capabilities in all these areas. They did so, with magnificent results. Furthermore, over the years, Ireland expanded in all of these categories and set an example of what a small, highly educated, freethinking society can achieve if willing to make the effort.

And in the early stages of this century, another small country, also full of Irish descendants, and about the same size as Ireland, has also achieved significant economic growth. I'm thinking of New Zealand, which is also a highly competitive sailing nation.

So we were off to Ireland, and it wasn't all business. The land of my father's birth is also the origin of self-deprecating "Irish Humor," which goes close in hand to "Sailor's Humor." There's always a laugh at the end of a story. It reminds me of that funny Irish movie, *Waking Ned Devine.*

The 1969 SORC and the Miami-Montego Bay Races played a major role in our preparation for the Transatlantic Race later that year. We'd had a good opportunity to test ourselves against the light, new *Windward Passage*, with its longer waterline, and the converted America's Cup racer, *American Eagle*, a strong upwind performer.

Based on those trials, we concluded that we needed more sail power and stability in the upper wind ranges. To address these matters, we lengthened the keel and added 3,000 pounds of lead ballast at the keel tip. This enabled us to remove some of the internal ballast and rework the yacht's basic floatation characteristics. We also completely overhauled our entire sail inventory to add sail area with more advanced sail shapes and made several changes to our spinnakers. Subsequent sail testing showed decided improvements. (We couldn't help but think how these modifications would have helped us in the 1969 SORC and the Jamaica Race.)

For the Transatlantic Race, our main competition would be *American Eagle* and Huey Long's new *Ondine*, a higher-rated yacht than *KIALOA II*. *Windward Passage* had opted to sail into the Pacific for the Transpac.

We'd learned quite a lot about racing in the North Atlantic in our 1968 Transatlantic Race from Bermuda to Germany. Our crew was especially fired up to win the race to Ireland. At precisely 1300 hours (1 p.m.) on the 22nd of June, our quest began. Here's what transpired:

June 22–25: The windward start, in an east-northeast breeze, was fairly uneventful. For the first 24-hours, winds varied between 10-17 knots and *KIALOA II* logged about 184 miles on a course of 108° magnetic (all compass readings in this chapter are in degrees magnetic). The air was foggy and moist. At about noon the second day, the wind shifted to the east and the velocity dropped. At 1900, we tacked onto starboard steering about 60° M, once again in moderate headwinds. (Note: all times are Zulu, or Greenwich Mean Time.) Eventually, the fog gave way to heavy rain and the wind filled in briskly from the southeast, blowing around 30-knots for several hours. Forty-seven hours after the start, *KIALOA II* had sailed 343.4 miles in fairly rough sea conditions. We were off and running.

Over the next 24 hours, the wind again increased in velocity to 30 knots from the southeast, though by 0400 on the 24th it had slowly dropped to around fifteen knots. We made several sail changes throughout this period—including reefing and un-reefing the main—and repaired two or three sails with our onboard sewing machine and, at times, by hand stitching.

The wind continued to move to the south, originally coming from a direction of 150° and moving through to 180° between 0800 on the 24th to 1500 on the 25th; from noon to noon on these two days, *KIALOA II* recorded a 219-mile day sailing under a full yawl rig using the No. 1 jib topsail, the full main, the No. 1 mizzen topsail and full mizzen.

June 25–26 (1200–1200): The wind kept moving aft, allowing us to set a spinnaker and large mizzen staysail by 1630, on the twenty-fifth. At 2000, KIALOA II jibed to port with the breeze blowing up to 20 knots for the next 7 hours. During this stretch, we jibed three times to sail the most favored angle and best speed, ending up on a port jibe steering 112° (closer to our desired base course) at 0300 on the morning of the twenty-sixth. Our position that day at 1510 was 43°30'N by 55°19'W.

Through that evening, the wind continued to drop.

June 26-27 (1200–1200): In the afternoon of the 26th, the wind increased to 13-20 knots. We had a good sailing angle, spinnaker reaching with the mizzen staysail until the early evening, when the wind went forward. At that juncture, we again dropped the spinnaker in favor of jib topsails, and continued to make frequent sail changes to optimize our speed. Steering an average course of about 113°M, we recorded speeds between 9.5-10 knots.

At 0800 on the 27th, we were "on soundings," some 55 fathoms over the legendary Grand Banks. Because of the heavy fishing-boat traffic, we needed to watch our navigation to ward off a possible collision. Luckily, though the sky was hazy, it wasn't as foggy as it had been during the 1968 Transatlantic Race. Our noon position was 43°49'N by 51°45'W, only 121 miles from Point Alpha, the iceberg mark we were obliged to leave to the port side of *KIALOA II*. The day's run from noon to noon was 213 miles.

June 27–28 (1200–1200): At 2316 on the 27th we rounded Point Alpha (44°N by 49°W), and altered course to 085°M. *Ondine* reported rounding Alpha some 4 hours and 45 minutes ahead of *KIALOA II*. It was a close race. Once around the iceberg mark, the strategy aboard every yacht was the same: Head north to sail a great circle course and save mileage.

Once past Alpha we were again "off soundings," and the wind dropped to about 5 or 6 knots. The fog rolled in and the water temperature quickly dropped six degrees, to 44°F. To keep *KIALOA II* moving in the light breeze, we steered variable headings from 20° to 60°M for eight hours, making only a few miles on course until 0900, on the 28th, when a new breeze came in. We jibed onto starboard tack, steering about 110°M and making around 8 knots. At 1200 the wind increased and allowed us to sail a course of 090°M. Our noon position was 45°33'N by 42°87'W… a beautiful 212-mile day.

I realize my short-form comments make it sound easy, but we had much to do: There were minor repairs to make, endless sail changes (which meant endless repacking), checking and servicing all equipment, and so on. Everyone was performing beautifully with their assigned duties, and we were having a great sail with plenty of concentration and camaraderie.

Our tactical plan was to hold a somewhat southerly track in relation to the great circle route as long as we were remaining within our handicap allowance with *Ondine*.

We felt that going straight north early, as *Ondine* was doing, would provide early gains, but that being too far north would diminish our options towards the end of the race. We were not willing to make this gamble. The *KIALOA II* crew had decided that we were going to win this race before crossing the starting line, and their efforts and determination were outstanding.

June 29–July 1: By noon on the 29th our position was 47°10'N by 36°49'W, after an excellent day's run of 253 miles. We were running hard under spinnaker much of the time, which put tremendous load on our afterguys and spinnaker pole end fittings. The wire guys sometimes popped out of the pole, which meant a 15-20 minute "all hands" fire drill to get things under control. We also had a few wire halyards and related blocks fail. Fortunately, we had adequate repair gear, and the great spinnaker rides made it all worthwhile. We were a happy, motivated crew.

At 1200 on the 30th, our position was 48°24'N by 31°13'W…a 237-mile day with 890 miles to go. At about 0030 on the first of July, we had a quick wind shift from 280° to 360° and our sailing angle went from about 85° to 50° at a wind velocity of about 15 knots. We trimmed sails for the new breeze.

July 2–5: The great sail continued until midnight on July 2nd when the wind dropped out and fluctuated through about 65° before settling in at 005°M. We tacked on to starboard and managed speeds of only 3-4 knots until 1100, sailing just 46 miles over the 11-hour period. We couldn't help but wonder what our chief competition was doing, while lamenting how hard it is to sail so slowly.

At 1200, our position was 49°04'N by 27°24'W. Fortunately, a 12-15 knot southerly breeze filled in soon after and we were back on a good course of about 095° making excellent progress. Our 2.2-ounce, heavy reaching spinnaker was a magnificent powerhouse in company with a forestaysail, full main and No. 1 mizzen staysail.

We were now having some very fast spinnaker rides while surfing on the waves, knocking off a series of daily runs well over 200 miles (during this stretch we had 24-hour runs of 253-, 237-, 244- and 222-miles), often times bettering 20-knots of boat speed on the long surfs.

The exhilaration was tremendous, particularly at night with the light of the stars above and the phosphorescence in the water below. Down below when off watch, you could actually hear the screams of joy and cheers from the crew on deck. It was exciting. It was fun. However, my bunk was just forward of the cockpit in the doghouse. I couldn't be a spoilsport and yell, "Shut up!" for keeping me awake. So, while I was thrilled and enjoyed the ride, I used my wakeful hours to calculate the noise level of the hollering. I discovered that George Bissell screamed the loudest, though Roy Bream was a close second.

It's impossible, when writing about the experience, to accurately record every sail change, but there were plenty of them: mizzen staysail spinnaker up, No. 1 mizzen staysail down, mizzen up, mizzen down, mizzen spinnaker up, mizzen spinnaker down, and on and on and on. We were continuously balancing the boat's power, and the fore and aft loads, doing all that we could, night and day, to optimize performance. Even when they were down below and resting, the off-watch crew was always available to be on deck to help.

Usually, when spinnaker reaching, we would not fly the actual mizzen. Instead, we opted for the biggest possible mizzen staysail, our big conventional reaching mizzen staysail or our spinnaker mizzen staysail. When steering became a burden or control an issue, we would then move the center of effort toward the middle of the boat by dousing or hoisting the mizzen.

At 1200 on July 3rd, after another 222-mile day, thanks to more downwind surfing under every sail we could fly—spinnaker, forestaysail, mizzen spinnaker staysail—we were north of the fiftieth parallel at 50°10'N by 21°58'W. The next day, we jibed to port with the wind angle changing to allow more spinnaker reaching on a new course of 100°M.

Our position at 1200 on the Fourth of July, after another great day, with 244 more miles in the bank, was 50°36'N by 15°35'W. We carried on with a 3.0-ounce spinnaker, and then, as the wind went forward, set a "ballooner" at 2150, only to change down again to a 2.2-ounce spinnaker an hour later. (The ballooner is a large, drafty headsail used for reaching when the apparent wind angle is too tight for a spinnaker).

At this stage, a seagoing trawler flying an Irish flag veered off course to inspect *KIALOA II* and signal hello, and we obtained the weather broadcast from Fastnet Rock, which showed the same weather as ours.

At 0645 on the July 5th, with the wind lightening and backing to the northwest, we made yet another spinnaker change, hoisting our 1.5-ounce chute to effect repairs to the 2.2-ounce kite.

At 0917, we were once again "on soundings" along Ireland's south coast. At 1520, with more wind, we changed back to a reaching 2.2-ounce chute with good speed and good seas.

After a 222-mile day, *KIALOA II* was off Galley Head, just 27 miles from the finish line. We knew *Ondine* had finished about 5 hours earlier. To win the race, the math was simple. We needed to cross the finish line in about 3 hours and 36 minutes, in what appeared to be a dying breeze. Could we save our time?

Yes, we could.

With 48 minutes and 20 seconds to spare, at 10:46 in the evening, *KIALOA II*…did it. The finish line was crowded and excited, with many of our wives, family and friends cheering and waving from a spectator fleet of many yachts and launches that had come out to greet us.

We knew we'd saved our time on *Ondine* (which ultimately corrected out to second in class and second overall), but we now had to check on the boats behind us. We were okay on Ted Turner's *American Eagle*, who finished 15 hours behind us on elapsed time and about 7 hours behind on corrected time for third overall and third in class. Dick Nye's *Carina* finished 2 days and 10 hours behind us, and after their handicap time allowance was applied, they were declared winners of Class B and fourth overall.

But *KIALOA II* had done it, winning the '69 Transatlantic Race, just as her crew predicted. The victory was a testament to the skill and tenacity of our crew, who sailed a fast, technical race. The numbers bore this out. Over the 2,750-mile racecourse, we'd averaged 8.8 knots and 211-miles per day. (Actually, due to our uncountable tacks and jibes, we sailed a distance much farther than 2,750 miles at higher average speeds.)

What a victory it was for our dedicated team. As always, they were outstanding. I salute them all.

And a further salute to the almost 6-year-old *KIALOA II*: What a boat.

The reaction by the Irish people to a first-generation American Irishman, and several Irish crewmembers, winning the race in honor of the 250th anniversary of the Royal Cork Yacht Club, was simply unbelievable. The Irish humor and celebration now began in earnest. It lasted for quite some time.

Wherever we went in Ireland, we were congratulated and thanked for coming home. Later, when anchored in various coves, the locals would row out to *KIALOA II* bringing Irish soda bread under one arm and a salmon beneath the other, as a gift to the boat and her crew.

We met many of the leading members of Cork's and Ireland's community at a lovely afternoon party hosted at the residence of U.S. Ambassador John D. J. Moore, and again at the trophy presentation. The trophy was presented by Jack Lynch, the Irish Taoiseach (Prime Minister), and his lovely wife.

The trophy for winning the 1969 Transatlantic Race was, and still is, magnificent. Crafted in Waterford crystal, the hand-blown glass globe stands 20-inches tall and 14-inches in diameter and is accurate in every detail. The one-of-a-kind piece was designed and fashioned by one of the world's greatest glass blowers, 36-year-old Tommy Wall of the Waterford Glass Company. It took 150 hours to complete.

My wife Kathy and I were honored and delighted, and extended our sincere thanks for such a unique, unusual prize. We were concerned about how to take the trophy home until Ambassador Moore offered to transfer it to Los Angeles with the U.S. Air Force, an offer we gratefully accepted.

All in all, it was a great race with a great crew

and great results, and we made many new best friends with whom we continued our acquaintance: the Taoiseach Jack Lynch and his wife, Máirín O'Connor; the U.S. Ambassador John D. J. Moore; Clayton Love Jr., the Commodore of Royal Cork Yacht Club, his wife and family; the Commodore's father, Clayton Love, Sr., a former Commodore himself; and Clayton Love Minimus, the grandson, who later sailed with us on *KIALOA III* and *IV*.

The enthusiastic reception by the Prime Minister, the Commodore, the U.S. Ambassador and the Irish people was overwhelming. What a story, if I do say so myself; who could've imagined an Irish American winning this great race, from a family who had left their beautiful country because of the years of repression?

Afterwards, we joined Clayton Ewing, the commodore of the Cruising Club of America; Tom Watson, the chairman of IBM and owner of the fine yacht, *Palawan*; Dick Nye and his yacht *Carina*; and several others to cruise aboard our individual yachts to the south coast of Ireland. We visited Kinsale; Castle Townsend, Baltimore; and carried on to Schull.

Schull!

Schull is where my father was born in 1875. I tried to imagine the changes of time over 94 years…I could not.

I have one last story to tell of our race to Ireland, one of the most memorable of my life. Shortly after Huey Long and *Ondine* had finished, Huey called to ask where we were. This reminded me of the 1959 Honolulu Race when *KIALOA I* was less than fifty miles from the finish line, sailing well in fresh breeze. Don Haskell of *Chubasco*, who had already finished, called to ask our position. When I told Don where we were, he said, "Congratulations, it looks like you are the winner."

I thought back to that unlucky year and the friendly call from Don Haskell, and what transpired almost immediately thereafter. The wind totally died. In big, sloppy seas, with *KIALOA I* rolling, slatting and banging around, we fell to fifth overall. It was sheer misery.

I could not and would not do that again. So, when Huey called, I told him we were well off Cape Clear, about 60 miles out, when in fact we were really at Galley Head, about 27 miles from the finish.

Sorry, Huey, I didn't mean to deceive you; at least we gave you a few hours of happiness. I just didn't want the wind to go away.

Lure of Sea Smoothes Business Waters for Yachtsman Kilroy

I feel that at times, perhaps most of the time, I am too close to the specific details related to my sailing and business careers, to adequately express my thoughts. Perhaps the following article by Dwight Chapin, from the Sunday edition of the *Los Angeles Times*, on July 27, 1969, may offer some specific insight:

TRANS-ATLANTIC WINNER

Lure of Sea Smoothes Business Waters for Yachtsman Kilroy

BY DWIGHT CHAPIN

Times Staff Writer

"The longer you sail," said John B. (Jim) Kilroy, "the more you'll find what an indefinable subject it is. You open one door and you find two. You open two and you find four."

"Perhaps the main thing the sea holds for you is that it's never the same. The water, the clouds, the navigation, the wind….they're always changing."

Jim Kilroy, highly successful businessman, head of Los Angeles' 1976 Olympic Games effort, and sailor, was talking about a subject about as old as the earth itself.

He was talking about what makes a man get into a boat and go out to sea.

"Sailing shows the relative insignificance of the individual," he said. "You're engaging in a fundamental relationship with nature, an attempt to harness nature for your own benefit.

Forgot Business

"I know when I'm out there on an ocean I forget all about matters of business. And everything seems so much easier when I get back. Maybe it's because my staff cleans up everything when I'm gone—but it isn't as difficult to get to the core of the problem, to strip the problem of its unessential details."

Laid out before Kilroy on his eight-floor office in a downtown Los Angeles bank building was a jumble of charts and log books, maps and newspapers.

He is one of the area's best-known businessmen but he now was completely lost in talk about a subject that was light years away from his telephone, his conference room and his multi-million dollar investments.

Won Irish Race

No one intruded as Kilroy discussed his latest and perhaps largest yachting triumph, victory in the recent Trans-Atlantic race from Newport, R.I. to Cork, Ireland.

"People ask me about it," he said. "What it was like out there, what happened? What can I tell them? When you sail that far (2,790 miles) on the Atlantic, everything happens."

Kilroy's yacht, the *KIALOA II,* and his 13-man crew survived a flood of minor difficulties to beat *Ondine* on corrected time, 12 days, 21 hours, 6 minutes, 35 seconds.

The Atlantic was its usual, unpredictable self. *KIALOA II* encountered fog, heavy rain, reefs and challenges of every sort. But they were met by a dedicated crew that includes just one salaried hand. And because the challenges were great, so is the satisfaction.

Kilroy displayed a picture of a Waterford crystal cut-glass trophy that was awarded to the winning boat. The trophy is in the form of a globe. "It took over 150 man hours to put it together," he said, "and it's so accurate in detail you can navigate by it. The State Department has charge of it now, and we've heard it might be presented to us in an official ceremony in Washington, D.C."

Appropriate Win

This was the first year the Trans-Atlantic race finished in Cork and a uniquely appropriate year for Kilroy to win it. "My father," he said, "was born in County Cork. I'm a first-generation Irish-American."

After the race, which helped celebrate the 250th anniversary of the Royal Cork Yacht Club, the world's oldest, the competing yachts and other boats from around the world went on a cruise of ports throughout Ireland.

"The ports, and the terrain, were just beautiful," Kilroy said, "and the people were wonderfully considerate. Soda bread is common throughout Ireland and everywhere we'd visit they'd give us some. We'd come out of a pub or a traditional meeting place with a loaf of bread and a bottle of ale under one arm and a big salmon under the other."

Kilroy and the *KIALOA II* have sailed in the Transpacific yacht race (and were class winners) as well as the Trans-Atlantic and the skipper says the latter is generally much more of a test.

"The race to Honolulu is one of the world's great sailboat races," Kilroy said, "but it's primarily an off-the-wind and warm weather race. You just don't have the shiftiness of wind and the changing sea conditions you have in the Atlantic, which is pretty much an on-the-wind race."

Kilroy said that he and his crew "played it on the conservative side" on the way to Cork. *Ondine* finished first and *KIALOA* second before corrected-time calculations, but Kilroy indicated that didn't upset him at all.

"*Ondine*, which is damned good competition," Kilroy said, "gambled on speed. We were interested mostly in position, in sailing to cover our competition from behind and against *Ondine* in front."

KIALOA II will not pause long on it laurels. Kilroy and his crew will leave with the yacht next week for an English Channel race and three more August races in Europe.

Then Kilroy plans to use the boat for another purpose—to entertain European sports dignitaries in his role as leader of the drive to get the '76 Olympics for Los Angeles.

And then it will be on to the winter racing circuit. The lure of the sea is still the main lure. "You're playing chess out there," Kilroy says, "with some very sophisticated equipment, and you're working with and against some awfully stimulating, interesting people.

"There's a commonality of people of the sea. You're one of them. You ask a sailor a question, and you KNOW you're going to get a straight answer."

He looked at his watch. "An hour-and-a-half!" he exclaimed. "Have we REALLY been talking an hour-and-a-half?

KIALOA Approaching Fastnet Rock

The Summer of '69

For *KIALOA II* and her crew, the 1969 Transatlantic Race to Ireland was a huge success. A decade later, aboard *KIALOA III*, we would once again race across the Atlantic. But that was in the future. In the summer of '69, we still had unfinished business in the United Kingdom.

After celebrating our victory with a cruise along the coast, our Irish episode was over, and it was back to Los Angeles for family, business and community. Meanwhile, *KIALOA II* sailed from Cork to the English port of Cowes on the Isle of Wight to prepare for Cowes Week, in which we only sailed two races, the Channel Race and the 605-mile Fastnet Race. After returning to England, I was busy making contact with International Olympic Committee (IOC) members and National Olympic Committee (NOC) members from several European countries, trying to sell the 1976 Los Angeles Olympic Committee bid for the XXI Olympiad. As chairman of the committee, it was essential that I contact as many IOC, NOC and Sports Federation members as possible.

KIALOA II and *American Eagle* were both measured under the RORC rule in Cowes and received their rating and handicaps. *KIALOA II's* measurement provided a handicap of 1.0598 (elapsed time). *American Eagle* was slightly less, 1.0484 (elapsed time). The coefficient was a multiplier of each yacht's elapsed time.

The '69 Fastnet Race, along the south coast of England with the turning point at Fastnet Rock, was a very slow affair with little wind and a strong, adverse tidal current. On the morning after the start, we were forced to anchor for several hours while all smaller yachts—without even moving!—were gaining substantial handicap time due to their lower handicap coefficients.

For the first twenty-three hours, in fact, our ship's log showed a gain of only 67 miles. Off Start Point, according to a log entry, the sea was calm and glossy, and while some yachts were making slight progress, others were going around in circles. It's important to note that this wasn't a normal Fastnet Race. Ten years later, in the infamous 1979 Fastnet, *KIALOA III* was part of the fleet that was pummeled by a Force 10 storm in which 17 sailors, and several yachts, were lost at sea.

At the finish of this slow, variable contest, *American Eagle* was first home, four minutes ahead of *KIALOA II*, with a corrected time of 93 hours and 16 minutes; however, with her lower CTF, she gained an additional credit of 1 hour and 37 minutes over *KIALOA II*. In spite of the calm weather and the time spent at anchor, *KIALOA II* finished third in class and fifth overall on corrected time, while *American Eagle* was second in class and fourth overall. After a 0.8070 time correction was factored in, *Red Rooster*, a 43-foot Dick Carter design, was first overall on corrected time.

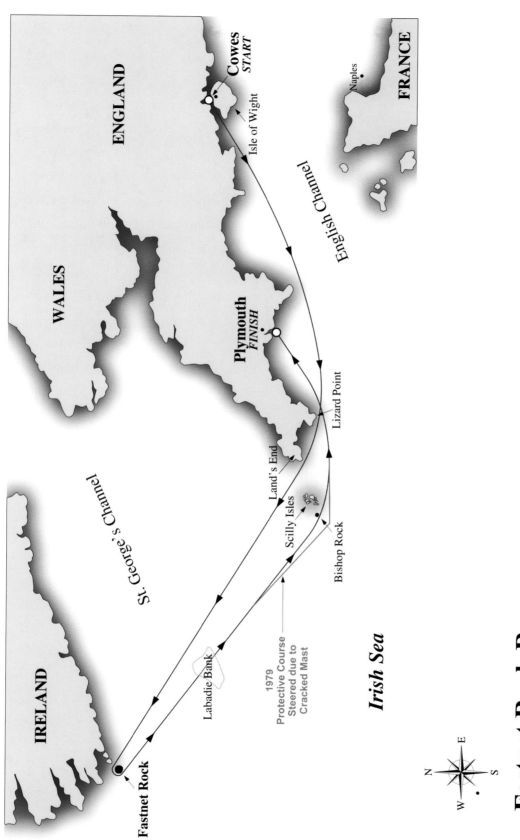

Fastnet Rock Race
605 Nautical Miles

The 225-mile Channel Race, with more heavy tide and fluky breeze, was just about as bad. With a 0.7690 time factor, a yacht called *Rainbow II* was the winner. Ted Turner's *American Eagle* was second and *KIALOA II* was third, three hours behind *American Eagle*. Though we had different strategies on how best to work the adverse tides, nothing conclusive could be defined from these "crap shoot" conditions.

After the races, before returning back to Los Angeles, I continued making IOC contacts in Portugal, Spain, France and Switzerland, as well as meeting *KIALOA* in the French Riviera and onto Sardinia. *KIALOA II* was then delivered to Florida for the 1970 SORC, which was sailed under a new revision to the Cruising Class of America rule. The new rating for *KIALOA II* was now 65.0 (for the Transatlantic Race, it had been 63.8), which underscored the general confusion in advance of the new IOR Rule. Since the rating numbers for most yachts were reduced, *KIALOA II* now owed more time allowance to smaller yachts.

12

THE OLYMPIC CREED

*The most important thing in the Olympic Games is not to win
but to take part, just as the most important thing in life
is not the triumph but the struggle.
The essential thing is not to have
conquered but to have fought well.*

THE OLYMPIC MOTTO

*"Citius, Altius, Fortius."
Swifter, higher, stronger.*

The Creed and the Motto are intended to spur all athletes
and participants to embrace the Olympic Spirit.

With respect, I call to the attention of those who read this book,
the fundamental rules apply to all who participate in phases
of the games of the Olympics, including athletes, organizers,
administrators and managers.

Backstabbed by Brundage

*Hope and Deception
in the Quest for the '76 Olympic Games*

In early 1968, the mayor of Los Angeles, Sam Yorty, asked if I would chair a committee to bid for the 1976 Games of the Summer Olympics on the city's behalf. My response was that it would be a wonderful tribute for our nation to host the Olympics during our bicentennial anniversary, and yes, I would be honored to do so.

Though the circumstances were quite different now, it wouldn't be my first experience with the Olympics in Los Angeles.

Some simple math revealed that 1976 would also be the 44th anniversary of the city's "no cost" Olympics of 1932, which had been a great spectacle for my brother Walter and me, at the time 13 and 10, respectively. Though we didn't have tickets, we did watch the Games inside the great, expanded new Coliseum. We were street kids selling newspapers, which advertised the Olympic program on the front page; we worked our way in to sell those programs to the paying customers. Once again, it was fortunate that we were pretty big kids for our ages.

The fact that those '32 Games were staged at "no cost" to Los Angeles was a big deal. That was our game plan for 1976, as well. The Olympics would need to pay for themselves.

With that goal in mind, we arranged a preliminary meeting with a few of my close associates and Bill Nicholas, now the general manager of the Coliseum; Paul Zimmerman and Bill Henry, the sports editors for the city's major newspaper, the *Los Angeles Times*; and John Ferraro, a former USC football star and a city councilman. After discussing our objectives, we placed calls to Jack Garland and Bill Schroeder, who'd served on the committee for the 1932 Games. We were eager to have their guidance and learn the secrets to their success.

We also discussed the quality of the facilities that were already available, ranking them from good to great, and noting which might need a little improvement. We were lucky that Southern California was already blessed with outstanding sports and event facilities. As far as fund-raising was concerned, the vastly experienced Bill Nicholas was a great resource. Plus, in this regard we had a possible ace in the hole: television rights. Obviously, worldwide television broadcasts didn't exist in 1932. TV alone had great potential to cover a major cost of hosting the Summer Games.

Bill Nicholas introduced us to Thomas Gallery, the former vice president of sports for NBC, whom we immediately drafted as a member of our Los Angeles Olympic Committee. Soon, other heavy hitters from the realms of television, entertainment and sports also signed on. With their expertise, we commissioned a study that showed us that, with the cooperation of the International Olympic Committee (IOC)—who would also contribute special fees—an international television package could put our budget over the top.

Together, Bill and Tom designed a complete TV package and presented it to the IOC, which accepted the plan. All of our consultants agreed that we were in the ideal time zone for international distribution. A substantial foundation for the staging of our "no-cost" Games had been successfully established.

Our job now was to target and organize the facilities in both physical and technical terms, and sell our concept to the IOC and their related organizations—the National Olympic Committees (NOC) and Sports Federations (FISA) of various nations—as well as to the international press corps.

We left no stone unturned, analyzing not only the facilities we'd use, but also the related infrastructure, including hotel accommodations and living quarters for the visitors, officials and athletes; transportation; and even sightseeing attractions and other activities that visitors from around the world might like to visit and enjoy.

Housing was a big issue for our committee. Though we had plenty of facilities and attractions in Southern California, quality-housing assets did not surround our "Central City" area in downtown Los Angeles. In fact, the area was largely comprised of older properties that on the whole were poorly maintained. However, there was also an opportunity here. Not only did the Olympics require better housing, but if we wanted to retain a vibrant downtown atmosphere, so did the Central City. As it was, due to the lack of good housing, businesses were already moving out to Century City, Beverly Hills, Glendale, Westwood, Pasadena and other residential communities.

So, in drafting our concept for Olympic housing, we decided to place the Olympic Village across the freeway from the downtown Music Center and Civic Center. It was a wonderful, central location. We'd develop the area with apartment blocks, tennis courts, parks and athletic facilities, all the things the athletes would want and need during the Games. Afterwards, the development would already have all the features attractive to corporate executives, office-building tenants and employees. In short, it would be the centerpiece for growth and stability in the Central City.

There was funding available for this aspect of the project. We envisioned this development as a future profit center for the ownership foundation, a joint venture between our Olympics Foundation and private enterprise, who'd been involved in planning and refining the overall concept. The proceeds of these profits, in turn, would be set aside for youth development and sports.

Things were moving quickly, and productively. After reaching out to international outlets, our Television Committee felt confident that the broadcast rights would also be profitable, with benefits for both our Olympic Games Committee and the IOC. In fact, our financial analysis showed that we could hold an exceedingly successful, high quality Summer Olympics with a substantial profit for all concerned, and which included the new downtown development, which would be a lasting legacy for Los Angeles. Mind you, we were very conservative with our projections. But we were also convinced that we had a plan in place to stage a profitable, no-cost 1976 Olympic Games.

We invited officials from the IOC and the various national federations to come visit Los Angeles and help with the planning. We received many good suggestions and recommendations and were pleased with the "excellent" ratings bestowed on our work from our visitors. In turn, several members of our committee traveled to Mexico City on a fact-finding mission and attended several events. We were making strong friendships abroad—and established a relationship with the Munich Olympic Committee, who'd been awarded the 1973 Games—that we hoped would be beneficial to our bid.

Our Transatlantic Race to Germany had also enabled me to meet many leaders in the German sports community. Everything seemed to be working in our favor. Our one liability was surprising: Los Angeles was so well known for staging successful events that some people believed we might be *too glamorous* compared to other potential venues.

In October, 1969, it appeared that the field of contenders had been narrowed down to two possible cities: Los Angeles and Montreal. Representatives from both cities were invited to a joint meeting in Dubrovnik, Yugoslavia, to make presentations before the IOC and the other international sporting organizations. We prepared detailed reports, with graphics, for each Olympic event, and had all our financial spreadsheets in order. We were ready and prepared to answer each and every question about our plans.

I was waiting in our designated display area when one of the delegates to the presentation asked me if we could speak privately in fifteen minutes at the nearby boat dock in front of our hotel, which was situated right on the Adriatic Sea. I said, "Yes, of course," and suddenly found myself in the midst of a very interesting discussion.

"I am the social and cultural administrator of Romania," the man explained. "I do not believe that you Americans understand the purpose of sports in Russia and the Iron Curtain countries."

"We use sporting events and sports to constrain the potential uprising of our people. When there appears to be a problem in a certain area, we stage a sports event, frequently with potential opposition involved. It is a significant way of controlling our people."

"And, why do I tell you this when I am the Social and Cultural Minister of Romania? I do it, because I am opposed to Communism. I do it, because I am a family member of the deposed king. I do it, because we need the help and support of America. I do it, because you should know."

I thanked him, and he departed. It's perhaps noteworthy that in 1984, during the Summer Olympics in Los Angeles, Russia and other Iron Curtain countries boycotted the games, but that Romania sent a full team and participated in the entire event.

My brief talk with the Romanian official was surprising. A day later I had another one that was even bigger and more astounding.

Once again, I was asked to step outside and speak privately. This time, the request came from Jerry Snyder, the chairman of the Montreal delegation. After a few minutes of polite, informal chit-chat, he got to the heart of the matter.

Basically, what he told me was this: The city of Montreal had a substantial loan from West Germany that would soon be due and that needed to be restructured. His committee had no commitment from the Canadian National Government to provide any financial support for the Olympic Games, and it appeared that there would be none forthcoming. Montreal officials knew that there would be substantial losses from the Games that they could not afford and could not allow to occur. Given all that, he'd been instructed by Mayor Jean Drapeau to provide me with this confidential information, and they would, at the appropriate time, withdraw.

Jerry Snyder then congratulated Los Angeles as our probable winning bid for the 1976 Games. On behalf of our committee, I thanked him for this information and told him that I would await Mayor Drapeau's forthcoming statement before making any response. I believed that I could trust Jerry to provide accurate and honest information, yet days passed and there was no public announcement from Mayor Drapeau confirming that Montreal would withdraw.

I pondered this situation and then heard from a key source that Avery Brundage, the IOC President, was sending messages to Mayor Drapeau that Montreal should not withdraw their bid. And furthermore, Brundage reportedly hinted that he would soon have very good news for Montreal. I actually heard this rumor on more than one occasion.

There was really only one conclusion to draw from all of it. Somehow, Mayor Drapeau must have advised Avery Brundage of Montreal's intention to withdraw, and Brundage was doing everything he could to keep Montreal's bid alive.

Soon enough, the waters became even more muddied, as our sources revealed that Moscow might be making a late bid for the 1976 Olympics. It was now late in October, 1969, and we anxiously looked at the IOC Constitution to determine the "terminal date" for applications—the day after which a city could not apply for the '76 Summer Games. According to the Constitution, no city could apply within six months of the date on which the Games would be awarded. The IOC had announced that it would reveal its decision on May 12, 1970. As far as we were concerned, that meant the final day for applications was November 12, 1969, which was rapidly approaching.

The day came and went, and there was no word from Moscow. We were now cautiously optimistic that either Montreal would withdraw, or that we would still be selected to host the Games on May 12th at the planned ceremony in Amsterdam.

So we were later surprised by an article that appeared in the August 8th, 1970 edition of the *Los Angeles Times*, with remarks attributed to Konstantin Andrianov, the chairman of the USSR Olympic Committee and a vice president of the IOC. It read, "Andrianov rejected contentions 'from some periodicals abroad' that Moscow entered the list of contenders too late… He said there was no IOC rule that the site would be selected on a first come, first choice basis. Besides, he said, Moscow applied well before the Dec. 31, 1969 deadline."

This was stunning news. In the meantime, we continued to be informally advised of the discussions between Avery Brundage and Mayor Drapeau. We also learned that Brundage was involved in intense, ongoing negotiation with his fellow IOC officers over the future of IOC leadership, particularly who might ultimately succeed Brundage and other IOC officers. The rumors persisted, but my (unofficial) sources continued to tell me not to worry. It was just business as usual in "international competition."

I believed it right up to the moment that I heard that Montreal would be awarded the 1976 Summer Olympics…and Moscow earned the right to host the 1980 Games!

My official comments on learning about this unfortunate geopolitical prize to Montreal are as follows:

"On 10 May 1970, our Los Angeles 1976 Olympic Committee made its official and formal invitation to the International Olympic Committee to hold the 1976 Summer Olympic Games in the City of Los Angeles.

This official invitation, made before the International Olympic Committee and the International Sports Federation, was given by Mayor Sam Yorty; Mr. John B. Kilroy, President of the Committee; Ambassador Preston Hotchkis, Vice President of the Committee and the Official Representative of the County of Los Angeles; Mr. Stanley Wright, Coach of the 1968 United States Track Team, Coach of the 1964 Malaysian Olympic Track Team and a Director of the United States Olympic Committee; Mr. Thomas Gallery, former Vice President of National Broadcasting Company and a leading figure in international sports television; and Mr. William Nicholas, General Manager of the Los Angeles Memorial Coliseum and Sports Arena.

As part of the presentation, a 21-minute multi-media film, narrated by Lorne Greene, depicting the way of life of Southern California, along with our outstanding sports facilities, was shown to the members of the I.O.C. This film, which was received to resounding acclaim, was produced by

Mr. Wilson Brydon.

On the 9th of May, 10th of May and 11th of May, an exhibition booth of photographs, renderings and other display material, along with an orange juice fountain and gifts of Los Angeles baseball caps, was open for visits by the International Olympic Committee, National Olympic Committee, Federations and World Sports Press. The exhibition booth was manned by four attractive hostesses, interpreters loaned to us through the courtesy of TWA (Trans World Airline), and by members of our delegation.

By the evening of the 10th, the comment of the I.O.C. and members of international federations was that Los Angeles had made the most outstanding verbal, visual and technical presentation ever made by a bid city for the Summer Games. Our delegation had continuous, yet discreet, contact with each of the 70 I.O.C. members present to discuss any questions they might have relative to our brochures and technical data previously submitted to them through the United States Ambassador in their home country (additional brochures were given to them in Amsterdam). Such contact was made only after a personal visit with Mr. Avery Brundage by the Committee President and Mr. Lee Combs, President of the Southern California Committee for Olympic Games, to establish proper protocol.

The Los Angeles delegation consisted of the following. All should be complimented for their outstanding personal effort, statesmanship and long workdays:

Mayor Sam Yorty
Mr. and Mrs. John B. Kilroy
Mr. and Mrs. Guilford Babcock, III
Mr. Sam Bretzfield
Mr. Wil Brydon
Mr. Lee Combs
Miss Jeanne D'Amico
Supervisor Warren Dorn
Mr. Arnold Eddy
Commissioner Abner England
Councilman John Ferraro
Mr. Tom Gallery
Mr. Bob Golden
Mr. Preston Hotchkis
Mr. Norman Houston
Councilman Gilbert Lindsay
Councilman Billy Mills
Mr. William Nicholas
Councilman Louis Nowell

Commissioner Brad Pye

Mr. Rod Rood

Mr. Marty Samuelson

Mr. W.R. Schroeder

Mr. Charles Stuart

Mr. Fred Wada

Mr. Stan Wright

Mr. Paul Zimmerman

On 12 May 1970, the Congress of the 69ᵗʰ Session of the International Olympic Committee was officially opened by Queen Juliana of Holland in the Theatre of the RAI. At this meeting, Her Excellency M.A.M. Klompé, Social and Cultural Minister of Holland, spoke about the 1928 Summer Games held in Amsterdam and the need to reduce the Summer Games to a size and cost where they might again be held by small countries, and they – Holland – looked forward to a future bid.

Avery Brundage, President of the International Olympic Committee, in his address, stated that— to his surprise—Minister Klompé effectively gave his speech (Miss Klompé's speech had been previously 'cleared' through Mr. Brundage's office in "normal" protocol and the printed speeches were prepared for distribution), and that the Games must be reduced in size and cost in dollars to give all of the smaller nations the opportunity to reap the great rewards of the Olympic Games.

This, Brundage said, is particularly so in present times, at the time of the problems of Southeast Asia, anarchy and unrest, riots in the schools, civil disobedience and other disorder in the United States.

We should return to the heritage of the great Olympian of the past, citing Emile Zatopek from a small country, the great four-Gold-Medal-winner of the Helsinki Games (this was apparently a direct reference to the problem of Colonel Emile Zatopek, who became a garbage collector overnight as a result of his resistance to the Russian invasion of Prague, which was well known by all in attendance). There was no reference to Gold Medal winners from the United States or our Olympic contributions and absolutely no mention specifically of Russia or Montreal, except inferentially through Zatopek. The opening meeting was then closed and the I.O.C. adjourned along with the Federations prior to the vote for the award city by the I.O.C.

In meetings the day before, the Federations leaders desired to vote <u>individual ratings of the cities as to their technical qualifications</u>. Much opposition came, particularly from Commonwealth and East European members, to any such specific rating based upon the fact that each city had adequate time to build suitable facilities to hold the Games. <u>A vote against such specific recommendations barely passed</u>. As a result, Los Angeles was given no credit for existing capabilities. This vote, contrary to the wishes *of most of the Federations Executive Committee, was presented to Mr. Brundage and the I.O.C. The Federations were dismissed and the secret vote of the I.O.C. was then taken.*

While these deliberations were under way, the Los Angeles delegation hopefully wished that the addresses before the Queen and the opening session did not portend the defeat of the bid of Los Angeles. Unfortunately, we were wrong. Los Angeles was eliminated on the first round with only 17 votes. Montreal had 24 and Moscow had the firm bloc of 28 votes. On the second ballot, the Los Angeles votes switched to Montreal, the other bid city from the Western World, and they were awarded the Summer Games of 1976.

Incidentally, prior to the vote, Soviet news agency Tass announced on the international wire service that Moscow had won on the first vote. This was later withdrawn by Tass.

How was Montreal selected? They did not answer a number of questions submitted by the I.O.C. They had neither the financial support of Parliament, nor the Provincial Government, both of whom have denied them funds. They did not have the facilities; (and in 1969-1970) they had one of the highest tax rates in the world along with an 8% sales tax. They had a debt of over $25,000,000.00 to West Germany and had to negotiate a loan from Holland to pay the interest and carrying charges on this loan – yet they were awarded the bid.

The comment of various I.O.C. members, most of whom indicated to us that they supported Los Angeles (?), was the problem of the two great powers, U.S.A. and U.S.S.R., competing for the Games or, alternatively, if they were given to Los Angeles, that we would stage the Games in such a fashion that no one could equal the extravaganza and technical capacity of our performance.

After much discussion, we reminded many I.O.C. members that they and the Federations controlled the cost by technical requirements for facilities, village, etc., and that the costs were fairly uniform for each country – all very high – and why, then, would they put the Games in a city that would be burdened by these costs? The organizing Committee and City are the hosts subject to the direction of the I.O.C. and Federations.

Needless to say, no answer could be provided. No resolution of the great impasse could be obtained, nor should it be pursued.

Of all the groups making a presentation, we were the least conspicuous and the lowest keyed. The antics of our competitors were quite conspicuous.

Based upon volunteer commitments by I.O.C. members, verbally or in writing to our committee members, to our Ambassadors and the White House, and reaffirmed by indirect check, we believed we had 36 to 43 votes. Perhaps we were too cautiously optimistic and certain votes committed to us gave a consolation vote to Montreal. The difference was only seven votes. Perhaps no one wanted to face the reality of the competition of Los Angeles and Moscow. We do not know. All we know is that we lost, but Russia also lost.

We thank all of the members of our Committee, the City of Los Angeles, the County of Los Angeles, the Coliseum Commission, the business community and our technical staff: Bill Nicholas, Paul Zimmerman, Bob Golden and Jeanne D'Amico for their great cooperation in this cooperative venture. It was not a failure even though we were not awarded the Games. It was a great experience and effort of a divergent group of our community, working together, to sell the Los Angeles Metropolitan Area to the world. This was done exceedingly well and many future economic, sports and social benefits should accrue. Some have accrued already. The future will measure the rest.

Our Committee would make the following recommendations:

That the U.S.O.C. and the City of Los Angeles should not bid for the Summer Games earlier than those for the year 1988. (Note: Denver was awarded the 1976 Winter Games and subsequently withdrew their bid based upon voters' objections.)

That the U.S.O.C. should not authorize cities to bid for the Summer and Winter Olympics in the same year.

That the City, County, and Coliseum Commission should consider proposing a Sports Festival in our Bicentennial year in conjunction with our Bicentennial Commission, either prior to the Montreal Summer Games or after these Games to emphasize the great capabilities of this area. The Bicentennial Commission should be contracted and asked to financially support this project.

To the members of our committees, subcommittees, and associated committees, may I express my warm personal regard for your cooperation and support? Perhaps we may individually reflect upon some of the ideas we have discussed for the benefit of our community and find some alternative method of making them go forward."

John B. Kilroy
Chairman
The Los Angeles 1976 Olympic Committee

To think that it was "all about sports" is plain nonsense. Here's Avery Brundage's official note to Mayor Sam Yorty informing him of the IOC's decision.

COMITÉ INTERNATIONAL OLYMPIQUE

<table>
<tr><td>President
AVERY BRUNDAGE
Ten N. La Salle St.
Chicago, Ill. 60602, U.S.A.
Cable Address
AVAGE</td><td>May 30, 1970</td></tr>
</table>

Dear Mayor Yorty:

This letter will convey to you and the citizens of Los Angeles the appreciation of the International Olympic Committee and its thanks for the gracious invitation which you submitted to stage the Games of the XXI Olympiad in 1976.

We regret that despite your great enthusiasm and impressive presentation, your city did not acquire the necessary majority of votes. You must know it was a difficult decision to make. We hope that the intense Olympic spirit indicated by your countrymen will not be diminished. Perhaps on another occasion it will be possible to stage the Games again in Los Angeles.

Cordially,

Avery Brundage

The Honorable Samuel Yorty
Mayor of Los Angeles,
Los Angeles, California

AB:mcm
cc. IOC
    United States Olympic Committee

After the award to Montreal and our loss to both Montreal *and* Moscow, I reviewed and tried to answer a number of questions:

Was Jerry Snyder playing a game in Dubrovnik when he told me that Montreal was going to withdraw their bid for the 1976 Summer Games because of financial problems and loan obligations to West Germany?

I consider Jerry an honest and forthright man who was telling the truth. It is reasonably apparent that Avery Brundage sold a package to Mayor Drapeau in spite of Montreal's financial problems.

Was Moscow truly a bidder for the 1976 Games or were they merely accommodating Avery Brundage and others with the understanding that they, Moscow, would be awarded the 1980 Games?

Brundage and the Soviets had conspired with one another. There's no other conclusion.

Were the quality of facilities a fundamental consideration in awarding the Games to Montreal?

After having the opportunity to inspect internal IOC correspondence on this matter, the answer is a fundamental, "No."

In the aftermath, I was later given a copy of a note to Brundage from IOC member Jan Staubo, which I've excerpted here: "I think it is a great disappointment for all those who actively participated in commissions, working for years to achieve recommendations, which were not even considered in Amsterdam. If you also think of the personal sacrifices and expenses involved to travel over large distances to successfully discuss these Olympic problems, one can only be disillusioned. In my opinion IOC's prestige has, after the meeting in Amsterdam, decreased further, not because of the attitude of many sportsmen, which you so often mention, but because of the lack of leadership from the IOC.

"The outcome of the voting for the candidate cities resulting in Montreal and Denver was only to be accepted, however, the votes generally, which especially came to light during the election for the Executive Board, are more based on block opinion than personal points of view and decisions. The very basis of our Olympic movement should be individualisms (sic), and our members should be in a position to vote, given an opinion and discuss matters completely independently, without being affected by political, national, religious, language, color or continental considerations."

It was interesting to review the text of Avery Brundage's speech at the Olympic Congress, before and after the selection process, with actual events of the day. Brundage said, "<u>This is particularly so in present times, at the time of the problem of southeast Asia area, anarchy and unrest riots in the schools, civil disobedience and other disorder in the United States</u>."

Our 1976 Olympic Committee was severely harassed by the European press and other overseas media outlets, who vehemently objected to the Games being awarded to Los Angeles, with regard to the Vietnam War. While complying with the rules and protocol of the Congress, we objected to these attacks. Despite our objections, there was no effort on behalf of the IOC to intercede. Through it all, the Los Angeles contingent strived to take the high road and keep the conversation to athletics, not politics. At one point, all we could really do was smile.

As an aside, in late 1969, I had the opportunity to meet with Brundage in California on an entirely different matter. It was held at, of all places, the Montecito Country Club just south of Santa Barbara. The president of the IOC just happened to own the club. Chuck Stuart, who was our liaison at the White House, had answered me in response to our request that Brundage be awarded the very first Freedom Medal. The White House was willing to do so if I approved.

Paul Zimmerman, the sportswriter and editor at the *Los Angeles Times*, joined me for the visit to Montecito. Ostensibly, we were there on other business. But we were going to use the visit to decide if we should move ahead with the proposed award. Brundage kept us waiting for a while and we commenced a wide-ranging discussion, during which he hinted that the Country Club might be for sale.

I prodded him to talk, which he was quite willing to do, and asked him what was wrong with the U.S. Olympic movement. "You are missing something," he said. "Your athletes are not as strong as the rest of the world. They are spoiled. They do not pay attention to physical conditioning. Americans have the highest medical rejection rate by the U.S. military when compared to the rejection rate of all other countries."

I told him that wasn't surprising, as our physical and medical standards for military acceptance were the highest in the world.

He said, "By all standards, your athletes and young people are not as strong as in the past." He added that they didn't respect the value and importance of the Olympics, and that sentiment carried over not only to the U.S. government, but to the entire population.

"The United States does not look at the Olympics as the world's major sports and cultural movement," he continued. "Look at how I am treated in the United States as compared to the rest of the world. I am president of the International Olympic Committee. Wherever I go in the rest of the world, I receive the highest recognition, the 'red-carpet treatment,' the special recognition that the president of the IOC should receive."

"President Brundage," I replied, "isn't it true that you were involved in congressional hearings requesting that the U.S. government should have no direct relations with the IOC, and that all such relations should be through the U.S. Olympic Committee? And didn't Congress honor your request? How can you now raise such objections?"

He said he was personally very offended. "The U.S.A. does not show their respect to the International Olympic Committee and to its president as other countries do," he said. As the chat continued, Brundage continued to express his negativity towards the U.S. and our Olympic sports movement.

I thanked Avery Brundage for our meeting and told him what I truly believed. Los Angeles and all of California were respectful and friendly, and would have a great reception for the IOC and the world's Olympians. Furthermore, we had nothing but the highest respect for international athletes and competition. I also discussed my personal international sports interests and pursuits, and my mutual respect for competitors from other countries. Considering the tone of the meeting, Paul and I behaved like gentlemen, with reasonably courteous responses, and we followed up with very civil thank-you letters.

After the meeting with Brundage, I called Chuck Stuart at the White House as soon as possible and relayed the conversation. I also was very firm: Under no conditions could I give my recommendation that Avery Brundage be rewarded or honored by President Nixon as the recipient of the first Presidential Medal of Freedom, or for that matter, any subsequent ones. Paul Zimmerman, who was as shocked as I was by Brundage's bias against the U.S., fully concurred. Certainly Brundage enjoyed his right to prosper and succeed in the United States, the same rights afforded to every citizen.

Perhaps needless to say, Brundage didn't get the prize.

The stories, of course, go on and on. It's rather amazing that a man like Brundage was handed the stewardship that Baron Pierre de Coubertin, founder of the modern Olympics, originally advanced.

A subsequent newspaper article, entitled, "U.S. Olympic Games Bid May Be Shelved Until 1988," by local columnist Glenn White, offers some more insight into the period. White wrote:

Los Angeles' staggering failure to land the 1976 Olympic Games may result in the United States declining to bid for a future Olympics until at least 1988. In fact, such matter is on the agenda for this month's U.S. Olympic Committee meeting in Denver.

A USOC official in New York told this column that Los Angeles' presentation bid for the Games last May in Amsterdam, Holland, was the finest ever made by any country—without question. He called it well organized, well thought out and in good taste. Yet, it finished a dismal third in voting by the International Olympic Committee with Montreal and Moscow running one-two.

It was concluded by a number of observers that Los Angeles was defeated because of political fence straddling and because of one powerful man's destructive words in an address to the international voting group.

That man, octogenarian Avery Brundage (president of the IOC), apparently went back on the promise he made to LA representatives and reminded IOC voters of America's racial problems, campus disorders and involvement in Vietnam.

Paul Zimmerman, former sports editor of the LA Times *and a Los Angeles committee member, told this column Brundage had given his word that any mention of U.S. internal problems would be gaveled out of order.*

Yet Brundage's speech to the IOC voting body in part said: "Today we live in an uneasy and even rebellious world with a greatly discontented younger generation expressing its dissatisfaction with prevailing conditions in frequent destructive demonstrations in France, Japan, the United States and many other countries. The participants oppose war and demand the cessation of hostilities. They are against discrimination of any kind."

Asked by Brundage if the U.S. bid would be weakened by such comment, Zimmerman offered the following opinion: "Avery has always contended he represents no country in the Olympic movement. And there seemed to be a fear Russia would undermine the '72 Olympics in Munich by coercing Iron Curtain countries to boycott the Games like she threatened in 1968 when the question of South Africa's Olympic participation arose."

Zimmerman also points out another Brundage inequity to the U.S.—that being an extension of the bidding deadline for the 1976 Games.

Cities seeking the '76 spectacle were to have announced such intention by spring of 1969. Yet Brundage held that period open til December when Moscow made its belated entry in the effort to secure the prestigious world sporting event.

Arthur Lentz, executive director of the U.S. Olympic Committee, is one of those who feels it's a waste of time for America to bid for an Olympics after the infamous vote in Amsterdam.

He outlines some of his opinions in a letter to John Kilroy, Newport Beach resident who headed the LA Olympic Committee for '76: "We share with you the disappointment experienced at Amsterdam and for many days now I have been thinking that it is high time that the International Olympic Committee establish some very specific policies and patterns relative to the bidding for the summer Olympic Games."

Lentz continues:

"Too often, those who have been well qualified and have held to the line of proper conduct have been penalized because of an ambiguous idea being introduced after all the bidding has been concluded. It is my hope that the IOC comes to grips with this vexing problem. Otherwise, cities in the United States and in any other large nation will be wasting their time fighting intangibles which are introduced as arguments. I admire your ability to be gracious despite the bitter setback. You and your fellow workers are to be congratulated on an excellent presentation which certainly deserved a better fate."

Also of interest is an exchange of letters between Kilroy and Brundage:

Dear Mr. Kilroy:

I regret your reaction to the results of the voting in Amsterdam. Also, I fail to understand the reasoning which prompted your conclusions and your adverse criticism of the International Olympic Committee.

Adverse international publicity on racial and student disorder in the U.S.A. had appeared long before the session as was mentioned and deplored when you and Mayor Yorty visited me at Amsterdam. My remarks were designed to establish what these conditions were world-wide and not exclusive to the United States. You may be sure that my remarks did not change one vote.

Otherwise how do you account for the success of the Denver Committee?

The fact that Avery Brundage has been blamed publicly and privately for the failure of the Los Angeles invitation, I resent. If you remember, I warned you many months ago that the United States had few friends when it came to matters of this kind and your type of campaign quite obviously did not help to correct this situation.

Should you have attended other award sessions you would know that the method of voting was not changed and the system used was the same as before. From the reports I have heard, I fear that your Committee left in Europe the impression that it was a bad loser.

Avery Brundage

Dear Mr. Brundage:

The report of our Committee, submitted to you, did nothing but state the facts surrounding the Amsterdam meeting in May of the International Olympic Committee and the selection for the city to bid for the Summer Games in 1976.

Our report neither criticized nor commended. Should you accept facts as criticism, then you should be the most qualified judge. We have neither blamed the IOC nor Avery Brundage for our failure to receive the award of the Games. There is no question that the IOC has the sole right to make this determination whether they follow their own rules and regulations, whether they give equal treatment or whether they do not.

There is also no contention that the receipt of personal assurances from Avery Brundage to not publicly discuss or permit discussion of certain items, which items were to be ruled 'out of order' does not legally bind him if he desires to ignore such personal assurances and forsake his given word.

The question I have raised is clearly stated in my letter to you which I shall again restate, 'We are saddened by this experience—by the failure of the International Olympic Committee and its leaders to impose upon themselves the same disciplines that they insist be imposed upon all other participants. How then can this illusory goal, the traditional and oft-stated objective of the Olympic ideal be extended to and understood by youth, if it is not understood and practiced by the Committee?

Jim Kilroy

In short, the United States was believed to be a victim of hypocritical voting and a political hot potato in the ballot that shockingly gave Montreal the Games, apparently to save a U.S. confrontation with the Soviet Union. Why go to the expense (LA coughed up $330,000, Denver $1 million) to make the pitch when the deck is already stacked?

Finally, here's a quote by Mayor Drapeau of Montreal, soon after his city was awarded the 1976 Summer Games. When asked by the press about the probable cost of the Games, he said: "The Olympics can no more lose money than a man can have a baby."

Following the '76 Games, Montreal was left with a debt of $1 billon.

Before Peter Ueberroth was appointed to spearhead Los Angeles' 1984 Olympic Committee, I was asked to again become involved. Though it had certainly been an interesting and singular experience, once was enough. So my response was simple: "Thank you, but no." In my case, one instance of being involved in such illogical "logic" was plenty.

But many of my colleagues from the earlier bid did come back for the '84 Games, and with Ueberroth's leadership they did a fantastic job. I salute them all. In many ways, they followed our "no cost" game plan that we'd structured for the proposed '76 Games, and when all was said and done, they netted a profit of $200 million, much of which was funneled into non-profit sports groups. They targeted television rights as the primary source of funding, as we had. All of us in the sports world should again thank Bill Nicholas, Tom Gallery and the many others from the '76 team that laid the groundwork for the television model and helped the 1984 committee meet and surpass its expectations.

Looking back to my tenure, I know that we had many tough decisions to make but we always did so as a team; I am thankful for the critical mass of intelligence provided by our close-knit group, who all worked in close harmony and consideration of all the other members.

With respect, I call to the attention of all who read this book, the fundamental rules for those who participate in all phases of the Olympics, including athletes, organizers, administrators and managers.

THE OLYMPIC CREED

The most important thing in the Olympic Games is not to win but to take part,
just as the most important thing in life is not the triumph but the struggle.
The essential thing is not to have conquered but to have fought well.

THE OLYMPIC MOTTO

"Citius, Altius, Fortius." Swifter, higher, stronger.

The Creed and the Motto are intended to spur all athletes and participants to embrace the Olympic Spirit.

After our efforts to gain the 1976 Summer Olympics for Los Angeles, I was gratified to receive complimentary letters from members of our Los Angeles 1976 Olympic Committee and others. I was particularly pleased to receive the following letter from Bill Nicholas, General Manager of the Los Angeles Memorial Coliseum Commission and a key player in direct negotiations with the IOC on major international television and communication issues.

My thanks to you, Bill, and to all of our outstanding committee members.

OFFICERS

WARREN M. DORN
PRESIDENT

JOHN FERRARO
VICE PRESIDENT

WILLIAM H. NICHOLAS
GENERAL MANAGER

H. AUSTIN MAHR
ASST. GENERAL MANAGER

COLISEUM COMMISSION

STATE OF CALIFORNIA

QUENTIN W. BEST
STEPHEN BILHEIMER
ARNOLD EDDY
——
GEORGE E. KINSEY
ALTERNATE

COUNTY OF LOS ANGELES

ERNEST E. DEBS
WARREN M. DORN
KENNETH HAHN
——
FRANK G. BONELLI
ALTERNATE

CITY OF LOS ANGELES

A. E. ENGLAND
JOHN FERRARO
BRAD PYE, JR.
——
GILBERT W. LINDSAY
JAMES MADRID
ALTERNATES

LOS ANGELES MEMORIAL COLISEUM COMMISSION

COLISEUM, 3911 SO. FIGUEROA ST. • 747-7111 — SPORTS ARENA, 3939 SO. FIGUEROA ST. • 748-6131
LOS ANGELES, CALIFORNIA 90037

June 9, 1970

Mr. John B. Kilroy
Kilroy Industries - Suite 850
626 Wilshire Boulevard
Los Angeles, California 90017

Dear Jim:

Now that the dust is settled from the big explosion and I have time
to reflect back on the past year or year and a half, all I can say
is, "Chief, I am sorry that we didn't do it for you."

I was so confident that we were going to win this one that I would
have almost been as foolish as Fred Wada. But, you notice that I
didn't put my money where my mouth was.

There is no question that your '76 Committee was royally double-
crossed. I am just waiting for the day when, I am convinced, some
of those people who did everything they could to hurt us will be
forced to come crawling, asking for Los Angeles' support.

The real problem with Los Angeles is that we have so much going for
us. We have such a full program that we have been used by the leadership of the International Olympic Committee to the extent that our
relationship with other countries has alienated these people against
us.

Jim, one of the real pleasures and real opportunities derived from
this experience and association has been the privilege of knowing
one Jim Kilroy. You are a tremendous leader, a superb salesman, and
a real all-around fellow. Through your leadership and the Olympic
bidding, the City of Los Angeles and Southern California have been
extolled throughout the world, and the benefits will continually flow
to our community.

It was a real pleasure being associated with you. Any time that I
have the opportunity to again have this privilege, I will be happy
to do so.

My sincere thanks for your friendship, your counseling and your
understanding.

Sincerely yours,

W. H. NICHOLAS
General Manager

13

Racing *KIALOA II* in Cowes Week and the Fastnet Rock Race
in the Irish Sea and English Channel made all aboard *KIALOA II*
aware of the sailing skills of the Australians and New Zealanders
and their challenging races, the 630-mile Sydney Hobart Race
and the 1511 mile Tasman Sea Race.

We decided to join them in December after the 1971 Transpacific
Race, cruise through beautiful South Pacific Islands,
Tahiti and French Polynesia, Tonga and Fiji and then challenge
their major races, with outstanding results.

Because of our close association with the University of
Southern California, we invited their marine biologists to join us.

Come dive with us in the beauty of the Southern Seas.

1971 Transpac
and into the South Pacific
Riding the Trades to New Zealand,
Australia and the Tasman Sea

The year 1971 was shaping up to be a most interesting one. Once again, *KIALOA II* would be racing in the Transpac, but afterwards, the schedule was very ambitious. From Hawaii, we would cruise through the South Pacific to New Zealand, and then carry on across the rugged, historic Tasman Sea to compete in the legendary Sydney-Hobart Race, a challenging 635-mile event into the Roaring Forties. From there, *KIALOA II* would return to Auckland in another demanding contest, the 1,500-mile Tasman Sea Race.

But before all that, with the bid for the 1976 Olympic Games behind us, it was time to concentrate on business and family.

We did sail *KIALOA II* in two of the three races in the 1970 St. Francis Big Boat Series with surprising results. A brand new 50-footer designed to the new IOR MKII Rule—with the highly appropriate name of *Lightning*—built and sailed by the boatbuilding Stevens brothers—"cleaned everyone's clock," including *KIALOA II*'s.

That winter, *KIALOA II* again went south of the border for the Mazatlan Race, which was conducted in virtually no wind, but which gave us a good excuse for a lovely holiday cruise off Baja California. We returned home for the '71 Whitney Series, where *KIALOA II* had excelled in the past, but once again *Lightning* won Class A decisively while *KIALOA II* finished back in the pack. A trend was developing: In shorter races, *KIALOA II* no longer excelled. Part of the reason was light weather, but new technology was another factor.

Around this time, the owners of *Lightning* received some shocking news. The new IOR MKII rule, the basis of *Lightning*'s design, had miscalculations and was superseded by IOR MKIII in 1971. "Transitional confusion" was blamed, but it sounded like the same old refrain to me. Instantly, the boat was basically obsolete.

Once again, the changing measurement rules were a source of great confusion and frustration. As mentioned previously, this was compounded by the fact that many races were scored with time-allowance factors that did not coincide with the reality of the racecourses.

Over the course of my racing career, from 1955 to 1990, the primary handicap systems were the CCA Rule and the IOR, which became effective in 1971. Both of these systems assigned a rating number (or speed number) based on a yacht's measurement. Corrected-time scores were based on these figures, which were actually a seconds-per-mile time allowance or reduction. Once a race was concluded, the elapsed time was "corrected" using the North American Yacht Racing Union's time-allowance table. The problem, again, was the NAYRU tables were based on courses composed of equilateral triangles. But the logic was skewed, because tacking to windward means longer distances. And in the Transpac, the thinking was truly flawed, because in most years the vast majority of the race is downwind.

With *KIALOA II* once again poised to race in the Transpac, the issue resurfaced. There's no question that the Transpac race committee tried to be reasonably fair to every yacht. But the matter was further complicated because of the unique nature of the event, where bigger, faster, lighter yachts, and the smaller yachts astern, are often sailing in altogether different wind patterns. And sometimes, before the quicker boats finish, the small boats have the added advantage of bringing fresh wind from astern while the leaders wallow in little or no breeze.

So, again, the use of the NAYRU tables in handicapping the Transpac race, in mathematical terms, seemed manifestly unfair, and I challenged the race organizers on it. After all, there was only about one percent of upwind sailing in the 2,225-mile racecourse. The handicap formula has since been modified, but it was a particularly thorny issue in the '71 race, when the CCA Rule was being superceded by the IOR rule, something the crew of *Lightning* learned prior to the race.

A year earlier, I swapped letters about the problem with Olin Stephens of S&S, the primary designer of *KIALOA I*, *KIALOA II*, and later, *KIALOA III* (see letters next page).

In essence, Olin agreed with my position. "Each race seems to have its own particular problems when this subject is considered and consideration of this subject, in general, has generated so much more heat than light that I am very reluctant to go along with any argument that I have not investigated myself," he wrote.

Olin went on to say that he hoped I understood his position and that I'd forgive him for not providing more support because, though he thought I was right, he wasn't a hundred percent positive. But this seems to contradict an earlier portion of the same letter, where he says, "I think you are right that a primarily downwind race should be sailed with less time allowance than a triangular one for which the time allowance tables seem to have been prepared."

Until now, I've never disclosed these details. And yes, the Transpac organizers eventually revised their handicap formula to reflect the reality of the racecourse. But that was well after the '71 race, the year the IOR measurement rule became effective, when a strange situation unfolded.

When *KIALOA II* sailed in the '67 Transpac, under the old CCA rule, we owed the winning Cal 40, *Holiday Too*, a net time allowance of 56 hours, 26 minutes and 22 seconds. But in the '71 Race, under the new IOR rule, *KIALOA II* gave a virtually identical Cal 40 yacht a time allowance of 71 hours, 4 minutes and 16 seconds—a bonus of 14 hours, 37 minutes and 54 seconds. One might ask why a Cal 40, a design that won multiple Transpacs, received a bonus handicap of over 14 hours under the new IOR rule? We certainly did. Ultimately, the discrepancy was caused by an incorrect coefficient in the IOR rule that was subsequently corrected in the MKII version.

Normally, all owners are pleased when the rating number of their yacht goes down. They should be if their yacht is the singular lucky one; however, if all yacht ratings or most ratings go down, the larger yacht owes all of the smaller yachts much more handicap time. The allowances between the yachts with lower ratings have much more time spread than in the higher ratings.

In any event, even the "wind gods" objected to the new time allowances by creating Hurricane Denise, which forced the high-pressure cell to move further north than usual, leaving sloppy seas and frustrating winds for the smaller yachts. *KIALOA II* averaged 8.97 knots in the '71 Transpac and was the fifth boat to finish, sixth in class and sixth overall. (*Windward Passage*, the largest yacht, was first to finish, first in class and first overall.)

Afterwards, an article in the September, 1971 edition of *Sea and Pacific Motor Boat* magazine captured my feelings succinctly:

"It was an easy ride, but exceedingly frustrating," Kilroy commented. "We don't come out here to sit on the deck and play dominoes and not be able to do anything. But you sail apparent wind angle and that's it. There was nothing to trim, nothing to do. We had a lot of crew boredom. You look at the Honolulu race as one in which you are going to be throwing spray off the bow and shooting a stern wave up in the air, but it just didn't happen that way this time."

Although Class A swept the top nine places overall, Kilroy still is highly critical of the handicapping system used for the Transpac.

"In spite of the fact that everyone was parked in a parking lot, we knew 24 hours later that every one of those boats could have kicked the hell out of all of us who finished early. This just emphasizes the disparity of the handicap formula for the Transpacific Yacht Race."

Kilroy's chief complaint is that the time allowance table used is based on a triangular course and is weighted to consider entries will sail 114 percent of the course distance in such a configuration. Kilroy contends the distance factor should be about 103 percent for the TransPac.

"You can't take a 114 percent distance rule and sail a 103 percent course with it and have an equitable race," he argues. "The only reason the A boats won is because the wind was shut off."

Kilroy also contends that the allowances do not take into consideration the surfing time and the current assistance the smaller boats get when they are at sea up to 50 hours or longer than the big boats.

KILROY INDUSTRIES ▪ 213/624-9731 ▪ SUITE 850 ▪ 626 WILSHIRE BOULEVARD ▪ LOS ANGELES, CALIFORNIA 90017

24 December 1970

Mr. Olin Stephens
Sparkman & Stephens
79 Madison Avenue
New York, N.Y. 10016

Dear Olin:

I have been corresponding and discussing the matter of the handicap allowance for the Honolulu Race with the Board of Directors of the Transpacific Yacht Club since 1968.

In my opinion, it is not equitable to all yachts to use full course distance and the Cruising Club of America time allowance tables to determine the time allowance of each yacht. The CCA time allowance tables contemplate that a yacht will sail a triangular course about 1.14 times course distance. In the Honolulu Race, an off-the-wind race, a yacht sails only slightly above true course distance. A yacht is also materially aided by both current and surfing, lessening sailed distance even further.

I have therefore recommended that the rated course distance be shortened. I enclose copies of my correspondence as well as correspondence from others relative to this matter.

Bill Lapworth has endeavored to justify the continuance of the use of full course distance by the graphs which are enclosed. My letter of comment on Bill's graphs is also enclosed. I would appreciate your frank comments on these.

The Transpacific Yacht Club Board of Directors has voted to continue using full course distance in the 1971 race. Kialoa II will participate accordingly; however, I will continue to work for a change in subsequent races if it is not possible for 1971.

Yours very truly,

John B. Kilroy

JBK/mgm
Enclosures

REAL ESTATE AND INDUSTRIAL INVESTMENTS

SPARKMAN & STEPHENS
INCORPORATED

NAVAL ARCHITECTS — MARINE INSURANCE

YACHT & SHIP BROKERS

79 MADISON AVENUE, NEW YORK, N. Y. 10016
Telephone Murray Hill 9-3880 · · · Cable Sparstep

31 December 1970

Mr. John B. Kilroy
Suite 850
626 Wilshire Boulevard
Los Angeles, California 90017

Dear Jim:

I have your letter of the 24th with further reference to the
course distance of the Honolulu Race. I applogize for not writing
you sooner and in more detail on this subject but I have been so
much up to my neck with work at the office on top of which I.O.R.
work has been added that I simply have not had time to restudy this
particular problem. I have also been reluctant to stick my neck out
without taking a good deal of care to understand the background
because I seem to have become something of a target for criticism
in regard to the I.O.R. situation and I think it is good policy to
keep quiet unless I am pretty sure that I know what I am trying to
say.

Offhand and between ourselves, I think you are right that a primarily
downwind race should be sailed with less time allowance than a triangular one for which the time allowance tables seem to have been
prepared. To add further reservations, however, I have to say that
each race seems to have its own particular problems when this subject
is considered and consideration of this subject in general has generated so much more heat than light that I am very reluctant to go
along with any argument that I have not investigated myself and I
simply have not the time to go into this one just now. I hope you
will understand my position which I should have explained to you
some time back and that you will forgive me for not providing more
support because I think you are right but I am just not 100% positive.

I also have a copy of the letter addressed to you by a Capt. Wakeland
in regard to conditions on KIALOA's underwater surface. Frankly to
me painting problems on the bottom of a metal boat must be considered
a part of the routine maintenance and the fact that no deterioration
was found is of course satisfactory. The aluminum spray seems a
little unusual but may actually have been a very good method of
accomplishing the necessary fairing. Since you sent the letter without
comment and I am not sure why it was sent to me, this is about all I
can say for the present. Best wishes for the New Year.

Sincerely,

Olin J. Stephens II

OJS:vm

With the race and the parties behind us, we could begin to make more coherent plans for the future, subject, of course, to the possibility for further modifications to the new IOR rule. *KIALOA II* had been measured and re-measured twenty times in the last few years. For a while, it was good to have that behind us. Kathy and I relaxed for a few days in Waikiki before returning home. We had lots to do so we could join *KIALOA II* a few weeks later in the South Pacific.

We had invited three marine biologists from the Captain Allan Hancock Foundation of the University of Southern California to conduct research on this great cruise, which would begin with a 2367-mile voyage to Papeete, Tahiti, and then carry on to Moorea, Huahine, Tapa, Bora Bora, Tonga and Fiji en route to Auckland. Everyone aboard was an active SCUBA diver and we were all very enthusiastic about the sailing and the islands, as well as the possibility that our research would be productive and beneficial.

Our daughter Dana—on a special "free pass" from studies at Newport Harbor High School— was also part of the sailing and research crew. Dana was on board because of an incident with an irresponsible teacher at her school. The teacher had criticized churches and everyday citizens for not doing more to help the poor, comments that left Dana very upset. He said that churches should be stripped of their artwork and gold, that it was money that shouldn't have been spent on such things, and which should've been given directly to poor people. He finished this rant by telling Dana, "And your father, to spend so much money on a maxi boat! That money should have been given to the poor as well."

Dana and I discussed the matter in detail. I pointed out how the construction of cathedrals offered jobs and construction skills to the workers, that it in fact it helped reduce numbers of the hungry and the poor, and gave them opportunities and crafts that would help then obtain new jobs in the future.

And as far as *KIALOA II* was concerned, I suggested she tell her teacher it wasn't a maxi-yacht, but a "Marxi boat." It redistributed the wealth and also gave people jobs and new skills. It was exactly what Karl Marx said he wanted.

We ultimately decided that the cruise through the South Pacific would offer the chance to see how people with little money lived and helped themselves by working with others, and would provide Dana with valuable experiences. So she joined the cruise and had a magnificent time, while learning a lot in the process.

Calvin Hurst was the leader of the USC marine biologists and later wrote a great article for a 1972 edition of *Oceans* magazine entitled, "Nohu: Devil in Paradise." One of the objectives of Cal's team was to catch and remove the venomous poison from what the villagers call "the Nohu," or stonefish. They planned to take the poison back to USC and develop an anti-venom serum for fishermen and islanders who accidentally step on the lethal spines of this horribly ugly, dangerous fish.

These stonefish hide under a shallow layer of sand, and those unfortunate enough to trod on one must seek immediate medical attention; even then, they may be disabled for life. The ten-inch long Nohu, covered in wrinkles and warts, dwells in barrier reefs and is as venomous as it is ugly; weighing up to four pounds, it has fourteen venomous spines, very sharp points that inject the serum. Its displeasing appearance provides ample camouflage, particularly under a layer of sand. You can find them by looking for slightly disturbed patches of sand, which unfortunately are a logical place to step when wading.

Along the way we did discover and catch some Nohus, and the scientists extracted the venom by making a clamp that held the sides of the fish, then touching the spaces between the projecting spines with a metal rod. The venom would squirt a foot or more into the air. Some of it was saved and frozen, and then taken back to USC, as were some live specimens. Later, the biologists made strong progress developing their serum.

It was odd to compare the Nohu to its distant cousin, the Lionfish, which is also venomous and

deadly. But while the Nohu was unbelievably ugly, the Lionfish (*Pterois Radiata*) was incredibly beautiful. Furthermore, it didn't hide like its unsightly cousin, but can be readily and easily seen. The research continued with other species of sea life, which gave everyone aboard deep satisfaction.

The leg from the Isle des Sous Vente to Tonga was especially beautiful, and we called at many small islands. We learned much about the cheery islanders and it gave us a fresh appreciation for the history of sailing ship exploration. While visiting such places as Raiatea, Tapa, Huahine and Bora Bora, we were reminded that we were sailing the home waters of the early Polynesian explorers who sailed to the Marquesas and then onto Hawaii or Easter Island. It was an amazing era of discovery.

Once we'd put the commercialism of Papeete behind us, we were also mindful of the culture and traditions of the Polynesian and Melanesian people. When you anchor near a village, you must be respectful and you must make "*savu-savu*" with the chief. The ritual is always the same. As soon as the yacht is securely anchored, a younger member of his family meets you and escorts you to the chief.

We would usually give the relative a tennis ball or some candy. And while paying respects to the chief, we would offer a small gift and respectively listen to whatever he cared to say. When the meeting was over, the chief would grant permission to anchor off their island. Failing to engage in a *savu-savu* ceremony would be like parking on your neighbor's lawn.

You must also be cautious and careful if the chief offers you a swig of that noted South Pacific drink called *kava*, which is served in a coconut-shell cup. If you can down it in one gulp, you are manly indeed…but most people can't! One cup of *kava* is plenty. If you have two, you're at your own risk and better watch out on the dinghy ride back to the boat.

In our experience of cruising the South Pacific over the years, we found the islanders to be happy, well-fed and courteous people with much to talk about. In general, they are self-satisfied, trustworthy and respectful. They are interdependent and recognize their interdependency. Are they poor? Well, how does one measure poor and rich? Would a "first world" agency classify them as wise or as uneducated? A person who lived his whole life in Southern California might have one answer. Someone who'd spent all their lives in the islands would surely have another.

But this was the precisely the sort of experience I wanted my daughter Dana to have, to look at the world from a completely different perspective. We came from thousands of miles away to hear their stories and see the world through their eyes, and in doing so gained a better understanding of life, and of ourselves.

Due to clearance problems, as we traveled west through the outer Tongan and Fijian islands, we didn't stop, calling instead at the city of Suva on the southeast corner of Viti Levu, the biggest island in Fiji. Over the years, we stopped there on several *KIALOA*s, and we never tired of its changing vistas, mountain peaks and overviews of the many smaller surrounding islands.

Suva was a bustling commercial port, as well as a center of banking and finance. A few miles to the south, in the middle of a surrounding reef, is the island of Mbenga, the home of the firewalkers, who practice an ancient religious tradition. Yes, they do walk across the red-hot coals in their bare feet. I've witnessed this many times and cannot tell you how they do it. The firewalkers draw audiences from the hotels along the south coast of Viti Levu, about 20 miles away.

Further to the south is an interesting circular reef, the Astrolabe Reef, which is surrounded by an inner circular bay of about two miles in diameter. There's only one entrance through the reef, and once inside there's a tall lighthouse right in the center of the inner bay. It's a good anchorage with fine SCUBA diving on the outside of the reefs, particularly on the east side when the surf is down, which is fairly rare.

KIALOA II had an interesting experience in these waters. A few miles to the south of Astrolabe were several smaller islands and another big reef. There was a local canoe with an outboard motor that broke down, and the people aboard, on their way home from church, were blown onto the reef.

We were out in the Zodiac, saw what happened and came to the rescue, towing them to the major village nearby, the home of the chief. Soon after, we received a message from the chief to re-anchor at their island and join them for a *savu-savu* with an excellent barbecue of fish and pig, a native orchestra and a chorus. The songs and native dances were beautiful. After a cup of *kava* or two, we were invited to join in the singing.

The seating order was quite orderly and controlled. The chief was in the center of a semicircle, with me to his immediate left, then Kathy, and then the rest our crew in order of "seniority." To his immediate right, the villagers were seated in a similar fashion. At 6'3" and at about 205 pounds, with a shoe size of 12.5 and the hands of a basketball player, I'm a reasonably sized man. But I felt small next to the chief, who packed over 250 pounds on his 6'8" frame. His feet had to be somewhere in the 15-18 size range, and his hands were huge.

Every time he laughed, in a gesture of friendliness, he'd hit me hard on the back. He was basically clobbering me. I did my best to return the compliment, and both of us would slide across the floor before doing it all again. It was a fun, crazy evening. When we returned to *KIALOA II* in our Zodiac, a bunch of locals escorted us, singing from their canoes.

The next morning, we planned to leave early for a bay off Viti Levu. At first light, we heard footsteps on the deck and came topsides to see a bunch of villagers tying bunches of bananas on the backstay and placing baskets of fruit all around. We thanked them; paid our respects to the chief, his wife and their family; and got underway while being serenaded by the beautiful Fijian song, "Isole."

It was all a very emotional scene, and we were pleased that Dana could see with her own eyes this mutual display of affection and courtesy. Perhaps she would even convey the spirit of the moment with her clueless high-school teacher, who had no understanding of the world and the simple dignity people can display as they help one another.

Our trip continued on to Viti Levu. First we stopped at a new, small tourist hotel owned by friends from Hawaii in a beautiful bay on the island's south shore. The next morning we sailed up the west coast and spent the night in the Mamanutha Islands before carrying on to the northwest to enchanting isles around the Blue Lagoon. There was so much to see, the villages were delightful, and the diving was spectacular. Years later, we'd call in Fiji again aboard *KIALOA III*. The islands were just as fantastic.

The cruising season was growing short, however, and it was time to keep moving for our full slate of regattas: the Southern Cross Series, the Sydney-Hobart Race, and the Tasman Sea Race from Hobart to Auckland. As the boat got underway for the fast thousand-mile reach across the Southern Ocean, that lovely tune, "Isole," was still ringing in our ears. Soon enough, *KIALOA II* was sailing through the fantastic Bay of Islands on the northeast coast of New Zealand before entering

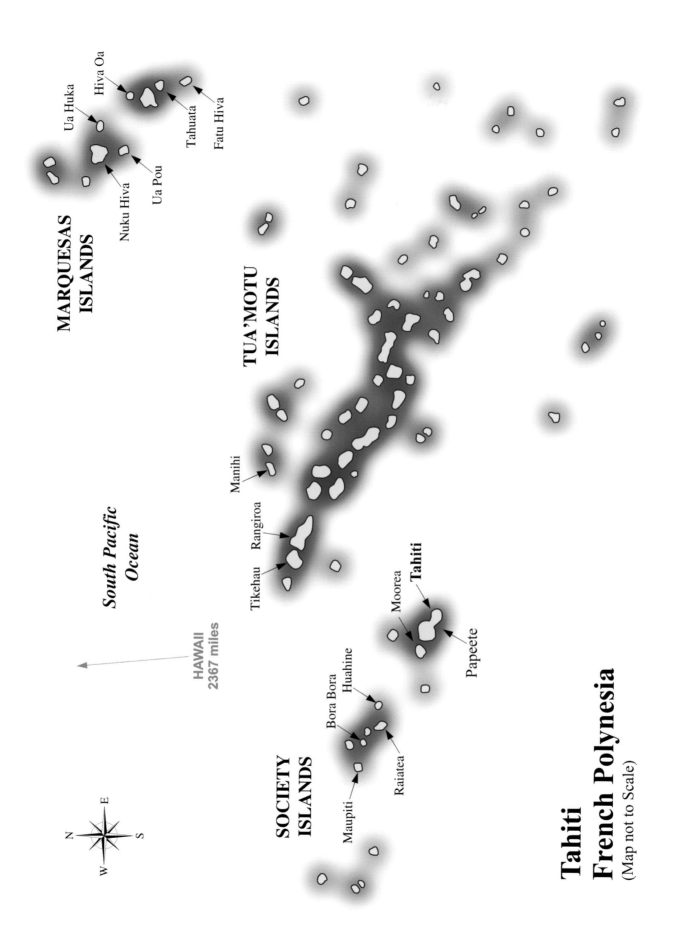

Tahiti
French Polynesia
(Map not to Scale)

the Hauraki Gulf and the country's sailing capital, Auckland—the City of Sails—which was home for many of the *KIALOA* crew.

Unfortunately, I wasn't aboard to join the festivities, but Bruce Kendell and many of his Kiwi mates were. A small fleet of local yachts came out to greet *KIALOA II* and guide them into the yacht harbor. It was an emotional moment for all the New Zealanders. *KIALOA II* was looked upon as a Kiwi boat, and the *KIALOA* crew, whatever their homeport, became New Zealand sailors.

Soon, Bruce and the crew, with a handful of extra Kiwis, sailed *KIALOA II* across the Tasman to Sydney to prepare for the busy race schedule. For a lot of us, this would be our first competition "Down Under"—a place we'd only read about—which had the reputation for being an aggressive area to sail and a focal point for modern sailboat racing. It was *KIALOA II*'s first visit too. Our initial impression of New Zealand and Australia, and later Tasmania, was of the magnificent beauty of the coastlines and harbors.

Most of the racing crew joined *KIALOA II* at the Cruising Yacht Club of Australia (CYC) in Sydney, virtually right next door to the Sydney Opera House, which was then nearing completion. We were offered an extensive tour of the place and learned all about its design, construction techniques and its ultimate finish. With its many bays, rivers and hills, Sydney is a wonderful city, and as we prepared for the racing, we test sailed and tuned up as much as possible with our Aussie competitors. They couldn't have been more courteous or obliging.

The Australian yachting authorities were also very forthcoming in offering views and advice on their forceful style of sailing, their love and enthusiasm for the sport and their handicapping formula. One of Australia's senior yachting officials, Gordon Marshall, and I had extensive discussions about their "Time-on-Time" formula, which was slightly different, and even more favorable than the British handicap system. Marshall clearly stated that they had centered their rule on boats ranging from 30-45 feet, and as a result, it was virtually impossible that *KIALOA II* could win overall honors on corrected time in any race in Australia or New Zealand. He said that we should instead set our sights on first to finish on elapsed time, and first in class.

I accepted and appreciated the frankness of his comments and said *KIALOA II* was prepared to meet the greater challenge. We also talked about the effect of the IOR rule and its favoritism toward small boats. Marshall was unapologetic; he said small boat sailors where their basic clients and stockholders.

This was our mindset for all the racing in Australia that would follow. Our biggest competitors would be our fellow Americans aboard Huey Long's *Ondine,* Bob Johnson's *Windward Passage* and Ted Turner's *American Eagle*, as well as the Australian yacht, *Ballyhoo.* That said, in the Southern Cross Series, our main competition would also be our teammates; the regatta is composed of three-boat teams, with *KIALOA II, American Eagle* and *Ondine* representing the United States. (Each country was allowed one team, though each state in Australia could field an entry.) Yachts were also scored individually.

A pair of closed-course, 30-mile races, and a longer 180-mile distance race kicked off the series. The longer contest started late in the afternoon and provided all the diurnal wind shifts that require local knowledge. For that reason we recruited Aussie sailors Jock Sturrock and Magnus Halvorsen to crew aboard *KIALOA II*. But the handicaps did indeed favor the smaller boats and our American team fared poorly.

With a sixth, eleventh and twelfth, *American Eagle* was the top U.S. point scorer. *KIALOA II* registered a fourteenth and a pair of sixteenths. *Ondine* took a nineteenth, twentieth and twenty-first. We did have a strong finish in the so-called Trophy Race, a 30-miler. Still, our final individual result in the Southern Cross series was twelfth overall. Even so, it was a fun event and good crew training after months with no racing.

Plus, our next big event, the 1971 Sydney-Hobart Race, was right around the corner. Over the next several days, we formulated our game plan for this offshore classic.

In looking at the charts of the waters between Sydney and Hobart, the most dominant feature was Bass Strait, the fairly shallow, 80-mile-wide open stretch of ocean between mainland Australia and the island of Tasmania. Due to its positioning, the current flowing into the strait from the Indian Ocean is accelerated, and there were obvious current vortexes at its easternmost exit point. It was obviously a great place to encounter "reverse-current" eddies and a horrible place to encounter the current head on.

My strategy took all of this into consideration. I felt we needed to follow a track that would permit us to get a favorable southerly ride on the reverse eddy along the southeast coast of Australia. Then, we'd want to use the eastbound current to our advantage to get back on course towards Tasmania, and a southbound eddy to set us up for the approach to the island. Overall, the idea was to stay slightly west of the straight-line course south from Sydney. Once approaching the island, while keeping a close eye on the breeze, we didn't want to get too close. There was the possibility of a reverse current along the coast, as well as big wind shifts and/or blanketed breeze.

We discussed all this with Halvorsen, a former winner of the race who also had a lot of experience fishing these waters, and Sturrock. Both agreed with our analysis. (We'd later use this strategy in the '75 and '77 Hobart Races aboard *KIALOA III*).

The race started at precisely 1100 on Boxing Day, December 26, 1971. The starting line was crowded, as was the racecourse out to the famous Heads at the mouth of the harbor. Along with other race boats, spectator boats and even surfboards, it was tough going to power through the sloppy seas and the wakes of the other vessels in about 2-8 knots of wind.

At about noon, we were abeam of the light on South Head, and changed headsails as we cracked off to a reach. An hour later, we hoisted our light spinnaker, making about eight knots. Finally, another six hours later, we felt blessed as a 20-25 knot north-northeast wind filled in from astern. We changed spinnakers and staysails in the squally, shifty winds until about midnight, when the wind went forward and we went with regular headsails. As we were headed, we tacked from starboard to port and steered a course between 185° to 220° until noon of the second day. In spite of the light early conditions, our first 25-hour run was about 189 miles. So it was a good first day, with fine crew work. *KIALOA II* was a happy ship.

The second day, we continued to tack on the wind shifts, as if we were sailing a round-the-buoys race, as the wind pumped out of the southwest at 30-35 knots, with the seas big and building. Through all of it, the barometer remained steady at 29.80 inches.

Early in the morning of the 28th, the wind shifted slightly west and increased to 40 knots, which allowed us to ease the sheets, tuck another reef in the main, and change headsails to the smaller No. 4 genoa. Now the seas were even bigger, and more confused. By noontime we'd put another 195 miles behind us and had covered 384 miles of the course, which didn't meet our expectations because of the slow start and the squally, shifting headwinds.

That afternoon, the wind moved more into the west and settled at about 25-knots before slowly dropping and oscillating from the southwest to south-southwest to the south. Finally, it swung into the northwest, but only at around five knots with occasional puffs to 8 knots. Over the next 13 hours, it more or less stayed there, with the exception of three hours when the breeze slid to under three knots. It was tough, hard sailing in extremely sloppy seas, and though the going was slow, it kept the crew very busy.

Under these conditions, we felt the race had truly turned into a small-boat affair. This feeling was confirmed at 1400 on the 29th, when a new 12-knot breeze filled in from the north-northeast, bringing the smaller yachts that had been well astern with it. For a spell the wind increased to 25-knots before settling in at around 18-knots, still from the north-northeast.

On port jibe, steering a course of 185° with all possible running sails flying—spinnaker, forestaysail, main, mizzen spinnaker—we were enjoying some great sailing, with continuous sail trim and sail tending, even though it was clear we were being attacked by the smaller yachts behind, who received the new breeze earlier and were bringing the wind down with them.

In the later afternoon hours of December 29th, *KIALOA II* rounded Tasman Island on a fairly wide angle, as we planned on using a reaching chute in this latter portion of the race. As we began setting a headsail and dousing the spinnaker, we were hit by a big puff of breeze, about fifty knots, which blew out the head of our heavy reaching chute.

If a kite is going to blow, it's always best if it happens close to the finish line when you don't need it anymore. So we were pretty philosophical about losing the sail, as the remainder of the race

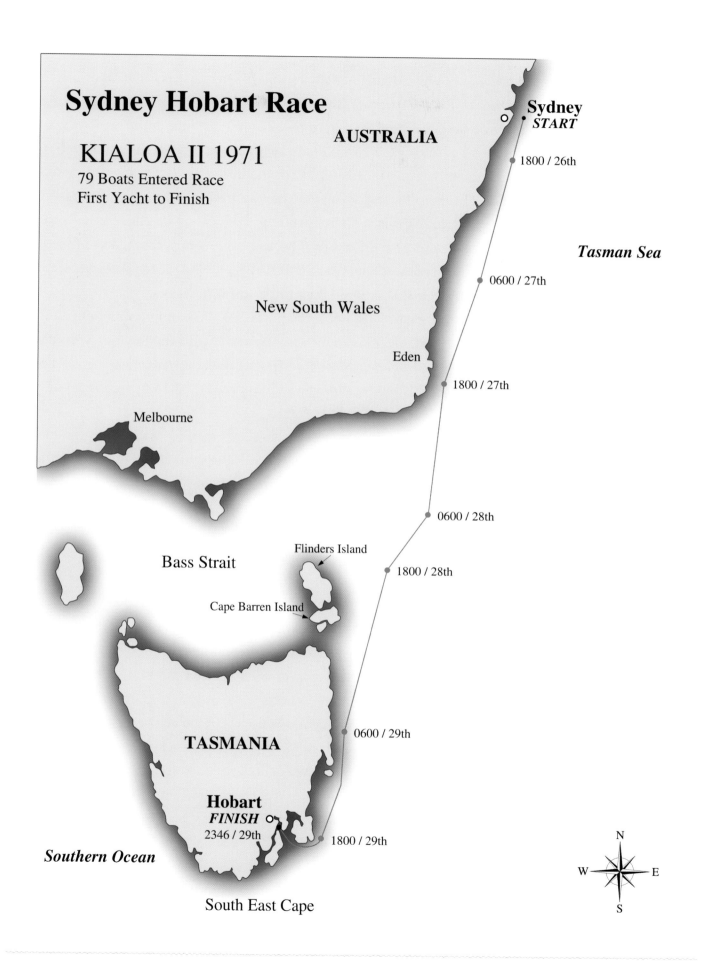

Sydney Hobart Race

KIALOA II 1971
79 Boats Entered Race
First Yacht to Finish

AUSTRALIA

Sydney
START

1800 / 26th

Tasman Sea

0600 / 27th

New South Wales

Eden

1800 / 27th

Melbourne

0600 / 28th

Bass Strait

Flinders Island

1800 / 28th

Cape Barren Island

TASMANIA

0600 / 29th

Hobart
FINISH
2346 / 29th

1800 / 29th

Southern Ocean

South East Cape

N
W   E
S

would be close reaching or on the wind, which is good for the reporters and photographers.

For three-and-a-half hours, *KIALOA II* reached under headsails across Storm Bay at a speed of 10 knots right up to the "Iron Pot," the entry to the Derwent River on the final approach to Hobart. It took an hour and 36 minutes to sail the last 11-miles up the narrow river, and what an interesting ride it was…on the wind, tacking back and forth, with cars and headlights lining the river banks, honking their horns as *KIALOA II* passed by. And once across the line, we had a tremendous greeting from thousands of people—not to mention our friends and wives—as we entered the center of town. Kathy said that as she was rushing down to the dock she was almost crushed by group of Catholic nuns running down the street to be there first. The champagne and the television reporters arrived, just in time to watch us celebrate our line-honors, first-to-finish victory.

KIALOA II's elapsed time was 3 days, 12 hours, 46 minutes and 12 seconds (84 hours). However, once the handicap multiplier of 1.0413 was applied, our corrected time was another 3.5 hours, or 88.27 hours. The winning yacht was a 40-foot, One Ton-design called *Pathfinder*, with an elapsed time of 96.035 hours. (Their Time-on-Time correction coefficient was 0.7835, which reduced their corrected time to 75.233 hours.)

Again, I must emphasize that we sail under the race and handicap rules set forth by the race sponsor and honor the results, even though we may disagree with the formula. Before the start, as mentioned, we'd been clearly advised of the bias in the handicap system.

KIALOA II sailed on average speed of 7.55 knots over the course. *Pathfinder* sailed on average speed of 6.56 knots over the course. Her corrected time speed under their Time-on-Time formula was 8.51 knots. Gordon Marshall hadn't lied. Our final result: first to finish, twentieth in class and thirty-ninth overall.

Over a 630-mile course like the Sydney-Hobart Race, yachts become widely separated and can have substantially different wind and sea conditions. As *KIALOA II* was finishing the race, a little after midnight, we were in exceedingly light-weather, upwind conditions. *Pathfinder* finished at about 1200 noon the following day under much more favorable conditions.

A frequent problem under the Time-on-Time correction factors used in England and Australia occurs in very light air when yachts are barely moving, or in some cases, when yachts may even be anchored in a foul tide. In the Fastnet Race in England, we were either anchored or barely moving for about 12 hours and were again beaten by three yachts on Time-on-Time Correction (or T.C.F. corrected time), solely based on the time the other yachts gained when we were not moving through the water.

No rule is perfect, but I prefer handicapping calculated by Time on Distance, a credit defined as seconds per mile over the racecourse. Based upon their rating (speed allowance), different-sized boats receive an allowance credit of seconds per mile times the racecourse distance. Larger yachts

receive fewer seconds per mile and smaller yachts receive more seconds per mile, based upon the rating number (speed number). In any event, we were happy with our line-honors victory in the '71 Hobart Race, which was really the only part of the event over which we could control our destiny.

Jim Kilroy's *KIALOA II,* Ted Turner's *American Eagle* and Bob Johnson's *Windward Passage* continued their rivalry to be "First to Finish" in the world's most famous sailboat races. All three yachts were preparing for the 635-mile 1971 Sydney Hobart Race.

The photograph of all three yachts anchored together at a party in Sydney, Australia, shows the readers of this book the difference in beam width.

KIALOA II was the first yacht to finish in the 1971 Sydney Hobart Race and the winner of its "First to Finish" rivalry over its two Maxi competitors.

The owners-skippers, friends, while intense rivals, grouped together at the wheel of Windward Passage a short time before the start of their new challenge.

The entirely different yachts—American Eagle, a former America's Cup Yacht with its narrow beam, KIALOA II, a CCA-yacht, with a moderate beam, and Bob Johnson's Windward Passage, wide beam following the theory of beam stability in moderate and downwind races—in a decidedly light-weight hull and keel.

Sydney and Hobart, of course, are important Australian seaports. As the Port of Los Angeles is one of the largest seaports in the world, and I served as one of its commissioners, in both Sydney and Hobart we invited our Aussie counterparts for a luncheon and an afternoon sail aboard *KIALOA II*. It was a mutually beneficial meeting and I was pleased to offer the use of *KIALOA II* to the city of Los Angeles to serve on the Los Angeles Harbor Commission for many interesting years.

EXECUTIVE OFFICES: P.O. BOX 151 • SAN PEDRO, CALIFORNIA 90733
TELEPHONE: (213) 832-7241 • 775-3231

ADDRESS ALL COMMUNICATIONS TO THE BOARD
CABLE ADDRESS: LAPORT

BOARD OF HARBOR COMMISSIONERS
CITY OF LOS ANGELES

SAM YORTY
MAYOR

February 10, 1972

JOHN J. ROYAL
PRESIDENT

JOHN B. KILROY
VICE PRESIDENT

FRANK C. SULLIVAN
COMMISSIONER

ROBERT A. DAY
COMMISSIONER

MANUEL K. INADOMI
COMMISSIONER

ROBERT D. HUDSON
SECRETARY

BERNARD J. CAUGHLIN
GENERAL MANAGER

Mr. John B. Kilroy
Kilroy Industries
626 Wilshire Boulevard
Suite 850
Los Angeles, California 90017

Dear Jim:

On behalf of the Board of Harbor Commissioners and
the Port of Los Angeles I would like to extend my personal
thanks for the use of KIALOA II in Sydney, Australia; Hobart,
Tasmania and Auckland, New Zealand.

As you well know, the expansion of the Port of Los
Angeles is vital to the economic stability of Los Angeles and
along this line trade to and from the South Pacific is taking
on much greater importance.

The success of our recent Trade Mission was greatly
aided by our identity with KIALOA II and your participation
in the Sydney, Hobart, Tasman Sea, and Southern Cross Races.
We found that the manufacturers, shippers and steamship operators
were familiar with the races taking place and the participation
of KIALOA II and the Vice-President of our Commission. This
made our contact easier, more meaningful and on a personal basis.
Your personal acquaintance and contact with the U. S. manufacturers
who had major branches in this area was also helpful and I am certain that they will report meeting you to their home office.

Page Two

Mr. John B. Kilroy

February 10, 1972

I might also add that everyone likes to do business with
a winner and KIALOA II was not only a winner in the sailing events
but also a winner for the Port of Los Angeles in helping to establish a close relationship and specific commitments which should
be exceedingly beneficial to the City of Los Angeles.

Sincerely yours,

BOARD OF HARBOR COMMISSIONERS

John J. Royal, President

JJR/mt

cc: Mayor Sam Yorty
     Councilman John Gibson
     Councilman John Ferraro
     W. Morton Jacobs
     Commissioner Frank Sullivan
     Commissioner Manuel K. Inadomi
     Commissioner John Y. Chu

A Tasman Tale by T.E. Lalonde

With our first Sydney-Hobart behind us, we understood how challenging the race was and how difficult it would be for a big boat to win. But we'd be back.

But for now, it was time to race across the Tasman in the Tasman Sea Race, a 1,507-mile event from Hobart to Auckland, which many of the Kiwi boats entered to return home. Unfortunately, before the race, I received word that I had to immediately leave for a meeting with Shah Pahlavi and Mayor Nikpay in Tehran, Iran, in connection with a 1,400-acre development north of the city. I asked Bruce Kendell if he would skipper *KIALOA II* in the race to his home city and he enthusiastically agreed. Terry Lalonde—who, like Bruce, became associated with our business—was also aboard, and what follows is his account of *KIALOA II's* record-setting participation in the 1972 Tasman Sea Race. We pick up the story as Terry finished the Sydney-Hobart Race aboard *Ondine* before the start of the Tasman Sea event.

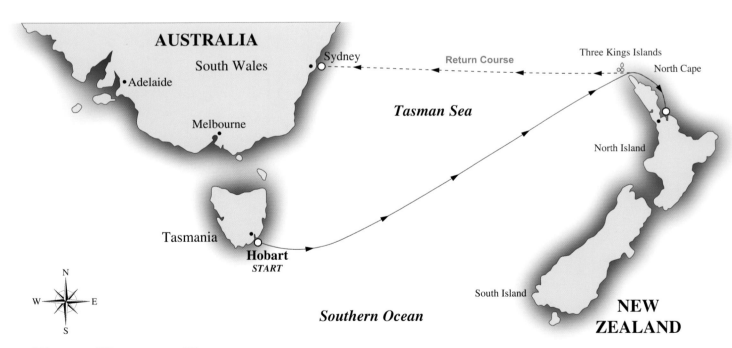

Trans Tasman Race
Hobart to Auckland

The wind was blowing lightly down the Derwent River and as such we aboard Ondine *were slowly working to weather with our huge number one Genoa. Damp and tired, I had gone forward for some quiet contemplation and positioned myself on the lee side of the headstay leaning against the rather substantive pulpit. This is one of the few isolated places on the yacht. I was just enjoying a moment's solitude as well as keeping a watch as we progressed up this dark estuary. Upon reflection, however, I realized I was a bit depressed, for not only did we not set a record in the esteemed Sydney to Hobart race, but* Ondine *would be finishing behind KIALOA II…again. We had finished behind KIALOA, or KII, in every one of the races in the series, and this was the last chance to get even. My slight feelings of despondency were the result of our not having sailed very well, at least in my opinion.*

Eventually a spotlight lit up the night, and we were officially clocked in as having finished the race. As this occurred we began our turn to port and into Constitution Dock. This basin is a historic center in Hobart and is surrounded by old, granite buildings testifying to its importance over the last couple of hundred years. Every year, just after Christmas, the harbor is emptied of its collection of working vessels and yachts, and becomes the finish point for the Sydney to Hobart race, arguably the most prestigious ocean race in the world. There, tied to the pier, in her typical first-to-finish fashion, was KIALOA II. She looked particularly proper and attractive with her more traditional lines including overhangs forward and aft, a pleasing shear line and stately bow. She was one of the most beautiful of the big ocean racers. This stood in stark contrast to the craft I was on, the rating-maximized Ondine, *which had been designed to stretch the handicapping rule to the limit. She should have been a ninety-foot yacht, but had her ends cut off to accommodate nuances of this rule.*

To add insult to injury, KIALOA II had been properly put away and made to look ship-shape, including sail covers on main and mizzen. She had her Los Angeles Yacht Club burgee hoisted and even had the colorful blue and white flag of the Los Angeles Harbor Commission flying as Jim Kilroy, the owner/skipper, was a commissioner. (This flag was later pilfered.) For yachts capable of gaining line honors, finishing first, this is always something to strive for, that is to have everything cleaned up and put away, and the crew enjoying libations at the bar before the second yacht finishes. There was a pattern here, as even in the Whitney Series raced in Southern California I had chased her aboard the beautiful and older yacht Baruna. *In the Whitney series KIALOA II, or KII as the crew refers to her, set five new records in six races.*

Positioned not as noticeably in the basin was another yacht, new, fast, shiny-black, which had beaten us by about five minutes. She had finished first in the previous year's Sydney to Hobart, and would be heading home with a plethora of local knowledge in the Tasman Sea

Race as scratch boat, allegedly fastest with the highest rating. Buccaneer *was her name.*

Ondine *was not going to do the Tasman Sea Race. On the other hand,* KIALOA II *was to do the upcoming race and a number of her crewmembers were heading home, leaving her in need of crew. So, four of us from* Ondine *talked with the skipper about joining* KIALOA II *and were honored by being invited to join her, the premier racing yacht in the world.*

Surprisingly it was Jim Kilroy, the owner and captain, who had to drop out at the last minute. His reason was work-related, which in itself was most unusual as Jim's philosophy included a need to put scheduled yacht racing commitments as a priority over work in order to assure their occurrence, and more importantly, in order to "recharge" certain recesses of the brain. This particular instance, whereby he would break priority, included a flight to Tehran. Knowing Jim Kilroy, he would much rather have done the race, but, he had committed earlier to be in Iran and had just gotten a "command performance" telephone call. He would be meeting with the mayor of Tehran and others, including the Shah, about a massive redevelopment project. This meant that for the first time in KIALOA's *seven-year history she would sail without him, and under the guidance of a twenty-three year old transplant New Zealander, the yacht's able skipper Bruce Kendell.*

Hobart, one of Australia's earliest settlements, is tucked down in the lower right-hand corner of that arrowhead-shaped landmass known as Tasmania, a large island wedged between the Indian Ocean and the Tasman Sea. It is accessed via a long inlet making it necessary to travel some distance to the open sea. And so it was on a relatively nice sunny Tuesday, January 4th, 1972, we, a crew of fourteen, motored to the start near Hobart Light. The wind was a light five- to fifteen-knots and would require the contestants to claw their way to weather in their efforts to reach New Zealand first. The course was 060°, but we were only able to make 045° and 095° depending upon which tack was selected, thus zigzagging across the desired 060°.

The next day, Wednesday, the wind increased to about 14 knots out of the east and east-southeast, and we were able to start reaching. We were able to go to a large number one jib-top and mizzen staysail. This is a sail combination with which KIALOA II *excelled and it would help offset the formidable reaching characteristics of the newer and faster* Buccaneer. *We had been sixteen miles south of course but were able to now steer the course. Tactically, we had elected to sail to the north end of New Zealand via the great circle course, which compensates for the curvature of the earth as opposed to the course represented by a straight line drawn on a chart.*

The days became consistently overcast and the wind became anything but consistent. It varied in strength and direction. This required constant sail trimming and changing. We would be dragging the rather substantial main boom in the water one moment and trying to figure out how to increase the amount of sails carried the next.

Ocean racing is generally an unheralded sport, not one chosen by those who seek recognition and/or fame. Its battles are typically fought out of sight and recognized only by the participants. Also, it is inherently dangerous and the notoriously changeable Tasman Sea has a reputation for trying those who venture upon it. The earth's land area is predominantly in the Northern Hemisphere. When one looks at a globe, it is obvious that there is little land area in the Southern Hemisphere below the latitude of 30° south, as opposed to latitude 30° north in the Northern Hemisphere, where the majority of the earth's land and civilizations exist. There is nothing to inhibit or mollify the angry storms that come spinning from and around Antarctica and rush unmolested around the southern ocean. They simply charge headlong across open seas towards Australia and New Zealand, often across the Tasman Sea. During this race, however, we were spared the experience and hostility of such southerly-generated storms, known as the "Southerly Busters."

This race seemed destined to become routine. The days began to appear one as another. Not that routine meant boring nor of limited efforts; as quite the contrary, these middle days were full of work and constant action. We were following along the top of a high-pressure system, which seemed to pulsate on a daily basis, such that we would start the day on a close reach, the wind more on the side of the boat, which would gradually freshen and turn to a broad reach. Eventually, each day we would go to reaching with spinnakers with the wind freshening and subsiding. The increases in wind velocity, and its tendency to move aft during the day, required untold sail changes. None of us on the boat had ever experienced so many sail changes in one race, and, I suspect, none were to experience as many again. Bruce was later quoted in a newspaper as saying "(he)…never worked so hard nor changed so many sails."

On KIALOA, it was not unusual to have an available, daily beer allocation. This was perhaps a tribute to the historic ration of grog used to keep an overworked and often abused crew from mutiny. Beer had been loaded on before the race, chilled and been consumed at the rate of two beers per day, per crewmember. As we neared the north end of New Zealand and our repetitious, as opposed to monotonous, days ended, a seemingly unbelievable event occurred… we ran out of beer! Mutiny seemed not an option, but a considerable amount of abuse was directed around in search of some culprit. Various scenarios were vociferously and vehemently explored. Did someone or other drink more that their prescribed allotment? Had someone made a mess of a seemingly simple provisioning calculation, something that Bruce adamantly denied? Had someone used an unreasonable expectation of our ability to significantly break the record?

Regardless, we were out of beer and at a time when the real work was about to begin.

Bruce and the very able tactician and co-navigator, Magnus Halversen, kept a continual watch on the positions of other yachts as they reported in for noontime roll calls. We were extending our lead. As we neared Cape Reinga, which sits at the end of a long spit of sand dunes called the ninety mile beach at the top of New Zealand, we ran out of another, more important, commodity. The wind quit. Thus, the second untoward event presented itself.

With the loss of the wind, the inevitable occurred. Shortly after dawn on the horizon behind us appeared another yacht. Although seventy miles from Reinga, we had been forty-eight miles ahead of the yacht that had set the fastest time in the prior year's Sydney to Hobart race, but here she came, riding out the last vestiges of the breeze behind us. Buccaneer, long on local knowledge, closed on us. Late in the day we were again becalmed, this time off the Cavalli Islands. This small cluster of islands is at the north end of a beautiful area known as the Bay of Islands. Captain Cook in 1769 named the area when he stumbled across New Zealand in search of the South Continent. The greater area is comprised of secluded bays and 140 islands. It is beautiful, but a veritable obstacle course for yachts, especially in light air. Local knowledge would be invaluable. However, we were not without "an ace in the hole." KIALOA II had four on board who had sailed extensively in Southern California, a place frustratingly known for its light, fluky winds…especially at night.

Light air sailing can be very burdensome, and will tax one's perseverance. Seldom is there a complete absence of wind, but it will come in soft little gossamers from varying directions. The trick is to not let the yacht become completely becalmed, and to rapidly try to capture whatever trickle of air there might be about, being ever diligent to marshal any breath of airflow. In nighttime light air sailing in Southern California on a very competitive Class A yacht, an especially fast light-air yacht, the owner would smoke a cigar and we would watch the smoke gently, slowly move out across a blackened sea, allowing us to determine hints of wind and its direction. No one on KIALOA smoked, but we did know other tricks, e.g. we separated the two layers of toilet paper, and carefully tore it into thin strips which we hung all over the yacht. The slightest hint of air would gently move these paper tell-tales. The thinnest and most fragile of sails would be used. The drifter, a hank-less headsail, would be used when the air tended to move forward, while a half-ounce spinnaker would be used as the whispers moved aft. Sometimes these sails would be exchanged a number of times within mere minutes. I do not think any of us had sailed so intently as through this night and the following day.

Later in the evening Buccaneer went inside of us and got about one half mile ahead of us with only 89 miles to go. We had chosen to stay farther offshore heading towards the Hen and

Chickens group of islands, named by Captain Cook who first sighted them in 1769. We were experiencing light rain, making the lighter sails less effective in the slight wind conditions.

The close sparring and frequent changing of the lead made for great news coverage. New Zealand and Australia closely follow yachting events. Aircraft throughout the day had buzzed us, and though we were not listening to the radio, there were continuous news flashes as we sailed down the coast. Even Bruce's mother was interviewed on the radio, and there were front-page pictures of both KIALOA and Buccaneer on all the papers. The degree to which New Zealanders were following this race, in large part due to the return of a warrior son as well as the largest American racing yacht ever entered, would become much more apparent as the race unfolded.

Bruce had left New Zealand, via Sydney, in 1969 to oversee the American yacht Rapture, *a Columbia 50, while it was shipped to Europe for some cruising and racing. Stuart ("Stuey" or "Stu") Williamson, a dynamic bon vivant, had sailed on* Rapture *in San Francisco and joined up with her in Sweden during the summer to race in the Scaw race. Here he met Bruce and they became best of friends. They both sailed in the Cowes Race Week and, as fortune would have it, tied up on the outside of Ted Turner's* American Eagle *and Jim Kilroy's KIALOA II. Bruce and Stuey had to traverse both KIALOA and* Eagle *to get to their boat, being on the outside of the dock. Stu was flying back to the States to teach his biology classes and asked Bruce what he was going to do as his employ on* Rapture *was coming to an end. Bruce, ever positive, said, "he would crew on KIALOA," and he, being Bruce, would do what it took to make that happen. He not only crewed, he soon became skipper of KIALOA when the original skipper retired. He had done well in his chosen field of endeavor and was now returning home triumphant in charge of a multimillion-dollar yacht after but two years aboard her. This speaks highly of Bruce's abilities and Jim's ability to recognize and trust in them.*

Thus, as we battled in a chess-move fashion down the east coast of New Zealand, we had become the primary news event. This must have been to the great chagrin of Boeing Aircraft as they were vying for the news with the arrival of the first Boeing 747 into the country. KIALOA vs. Buccaneer commanded page one of every paper.

I must admit, the first time I saw KIALOA II, I was duly impressed. You might say awed. It was before the start of a race near the Los Angeles entrance buoy. I was on a pretty, thirty-five foot Holiday yawl named Ghoster *and KIALOA motored past with just her mainsail up. Her bow towered over us, not to mention her mighty sloop rig. This was in late 1964 or early 1965. She represented many firsts, not just in her race history but in her design and construction. She was the first yacht of her size to have her lines lofted and structural engineering done by computer. A company was created primarily to build* KIALOA II, Yacht Dynamics, *and it was to build but a few other aluminum yachts. It was a consortium involving Kilroy, Douglas Aircraft, Alcoa, Reynolds and Kaiser aluminum companies all having a hand in her construct, the end result being the first yacht of her size constructed of aluminum.*

For our race in early 1972 she was in peak performance. And fortunately she was doing as well as she ever would in light air conditions.

The sailing was as keen as it could get. No opportunity was missed, nor any slacking of diligence witnessed. We simply sailed KII as well as she could have been sailed. We were constantly working the sails with subtle changes that would have been imperceptible to most sailors. At night there was always someone with a flashlight checking sail trim.

There were a couple of times where Buccaneer *got close enough for us to call back and forth as there were many friends on both yachts, and it did make for some lightening of the otherwise tense situation. There was another possible factor that could influence our ability to outperform the competition. On one of our close encounters, around six in the evening, the* Buccaneer *crew advised us that they were enjoying cocktails in their comfortable, enclosed cockpit. This was done somewhat as a good-natured rub as they already knew of our dearth of beer.*

The log entry for midnight, 2400, on January 11, 1972 simply says "Passed Buccaneer *to windward about 50 yds apart." This in Bruce's handwriting, and no doubt he was both slightly relieved and excited to make this entry. But there was surely little to celebrate as the very next entry—0045 January 12, 1972—reads "Abeam Tutukaka Light – with* Buccaneer *100 ft back." It was a long, hard-fought battle that night. No one slept. By early morning we were in a flat calm trying to make progress with the drifter up and concentration strained to recognize the slightest bit of air movement.* Buccaneer *was to starboard, closer to the land once again. In a game of inches, we worked our way around the east edge of a large calm area. Slowly, we managed to crawl towards little hints of air and on to Auckland and the finish. The area is full of little islands, and we had been dogging in and around them as we sparred.* Buccaneer *being west of us, maneuvered into a bit of the lee of the 1300-foot Hen Island and as the owner/skipper, Tom Clark, said after the race, "we followed her until we fell into a big flatty."*

By dawn, Buccaneer *was not to be seen, but we were barely moving towards the finish, and she seemed sure to re-enter the picture. The crew, which had a demonstrated capability of celebrating boisterously ashore, had exhibited the seriousness, intensity and concentration necessary to beat all other contestants. Importantly, the crew had acted in a very cohesive manner, especially considering more than 40% had never sailed on* KIALOA *or on the same team together. There was a clearly identified time for celebration necessary to ease the tensions of racing, and there was a time to work seriously and develop the tensions that would need to be released through a celebration.*

We were worried about our primary competition. This was especially so when by 0700 in the morning, we once again became engulfed in a "flat calm," and out came the drifter and the tissue "tell tales." This occurred off Rodney Point, which is about 30 miles from the finish. Buccaneer had to be lurking somewhere, but where? However, gradually an east-south-east light breeze began to fill in and started us moving. By one o'clock, we were able to raise a spinnaker and start a proper march towards the finish.

Entering Hauraki Gulf and crossing to the entrance into Auckland, we were running mostly square to the wind in a nice twelve- to fifteen-knot breeze. The finish was well inside Auckland harbor. As we began to get closer to the land, which was slightly elevated with a bluff running along our course, we all began to wonder what we were seeing along the hillsides and beach areas. We already had noticed quite a bit of small motor yacht traffic, more than one would expect for a Wednesday afternoon. Soon it became obvious; this unusual ornamentation was comprised of people and cars…lots of them. Slowly, as if in a dream sequence, we began putting the pieces of the puzzle together. The armada of small craft was trailing along to see us finish!

One speedy craft full of good-natured sailors pulled alongside to wish us well and even offered some beer. They managed to throw us enough beers for the crew. Parched by now and just this side of mutiny, we all enjoyed our first cold New Zealand beer. In retrospect, this receipt of victuals was technically probably illegal, but the New Zealanders would never have protested once they understood our plight.

Ah, but the best was yet to come. We were unable to lay the finish on our present downwind tack and it would be necessary to execute a jibe, which is to put the wind on the other side of the sails. Now none of us were self-conscious enough to suffer stage fright, but this was the first and probably the only time we would have to perform a jibe maneuver in front of ten thousand people! It was an absolutely flawless jibe. The spinnaker did not even move an inch, its luff was motionless, the main went through the wind and onto the other side as if a well lubricated, smooth, swinging door. In addition, Stu, who had been advised by Bruce to put up the biggest mizzen staysail on board, jibed the mizzen and reset the staysail flawlessly. We had finished in 8 days, 2 hours, 10 minutes and 28 seconds and beaten Buccaneer one-and-a-half hours. At the finish, the Royal Akarana Yacht Club played The Star-Spangled Banner *to round out the spectacular reception.*

Jim Kilroy had courageously turned over his world-famous yacht to a young New

Zealander for a triumphant return to his native land. What an honor for this young sailor, and what a trust exhibited by the yacht's owner. Jim was an excellent judge of character and was able to see people's abilities. He was not let down as KIALOA II *was first to finish, beat the local favorite, and in spite of being becalmed several times, broke the existing record held by* Fidelis *by 25 minutes and 20 seconds. As with winning in most endeavors, there were a multitude of facets involved. We had a proven fast yacht, and we were able to accurately predict and utilize the weather and conditions, but most importantly we sailed harder than the competition. Additionally, we had not taken a "flyer" in any sense of the word. We constantly assessed all information and alternatives available to us and made reasoned decisions. We were the only yacht to sail the great circle route to Cape Reinga, which is 13 miles shorter than a straight line as placed on a chart, the "rhumb line." This decision, no doubt, caused us a portion of the plethora of sail changes we experienced, but it paid off. In those elements of an undertaking upon which you can have control or influence, it is important to maximize one's efforts. We could control how the yacht was sailed. We never let up and were rewarded by winning.*

14

The final comments on my book are made as we transition
from 2011 into 2012, 41 years after my acceptance of
Mayor Yorty's request to become involved as a commissioner
of our Los Angeles Port Authority.

Over these many years, starting from a restructured foundation,
it has become one of the leaders in our world of Maritime Transport.

I compliment the many commissioners and managers
that have followed.

Community Service
The Los Angeles Port Authority

In 1970, I was asked by Mayor Sam Yorty to become a Member of the Harbor Commission, which had been troubled by many things, including finding a former commissioner (the President of the Commission) floating in the bay. Sam wanted to know if I would go down and do my best job to represent the Mayor and the City, and I told him I would do so.

I recognized that there were many problems that needed to be ferreted out, and I had to study what the Los Angeles Harbor Commission and the Port of Los Angeles were all about. Actually in the San Pedro Port area, there were two harbor entities. One was Los Angeles Harbor, run by the Los Angeles Harbor Port Authority, and the other was the City of Long Beach Harbor, run by the City of Long Beach Port Authority.

When I arrived on the commission, I studied the interrelationship between the two and found none, except that they were truly competitors, and the idea was to underbid the other port so that you would get the contract with whomever the foreign shipping lines might be. It might be for containers. It might be raw material. It might be whatever, but the idea was for the City of Los Angeles Port Authority to beat out the City of Long Beach Port Authority. Both were losers in this competition.

Another issue I found at the first meeting I attended was that there were rules—rules for the civil servants of the City of Los Angeles and guidelines that you had to operate within. At a special meeting—my first meeting—the big issue was that the terminal island drawbridge operator was having coordination problems, mental problems, or perhaps, alcohol problems, and had dropped the bridge upon the top of a marine vessel. Fortunately, the marine vessel was only damaged. No one was hurt. But, this was very, very serious.

As the case was coming before the commission, I asked, "Was the operator still on duty?" And the answer I received was, "Yes, he is now on duty." It was incomprehensible to me that this person could stay on duty regardless of whatever the civil service rules and regulations were.

I demanded at that point, for the pure safety of the vessels and the people, that he be taken off his duty on the drawbridge and someone else be substituted. This was done. This was a case of not using executive judgment and not protecting other people simply because of some old-fashioned civil service rules.

That shocked me into investigating further. As I looked at the competition between the two ports, I came to the conclusion that there was a finite amount of ground and water area, and that we should not be competing with each other. We should offer shipping lines proposals that were acceptable and financially responsible to give our port a good return, and we should also take a look at the rates that our primary customer, Japan, was charging for shipments going into Japan and elsewhere. We should have comparable rates if they were favorable to us. And since there was a finite amount of land, if the city of Long Beach made deals reducing their available land area on a low bid price, they didn't have a great deal. At a later date, we would effectively be able to quote whatever rate was commercially responsible, and ethically responsible, as their land would be committed.

I talked to the Port of Long Beach commissioners as well, and I said, "This is nuts. I don't think that we can necessarily coordinate on every transaction, whether that would be legal or not, but you have to calculate a deal that makes a profit for your community and a profit for your port."

The ports are here to do a good job in receiving the commodity that is being brought into the area, which may not be just for Los Angeles—it may be transported elsewhere. Jointly, Los Angeles and Long Beach were the leading port. We should only do transactions that were profitable to us. We should not subsidize foreign nations or foreign lines. They should pay an amount predicated upon a profitable formula, "We are a real estate development company. We must amortize our assets. We must have a net profit after amortization—a reasonable and responsible profit." We instituted responsible and profitable deal making after much haggling within the harbor area.

Now, it was a change. It was a management change, as the prior manager had a very different understanding as to what should be done. I'm fearful that he liked the game of competition with Long Beach, and it was a case of trying to get one up on the opposing port instead of getting an economic deal that was equitable, fair and responsible, which considered all the aspects you would normally consider within a profitable real estate development.

I then suggested that we look at the types of tenants that we already had, what their leases were, when they were coming up and whether we wanted them back or not. And if so, what appropriate rate should be charged for the facility. We had one tenant who was a scrap steel operator. It was not attractive, it was not economical, and of course, we needed to recognize that we had to receive and ship scrap steel. But, it was a secondary operation, not a primary one. It should be placed in a secondary location. It should be at a rate that was suitable in comparison to what other rates would be. They had to compete with other businesses, not just compete with what a scrap dealer wanted to pay.

That was a tough negotiation. We did improve the return from that particular asset, and I don't recall now whether it was with the same tenant or a new tenant.

We had another situation with a bulk loader. For some reason, the city ended up owning a bulk loader for coal and related activities. Any way you looked at it, it could not be a profitable operation predicated upon environmental matters and its primary location. And so again, it was a hard decision to say, "This is not a good economic deal. We have to do something. We have to re-engineer the area."

The bulk loader was downgrading the value and use of the property and the contiguous property. We analyzed our engineering process. Our engineering department was not necessarily geared to flexibility. Add to that the fact that when we made an investment, we did not want that investment to be just a singular-use investment. We wanted it to have turnover capabilities so it could be used in connection with other tenants, so that in any event, even if the same tenant was there, we could not allow him to negotiate and say, "This is only good for this operation. This is all I'm going to pay you."

We looked at the port as a responsible real estate development. Again, this was somewhat shocking to the manager and somewhat shocking to others, but we had a good enough team on the Board to pass responsible transactions and resolutions. And in turn, the management would have to proceed accordingly. We did have certain other issues in how we managed engineers, and in how we managed the employees. I had the strong feeling, again, that this was to be treated as a real estate development, and we had to look at it with the same skills that we would in the management and the development of real estate. And, we slowly, slowly moved in that direction.

Another issue that concerned me was the fact that the port had no regard, or little regard, for the surrounding areas of homes and commerce. They did not try to do anything to disguise that we were anything other than a port. And, ports are not very attractive and not very nice to look at, and environmentally undesirable unless controlled. We set up a plan to beautify the port and to make the area responsible in connection with the economic benefits to the balance of the community. There was a plan to build the headquarters office facility for the port in the center of Terminal Island, which was strictly for industrial port use, including canneries and unattractive outside storage.

It did not seem logical to build an office building there. It certainly had no flexibility. And certainly, there was no point in taking office personnel into that type of community. The ground could be better used for other port activities. And so, we relocated it into the area of commerce within the City of San Pedro. It became an asset to San Pedro and a greater benefit to all of the employees in San Pedro.

We had various types of leases. Some leases provided for the sole use of that specific site by the lessee who generally installed tenants' own special equipment.

We had other facilities, which were general use facilities used by different tenants as needed. We provided the equipment at these sites and charged a bulk rate based upon the appropriate measurements, such as a barrel of oil, ton of steel, etc. Our pricing had to be modernized and set at a suitable rate so as to make a profit to amortize equipment and improvement cost and to continually update the property for new ongoing use.

Ultimately, there was a change in the Mayor. I was asked to resign, and customarily, you resign. I did not resign. In turn, I told them that I would resign when they had adopted a revised plan for the continuing and successful operation of the Port, which was described in a letter to the Mayor dated 10 September 1973. (See letter on the KIALOA—US1.com website).

I had previously filed reports in connection with what I thought should be done with the Port and with the Chief Administrative Office (CAO) of the City, as well as with the City Attorney when appropriate, which were on file. The Board authorized a resolution that the CAO perform an audit of the Harbor Department. One of the things that I did insist on—and it's not a happy situation when you do this—was that the general manager be replaced. And when they had a plan to replace the general manager who would implement our revised plans, I would then resign. I would coordinate on other matters with the new president of the Port Authority. At his request, we worked out a mutual relationship in this regard. And, the Port substantially enhanced their value, substantially enhanced their flexibility, and substantially enhanced their earnings. I think that it was a simple matter of defining what the Port was all about, and its comparative nature to the commercial world. A port is a real estate development, and it was regarded that way. I think it's been profitable and successful ever since. I was pleased to become involved, to use real estate and management skills to convert the Port to a reasonable and equitable profit-making facility.

15

As one can read from my writings, the Transatlantic Race from Bermuda to Bayonna, Spain with the Azores Islands and Isla Flores being a mark of the course was not one of my favorite races. I have felt that the Race Committee should have read the same book privately given to me by a noted European sailor.

This book seems to say that Columbus was given specific instructions on the course to the New World and that he must sail the reverse course on his return to Spain. The course to be sailed to the New World would be a reasonably comfortable sail with the wind and seas from the east. Sailing the reverse course on his return to Spain would have meant head winds and headseas, much longer sailing, probably, tacking back and forth across the ocean.

The book I read states that Columbus did not follow his instructions on his return. He sailed to the north over the center of the North Atlantic High Cell and then southeasterly to Spain.

We could see why Columbus chanced the sailing to the North as we were becalmed to the west of Isla Flores. However, as we were going nowhere, we could swim, we could try to move *KIALOA II* to the east and we could have a pleasant dinner along with enough fuel reserve to take us to Horta, which we promptly used.

We understand that Columbus went to prison for violating Torquemada's instructions. It appears that one must ask why these instructions were given.

KIALOA II: The Final Races 1972 Bermuda to Vigo, Spain

Stuck in the Horse Latitudes, a Gift to the Coast Guard

After our adventures Down Under, our next event would be halfway around the world and back in the Northern Hemisphere, an "abbreviated" Transatlantic race from Bermuda to Bayonne, Spain, a port in the Bay of Biscay on the country's northern coast.

A mark of the course, Isla Flores in the Azores Islands, would oblige the fleet to sail across the historic Horse Latitudes. In the history of discovery and exploration under sail, many vessels spent days, weeks and even months in the Horse Latitudes. Sometimes they'd have to jettison their livestock to survive, which is where the name was derived.

At the race briefing in Bermuda, the local weathermen advised skippers that the North Atlantic High cell was moving south and might generate fair winds on a great circle course all the way to Isla Flores. We'd initially been planning a more northerly track, but the optimistic meteorologist convinced everyone, including us, into the great circle concept.

The race began on June 31st, 1972, and indeed, the first forty-eight hours of the race brought good sailing, almost 400 miles. But on the third day, July 2nd, the wind velocity dropped and so did our speed—only a 155-mile day. It didn't get any better on the fourth, 130-mile day. Day 5 was even worse—62-miles—and yet we were still leading the pack of the maxis in the center of the high cell that had failed to follow the weatherman's forecast and dip south. On the sixth day, *Ondine* retired, and on the seventh day, we broke the windless barrier by recording 115 miles… but it didn't last.

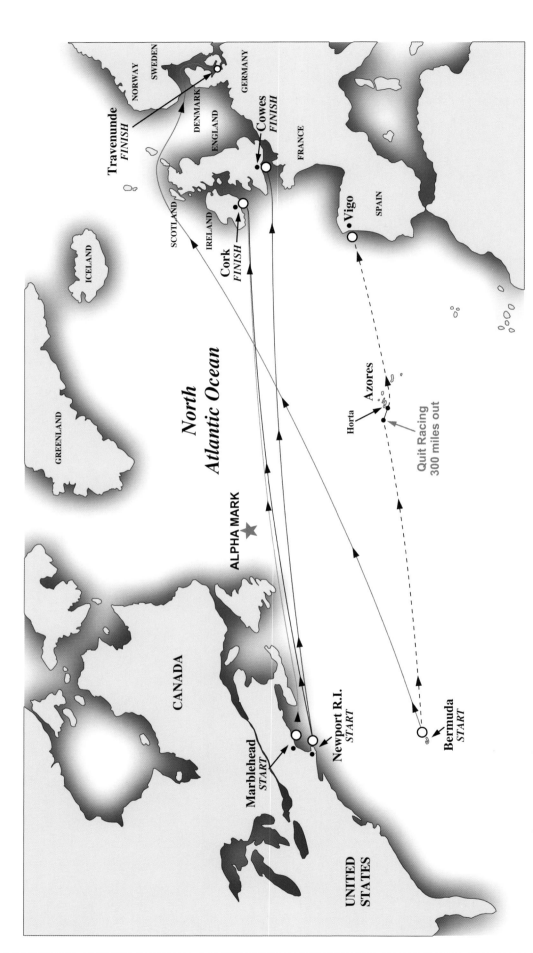

Trans Atlantic Races

- KIALOA II - 1968 Bermuda over Scotland to Travemunde
- KIALOA II - 1969 Newport R.I. to Cork Ireland
- KIALOA II - 1972 Bermuda to Vigo Spain
- KIALOA III - 1975 Newport R.I. to Cowes England
- KIALOA III - 1979 Marblehead to Cork Ireland

★ Alpha Mark - Notice of Location given day before Start of Race (moves with Iceberg Flow)

On Day 8 we made only 42.5 miles and were solidly stuck in the Horse Latitudes. There was no wind, but very pleasant swimming. We decided we'd give it one more day, and if there were still no breeze, we'd retire.

None of the crew enjoyed the idea of retiring. However, with 670 miles to Isla Flores, and many more miles to Bayonne, when would we finish? Our crew had commitments to their families and their businesses. Our navigator, a surgeon, had commitments for operations. We had no choice, really, so we dropped out of the race, a very rare occurrence on any *KIALOA*. We had minimal fuel on board so we sailed and motored to Horta, conserving our diesel, arriving on the twelfth of July. We spent two days there and met the locals, who accepted us as sailors and men from the sea, like them, and not just as tourists. Then *KIALOA II* motorsailed with a delivery team to Bayonne while the rest of us caught the ferry to Tercera, which stopped in Pico and a couple of other places along the way.

The ferry ride was a great experience. In Pico, the locals boarded with commercial items and animals, including several head of cattle from a small corral. The crew then took the cattle on and off the ferry two times and recounted. They then announced that someone must have had a barbecue the night before, because they were one head of cattle short. As fellow sailors, we were asked to join the ferry crew for breakfast and somehow, we had an "Indian Arm Wrestling" contest with them. The stakes were high—which crew would have the right to dock the ferry at the next stops.

We entered two *KIALOA II* crewmen, cook Bill Clum and his son-in-law, a U.S. national kayak champion, who stood about 6'4" and weighed 220 pounds. However, the ferry crew representative was also a big, strong, arm wrestler, and he dispatched the son-in-law. Next up was 5'6" Bill, about 170 pounds.

Little did they know that Bill Clum was the Arm Wrestling Champion at the California Frog Jumping Competition, which draws a talented field. Bill was compact, with short, strong arms, and he had great leverage over the bigger man. Bill won and after another glass of good red Azores wine, the *KIALOA* crew took over the docking of the ferry with great humor and a lot of laughter by both crews. We took turns docking and I was first. Not too bad, if I do say so myself. Bill Clum was second, deservedly so, and after a couple more stops we were in Tercera. We stayed a day until flying on to beautiful Lisbon, which we enjoyed for several days.

So we had a good time, even though the race turned into a non-event. Peter Bowker, a highly qualified crew aboard *Windward Passage*, summed it up in an article in the October, 1972 issue of *Sail* magazine. Bowker quoted Dick Nye, the race committee chairman and also the skipper of the winning yacht, *Carina*, who said, "This race has probably set yachting back 50 years." We agreed, at least for this race!

But it did mark a milestone. *KIALOA II's* nine years of highly successful racing in the world's most challenging and competitive races was over. Yachts designed to the new IOR MKIII rule, which became effective in 1971, had taken over the game. However, one anomaly continued. Certain yachts designed in the last few years under the old CCA rule, or the initial IOR MKI or MKII (1970) rule were able to take advantage of old-age allowances under the MKIIIA rule, which increased handicap allowances each year. With this revised rule, owners could modify *anything* on an older boat—the rig, sail plan, displacement, etc.—as long they didn't touch the basic hull. For a boat like *Windward Passage*, the credit they earned was astounding; with a host of new modifications, the boat was suddenly rated as if she were ten or eleven feet shorter.

These old-age allowances increased their handicap allowance credits and gave them tremendous advantages, particularly in the SORC, which also instilled *an additional* handicap time allowance called the SORC/FORA (Florida Old Age Allowance) allowance. These combined old-age allowances provided tremendous reductions in corrected times—well beyond what everyone had anticipated—and Ted Turner and a few others immediately purchased and raced such MK IIIA yachts as *Tenacious* to their substantial advantage.

However, we recognized that *KIALOA II* was outdated and could not successfully race under the new rule, and that it was time to design, build and race a new yacht: *KIALOA III.*

In the meantime, we entered *KIALOA II* in the 1973 SORC, anyway. As before, the boat sailed well, but under the new, compromised rule and handicap formulas, all for "the betterment" of international yachting, we tanked the series. Though we didn't make all of the races, the results were horrible: twenty-first in class, ninety-ninth in fleet.

After the SORC and a few days before the 1973 Jamaica Race, we found a serious crack in our rod head stay and ordered a replacement. We were assured that it would be in Miami a day before the race as indicated on the bill of lading. Somehow, it was lost and did not arrive the day before the race. We were then assured of an early race day morning arrival. It did not arrive until after the race started, and we could not officially start the race as the official timer had left. However, we raced anyway, starting three hours later than the rest of the fleet, and we had a great, fast sail. We finished responsibly, but silently—no horn, no gun. It was like a ghost race, and how symbolic.

But *KIALOA II* was off to a new home, and a good one. We decided that the outstanding U.S. Coast Guard and *KIALOA II* could be a good marriage, that the boat could be a great training vessel for a dedicated group of men and women whose mission was to safeguard U.S. vessels and shipping in home waters and many places around the world. The Coast Guard agreed.

We delivered *KIALOA II* to the USCG Academy Foundation in New Haven, Connecticut, on July 20, 1973. After nine years of tremendous racing success, as well as many cruises with friends and family to beautiful places in our great world, we handed over the keys in an appropriate and thoughtful ceremony.

We gave *KIALOA II* to the Coast Guard because we knew that they would use it well in their training of new and young Coast Guard officers. More particularly, it was given in deep appreciation for the great service of our Coast Guard, who provide security and sometimes even rescue those of us who enjoy sailing across the beautiful sea.

When we conceived *KIALOA II,* we anticipated an excellent cruising and racing yacht. *KIALOA II* exceeded all of our expectations. As we raced, we found many ways to improve her racing and yes, even her cruising performance. The wonderful ideas that came from our crew, and from our friends in the aerospace and engineering world, made us continually think "outside the box."

In spite of all the rule changes, our non-stop testing and input into the development of the new IOR rule, and the slight modifications we made in an attempt to keep competitive under changing rule parameters, were intellectually stimulating and spurred us to sail and concentrate on a much higher level. But the decision had been made and the time had come for *KIALOA III.*

We had a lot of respect and affection for *KIALOA II*, and never could have sold her to someone who did not understand her value and years of success. As a sailing training vessel with the U.S. Coast Guard, she would have a good home.

AND, WE STILL REMEMBER HER WINNING WAYS:

OVERALL FLEET VICTORIES – 24.56%

OVERALL PODIUM FINISHES (TOP THREE PLACES) – 54.38%

16

I have questioned why I was asked to chair the Los Angeles emergency oil committee. It was well known that I was generally opposed to foreign oil, until we had adequate oil production under our full control to support our nation's own needs and to fully maintain our nation's security into the future. The 1973 Arab Oil Boycott certainly verified that we did not have enough oil under our absolute control to fulfill our needs and to guarantee our security. The distress to our economy was easily verifiable by counting the cars waiting at the local gasoline service stations.

We were being tested as to our future plans. We did not respond. The price of oil substantially increased while cash flowed out of our country, a tragic economic and security loss which we have never regained. Yes, our committee accomplished many things to the benefit of our community. I wish that we could have accomplished much more to protect our nation economically and its security. The reader should look at the huge increase in the price of oil per barrel over the years since the boycott.

January 1978   January 2003   April 2012

Source: U.S. Energy Information Administration

"A Test"
The 1973 Arab Oil Boycott:
October 15, 1973 to March 17, 1974 – 152 Days

I can remember the shock to the American people—long lines of cars waiting at each open service station for a few gallons of rationed gasoline. I immediately went to the *Webster's Unabridged Dictionary* to look up the word "boycott" to see what it might say: "Boycott—a means of intimidation and coercion." I can remember forthright and unprintable works, asking "Where is our national security? We must protect our nation—why don't we drill in our restricted reserves to protect our nation?"

The Mayor of Los Angeles, Tom Bradley, called and asked if I would form a committee to find enough oil to keep the City of Los Angeles and its Department of Water and Power (DWP) running. I said "Yes, I will do my best." I asked Bob Fluor, President of the Fluor Corporation, leading engineers of the oil industry, and Paul Sullivan, Senior Vice President of Bank America, to be co-chairmen. We three invited other community leaders to join us.

Our committee first looked at the needs of the DWP, their procurement policies and their storage capabilities. Shockingly, there were only 90 days of storage capacity with only a 60-day supply of oil, and procurement based on the spot market—no contracts. Our auditors also reviewed their needs and management policies. We immediately asked their rival in Southern California, the Southern California Edison, to volunteer cooperation with their more substantial reserves and received their cooperation.

Our committee held private meetings with senior executives of major oil companies to gain their cooperation in this challenging time. We mutually agreed that our meetings would be confidential without the press. As things can happen politically, the mayor's office advised the press of a meeting and they arrived before our oil industry leaders. We were able to isolate the press, and I advised them that I would hold a press conference after the meeting. I did, about 30 minutes after the oil industry leaders left, for which I was challenged. I reminded them that I had stipulated to the press that *I* would hold the press conference.

A shocking cartoon then appeared in the *Los Angeles Times* editorial section. It severely criticized Union Oil Company and Fred Hartley, the President. The foundation of the criticism was that Union Oil had two oil tankers enroute from Indonesia. One tanker was commandeered by the Air Force Pacific Theater and the other was scheduled for Los Angeles. The second tanker did not arrive —it was also commandeered by the Air Force. Fred Hartley and Union could not stop it.

The *LA Times* cartoon showed a wilted Christmas tree with oil dripping round balls on the tree. The logo number 76 was on each ball and the nasty comment, "Heartless Fred" was at the base of the tree; terribly incorrect, terribly inappropriate. Fred brought suit against the *LA Times*; however, the court ruled that he was a public figure and could not sue.

After 152 days of challenge and testing, those who organized "The Arab Oil Boycott" acknowledged that they had won the test, the challenge to which we would not respond with the strength of our nation. We, the U.S.A., had conceded that we were dependent upon the Arab oil, that we would not challenge with our own resources. How illogical. Our national security was in their hands. We could have submitted plans for rapid drilling in our reserved oil fields; we could have organized construction of nuclear plants. Basically, we did nothing. We acknowledged the success of their boycott and gave them the concept of oil at any price. Any price included the almost $150 a barrel in late 2008. And, now in 2011–12, there is little change except that we have a greater need for foreign oil, and so do China and other competitive nations.

China, with its tremendous industrial growth, buys about 40% of its oil from Iran, and is vigorously drilling for oil in its own reserves, acknowledging its needs, protecting its economy and its country. How much more will China grow? Will its needs from other countries increase? Will these needs be in direct competition with our needs, and what about the needs of India? The population of China is about four times that of the United States, and the population of India is about three times that of the United States. Together, China and India's population is about seven times that of the United States. What competitive impact does this have on the U.S.A.'s needs for foreign oil and on our security? Let us be logical when it comes to economics and national security.

Our nation is lacking in such fundamental analysis. We have competition for foreign oil. We have no way of controlling our foreign oil resources. We have no way of controlling the price of foreign oil resources. We should look at past energy issues. A good example is the "Greater Asia Co-Prosperity Sphere," controlled by Japan in the 1930's and early 1940's. The Japanese were becoming a powerful industrial nation. They had no real supply of minerals or oil on their islands. They formed the "Greater Asia Co-Prosperity Sphere," asking other nations to join them. In simple translation it meant "give us your oil and minerals or we will take over your nation." Korea, China and Manchuria were under substantial Japanese control. These nations appealed to the United States for help knowing that negotiations with Japan had been underway for some time. The U.S.A.

cut off scrap steel sales to Japan and ultimately advised Japan that oil shipments from Indonesia would be challenged. A challenge of no steel, no oil was destructive for Japan and they looked at their options, reviewing a war plan of Admiral Yamamoto, a surprise attack on Pearl Harbor. What options did Japan have except to hope that such a masterly bluff might scare the U.S.A. out of the Pacific to concentrate on the war against Germany?

History has shown that the Japanese ignored or did not read Yamamoto's second file, which stated that any such victory would be temporary and that Japan would ultimately suffer defeat as they did not have a guaranteed and protected source of energy.

The Japanese had no guaranteed source of energy; nor do we. Control of the U.S.A. is substantially in the hands of foreign nations. Our excuse is protecting our environment, which directly relates to the environment of the world. An oil well is an oil well. Does an oil well in the Arab world have less of an effect on the world's environment than an oil well in the United States? The same can be said for refineries and distribution facilities.

Logic says that we need to protect our nation, our economy, our security, and our economics. This can be accomplished to the best of our ability by drilling for oil in our major oil reserves, installing distribution facilities and necessary refineries and using them as necessary. It's necessary to protect our nation, to protect our economy and to protect against the excess cost of oil that we witness today. Such protection also applies to nuclear facilities. They can readily be tied into existing distribution grids and provide ongoing needed energy without the universal environmental problems associated with oil production.

If we consider the environment in the drilling of our own oil reserves, the new product would reduce the environmental impact of transportation and other related issues of foreign oil. Let us not deal in trivia. Let us consider the security and economics of our great country, the U.S.A. We can always be in transition towards more efficiency and a better environment based upon future and realistic technology, while focusing on reality. Without security, we have handed our future to others. Ideologies can create unknown consequences. We must protect our nation with our own resources. It is time to show that we have reviewed and even though late, we are prepared to win the Test of 1973.

17

Harmony, Beauty, Success
"I Name Thee *KIALOA III*"
KIALOA III and Kathy Kilroy

1974

Nicknamed "The Ordinary White Boat"

KIALOA III was now launched and test sailed. We knew that we had much to learn about our beautiful new racing yacht and rigorous test sailing and tuning would tell us much more.

We did not know that our newly launched *KIALOA III* would be one of the most successful yachts in the history of modern competitive yachting racing oceans of our world. We will further discuss her outstanding success throughout the remainder of this book along with the success of her big sisters *KIALOA IV* and *KIALOA V.*

A short time after launching, we carefully analyzed *KIALOA III's* IOR-MKIII measurement certificate. We found a serious technical error in *KIALOA III's* IOR-MKIII handicap measurement certificate, which calculated her displacement to be about 20,000 pounds lighter than her true displacement. This meant that we would give more handicap correction time to her smaller competitors and less handicap correction time from her larger competitors.

We enclose in chapter 27 a diagram which further describes this calculation error. We tried and tried over the racing career of *KIALOA III* to have the measurement calculation corrected, to no avail.

We knew that we had to sail harder, improve our sailing skills and tactical planning, all of which was accomplished by our outstanding *KIALOA* crew. We were forever amazed at their continuing success in sailing our outstanding *KIALOA III,* as set forth in the following chapter.

The "Ordinary White Boat"
The Christening, Testing and Early 1975 Racing Aboard KIALOA III

In the late fall of 1974, under a blue sky dotted by buttermilk clouds, our new racing and cruising yacht, *KIALOA III*, was about to be launched and christened. It was a beautiful day at the Palmer Johnson Boatyard in Sturgeon Bay, Wisconsin—perfect for a party. The yacht was beautiful. A large group of friends and crewmen were on hand, as well as the shipyard workers who'd built the boat. Everyone agreed that a yacht this handsome had to be a winner.

Pat Haggerty, Palmer Johnson's principal owner, introduced the builders and designers, one of whom was David Pedrick of Sparkman & Stephens, who had once again drawn the lines of our latest *KIALOA*. The boat's skipper, Bruce Kendell, who also supervised the construction, made some well-received comments about the design and the quality of workmanship, which was excellent.

With the formal speeches concluded, the local Catholic priest, who was also an enthusiastic sailor, made a wonderful invocation, followed by the actual christening. My wife, Kathy, did the honors with one artful swing of a champagne bottle and a tender statement: "I name thee *KIALOA III*."

It was now time for our first sail. The sails and deck gear were already aboard, and a large crew of guests and family followed. The racing crew went to their pre-assigned stations to gain familiarity with the new deck layout, and to see how things should be tuned and what changes might be required. We didn't bother with the spinnaker on this inaugural trial, but it was a great first sail under headsails and a full mainsail. The new *KIALOA* was remarkably speedy and close-winded.

Pat Haggerty—who skippered and owned the Admiral's Cup racer *Bay Bea*, and owned the great electronics firm Texas Instruments, as well as Palmer Johnson—carefully checked all the electronic instrumentation that is so essential to Grand Prix sailboat racing. The English company, Brooks and Gatehouse, had specifically designed new sailing instruments for *KIALOA III*, and Pat was having a great time seeing how well they displayed the vital information needed to race a boat at the highest level: boat speed, apparent wind speed, true wind speed, apparent wind direction and true wind direction, apparent wind angle, true wind angle and so on.

We were encouraged to see the boat's tight tacking angles, a vital characteristic for successful racing. At the helm, I had a wonderful time getting to know the boat and beginning to understand her sailing and maneuvering strengths. Bruce and others were enthusiastic about *KIALAO III*'s balanced helm and overall quality. The grinders were happy with the big, fast "coffee-grinder" winches. And the sail trimmers were excited about the efficient sheet leads and deck layout. None of this was an accident. We'd spent a lot of time on a mock deck layout and had tested the interrelationship of all the various hardware and equipment prior to settling on final design. It appeared that few changes would be required.

After our second day of sailing, we gathered for our traditional major dinner. Olin Stephens had arrived from New York and together we analyzed the two days of sailing and reviewed the list of "to-do" items.

With the preliminary trials over, it was essential to move *KIALOA III* to Long Island Sound for more detailed testing, starting with the mechanical and operating systems. Next, we needed to thoroughly analyze our sail inventory and sail shapes, and tune the rig. We were also keen to develop a new, accurate wind-based sailing performance program through a computer analysis of the output of our Brooks and Gatehouse instrumentation. But we had difficulty pinning this down because of an anomaly in the figures we were recording.

Our apparent wind angles, an instrument-calculated wind angle—a combination of the true wind angle and the speed of the boat—would not compute out to an appropriate compass course being sailed, which also meant that we received an incorrect readout of true compass courses.

Yes, we had large, separate magnetic compasses and could not be lost, however, it was now the modern quick-scanning electronic world, and we insisted upon being accurate.

We had a debate aboard as to what caused this issue and how we could correct it, understanding that it all began in the aerodynamics of what we were doing.

I called one of our crew and consultants, Arvel Gentry, the supersonic aerodynamics engineer at Douglas Aircraft, Long Beach. He said, "Call back tomorrow and I'll have an answer, I hope."

He did. First remember we do not sail directly into the wind. Let's assume that we were sailing a 35° angle to the true wind, and a tacking angle from side to side of about 70°. Now, the helmsman could assume that in about an 11-knot breeze, the apparent wind angle displayed on the instrument would be about 21° because of "upwind correction" caused by the speed and resistance of the boat, the sails, the mast and all items on deck against the atmosphere and wind about 150 feet ahead of *KIALOA III*.

In simple terms, the pressure of the speed and mass of the boat against the mass of the air 150'
ahead of the boat shifted the wind angle by 3°-9° dependent upon boat speed—9 degrees in light
conditions and 3 degrees in heavier wind conditions.

This may not seem like a big issue to many, however, in the precision of ultimate sailing, it can
mean a great deal for the helmsman in maximizing the performance of the boat.

Brooks and Gatehouse modified their electronic instruments to accommodate our requirements and this information became a benefit to all in the ultra competitive sailing world.

After our second round of testing on Long Island Sound, we sailed to Miami to continue tweak-
ing things and trimming the flotation. We knew we still had much to learn but we were also reasonably prepared for *KIII*'s first regatta, the SORC. As always in yachting, there are a lot of nicknames
for boats and sailors, and soon enough, our new yacht was being called "the Ordinary White Boat."
It was meant to be ironic and contradictory, as there was nothing at all "ordinary" about *KIALOA
III*. We had a lot of fun with the name.

More than a hundred yachts from the U.S., Canada, Europe and South America had gathered
in South Florida for the 1975 running of the SORC, which was being contested under the contro-
versial IOR MKIIIA/FORA rule, which we previously addressed in Chapter 15. We won the Governor's Cup Race and scored top ten finishes (a second, sixth and eighth) in three other events. We
also had two poor races—a 21st and a 72nd—but given the old-age allowances, the Gulf Stream issue,
and the fact that we were sailing our first regatta, we were pleased and enthusiastic about the results.

Next up would be the 811-mile Miami-Montego Bay Race, *KIALOA III*'s first real offshore race.
We had familiarity with the course after our challenging sail against *Windward Passage* and *American Eagle* back in 1969, as well as our repeat visit in 1973. I always enjoyed reviewing the charts of
the Western Caribbean. You can imagine the caution and care Columbus and the other captains in
his small fleet—the *Nina*, *Pinta* and *Santa Maria*—must've taken as they approached this uncharted
area in 1492. Think of it; they knew nothing of the Gulf Stream, the tidal currents, the many rocks
and shoals, or the wind patterns, which in these waters include the occasional hurricane. Many
people who have not actually sailed this area might imagine that it's an easy place to voyage with
reasonably steady breeze. Based on what I've read and experienced, this is a misconception. The
conditions are always changeable—you see a lot of winds, hurricanes and currents.

A quick aside about Columbus: At a luncheon in Madrid in the 1970's with the King of Spain,
Juan Carlos, and some other Spanish friends, we learned quite a bit more about the lifetime of
Columbus' and his navigational prowess. Juan Carlos was a highly qualified racing sailor who frequently crewed on our *KIALOA*s. He recommended a book that really probed into the Columbus
background. I'd known that Columbus had been trained in the Portuguese school of navigation
under Prince Henry, but I never knew that he'd voyaged to Ireland, to the Nordic seas, Iceland and

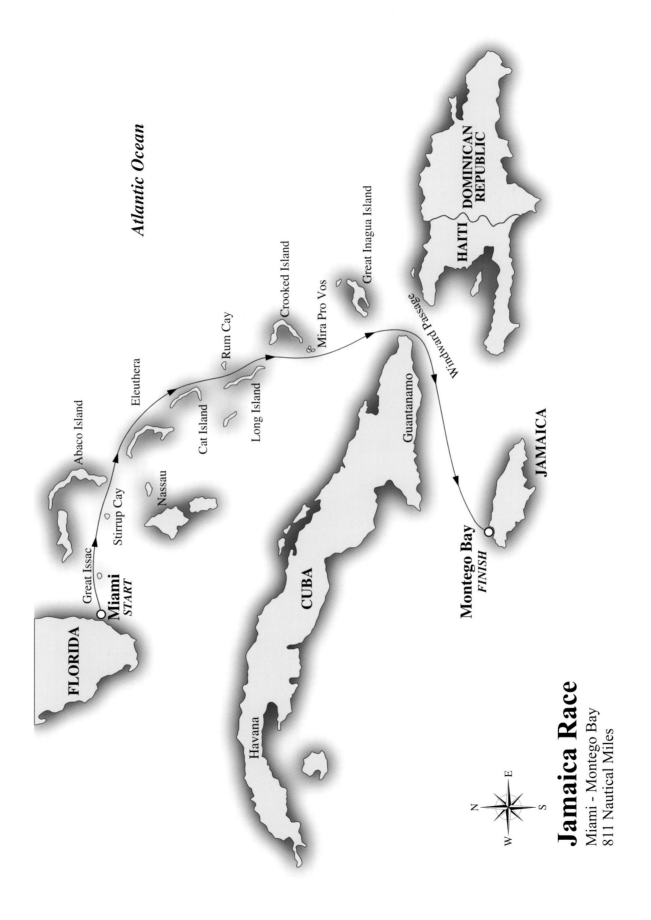

Atlantic Ocean

FLORIDA

Miami
START

Great Issac

Abaco Island

Stirrup Cay

Nassau

Eleuthera

Cat Island

Rum Cay

Long Island

Crooked Island

Mira Pro Vos

Great Inagua Island

Windward Passage

HAITI

DOMINICAN
REPUBLIC

CUBA

Havana

Guantanamo

JAMAICA

Montego Bay
FINISH

Jamaica Race
Miami - Montego Bay
811 Nautical Miles

N
E
S
W

The "Ordinary White Boat"   217

further west.

Columbus returned from his successful Caribbean voyage of discovery by sailing north, over the top of the North Atlantic high, and locking into the westerlies. This was in the late 1400s! Obviously he knew something about great circle navigation, global weather patterns and the Coriolis effect. Upon returning to Europe, he was roundly criticized for taking this route by Torquemada, and in a subsequent trip to the Caribbean, he was forced to sail home directly east, into the headwinds and contrary current.

I was, and remain, tremendously impressed by King Juan Carlos—as a man, a sailor and a friend, in recognition of his contributions to Spain and his forthright manner in discussing issues. And his wonderful partner, Queen Sofia, is a delightful lady with a tremendous sense of humor. The King and Queen were always welcome aboard *KIALOA*.

Back to the Jamaica Race: The course is challenging, taking the fleet through the shallow waters of the Eastern Bahamas, down to Cuba, through the Windward Passage and across the Caribbean to Montego Bay. In '69, we'd sailed close to Cuba while surfing under spinnaker in a strong blow,

but we were going so fast the patrol boat sent out to investigate couldn't keep up.

History repeated itself, to a degree, in the '75 event. We were again sailing under spinnaker along the south coast of Cuba, about three miles offshore and just west of Guantanamo, when a most unusual incident occurred. A Cuban bi-wing patrol airplane began buzzing *KIALOA III* at very low altitude. We confirmed our position—we were more than three miles offshore, outside of Cuba's legal jurisdiction—but it appeared the plane was trying to force us inside their territorial waters. Our crew thought the air show was great, and we all cheered, laughed and waved as we carried safely onward.

The biplane continued to circle, which was fine, until it banked sharply ahead of us and started flying directly toward *KIALOA III*'s billowing spinnaker. It was immediately apparent that the pilot knew little about aerodynamics, particularly the turbulence and disturbed air generated by a powerful spinnaker. When the plane hit this turbulence, it rolled up on a wing tip and barely cleared the waves ahead of *KIALOA III*. Fortunately for the pilot, it was his starboard wing tip, and he was able to roll the plane to port and clear *KIALOA III*. Of course, this brought another round of wild cheers, and we all joked about almost taking down a Cuban airplane with a most unlikely weapon—our spinnaker.

The rest of the race was uneventful, except when we crossed the finish line and discovered we'd earned a clean sweep: first to finish, first in class and first overall on corrected time. This was a testament to our speed, tactics and crew work, and a reinforcement that our efforts to bring *KIALOA III* to fruition had been worth all the hard work and effort. Well out of the Gulf Stream for most of the race, where its benefit to small boats wasn't a factor, we were truly able to evaluate the performance of the boat on a "level" playing field in variable conditions. It had been a fair, true test and *KIALOA III* passed with flying colors. The ensuing party and trophy presentation at the Montego Bay Yacht Club were excellent and we enjoyed visiting beautiful Jamaica, particularly its north shore.

Once the race was over, we enjoyed *KIALOA III*'s cruising capabilities. Our destination was Grand Cayman Island for a few days of sunbathing and scuba diving with our great friends, Lee and Patty Atwood. Lee was the president and chairman of North American Aviation and designed the P-51 Mustang fighter airplane that was so successful in World War II.

Two years later, we'd return with *KIALOA III* to again race from Miami to Jamaica. Though the conditions were different—the winds were much lighter—the results were the same. *KIALOA III* was again victorious—another clean sweep. It's interesting to note that we were successful in such different wind strengths. For comparison purposes, in 1975, our elapsed time was 92.23 hours; in '77, it was 100.07 hours.

For a racing sailor, comparing different sizes and types of yachts in relation to the weather experienced in specific events can be fascinating. This point was brought home recently with a note

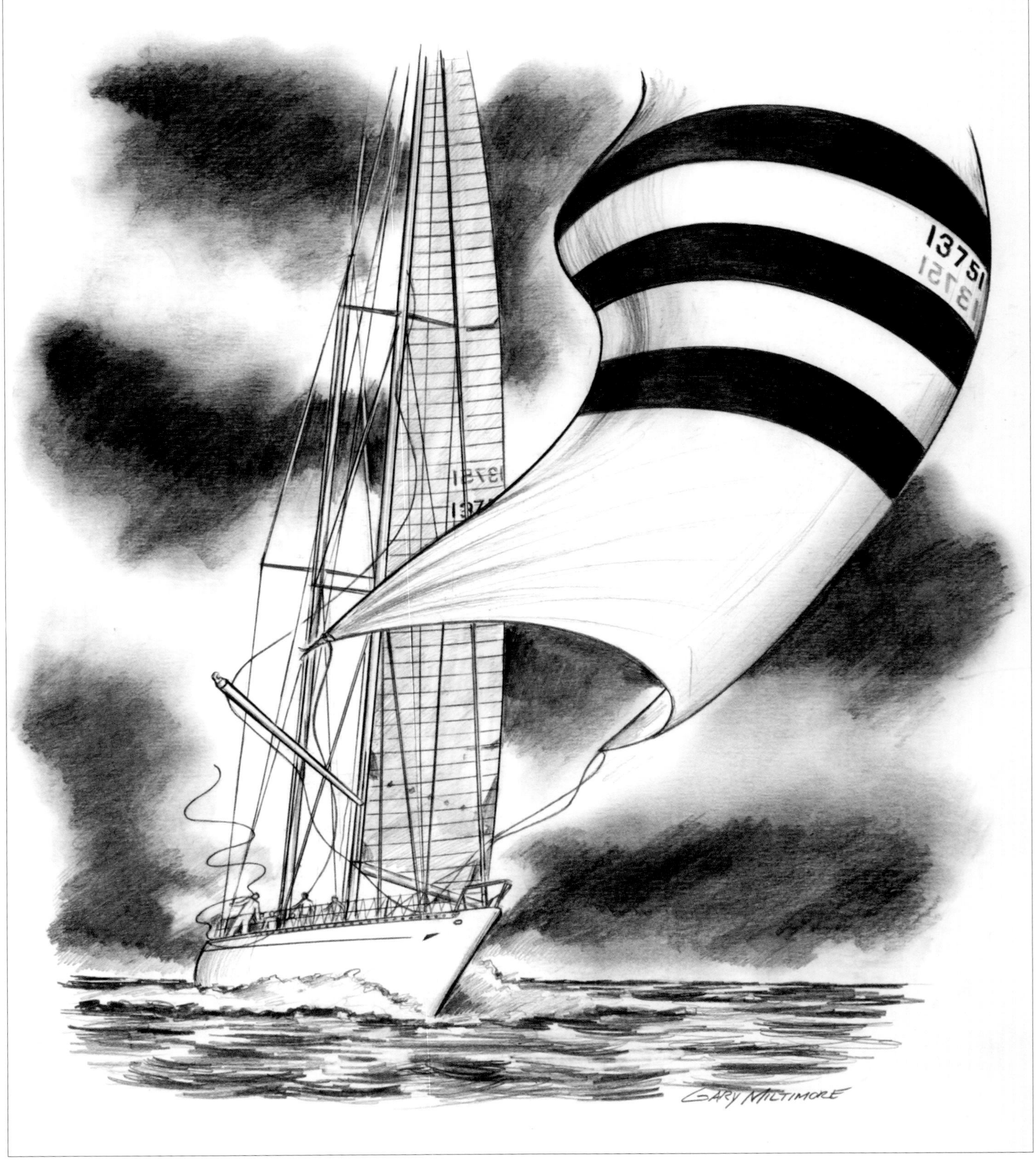
13751
13751
13751
1375
GARY MILTIMORE

from professional sailor Justin Clougher, who crewed aboard *KIALOA* before turning pro.

Justin sent a comparison of elapsed times of first-to-finish yachts in the Miami-Jamaica race from 1961 to 2003. And then he included *Rosebud*'s first-to-finish time in the 2009 race. *Rosebud*, a state-of-the-art contemporary yacht with water ballast, finished the 2009 race 33 hours faster than *KIALOA III*'s time in '75. Water-ballasted vessels like *Rosebud* carry a relatively small amount of lead ballast and induce stability, when needed, by pumping water in or out of water tanks. In this fashion, they save thousands of pounds of dead weight and can "dial in" their stability based on given conditions to maximize speed. Swing-keel yachts are also very versatile. Compared to fixed-keel yachts, both designs are akin to racing a jet fighter against a vintage, propeller-driven aircraft.

Still, the weather is perhaps the biggest variable. *Windward Passage*'s elapsed time difference between 1969 and 1971 was 31 hours. As mentioned, *KIALOA III* had a difference of 8 hours between 1975 and 1977. Seen in this light, *Rosebud*'s 33-hour "victory" isn't as impressive.

As you look down the list, you see boats that represented great leaps in yacht design: lightweight carbon-fiber flyers, Maxi IMS racers, and so on. But a race like Miami-Montego Bay can be a great equalizer. In recent years, Roy Disney's bigger, lighter, faster *Pyewacket* tackled the race to Jamaica, which should have played to her strengths as a downwind machine. But *Pyewacket* could not better the course record established by *Windward Passage*…in 1971.

This is what makes yacht racing such a challenging, rewarding sport. You can race the same course a hundred times and never see the exact same conditions. How we play the cards Mother Nature deals us is what's ultimately most important.

Our first races had given us plenty of reason for optimism. After Jamaica, it was time to return north to being preparations for the 1975 Transatlantic Race. We'd had no mishaps aboard *KIALOA III*, but unfortunately, that was about to change.

The almost 200-mile Block Island Race is perhaps the biggest annual event on Long Island Sound. The course is basically a leg out and around Block Island, then back to the finish line off the Stamford Yacht Club. For 1975, the race was conducted under storm warnings, and the breeze filled in appropriately.

In the latter stages of the race, *KIALOA III* had opened up a substantial lead, and we were up the Sound under spinnaker enjoying a terrific downhill run with all sails flying. Because we were so far ahead, we decided to sail conservatively and doused our 2.2-ounce full-sized spinnaker as well as the shooter and the mizzen spinnaker staysail, replacing them with our heavier and smaller storm chute.

With only 15 miles to the finish line in a huge puff of wind, there was a loud explosion; the shackle at the end of the 3/8th-inch wire after guy, which helps control the spinnaker pole, had blown up. The wire arched high above the deck like an uncoiled snake and then came slicing down, where it hit Bruce Kendell in the head three forceful times. Luckily, he was surrounded by able sailors who kept him from falling overboard. But Bruce was in great pain.

We dropped the spinnaker while our navigator got on the radio and called for assistance. Fortunately, a powerboat was nearby and quickly had Bruce on the way to the hospital, where he spent three days. Bruce quickly recovered in time to assume his duties as deck boss and starboard watch captain on the race to England. We were all very lucky, even though we regretted having to retire from what was almost assuredly a victory in the '75 Block Island Race.

Of course, we didn't want history to repeat itself, for safety's sake and for competitive reasons. So, the crew had a chance to discuss changes and together we came up with a solution. On each clew of the spinnaker, we attached a wire after guy and a 5/8th-inch Dacron trimming sheet. When the wire was in use to control the spinnaker pole, we didn't use the "lazy" Dacron sheet, which was draped over the after guy between the spinnaker pole and the turning block on the deck. It worked, and added an extra sense of security as we made our final preparations to once again tackle the Atlantic Ocean.

KIALOA III Results: First Five Major Races

	1st to Finish	Class	Overall
Nassau Cup (day race)	1	1	1
Jamaica Race (811 miles)	1	1	1
Annapolis-Newport (645 miles)	1	2	2
Edlu Cup (day race)	1	1	2
Block Island Race (186 miles)	Crew injured – withdrew		

The Early Days of *KIALOA III*:
Thoughts on Success, Danger and Motivation

In earlier chapters I've described how my brother Walter and I, two Depression-era kids in the 1920s and 1930s, set out to find a future. Many outstanding people motivated us and helped us realize our potential.

As I built a business, I found it essential to develop techniques to motivate my associates. I asked for and tried their ideas; gave them broader responsibility and authority; and requested their input on how to create new opportunities. It was a great and mutual success. As a result, I gained more free time for other activities.

I was fascinated by the history of exploration and sailing, and once I was exposed to it, I realized that it was wonderfully technical sport that I might really enjoy. Sailing seemed a natural extension of my activities. I was fully motivated and gained much knowledge from designers and competitors, and again, by asking my crew for their ideas. Through their active participation in the decision-making process, they became more active and capable sailors.

As in business, and much of life, focus is essential to victory. We would have our crew work together to develop individual and collective focus for every maneuver.

For example, in a given regatta the day's onboard focus might be a 25-mile afternoon race. Say you're beaten to the finish line by two boat lengths. Over that distance, in terms of sheer speed, what is the equivalent of two boat lengths? It's a simple equation: only 0.01 knots. Now could we have eked out another 0.01 knots of boat speed? We'd pose that question to the crew, and the input was instructive and valuable. Everyone agreed: "We could have done that."

Aboard *KIALOA*, we didn't pay our crewmen. They had to be accomplished in some other walk of life, not as professional sailors. We did have many recent college graduates sail with us, who had "temporarily deferred" an ongoing career. We let them know—as we did with all our crew—that they could sail with us as long as they were making defined progress in making and fulfilling a plan for their future. In the meantime, we welcomed their input and ideas on how to improve our performance and results. We'd try them in practice. Some were great, some didn't work out—just like my ideas. But the very process was productive and inclusive, and in the end, the consistently good results spoke for themselves.

We've followed our crew's post-*KIALOA* journeys and careers, which have been outstanding. Their many successes have been our rewards.

18

It was 1975, the first year for *KIALOA III* and our third race across the Atlantic by a *KIALOA*, a race full of many surprises. We were the overall victor in a race six years earlier to Ireland (the homeland of our Kilroy family) and we wished to be a two-time victor in this 1975 race across the Atlantic to the NAB tower off the Isle of Wight in the English Channel. In one way we were, and in another we were not.

If the true course distance, 2931 miles, had been used as the handicap distance, *KIALOA III* would have been a decisive victor. If a course 229 miles longer was used, we were almost the victor but not quite; we were blocked from a two-time Transatlantic victory.

We also call the readers' attention to a very special chart log, painted daily at sea, in the stormiest of conditions by our artist sailor, Gary Miltimore, an amazing performance in the roughest of conditions.

Read the story and make your own decision.

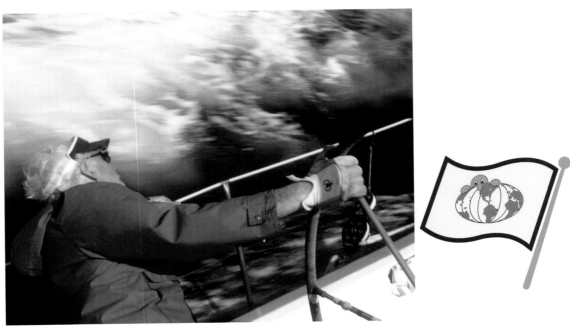

Our captain in lighter conditions before the storm.

Dancing with Amy
KIALOA III *and the 1975 Transatlantic Race*

Six years after *KIALOA II*'s triumphant performance in the 1969 Transatlantic Race to Cork, Ireland, in honor of the 250th anniversary of the Royal Cork Yacht Club, the *KIALOA III* crew was ready to test themselves once again in the North Atlantic. We all knew it would be a wonderful tribute to our ongoing campaigns if we could win "back-to-back" races across the rigorous Atlantic Ocean.

Ultimately, we would face two unanticipated challenges in the 1975 Transatlantic Race from Newport, Rhode Island to England's Isle of Wight. One would come from the weather, specifically a tropical disturbance called "Amy." The other would come from the New York Yacht Club race committee in charge of the event. Once again, the issue would be over handicaps and course distances. The handicap course distance for the race would be 3,160 miles, some 229 miles longer than the actual distance sailed, which was 2,931 miles.

The longer figure was quoted in the Notice of Race issued on May 1, 1975. An accompanying letter from the chairman of the race committee included this amendment. Basically it said that the 3,160-mile distance was included "for informational purposes" only, and that the *actual distance* could not be calculated until Point Alpha, a mark on the course, was established.

As in the 1969 race, Point Alpha was a waypoint in the North Atlantic that marked the southern limit of the icebergs, and was added to the course to keep yachts from sailing too far north and into the ice. The U.S. Coast Guard was responsible for determining the coordinates for Point Alpha, which they couldn't do until the last possible moment, when they knew how the ice was moving that season. Once they had that information, they pinpointed Point Alpha and passed the information to the race committee. The revised course was 2,931 miles.

At the skipper's meeting the morning before the start, as is usually the case, the race committee briefed the competitors on the weather, Point Alpha, the course distance, the handicap rules, and other related matters to the running of the race. They were forthcoming about Amy, a tropical storm that could be upgraded to a hurricane, which appeared to be in a stationary position south of the racecourse. However, they didn't voluntarily address the matter of the course distance as originally published and then amended after determining the position of Point Alpha.

On behalf of both *KIALOA III* and the racing fleet, I asked the committee chairman to define the course distance. His reply was that the scoring would be based on the 3,160-mile course originally published. This was a direct contradiction to the amendment he'd referred to in his original, accompanying letter to the Notice of Race.

We asked the chairman how it was possible to score a race at a distance that was about 8% longer than what the fleet would actually sail. The rather vague response was "weather fronts come from the west, which gives the bigger yachts the opportunity to stay in the weather fronts longer than the smaller yachts."

From our repeated experiences in the Transpac Race, we knew this was contrary to the facts. Boats in the back of the fleet always get the new wind first, and use it to make gains on the boats ahead. And again, based on speed differentials, the bigger boats ahead are often sailing in entirely different weather conditions. In any event, we asked the race committee to again review their speculative decision and advise a more appropriate handicap course mileage; they said they would do so and that the fleet would be advised by radio at the daily roll call or upon finish of the race.

Everyone assumed that the race committee had made a commitment they would stand by. Once underway, each boat would be obliged to radio their position so it was clear everyone would hear the race committee's decisions and updates. Because there was such a wide discrepancy among the boats in the fleet, which would spread out rapidly over the course of the event, relay vessels were appointed to pass along information to boats that were out of radio range. *KIALOA III* was the radio relay vessel for the front of the fleet.

Each day at roll call we would ask for the decision on course distance. Every day, there was no response. We were duly concerned. The 229-miles in question represented more than a full day of sailing for many of the smaller yachts. It was a significant number. For much of the race, this open-ended matter was very much in the back of our minds. But we also had a race to sail, and that became our overriding focus. And before all was said and done, Amy would also play an important role in the voyage.

The race started in a very light, 5-8 knot breeze at 1130 on June 29, 1975. For the first twelve hours we made little progress, but around midnight, both the fog and the wind rolled in. As the breeze rose from 19 to 26 knots, right on the button, the seas started to build and we made several sail changes in response. The log shows that we registered 160 miles over the first 24-hours.

On Day 2, still thrashing to windward, the breeze increased to 40-45 knots. Amy, whose status was wavering between a tropical storm and a hurricane, had suddenly become very active. *KIALOA*

III was to the north of the depression, and we knew that Amy would shadow us and then slowly cross our path as she followed the Gulf Stream to the north-northeast.

The third night was very rough. Sailing on port tack, we had *KIALOA III* fully reefed with our smallest headsail, the storm forestaysail, set on the inner forestay. It was a wild ride, but thanks to our excellent helmsmen and crew, we were always in control. At all times we had two capable drivers on station in the cockpit, one actually steering and the other calling waves or ready to lend a hand when necessary. When changing drivers—which in heavy weather we do about every 45 minutes—this routine also makes the transition much smoother. It may sound silly, but when driving in a serious seaway, I customarily sing what I think is an appropriate song; it helps me stay in rhythm with the conditions.

At that pre-race briefing, the meteorologists had said Amy was stalled and would be "no problem." That was then. Now, Amy was proving to be problematic for everyone. Aboard *KIALOA III*, the brunt of Amy's blow tore the boat's 29-foot spinnaker pole, which had been secured to the weather foredeck by strong aluminum fittings, off the deck and into the air. In the process, it stripped off the row of stanchions to starboard as well as all the safety lines. Luckily, it missed the crew as it went flying into the sea. This was unfortunate, but nobody was hurt and we still had our port spinnaker pole as reinforcement.

Besides, we now had a more serious issue in the continuously building seas. A bad leak was filling the boat with water at an alarming rate, even though our manual and electric pumps were hard at work. To address this situation, we had to run off before the wind to reduce our 30-35 degree heel and level the boat so we could pump the water out. It took about two hours before the interior was dry and we could resume racing on our proper heading.

After a thorough inspection, we'd found the leak in the lazarette under the cockpit, one of the tiniest, most compact spaces on the boat, where the mizzen staysails and other light sailing gear were stored. In this small, rough space, a couple of crew had to squeeze in and move sails, life-saving gear and other items to discover and repair the leak. It turned out to be a simple problem; one of the hoses linked to a through-hull fitting for the engine's exhaust system had come loose—probably due to gear being stashed or removed—and the related pump was re-circulating water that was already in the bilge. Once the hose was re-fitted and clamped tightly with stainless-steel hose clamps, the problem was solved once and for all.

But, as anticipated, Amy continued to drift to the northeast, fueled by the warm Gulf Stream. Hoping to find smoother seas, we tacked *KIALOA III* to starboard. In a 60-knot gust, we watched the Omega navigation antenna fly off the afterdeck. Still, even though the seas were heavy and confused, *KIALOA III* was sailing well. But the ride was wicked, the crew was in safety harnesses at all times on deck, and the only way to move around was on hands and knees.

Ironically, one of the biggest challenges was simply changing watches, and finding a secure place to sleep in the violent seaway as *KIALOA III* leapt off one wave and went crashing into another. Simply taking off sea boots, oilskins and heavy clothing took several minutes while desperately holding on. We'd gone to our storm watch system—three hours on and off at night, four hours on and off during daylight hours—and no one was allowed to sleep in their on-deck foul-weather gear.

By the end of the third day, we'd sailed 498 miles. But on Day 4, as we sailed into cooler waters and weather, the wind moved aft and moderated and we had our first good day of reaching under our big headsails and spinnakers, recording a 221-mile day. Over the next several days, the weather patterns continued to change, and we worked hard to maximize our speed in the varying conditions, dousing spinnakers, setting headsails, hoisting mizzen staysails, and on and on. It was hard work in falling temperatures, but great sailing.

The logbook through this stretch is filled with crew comments about the course distance, with pointed messages to the race committee. There was still no response about the amended course. But there were also excited passages about the high speeds we were notching in the downwind conditions, and other entries about drying out the wet gear and opening the boat up to ventilate the interior. In a related note, someone mentioned the excellent sleeping weather.

As we neared and passed Point Alpha, a busy Atlantic crossroads with lots of shipping and fishing traffic, visibility dropped to about a hundred yards. To offset the danger, we would make open calls on the ship's radio advising all parties of our position and the fact that we were competing in the Transatlantic Race to Cowes, England. We were always happy when ships in the area would advise us of their positions in response.

At one point, the skipper of a supertanker hailed us. "Hello, *KIALOA*," he said, and then asked, "How can you be so exact on your navigational coordinates?" We told him about the electronic navigational equipment we had on board, and he replied, "We are many times bigger than you, carrying huge amounts of oil and we have nothing like your electronic navigational equipment."

"Steer more to the south, just in case you might be near to our course," I said. "Keep in touch!" he replied.

"Not too close!" I concluded.

Our course was excellent—we were steering right down the optimum track—and we were making good speed...210 miles one day, 234 the next. Now the water was slightly warmer, the sun was shining and we had a bit more breeze, allowing us to sail with what we called our "Sydney Opera House" sail plan: main spinnaker, shooter, mizzen, spinnaker staysail, good speed, sunshine and warmer sea water.

On July 9th, however, the wind moved forward and we were once again close-hauled, making only 182 miles after numerous sail changes. The next day, close reaching in 10-20 knots of breeze with an apparent wind angle between 45-60 degrees—and with the crew constantly trimming to maximize speeds—we were back over two-hundred miles with a roughly 213-mile day.

For the '75 Transatlantic Race, we sailed with a crew of sixteen. There were seven crew to each watch, with the cook and navigator "floating" between the two and available to help on deck if needed. Some might think, with great sailing conditions, that there was little to do besides relax, sunbathe, read or sleep. That was never the case.

For the on-watch crew, there was always something happening: inspecting the mast and all gear; sail changes; packing sails; resetting and inspecting halyards; servicing mechanical equipment; cleaning the decks and interior; and making sure everything was ready for the next maneuver, whatever that might be.

When racing, we were always *racing*, and by that I mean we were pushing the boat as hard as we could and constantly undertaking maneuvers at racing speed. Two or three crewmembers were ready at all times to instantly trim the headsails and spinnakers. One was always on the mainsheet, ready to trim the main. Another was always minding the mizzen, and standing by to assist the helmsman: each watch had three assigned drivers. My own duties, in addition to my role as *KIALOA III's* captain and primary helmsman on the port watch, was "crew boss" and back-up navigator.

Our "permanent crew," which included Bruce Kendell and two other sailors, were responsible for mechanical systems, the diesel engine and generator, battery charging and power consumption, and general maintenance, with assistance from the rest of the crew. You need to think of a yacht like *KIALOA III* as an isolated, self-sufficient entity—a vibrant, active habitat, like a space module—that always must be prepared for strenuous duty under rigorous and even dangerous conditions.

July 11th and 12th brought more shifty winds and many more sail changes: fourteen in one nineteen-hour stretch. This was followed by beautiful sunshine and a delightful beam reach in 18 knots of wind. In the middle of the night we saw several trawlers sailing north to their fishing grounds. They hailed us on the radio, requested our identity, and wished us "good luck" for the remainder of our voyage.

As we approached Lizard's Head along England's south coast, the end of the race was drawing near. Once in the English Channel, we would have another 135 miles to the finish line, the "NAB Tower" off Cowes on the Isle of Wight. Conditions were superb: an excellent reaching breeze coupled with a fair tide.

We maintained an offshore heading for a few extra miles to avoid some nasty head currents. Once the current eased, we sailed in closer to shore. Early on the morning of July 14th, we set a spinnaker and other running sails and enjoyed a great downwind sail. We were surfing the waves and earning "free" miles thanks to the fair current. The entire crew was on deck, the sails were always perfectly trimmed, there was spray flying and the beautiful coastline was flying by. We even had a visitor, a little bird that flew into the cockpit and was treated to a bit of water and food in a little

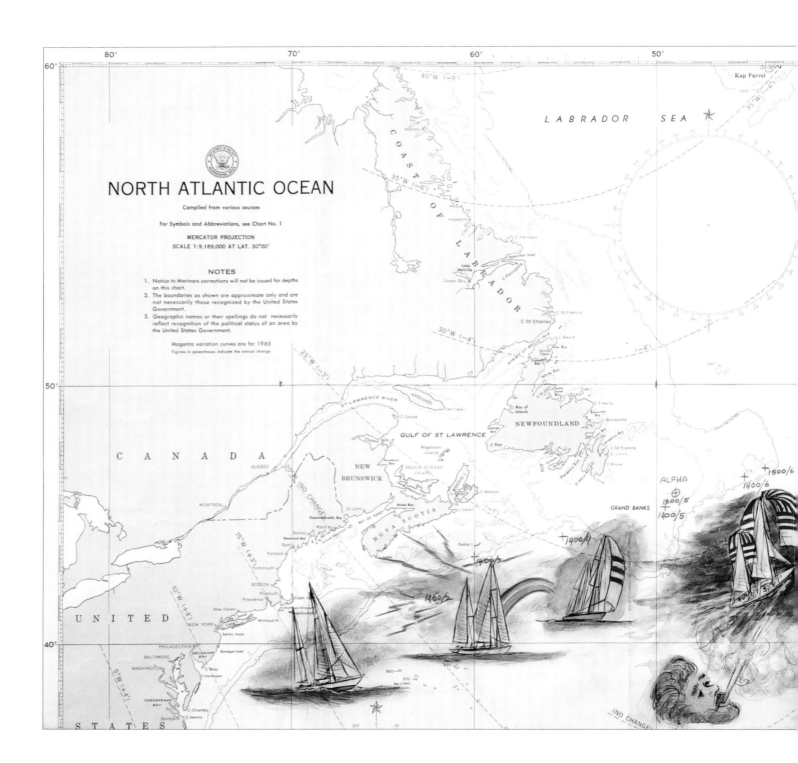

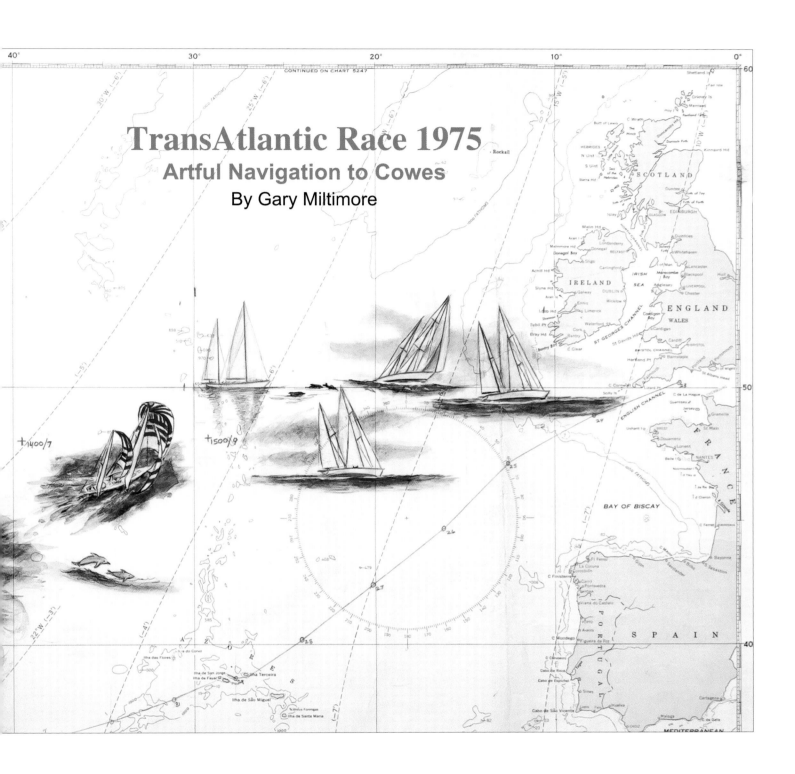

TransAtlantic Race 1975
Artful Navigation to Cowes
By Gary Miltimore

storage area out of the way. He was with us almost a whole day before flying off to England. What a great sail to the finish line.

We carried the chute right up to the NAB Tower, surfing and accelerating on each wave at about 14 knots, with every *KIALOA* crewmember at his station. With one final, perfectly executed, photographic jibe, we crossed the finish line first on elapsed time after a voyage of 14 days, 57 minutes, 12 seconds. Over the 2,931-mile course, we'd averaged 8.233 knots. Considering our early "dance" with Amy, it was excellent time. To cap it all off, we were all very pleased to receive a radio call from a fellow sailor named Prince Charles, extending his congratulations.

Despite the "additional" 229 miles we'd sailed, we knew a corrected-time victory was also a possibility. And we were confident that the race committee would reject the added mileage penalty once they'd reviewed the facts, as they promised to do. We were aware that the racing rules required a protest to be filed within 24 hours of a yacht's finish, but since the race committee had not yet announced their decision, there was nothing specific to protest. And again, we still felt that reason and logic were on our side. As more and more time went by, it appeared that we would be the winner under the normal distance handicap.

We'd had a wonderful reception after our arrival with our wives, family and friends at the event's co-sponsor, the Royal Thames Yacht Club. But then we received some unsettling news. The race's U.S. partner, the New York Yacht Club, ruled that there would be no change in the handicap mileage. Based on the 3,160-mile racecourse, the corrected-time winner was Ted Hood's *Robin II*, the smallest boat in the fleet, eking out victory over *KIALOA III* by just 1.05 hours. Had the actual distance been used, *KIALOA III* would've won on handicap, as well as elapsed time, by 7.06 hours.

We immediately filed a protest that was denied because it wasn't filed within 24 hours after the finish. At that juncture we filed an appeal and were advised that any appeal would not be heard until later in the year, which meant that I would be required to return to England or have legal representation.

We knew who the real winner was, as did the rest of the fleet and our friends on *Robin II*. The only thing missing was *KIALOA III*'s name engraved on the trophy. Reluctantly, we dropped the appeal.

KIALOA III *High Speed Downwind Sailing*

A Transatlantic Retrospective by Terry Lalonde

Y ou've heard my "official" take on *KIALOA III*'s experience in the 1975 Transatlantic
Race. What follows is Terry Lalonde's personal account—the viewpoint of one of our
outstanding amateur crewmembers. Choose whatever version you prefer.

"There is a tide in the affairs of men,
Which, taken at the flood, leads on to fortune..."
     from *Julius Caesar* by William Shakespeare

From the start at Brenton Reef Light—a temporary looking, spindly-legged structure
sticking awkwardly out of the water—the yacht did not have to go far before being swal-
lowed in an indistinguishable zone; soon, the land was gone.

In about three knots of wind, we ended up going to a drifter, the lightest of headsails.
Before long, and because we were the "scratch" boat, fastest per our handicap rating, we had
lost sight of the others in the race. Were you to look aft, all you would see was our wake
stretching in a straight line across the dull leaden grayness of the sea, disappearing into the
blankness where the horizon would have been.

The gentleness of this start would mask the fact that this endeavor would be overly
weighted on the experience aspect…as in an experience of a lifetime. Writing from the
perspective of thirty years since these events one might ask, "Why record it now?" Because,
it was a distinctive period of yacht racing that has not been accurately nor completely
recorded.

Every Maxi yacht racer starts a distance race with the hope of setting a record. The
record for the Transatlantic Race is a particularly renowned accomplishment. It had been
set as the culmination of numerous races across the Atlantic, the first of which was held in
1866. *KIALOA III*, or *KIII*, as the crew calls her, was known for having one of the best crews,
but no one was paid to participate, apart from the maintenance and delivery crew, and the
skipper and a deck hand.

At the skipper's meeting the race committee said, "There is a low off Hatteras…it will
move south and you will have a cakewalk." However, on June 26th before the start of the race,
and unbeknownst to the *KIALOA* crew, "the low" had a different idea. It planned to become
another race participant. It had begun earlier to take shape just north of the western Bahamas.
She was practicing her routine, strengthening and perfecting her moves. Her name was Amy,

and she was created to test *KIALOA*'s construction as well as the crew's fortitude.

Amy would ebb and flow in strength and approach, but not consistently remain above the threshold of hurricane status. This meant she had top wind speeds of just over 70 mph, and she happened to be the first hurricane of the season. In that she never made shore and was not, therefore, overly destructive, her name has not been retired and at some point in time some other mariners are likely to experience her namesake's wrath. We were to see wind strengths of her hurricane status first hand. She needed the nutrition of the Gulf Stream to keep her strength, and thus followed it north. By the 28th, one day before the start of the race, she had developed gale force winds, and that night as she skirted the North Carolina outer banks, she turned sharply east.

On the 29th, the start day for the Transatlantic Yacht Race from Newport, Road Island to Cowes, England, Amy was lingering to the south as if waiting for the start flag. She was idling at latitude 33°80' and longitude 71°80', somewhat holding position, while we started at roughly latitude 41°27' and longitude 71°16'. But Amy was building her strength and began riding the Gulf Stream like a military aircraft flying an intercept, arching its path so as to meet and test us in the worst of possible en route locations. From this position she meandered northeastward for three days, toying with us, lurking, awaiting a match with *KIALOA* in order to test the boat and the crew. The thrust of the storm was such, that with her counterclockwise rotation, as she moved north and east in front of us, we were forced to steer ever higher, as in these conditions we could only point about 35 to 40 degrees off the wind. The alternative would have been to tack, which would put us decidedly away from our course. There were two smaller-slower competitors, being farther behind and positioned differently in respect to Amy's winds, who were able to bear off to the south, and sail ultimately in more favorable winds. One of these was the yacht *Robin*, the smallest yacht in the race. She "kept getting headed southeast…and tacked to the northwest for about 5 hours, then tacked back," said Lee van Gamert, the yacht's skipper. By the next morning the breeze had started backing and she was able to start reaching, early on going to a jib top.

It was not long before we realized what we were in for…a hell of a ride, or perhaps the ride from Hell. The weather built rapidly. We soon had a sustained 30 knots of breeze with gusts much above that figure. The sea began to build and take on an awkward, confused appearance. It reminded me of Bass Straight, the body of water separating Tasmania from the rest of Australia; a narrow venturi of water, driven erratic by the similar shallowness, currents and strong winds, prone to developing steep waves of an irregular nature. The sea became most uncomfortable.

KIALOA, new to the world, was like a charging horse prepared to look death in the eye, unafraid to tuck and slam her head meaningfully into a counter charging sea. She would do so with a great shudder felt from stem to stern, and gouging out a great abundance of water, which as the bow came tossing up, would be thrown down the deck in a torrent of angry surf, making it all but impossible to go forward. This was repeated time and again like a creature exchanging blows with an opponent, one concussion after another. Night brought a new element as we were unable to see the building fury of the sea. There is a different form of trepidation that develops when one knows what is out there but unable to see it. In this blackness, white crests rolled down towards us like some marching piebald walls about to take our measure. Occasionally after a deep fall and slam, bow lights would disappear for what seemed an interminable length of time as the bow struggled to rid itself of tons of foaming liquid.

The log entry at 0510 on July the 1st in Jim's precise handwriting states "Stb Spinn Pole Missing…" In only 1 and ¾ days, we had begun to break apart… Ordinarily there would have been gravity associated with an expensive and pertinent piece of equipment going astray, but under the current situation it became a jousting point between the two watches, each claiming the other watch had lost the pole during their respective stewardship.

~~~~~~~~~~

The man leading the efforts to make fun of the loss of the spinnaker pole was Jim Kilroy, which is interesting in that it would seem he had the most to lose by its absence. John B. Kilroy, known as Jim to all his friends, was the captain, owner, creator, patriarch, organizer and prime mover for all the *KIALOA*s. He is one of the most amazing people that you could wish to know. What men believe about themselves has a great deal to do with determining the success or failure of their efforts in the vicissitudes and opportunities of life. "Whether you think you can or think you can't, you're right," said Henry Ford. Jim always knew he could and surrounded himself with those who thought they could also, and had little time for those who thought they couldn't.

A captain of ships or industry, and Jim was both, must at the same moment be empathetic and decisive. He exhibited an incredible ability to listen to all opinions and to assimilate the inputs, reorganize them, analyze, and then recast them as his own ideas either in total or as a modification to an original premise he might have had. Jim always listened to everyone, and could rapidly access the viability of outside offerings.

A captain must also be the leader and manager of the crew. The speed of the leader is the speed of the gang. Jim could be hard to keep up with at times. You cannot be around someone as successful in so many facets of life, one who has developed distinct formulae for life's puzzles and challenges, without adapting or learning some of these traits.

To be competitive in business and yacht racing one knows winning is the reward, second is not an option. One must have a very accurate and realistic assessment of the competition and the task at hand. *KIALOA*'s preparation had begun years in advance through untold other races and experiences. Her design, engineering, construction, outfitting and crew had been painstakingly assessed and guided. This is the job of a captain/leader in any undertaking. Jim possesses unparalleled focus, drive and energy to attain these results.

Jim confided that when at the helm the waves were like vertical walls, and the yacht would climb their face at an acute angle. He fantasized the boat might be pitched over backwards. To rid himself of this vision, he would sing to himself and pretend to be dodging potholes in a highway. I, however, whilst on the helm would swear in the most contemptible manner each time I was slammed into the wheel when the yacht fell off one of these walls.

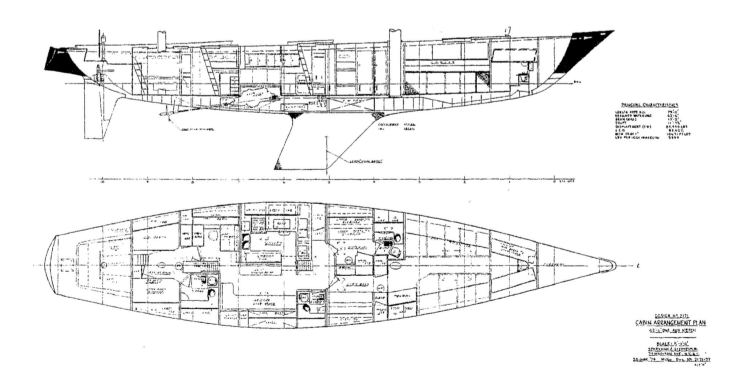

The wind began to peak at around 70 knots steady on the anemometer with outbursts whose sheer intensity would make the boat shudder as if momentarily shirking at the thought of it all. Communication became difficult as one had to rely on fragments of discourse as sentences and even words were shredded by the competing gale. The crew all wore safety harnesses that were clipped on to some secure bit of the yacht.

The sea is notoriously unforgiving. Never get presumptuous at sea, she will set you straight and you will be in store for a sobering lesson. Mankind has an innate self-misconception: the ability to think much more of its own significance than an impartial third party observation would support. This inflated self-assessment or overestimate of our significance and ourselves can be rapidly set straight by witnessing nature in its full force and glory. We are but "a poor player that struts and frets his hour upon the stage and then is heard no more …" Witness at sea level the truculence of a hurricane, and you will become properly adjusted as to the scale of your significance.

KIALOA was not only one of the world's fastest racing sailboats, but a fine yacht, richly detailed in warm woods and thoughtfully laid out below decks. From the helmsman's cockpit there was a hatch and a steep staircase to the master stateroom, which was comprised of an upper double berth to port and on starboard both lower and upper berths. There was a head forward on the starboard side of this stateroom that included a shower. On the port side of the head area there was a companionway that included a complete and modern navigator's stateroom. Just forward of this was the main salon containing the primary hatchway. The galley was on the port side with a center console. To starboard was a comfortable settee and dining area, above which was the cook's bunk…er sarcophagus (more on this later). Moving forward from the main salon there was another hatchway, and standing at the base of which there was a stateroom to the port with separate head and a companion way and head to starboard leading to the fore-peak area. This companionway could be closed off to create another stateroom. Ahead of this area were a small workstation and the sail locker with hatch to pass sails up onto the foredeck.

We were also fortunate that *KIALOA III* was beautiful, as a yacht must look proper. She had exquisite lines and to this day turns every head in any harbor she enters. At the time, who knew this was to become one of the most famous ocean-racing yachts…and crews. For example I can think of no other racing yacht that has had a drink invented by, and named after, her. The recipe for a "Kialoa" can be found in almost any good bartender's guide. I am sure this is because of the racing history of the yacht and not the party behavior of the crew…it must be.

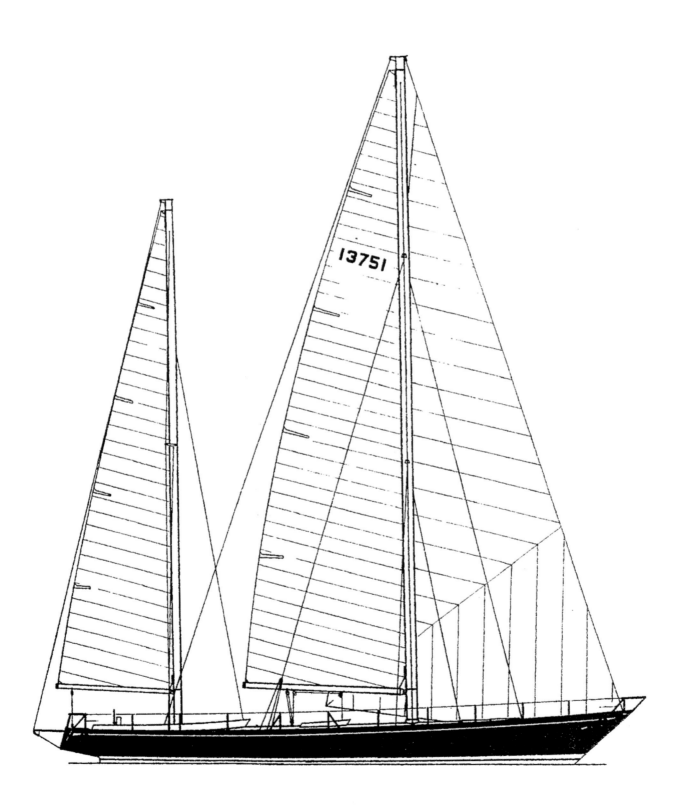

13751

No one was in a mood to drink "Kialoas" even though maneuvering below decks would seem serene in comparison to the cacophony of the main deck. That was until one of the charging walls of water would stop the boat dead, or the ocean would disappear from under the entire front half of the hull causing her to plummet and slam against the pit thus created. One would be driven to his knees, it being impossible to stand against the gravity force given off by such acceleration followed by an abrupt stop. This was made so much worse by having to negotiate in a world turned forty-five degrees to the horizon; any movement required grasping hand over hand the overhead rails while using a butting motion with your body along the bulkhead in the companionway in order to move.

The interior world was half deck, half wall…and everything wet…very wet and slippery. Moving forward past the navigator's stateroom and reaching the main saloon, the bulkhead ended, which required supporting all your weight by hanging on to the overhead rails and what cabinetry or anything else you could grab. The trick was to time a forward motion to throw your body towards the settee, most likely to be stopped by bracing against a couple of shipmates. The one in the most leeward position had to suffer the weight of those above him. At meals, food had to be passed about from hand to hand. Although there were gimbaled sections to the table, it was impossible to keep the food in place. Everyone had to curl up in some manner, bracing against anything available, and with food in lap, pocket, between the legs or some other contortionist cranny, eat like so many timid little rodents in their warren.

On a night watch, I was dressed and had worked my way forward to get a drink of water before climbing to the deck. In the dim watch-change lights of the interior, I noticed Nick Hilton, who was forward in the starboard stateroom, using gray duct tape to secure garbage bags onto his feet in preparation for going on watch. It seems this "ultimate sailor" had neglected to bring his boots, and his feet being of Herculean proportions, there were no others that would fit. Necessity had prevailed and he was improvising so as to keep his feet warm and dry. In keeping with absolute protocol, he did take considerable ribbing for this, which brought repeat smiles to everyone's faces.

I had been wise enough, I thought, to request the lower starboard bunk in the aft stateroom. This decision was made having consulted the North Atlantic wind rose charts for our time of year so as to determine which would be the favorable board or tack. For the majority of the trip this would mean not having to climb awkwardly upward to get into the bunk, and once there, having to sleep against a hard bunk board. In the era of great sailing ships, the trip from England to India would be made in the preferred, and more expensive, format of port-outbound and starboard-home from which we get the word posh. In this lower bunk position, one could better nestle for purposes of sleeping or reading. However, were a plumb bob hung from the overhead whilst on the wind to port, it would pass through this bunk and the drawer under the bunk, mine, as being the lowest level of the yacht. Thus it was a great place to collect water.

We had been pounded and exposed to a constant shower of water for three days, and clothing was soaked through and through. Due to the cold temperatures and submersing tendency of the yacht, all the hatches were kept well-secured, thus below decks was a veritable steam room of moisture without the heating element. Every three or four hours, the watches would exchange places, the off watch going below and bringing in a new round of water and soaked foul weather gear. The inside of the boat was dripping with condensation. The bunk blankets were wet, and it became normal to just crawl into a wet bunk to attempt any type of sleep. Just about the time I would drift off there was a "bink" on the forehead… too tired to care I would do nothing and would finally drift off again. "Bink!" A damnable drip of water would land on my forehead or face...a Chinese water torture… "All right I'll sign the papers…I confess!" Through necessity, it became a habit to tie a towel to the overhead handrails, thus catching the water, temporarily. Of course, this would allow only an hour or so sleep before the towel would get saturated; and it would start again…"bink." Out of the bunk, wring out the towel, tie it up, and jump back in before some violent motion of the yacht would put you on the cabin sole. I guess this was a just reward for such a well thought out plan for one's posh position.

By some quirk, one of several books I had with me was "Alive: The Story of the Andes Survivors" by Piers Paul Read. During the height the gale with its concomitant pounding and water dripping everywhere, I would burrow into my wet bunk, turn on the reading light and try for a respite in someone else's tragic adventure. It struck me as somewhat prophetic or ironic, yet humorous that I would be reading of others whose challenges seemed so much graver, and with such dire consequences. A true story, the book is about a 1973 plane crash in the Andes, where a young soccer team struggled for survival on a frozen peak. After ten weeks, they were rescued, but not before having to resort to cannibalism and other extremes to survive. Musing over the plight of their great endeavor put our adventure in better perspective. Furthermore, I felt much encouraged when Bruce Kendell reassured me that we had several weeks' worth of food on board.

Reading the book did draw some hypothetical parallels. The soccer team spent a lot of time contemplating imminent death. And though at times our little adventure would give one signs of the potential gravity of the situation, i.e. new and untested boat, truculent and changing weather etc., it never occurred to us, other than in a passing thought that life could end suddenly. Perhaps this was due to an underlying comfort that there always was a much greater plan for one's life. Lying in a soaking wet bunk, bouncing up and down, surrounded by sometimes thunderous noises created by opposing forces meeting so violently, did however make me wonder what my parents would have thought had they seen me… "He's really gone quite mad, you know!" This did bring a chuckle to my mind.

It was amongst this bedlam that Bruce had chosen to put a chart of the North Atlantic on the athwartships bulkhead, which runs across the yacht at the forward end of the main saloon. Upon this chart, he had marked our daily positions. Not one to put up with such a cold, clinical display of mere numbers and lines depicting our march across the sea, Gary Miltimore, the Artist, saw fit to illustrate on a daily basis our progress. The Artist, insouciant, incorrigible, full of a right brain innocence, was once described as having certain elements that the rest of the crew needed so as to enhance their own characters and become more whole. He never had an enemy. He is one of those souls who can go through life and befriend everyone, in whatever social status, without the least variation in approach or hint of adapting to a difference in cast or environment.

Having started this iconographic diary under the most adverse conditions, it was necessary for him to hold on to the overhead rails, hook one leg up and around the forward companion way bulkhead, wedge the other leg into the settee sofa and finally do his daily artwork with his free hand. In this manner his body was probably close to level with the horizon, but forty-five degrees to the interior of the yacht. This contorted stance was not unlike a gecko, which by means of suction cups stuck to some grossly angled wall. The fact that he found it necessary to twist his tongue outside his mouth, some times caressing his mustache, completed the reptilian visage.

During the height of the gale, his concentration and pen stroke would be interrupted or made to error by the jolting of the boat; this would entail an almost simultaneous expletive, which would resound throughout the interior. His efforts would lead to a great and anticipated daily enjoyment for the entire crew as it became a ritual to see how the previous day had been depicted. The Artist was a key and salubrious element of the crew. The strength of his soul and character are assured and demonstrated by the fact that, throughout the years, he has successfully managed to compete in the difficult world of supporting one's self and family by means of art alone. He has a well-justified reputation for paintings in oils and water colors, as well as graphic arts for racing yachts, all, as with his life, in a maritime theme. His subject matter for endeavors is favorably enhanced through experiences such as we had before us.

There are numerous routine functions of life that must be attended to regardless of the conditions, eating being one of them, though no one had a great appetite. Essential, unrecognized, and thankless is the job of cooking for seventeen hungry creatures. Cooking on a large yacht, at best, could be a stage for humorous venting or a means of sharing the camaraderie and the adventure. I have always questioned why someone would put up with this toil, but I was glad that someone did. It could turn wretched in a hurry. A yacht heeled heavily to one side, dripping with condensate, deck slippery with spilt food, the smell of various ingredients wafting around the nostrils would turn the galley into some great odoriferous pit. Bracing in the awkward-shaped stretch of a crippled yoga practitioner, trying to stir some bubbling cauldron of gruel with the boat taking a particularly hard slam, putting your efforts all over the deck would make one…well…swear. It would also make most cooks ill.

Bobby "Blue Eyes" Harris was a successful insurance broker, bon vivant, good natured and humorous man with a balding head, a little droll and always with the warmest of smiles and heart. And, of course, his enthusiastic, illuminating blue eyes rounded out his countenance quite well. In fact, his eyes were those of Santa Claus, and while one considers that concept, the realization comes that Bob was in many respects, visually and in demeanor, a Santa. He was also our cook, and prone to keeping all spirits high amongst the two watches, not that it was needed of course. You would slide into the settee for an evening meal and Bobby Blue Eyes would say, "You know you guys are my favorite watch. I'm not sure about those other guys, however." Of course this is exactly what he had said to the other watch a half-hour earlier and everyone knew it. It was Bob's way, always happy, always ready to act in a jocular manner.

It had gotten wretched. Early on, Bob became deathly ill—seasick. I remember going down below to see little more than his hooked proboscis protruding above the leeward bunk board. This was enough to permit the observation of a sea-foam, green pallor. He appeared motionless as in death, and the experience was as though one were visiting an open casket service for the cook. This lasted for days, as he was very sick, such that we were concerned. After the race and after his recovery, he was overheard to say, "That's it! I am selling everything related to the sea, including my Sabot!" It is enough to say that Bob did not enjoy this race.

But what to do? The crew was not in a particularly hungry state as the yacht had become so violent and unpredictable in the hurricane-created seas that keeping food down was an issue. Still, we had to have some sustenance. No one wanted to cook. Then, an improbable savior stepped forward—Richard.

Richard Colyear, the banker, was well-bred, well-schooled and affluent, and would have been an English aristocrat save for the lack of an accent, always proper in a very practiced sense. Either some of this came from, or was particularly beneficial to, his having to deal in that often ruthless world of high level finance, where there was a constant need to separate those certain charlatans from having access to your money, and where you had to keep those using your money on track and above board. This required a certain savoir-faire. However, it always seemed that Richard was on the verge of wanting to say, "Do you realize how hard it is to be Richard Colyear…being so proper all the time?" But Richard enjoyed the sailing and the crew, and I believe he enjoyed the lack of pretense in everything involving the crew. There was a truth and honesty about those on board that was not only on the surface, but went straight through to the core. This was no doubt refreshing for Richard, and a relaxing way of dropping his guard, to an extent. The crew liked Richard and he was accepted as a member. Furthermore, he made up one of the unique facets that gave character to the *KIALOA* crew.

Richard came up on deck after having finished the disdainful job of cooking and cleaning the galley. He had obviously cleaned himself, shaved, washed and combed his hair, something that none of us had done since leaving Newport and no easy task in these conditions. He, also, to the envy of all, wore a clean, dry, heavy-knit, expensive-looking white sweater. Being hot from all the work below, what he did not have was a top to his foul weather gear, just the bib overalls with braces. The only crew to smoke, he lit a cigarette, took one drag, which softly lit his dark curly hair and cleanly shaven face in an orange glow, when, with a bang, we slammed into a sea on the forward quarter. This sent a column of water arching up and over the weather lifelines and directly, as though through a funnel, onto Richard's head and down the flared opening of his overalls. Richard, with hair matted down his face, a half inch of his new cigarette between his fingers, and the rest at a right angle pointing, soaked, at the deck, maintained perfect aplomb, even though his overalls were full of water like some large, liquid, fat-man. In his absolutely unshakable manner and with perfect cadence to his elocution he said, "Well, you might have told me that would happen." The crew needed this, as it is a laugh we can still hear today upon those rare occasions when we get together.

On July 3rd, five days into our challenge, the log shows an entry that says "Steer no higher than 087 degrees magnetic to clear Sable Island." We were close to having to tack in order to clear Nova Scotia as Amy kept pushing us so far north.

Sable Island, a long wispy island looking like some giant protozoan organism, known for its wild horses and shipwrecks, is nothing more than a 20-mile long by 1-mile wide sand bar and shoal area. Since 1583, there have been over 350 recorded shipwrecks on this island, which has earned it the ignominious appellation the "Graveyard of the Atlantic." The ghosts of literally thousands of sailors lurk beneath the surface in this area. The Gulf Stream and Labrador Current converge at Sable and along the Grand Banks, causing a mix of strong and varying currents in the area. In addition, this brew of warm and cold water causes the habitual fog of this region, 125 days per year. The Grand Banks are a great crucible for storms because of these currents and the tracks that storms typically take, leading them to this area from their birthing grounds in the Caribbean, Great Lakes or off Cape Hatteras. In dense fog, one has to rely on the aptly named form of navigation known as "dead reckoning," whereby one keeps tallying track of the ship's speed and direction for navigational purposes. When the variables of strong current and fog are thrown into the equation, this form of navigation can be fraught with errors. The stacked bones beneath the surface duly record a history of these errors.

One could justifiably ask, "Why would you undertake such unheralded risks?" The answer is that it is about personal achievement and not for an audience or recognition. Being an inherently dangerous sport, racing a sailboat across an ocean is not for all, in fact probably for very few. Henry David Thoreau told us most people "live lives of quiet desperation." Most are never made aware of what they can do or what heights they can attain. First, one must accept that risks are a part of life; they are usually commensurate with the rewards. Along with having initiative, one must be willing to take some risks in order to advance beyond the norm in any endeavor.

~~~~~~~~~

Like the *KIALOA* crew, there are those who need to explore the limits of the real world, to experience the extremes in life and what it has to offer. It is not enough for them to read or hear of adventure, violence and tragedy, and then only to turn it aside. They must see it firsthand. Such experiences position these individuals to deal with the more mundane aspects of it all, and yield a greater perspective on the verity of the many other facets of existence. To experience the unreasonable strength and unmitigated fury of nature, in an exposed manner, enhances one's orientation for life's other situations. For example, in these situations, emotion is never allowed to dominate or reign supreme. A cold calculative reasoning is imperative under stress. Leadership, communication, focus and respect are essential. This teaches focus.

By Independence Day, the rage of "Amy" began to subside, but not before three yachts of the twelve-boat fleet had to drop out. Unfortunately, one of those was *Carina*, who had to go in to Nantucket when her Captain was thrown across the boat in a particularly hard slam and had been seriously injured. Her namesakes had made eight of the Transatlantics since this kind of yachting was revived in 1955. Another yacht, which was dismasted during the pounding, was *War Baby*. This had previously been Ted Turner's *American Eagle*, a 12-Meter, inshore bay-racer.

Amy, riding the remnants of the warm water Gulf Stream, moved to the north and *KIALOA III* sailed east into colder water with the wind from Amy's low cell now coming from the west. Now under spinnaker and reaching sails with dropping air and water temperatures, we were in dense fog. Hours later, the fog partially dispersed with clouds bringing the sound of thunder and obvious lightning strikes.

It was during a watch change when Bruce and I were in the cockpit and the off crew were sliding into their bunks, that we were hit, and I heard the loudest noise I've ever heard. It is difficult to describe such an explosion, undoubtedly amplified by our aluminum hull and tall aluminum masts. The incredible brightness of the lightning's intense blue flashed inside and outside of *KIALOA III*.

The electrical charge of lightning hit our mizzen and coursed down the mizzen's steel rod backstay into the aft cabin, seeming to explode in the very eyes of a sailor about to grab the backstay to swing into an upper bunk. How fortunate that he was a fraction of time too late.

Amy, the now extra-tropical storm, had passed almost this exact location 24 hours earlier heading north, and now being on the bottom of the low, we were sailing under main and mizzen spinnakers set on a port tack. We proceeded in these foggy conditions for a couple more days.

We could now smell the remnants of an electrical explosion in most of our navigational electronics. It was again time for Bruce Kendell to show his exceptional talents. I remember walking past the navigator's stateroom, seeing Bruce with solder, soldering iron and wire all over the chart table. He turned and said, "Look at this…here's where it burnt out." He

was holding a ten-inch by eight-inch circuit board, which clearly showed a "smoked" section. My amazement was that he would have thought to bring a spare circuit board for a sophisticated piece of navigation equipment. This was a tribute to his thoughtful, organized life, expertise and experience. I have yet to meet a person with talents in so many diverse disciplines; he was never intimidated by any undertaking.

~~~~~~~~~

In mid-ocean, after days of trekking remotely across its great expanse, far away from the normal distractions and comforts of life, there is a feeling that one cannot have much of an impact in the world other than concentrating on the work at hand. In fact, the world beyond the horizon of just a few miles does not seem to even exist. This realization allows the brain to explore deeper thoughts of existence and the journey of life associated with it.

This is less through a feeling of helplessness, and more of a removed aspect. No matter what may be happening elsewhere in the world, there is no element of it capable of touching you here in the middle of the North Atlantic. In fact, the only thing shared with the rest of mankind is the inexorable passage of time.

Once this mindset has manifested itself with reference only to the confined world and singular populace of the yacht, it is easy to incorrectly begin to regard the sea as a great and fallow void bereft of other life. This is never the case, and nature is wont to remind sailors of this possibly fatal error in perception. We had been lulled into such acceptance of our little world as being total, when someone spotted a large dolphin and then another and another. Before long the sea was almost horizon-to-horizon in dolphins, definitely the largest pod any of us had ever witnessed. They came up to the yacht and like so many times before played with us for miles, running and jumping off the bow wave, jumping beside us, chirping and whistling, darting in and out. I am sure they were as interested in us as we were in them. Perhaps they had been lulled into thinking they were the only things in or on the sea apart from their prey and were surprised to find us intruding into their perfect world…but I think not. This event, which was to go on for more than a day, gave the Artist the perfect representation for his requisite, daily artwork, and shortly after dinner our evening pictorial chart of crossing the sea was illustrated with "The day of jumping dolphins."

Once again alone on this imponderable and immense convex-surface, one has time to contemplate those who have gone before, perhaps on this exact spot, but without a trace. It is worthy to think of those thousands of settlers who challenged these same waters several hundred years ago in less dependable craft, their families and all their meager belongings carted with them. They were the bold, the brave, and the risk takers. They were willing to leave the lingering serfdom of Europe for a chance at self-reliance in a distant, unknown and wild country. This, in effect, was a Darwinian selection process. Those confident pioneers, opposed to autocratic dictates, would challenge a new upstart land for a piece of earth that they could leverage into their future. In contrast, those left behind would have a greater acquiescence to serfdom and aversion to chance innate to their genes. The French observer de Tocqueville, touring in the 1830's, would observe that the greatest differences between Europe and America was the reliance on government as opposed to self and community reliance. From the perspective of a few hundred years, it is interesting to observe this Darwinian path that lead to a singular super power, while those "who stayed behind"—those risk averse—appear to have been left with a destiny of broken, overly-supportive governing systems. And, they too often rely on their vituperative responses against those they perceive as successful and perhaps more confident as their only means of compensating, if only in their own minds, for their own lack of accomplishment. This affliction is a fundamental element of human nature, and is a reaction to envy. It can be witnessed on a national level but is most familiar on an individual basis. There was never any such "back biting" on *KIALOA* as the crew was much more confident and accomplished than that.

~~~~~~~~~

Drifting along at four or five knots under spinnakers, we proceeded through a damp void. The nights were dark as a coalmine without a light—dark enough for sensory deprivation—with overcast and fog precluding even a hint of light from the stars. Seven pair of eyes became so adapted that the subtle glow from the binnacle would seem enough to light up the cockpit area, the repeaters for the wind and speed instruments, a dim source of light amidships. The bow and stern lights seemed but a hint in the infinite darkness. These light sources are miniscule, and it is a tribute to the amazing flexibility and range of the human eye to be able to act in these situations. It was such that the crew, maneuvering as shadows in hooded white foul weather gear, could scarcely be discerned by one another, even in the closest proximity.

One had to know the boat, and furthermore, the current rigging of those particular sails that were serving. Flashlights were generally avoided because they could ruin the entire watch's night vision for minutes. It is amazing, but you could negotiate around slowly by a sort of sailing Braille, feeling your way, hesitating and thinking, "The mizzen sheet should be just ahead of my right foot." These periods could involve long stretches without conversation or noise, apart from the subtle hissing sound of the yacht parting the water. It was like this when someone emerged, phantom like, from below deck, momentarily allowing a soft shaft of light to penetrate upwards from the cave below. This weak glow seemed absorbed into the blackness a mere ten or twelve foot above deck height, thus defining the upper limits of our soft and very damp cocoon.

As this apparition came up on deck, Tripper Crisp, believing it was Stuey Williamson, gave a gigantic, surprise bear hug from behind at the same time exclaiming "Stuey!" This seemed to fit into the setting of the rest of the crew and was not regarded as an out of place reaction to Stuey's arrival. However, the otherwise peaceful and quiet situation was interrupted by "Ah...Tripper...I'm not Stu..."

"OH! Sorry JIM, I thought you were Stu," Tripper said in his grassroots Aussie accent. This of course did interrupt the quietude as all hands within earshot burst out laughing... including Jim. Even though this was a free and even society, there was a certain protocol expected in regards to the owner of the yacht. Jim, however, required no special treatment, and in fact, immensely enjoyed the camaraderie and just being part of the crew.

During this period of yacht racing a large part of the special nature of the experience was due to the unique collection of characters that acted out their roles together upon a stage of ocean. I question the probability of the coming together of so many unique, strongly defined and energized personalities. It might have been an example of the Theory of Complexity, at the edge of Order and Chaos, or perhaps some Divine Intervention or experiment. Whatever, the siren call of a yacht race would bring these individuals from all corners of the world, less like a trek to Lourdes or the pilgrimage to Mecca and more like the Green River Rendezvous of legendary trappers of the early 1800's. All shared components of the combined successes of *KIALOA* in some form or other. The relationships were rich and enduring.

After some thirty years, the lives and personalities still fit, seamlessly, back together as though time and the currents of life had not mattered nor take a toll, such that, the drifting in different directions has had no effect. Perhaps this is because we were all integral in the shaping of one another's character. We all had some of the same building blocks, in a state of disarray perhaps. But it was the events played out on and around the sea with others, of similar composition, that helped to arrange our individual building blocks to be even better fitting and defined, and thus yielding a greater result. We learned from one another. Life was profoundly molded by these experiences. Further, one's personal clay is never completely dry, or at least should never be considered as such, but there are times when the molding process can be accelerated or magnified by events and experiences. The adventures on *KIALOA* were such times.

It was not unusual for members of the off watch to come up on deck to enjoy the humor and comradeship of the others. However, Stuey was part of our watch and shared the aft stateroom with the Artist and me. Stuart Williamson, Stu or Stuey, a biology teacher, could join the race without excuse in that it was summer vacation. Were it during the school year, he would have taken leave from his job based upon, perhaps, the fourth or fifth time his grandmother had passed away or become seriously ill. He had sailed on *KIALOA*'s for over four years, and is best described as an effervescent individual who has a passion for travel, people and the sea. I am sure his picture is in the dictionary next to the word "globetrotter," and if it is not, it should be.

Stu has a remarkable, confiding, unfeigned personality with more than a modicum of humor in his presentations of, and interactions with, life's twists. He is a romantic and a driving force to make all recognize the import and relevance of the situations at hand. One could always depend upon Stu to perform his task and beyond, each undertaking most often accompanied by a rambling, humorous soliloquy. Stu was in charge of the mizzen, no simple task considering its size was greater than many of the other Class A yacht's main masts. Often you could hear Stu at the back of the yacht as he raised sails on the mizzen, carrying on a multi-sided conversation such that, were you to turn around, you would expect to see a five or six man crew at work. He would invariably race the main mast crew in setting sails and getting his portion of the ship squared away.

There was no task below any member, all tasks were distributed or taken equally. This was certainly no faux Marxist experiment; it was simply the description of a perfectly organized team effort. Of course, every person played a key role in select maneuvers, and should one let you down it could unleash consequences that could be quite dire. During the general operations of the yacht everyone knew what needed to be done, the chores less attractive than others were always undertaken without having to be assigned. There were other yachts with a more structured hierarchy, which, I am sure, never allowed them to tap into their complete potential. *KIALOA*, a reflection of Jim's philosophy, had one mission, to get the best out of the yacht without barren pretense.

By the eleventh of July, the sailing had settled into more of a routine, rhythmical nature. We finally had plenty of breeze and there were ongoing sail changes, but there was not anything out of the ordinary; except, we had a visitor from land—a small bird. We welcomed this non-aquatic life form, and took it as a good omen. Stu, our resident ornithologist, went so far as to provide it with water as it hid in one of the winch handle compartments. After two watches it had rested enough and flew off.

There was unstated excitement as we approached the tower and the finishing line. The sky had opened, and the sun was shining brightly with *KIALOA III* surfing downwind, averaging 14 knots over the bottom and all aboard were at their stations in case we had to jibe and finish on the other tack. It was marginal, and then as we began to close with the tower, we had a wind shift, probably a deflection by the mass of the tower.

Jim called, "jibe," the mizzen spinnaker was doused, the shooter was quickly dropped and the spinnaker pole had not been as quickly eased forward which induced a weather roll. As Jim at the helm corrected the sail, the huge shooter caught and tore on some obstruction—not a typical jibe event, and we completed the jibe resetting all sails for the short run to the finish. And, the big leeward setting shooter exploded as we crossed the line on the new tack, the end of our 2,931 mile race: Fourteen days, twenty two hours, forty-seven minutes, twelve seconds (14d, 22h, 47m, 12s), first to finish, first in class.

We finished on July the 14th, Bastille Day. Motoring into Cowes on a nice sunny day was a reflection that our trial or performance was over and that we had passed. It was a colorful spectacle with yachts from all over the world gathered for the Cowes Week Regatta. As we slid into our slip, Royce Neville, Dick's father and trade representative to the UK from Tasmania, met us. More importantly, he wisely had a couple of cases of cold beer with which to celebrate our arrival. We were very grateful for Royce's thoughtfulness, and it was to be the only recognition of our having completed a race across one of the world's oceans. This finish was in contrast to most race finishes in this regard, quiet and unrecognized, which seemed unusual as the race had been sailed to commemorate the Bicentenary of the Royal Thames Yacht Club.

~~~~~~~~~~

The peculiarities of the race did not end with the unheralded finish. The race distance for purposes of calculating the handicap rating was calculated incorrectly on a distance of 3160 miles, however, the actual distance was 2,930.35 miles, if one averages the computations of the British Admiralty and the U.S. Coast Guard. This inaccuracy was brought to the attention of the race officials both before and during the race, and was filed as an official protest the day after we had arrived. Even though the race officials had said they would "make a decision after all the yachts had finished," they chose to "sweep it under the rug" by having the International Jury declare, due to a technicality, that the official protest was not valid. Lesson learned: officials will opt for the solution that involves the least efforts on their behalf when they can. Had this error been corrected, KIII would have won in a clean sweep. However, there was no ill will felt against Robin. In fact, when her engine would not start after her finish and she had to sail into the marina late at night, she side tied to *KIALOA* and was offered dry bunks in which to sleep by Bruce.

It was, however, a great race and enjoyed by all. Little did we know that there would not be another significant Transatlantic for yachts of this type until the New York Yacht Club's 1997 Transatlantic Race followed by the DaimlerChrysler North Atlantic Challenge 2003, from New York to Germany.

On the evening in Cowes after the finish of the race a number of us, including a couple of wives and girlfriends, were gathered below deck enjoying cocktails, and more importantly the humor, wit and repartee of such gatherings. Tall tales of survival, sailing fast and jobs well done were being woven. At some point Jim was standing at the end of the settee telling of awakening the night before and complaining about itching under each arm. As he was telling of this, somewhat hunched over and in a simian posture, he tucked each hand up under his armpits and made a scratching motion, at which point I interrupted and said, "Don't tell me you had an overwhelming craving for a banana…right?" A peal of laughter interrupted the story. The loudest participant of which was Jim.

Humor, when used as a social lubricant, and particularly when it is comprised of numerous teasing or potentially taunting comments, requires intelligence as well as sophisticated knowledge and wisdom about the intellect, disposition and reactions of other people. To anticipate what is and what others will find funny, one must have subtle and tacit knowledge about other people's tastes. The crew knew one another through and through, and this crew included more than a mainstream collection of intellect and ability for lightning fast repartee. Humor was a mainstay, a cement, an ameliorating potion. No one was spared or allowed not to participate, including Jim, who would revel in such times.

The repeated laughter of the evening could be heard all over the quaint and historic marina. We were asked the next day what on earth could have been going on as people were expecting that there must have been a full and large party underway. The setting of the historic little town, boats with multi-colored pennants from many other nations gathered to participate in Cowes week, and the finest of all, stately tied at the end of the dock, with the *KIALOA* family laughing in grand form drew an apt conclusion to an adventure of a lifetime.

19

After the stormy 1975 Transatlantic Race to Cowes, the Isle of Wight, England and the further challenge of the proper course handicap distance, *KIALOA III* competed against Europe's greatest sailing yachts in Cowes Week, off the Isle of Wight in the Solent, along the English Channel and thereafter the Fastnet Rock Race 605 miles across the Irish Sea.

In the middle of chapter 19, we commence the delivery of *KIALOA III* through the Mediterranean, the wonders of the Aegean Sea, the islands off the coasts of Greece and of Turkey, thence sailing through the Red Sea to the Indian Ocean and on to Australia.

Our story begins…

Best of Both Worlds
Racing in England, Cruising the Med

KIALOA III was designed and conceived to be a true dual-purpose yacht: a powerful, winning Grand Prix racer and a comfortable, long-range cruiser. Following our memorable ride in the '75 Transatlantic Race, we were in an ideal place to take advantage of *KIALOA III's* versatility with the major races of the United Kingdom and an extended cruise to the Mediterranean.

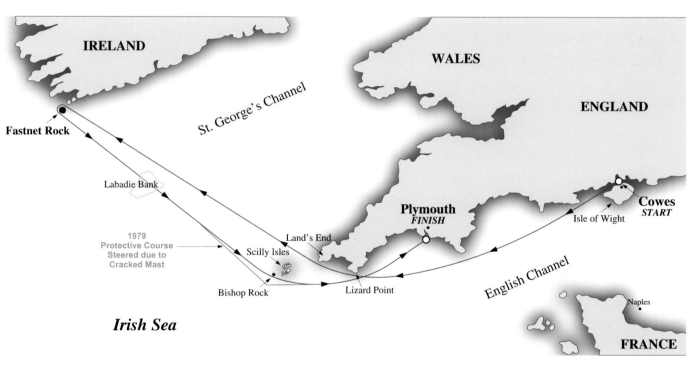

IRELAND

WALES

ENGLAND

St. George's Channel

Fastnet Rock

Labadie Bank

1979 Protective Course Steered due to Cracked Mast

Scilly Isles

Land's End

Bishop Rock

Lizard Point

Plymouth
FINISH

Cowes
START

Isle of Wight

English Channel

Naples

FRANCE

Irish Sea

Fastnet Rock Race
605 Nautical Miles

First up was the 200-mile Queen's Cup Channel Race. However, two days before the start of the Channel Race, I received a telephone call that my mother had passed away, and that I must return to Los Angeles. I asked Bruce Kendell and the crew to race *KIALOA III* without me, and they performed exceptionally: first to finish, first in class and first overall. I returned for the short Brittanea Cup Race, an event in which the wind and tides conspired against the bigger boats, and we did poorly. But we were also looking ahead to the next big test, the 605-mile Fastnet Race.

We knew the course well and knew the Irish Sea intimately, and we understood that there was a good chance of heavy weather causing a high percentage of upwind sailing. But how much? Would the breeze be fickle and variable? Would there be a heavy northwest sea? Or would we see a little of both? Those sorts of questions always linger at the start of an offshore ocean race.

As it turned out, it was a challenging, tactical sail. Along the southerly beaches and cliffs along the English coastline, we had light headwinds in a shifty westerly breeze. At Lizard Point, we encountered the northwest headwinds more typical of the Irish Sea and spent the next 42 hours tacking into them. There were many headsail changes before rounding Fastnet Rock about fifty hours after the start.

Our reciprocal course heading back toward the finish was south-southeast. But a big wind shift in an accompanying squall practically turned us around, and as the breeze lightened up, it continued to be very shifty. One thing about the Fastnet Race: it keeps the skipper, navigator and crew constantly on their toes.

The variable conditions persisted past Bishop Rock and along the south shores of the Scilly Islands. As we regained contact with the southern shore of England, the winds hovered in the 3-8 knot range with *KIALOA III* averaging a little under six knots over the bottom.

The final challenge was negotiating the entrance to Plymouth—which is a tricky harbor, with cliffs on each side—against an ebb tide and a very light, offshore breeze. If a crew is lucky, the last mile or so can be successfully navigated in an exasperating but reasonably short time. If unlucky, it can take hours…until the tide changes. *KIALOA III* was not lucky, and it took a long, long time to negotiate the entrance. When we finally finished, we wondered how our competition was faring in this very unusual edition of the Fastnet.

With our racing schedule over for the time being, it was time to go cruising. *KIALOA III* was first to finish in the 605-mile Fastnet Race with an elapsed time of 89.43 hours. The handicap-corrected time to determine race results for the fleet of smaller and larger yachts was determined by multiplying the actual elapsed time by a handicap coefficient determined by each yacht's speed rating.

KIALOA's elapsed time of 89.43 hours was multiplied by its handicap coefficient of 1.3597 to determine the handicap-corrected time (under the RORC measurement rule), which came to

121.4332 hours, which equals a 32-hour handicap penalty...more than a day.

Surprisingly, *KIALOA III* placed very well, first to finish, first overall Class A, and third overall in fleet. Our Cowes Week and Fastnet Rock racing were not over, and our outstanding cruise and delivery to Australia began.

From Cowes, *KIALOA III* sailed along the coasts of Portugal and Spain before heading into the Mediterranean Sea and carrying on to Vouliagmeni, the yacht harbor closest to Athens. We spent a few days in Athens and then continued on into the Aegean Sea to go through the Cyclades Islands and the Dodecanese Islands. Our first stop was the popular tourist island of Mykonos, with its many beautiful beaches. From there, we visited the small adjacent island of Delos, noted for its ruins and sculptures, and as a resort island of Cleopatra and other historical figures.

From there we carried on to Ios, where we enjoyed excellent diving at day and glowing beaches at night. Next up was the historic isle of Thera, also known as Santorini, the highlights of which are the world-famous volcano and the beautiful homes high on the hills. The yacht anchorage is actually the blown-out core of the volcano and the houses are stationed adjacent to the crater. Much has been written about the massive and historic eruption of Thera in the second millennium BC. It has been theorized that the immense explosion and the high, resulting waves were what parted the Red Sea, allowing Moses and his followers to pass through.

From Santorini, we sailed northeast through the Dodecanese Islands group to the beautiful historic island of Patmos. After a lovely two-day visit, we called at the Turkish port of Kusadasi to visit the antique Grecian city of Ephesus, with its historic library and well-maintained ruins.

The history of the Aegean, its islands and coastal cities is anything but straightforward. The Greeks and Turks waged many wars over the centuries and boundaries constantly shifted. When one thinks of the Persian Empire, the Ottoman Empire, the Battle of Marathon in 460 B.C., and other wars and historical events, it's even more confusing. But it's also very rewarding to read the past history of these great empires.

After our visit to Ephesus, *KIALOA III* cruised slowly along the beautiful west coast of Turkey to Bodrum, Marmaris, and Fethiye to the small port of Kas, and on to the tiny, beautiful island of Kastelorizo, which is also known as Megisti. In the first half of the 20th Century, Megesti was known as the Monaco of the Aegean.

We then sailed on to the larger island of Rhodos, a major marine and farming region, where we were pleasantly surprised. A large group of expatriate Greeks who had emigrated to Australia were visiting home and came down to the docks to greet *KIALOA III*, which had several Aussies on board. We arrived to cheers of "Welcome!," gifts of wine and flowers, and even a speech by the local mayor. It was a warm, pleasant arrival, and our subsequent stay in Rhodos was a comfortable one.

The welcome in Rhodos was especially appropriate because we would soon return to our next series of races back in Australia. After we flew back to Los Angeles—pleased to know that *KIALOA III* was a wonderful cruising yacht as well as a world-class race boat—a delivery crew started sailing for the Southern Hemisphere. Little did we know what record-setting adventures were ahead of us.

KIALOA III: The First Nine Months

Before setting sail for Australia, it was time to analyze the first nine months of our first year of racing aboard *KIALOA III*. For this review, we deleted the first five races of the SORC because of the tremendous Gulf Stream and old age allowance advantages given to other yachts. We did, however, include the last race of the SORC because the Gulf Stream impact was minimal, even though the double old age allowances were included.

KIALOA III – 1975 Racing Results through August 1975

Excluding first five races of 1975 SORC
due to double old age allowance and Gulf Stream benefits

	1st to Finish	Class	Overall
Nassau Cup	1	1	1
Jamaica Race	1	1	1
Annapolis-Newport	1	2	2
Edlu Cup	1	1	2
Block Island Race	*	*	*
Transatlantic	1	1	2**
Queens Cup	1	1	1
Britannia Cup	poor	poor	poor
Fastnet Rock	1	1	3

* Crew injured – *KIALOA III* well ahead – 15 miles from finish

** Incorrect Handicap – *KIALOA III* would have been 1st overall if correct handicap distance had been applied.

Deciding the Winner: The Handicap System

Throughout the sailing portion of this book, you will find many comments about handicap formulas and the handicap allowances given to bigger and smaller yachts. This is a highly technical process with many complications and differences of opinion, particularly true because of the continuous advent of new technologies, materials, and approaches to sailing.

With thirty-three years of racing aboard five different *KIALOAs*, we brought to yachting many new ideas for increased speed, all within our understanding of the limits of the measurement and handicap rules. It is exceedingly hard, if not impossible, to design a measurement rule that fits yachts of all sizes, weights and sail plans, taking into account the different types of seas and wind conditions encountered all over the world.

In the structure and design of such a rule and handicap formula, it is only logical that the formula be structured to fit the central volume, or mass, of the ocean racing fleet, which would be in the medium to small size of the fleet. Anomalies will always occur as the size of a yacht moves up and down from the center of the mass of such yachts.

KIALOA I was a mid-sized yacht, about 50-feet long. *KIALOA II* was a 72-foot yacht, the maximum length allowable at that time for the Bermuda Race.

KIALOA III, *IV* and *V* were all about 80-feet long, minus a few inches, and maximum-sized yachts for their racing periods. For Maxi (ICAYA) races in which we participated, the rating could not exceed a rating number of 70.5. This is a handicap number, not the length; *KIALOAs III*, *IV* and *V* were intentionally rated slightly lower than the maximum number for psychological purposes.

During the period that we campaigned *KIALOA I* and *KIALOA II,* one of two different measurement formulas were used, dependent upon the location of the race. The Cruising Club of America (CCA) measurement formula was used in the United States and Canada. The Royal Ocean Racing Club (RORC) formula was used in England, Ireland and much of Europe, Australia and New Zealand.

All racing yachts were measured under the CCA or RORC formula (hull length and displacement, sail plan, stability, etc.) and a speed number, also called the rating number, was produced for each individual yacht. The rating number was then applied to a formulated handicap allowance that would adjust the elapsed time of each yacht at the end of a sailboat race to provide a corrected time.

Each different measurement system—RORC or CCA—also had a different handicap system to provide the corrected time. The RORC handicap system provided a Time-on-Time adjustment based upon the rating number. A percentage multiplier would be produced for each rating number to be applied against each yacht's elapsed time for a specific race.

As an example, for the 1969 Fastnet Race, *KIALOA II* had an elapsed time of 89 hours, 2 minutes and 10 seconds. *KIALOA II's* RORC Time-on-Time handicap percentage was T.C.F. 1.0598. When *KIALOA II's* elapsed time of 89 hours, 2 minutes and 10 seconds was multiplied by their designated handicap percentage (T.C.F. 1.0598), the corrected time was determined to be 94 hours, 21 minutes and 38 seconds. As a further example, compare the 1.3597 handicap penalty applied to the bigger, faster *KIALOA III* set forth earlier in this chapter (121.4332 hours), which added 32 hours to the *KIALOA III's* elapsed time.

A similar system was used in Australia; however, they slightly modified their percentages to give smaller yachts even more time according to Gordon Marshall, a key figure in Australian Racing.

The handicap system used in the United States and Canada was entirely different. Here, race organizers took the rating number and applied this number under a Time-on-Distance formula set forth in the North American Yacht Racing Union Time-on-Distance manual, which provided a seconds-per-mile allowance. The seconds-per-mile would then be multiplied by the specified course distance in the race instructions for that particular event; the product would be deducted from the elapsed time to establish the corrected time. The yacht with the lowest corrected time would be the winner.

The RORC and CCA negotiated a joint measurement rule over a period of about five years in the late 1960s that would modify the design of the new racing yachts and would change the ratings of existing yachts. This new, compromised measurement rule adversely affected some of the most competitive yachts around the world and benefited others. The new measurement rule was entitled the International Ocean Racing (IOR) rule and went into full effect in 1971.

However, in the four or five years prior to the 1971 merger, various adjustments occurred in the CCA rule which appeared to be testing the CCA rule toward a fit with the RORC rule. These changes created peculiar race results in certain races in 1967-1971. While this is past history, such interim rule changes were disruptive to quality results, and such testing could have been accomplished by a "paperwork analysis," after the results of races were established under the already existing handicap formula.

A complicated component of the United States NAYRU Time Allowance system is the course distance component. The fundamental concept for handicapping under the NAYRU Time Allowance tables was clearly stated in a paper entitled *Handicapping Rules and Performance of Sailing Yachts,* by John S. Letcher, Jr. submitted to the Society of Naval Architects and Marine Engineers, dated January 19, 1974, which states:

"If potential elapsed times are to be computed in advance for handicapping, some assumptions must be made about the probability distribution of operating conditions. The CCA Rule, for example, contains in its introduction the statement that it 'is based upon the assumption that a triangular course will be sailed with approximately equal legs of close-hauled, running and reaching conditions,'[1] though how this assumption is incorporated into the rule is never made clear."[2]

As confirmed by John S. Letcher's paper, the NAYRU Time Allowance Table is based upon a yacht sailing an equilateral triangle with the three legs all being equal linear distance; however, one leg is a windward leg where the sailed distance is much longer than the linear distance because of the requirement for tacking upwind the full length of the linear distance.

Assuming 80° to 90° tacking angles, the actual distance sailed on the windward leg would be about 139% of the linear distance. Therefore, the course sailed in compliance with the NAYRU formula would be about 113% of the handicap distance set forth in the race instructions (1.0 + 1.0 + 1.39 ÷ 3 = 1.13%). A quick example of handicapping problems under the NAYRU Time Allowance formula is the Transpac Honolulu Race. The handicap course distance is 2,225 miles; an off the wind reaching and running race has only about 30 miles of upwind sailing.

The NAYRU tables are based upon the course distance plus about 13% caused by sailing one third of the distance upwind, for a total added distance of 289 miles. There is no credit for this unsailed distance in the Transpac Handicap formula, which determines the handicap winners of the International Regatta. Nor is there such a credit defined in many other long distance races in the world of yachting. Some long distance races have shortened the handicap distance to accommodate this issue. Others recognize that sailing to weather may occur in storm conditions or diurnal nighttime shifts to offshore winds typical of the Mexican coasts, or the general weather patterns which may produce windward sailing.

Even in off the wind racing, wind shifts, or jibing under spinnaker will cause added sailing distance which somewhat offsets the lack of windward sailing under the NAYRU Tables.

In the Honolulu Race, a yacht customarily sails an arc to the southwest to stay in the best wind sailing Isobar of the North Pacific High, about the 1020 gradient of the High.

---

[1] Cruising Club of America, "Measurement Rule for Racing," New York, 1967

[2] John S. Letcher, Jr., The Society of Naval Architects and Marine Engineers, *Handicapping Rules and Performance of Sailing Yachts* paper presented at the Chesapeake Sailing Yacht Symposium, Annapolis, Maryland, January 19, 1974

The argument prevails in the Honolulu Race Handicapping. Should the course handicap distance be shortened to accommodate the lack of sailing to windward? If so, how much of a reduction?

In the years of *KIALOA II,* I suggested verbally and in writing that there be some shortening of course distance, perhaps 50% of the calculated "un-sailed" distance which would be a reduction of about 130 miles. My suggestion was rejected. Under the current and then handicapping, this would provide slight benefits to the larger yachts. However, if the reader were to browse through the Official Transpac Race Book, entitled *Transpac, A History of the Great Race To Honolulu, 1906-1979,* it becomes obvious that the Race Handicap Committee has been using different handicap formulas along with Transpacific Yacht Club revisions in an attempt to improve the equity of results between large and small sailing yachts.

There is no simple solution because of the substantial course distance. At the finish, there are often several days separating the larger and smaller yachts, who have also sailed in different wind conditions. Handicapping such races is a very complicated issue. My comments are not in conflict with what the Transpac Race management has tried to do; in actuality, I compliment the Transpac Committee for addressing this problem as there are no certainties in ocean sailboat racing. My comments are based upon technical issues and yes, I believe that this would have helped the larger yachts. *KIALOA III* won the 1977 Transpac Race and *KIALOA II* and *KIALOA I* did well in the event. By shortening the handicap course distance, we would have benefitted in all seven races we sailed.

20

KIALOA III followed the lead of *KIALOA II* and was again first to finish in this 1975 world famous race, setting a new elapsed time record, 11 hours faster then any prior yacht and 23 minutes ahead of *Windward Passage,* symbolized by the gift of the shell casing from the first to finish gun.

It was rewarding to set a new record, to be the fastest yacht, while realizing that records are always set to be broken by newer, faster latest technology yachts.

There is much more to this story, 21 years later in 1996 the *KIALOA III* record was broken and then only by 28 minutes.

We again congratulate the outstanding amateur *KIALOA* crew and ask the reader to review their wonderful success.

The Floating Opera House
Setting the 21-Year Elapsed Time Record

KIALOA III's first racing year was 1975. She had raced in the SORC, sailed the race to Jamaica, the Annapolis Newport Race, the Edlu Cup, the Transatlantic Race, England's Queen's Cup and the Fastnet Rock Race with three first places, three second places, and one third place. *KIALOA III* had sailed and cruised across the Bay of Biscay, across the Mediterranean and the Aegean Sea, through the Red Sea and across the Indian Ocean to race the 1975 Sydney Hobart Race and its Australian, New Zealand and international competitors. *KIALOA III* and *Windward Passage* would challenge each other, as well as yachts from around the world, in the great 1975 Sydney Hobart Race.

When we first raced in the Sydney Hobart Races, we, and many Australians, were amazed by the geometric comparison of the Sydney Opera House and the sail plans of *KIALOA II* and *KIALOA III*. Many Aussies call the *KIALOAs* the "Floating Opera House," a true and friendly honor. We had noted Australian sailors aboard which increased the Aussie's enthusiasm and the enthusiasm of our entire crew. The Sydney Hobart Race was one of the most challenging races of our International Sailing World.

The Australian handicap system (adjusting elapsed time results to corrected time results) favored the smaller yachts as explained to us by major Australian sailing leaders, which we understood, but we strongly believed that records and victory concepts existed to be beaten by the exceptional performance of the yacht and the crew. Also, Magnus Halvorsen, a previous victor of this race, and Jock Sturrock, a leading Australian sailor, were there to join us.

KIALOA II was the first to finish in 1971 and we were again challenging the elapsed time record and a potential victory over the other yachts from Australia, New Zealand, Asia, Europe and the United States. Dependent upon the changing winds, we would sail the same tactical course as in the 1971 race, as set forth later in the chapter.

The challenging and amusing start, on Boxing Day, (the day after Christmas), again had the thrill and confusion of hundreds of spectator boats, including surfboards in the center of the Sydney Harbor as participating spectators, challenging and cheering the participants.

KIALOA III and *Windward Passage* had excellent starts, quickly separating from the fleet of racing yachts and spectators, reaching on headsails through the night until the next morning when the wind went aft and both yachts set spinnakers and mizzen staysails and began running at high speeds.

KIALOA III was ahead, tactically covered and kept pressure on *Windward Passage,* gaining mileage over the next few hours and sailing as much as possible on our preplanned course.

With our fastest downwind spinnakers and staysails set, surfing on every wave we continued covering *Passage* to the rear and listening to the race communication vessel for an update on the weather and the smaller yachts behind. The race communicator vessel speculated that *KIALOA III* could break the existing elapsed time record.

All aboard *KIALOA* continued their concentration on sail trim, fine tuning our speed under sail and maximum speed rides on the waves of the windblown sea. Our navigation and calculations showed that we were indeed breaking the existing elapsed time record; we hoped to reduce the record to about 60 hours. However, the wind and seas reduced their force when we were still north of Tasman Island, and we prayed that the wind would not die.

As we rounded Tasman Island and were changing sails from spinnakers to headsails for close-hauled sailing across Storm Bay, we blew out our biggest spinnaker which was quickly doused as the headsails were raised. As we were sailing towards "Iron Pot," the entry to the Derwent River, our navigator calculated that our elapsed time would be closer to 62 hours than our hoped-for 60 hours. Quickly, we rounded the Iron Pot Buoy, the entry to the Derwent River, tacking five times, toward the finish line, while cars parked along the river honked their horns and flashed their headlights as a "first to finish" greeting to *KIALOA III* and crew.

At about 2:30am in the morning of December 29th, *KIALOA III* crossed the finish line and the shot gun fired its "finished" shell for the first yacht to finish, and our navigator quickly calculated our elapsed time record of 2 days, 14 hours, 26 minutes and 56 seconds, shattering the existing record by almost 11 hours. It was not the 60 hours we had hoped for, however, the *KIALOA* crew was still totally thrilled by our tremendous record-breaking performance. *Windward Passage* also broke the prior record, arriving 23 minutes behind *KIALOA III*.

When we arrived at the Hobart Dock the finish line judge, Don McIndoe, congratulated *KIALOA III* and we proudly accepted the shell casing from the finish gun, which was placed in its decorative base at a later date.

KIALOA III was not the handicap victor in this high speed race, however, all aboard were intensely proud of sailing the 635 mile course 11 hours faster than any other yacht in the Sydney Hobart race history. Under the handicap formula, each yacht is assigned a coefficient to apply to their actual finish time, the yacht with the lowest calculated time is the corrected time winner.

KIALOA III was first to finish, and our elapsed time would be multiplied by a coefficient of 1.0575 to provide our corrected time. The corrected time winner *Rampage* had a coefficient of about 0.75 and its corrected time would be 75% of its elapsed time. This yacht, after adjustment by their coefficient with the lowest corrected time, would be the overall winner of the given race.

We salute *Rampage* and their crew for the corrected time victory of the 1975 Sydney Hobart Race. However, because of press coverage, the local and worldwide newspapers, the big story was the high speed "first to finish" victory of breaking the former elapsed time record by almost 11 hours in one of the world's most challenging distance races.

Aboard *KIALOA III* ,we wondered how long our new elapsed time record would hold. Because it held for several years, the yachting world and advertising world thought that a challenge against our record would be a good promotion of this race.

$100,000 was then offered to any yacht that would beat the *KIALOA III* record. There were no specific limits to the size, weight or rating of such yacht. *KIALOA III* was 78' long with an actual displacement of about 85,000 pounds. Larger, purportedly faster, bigger sail plans, lighter displacement yachts challenged the *KIALOA III* record for years. The bonus was raised from $100,000 to $300,000 for the yacht that could beat *KIALOA's* record.

Twenty-one years later, *Morning Glory*, a bigger, lighter carbon fibre hull and mast IMS yacht challenged the *KIALOA* record. This lighter, longer and latest design IMS yacht, skippered by Russell Coutts who was skipper of New Zealand's America's Cup Victory and crew, broke *KIALOA's* 21-year-old elapsed time record by only 28 minutes and won the special prize award of $300,000.

All *KIALOA* crew were exceedingly proud of their victory and the acknowledgement of the tremendous record held for 21 years. The record setting course of *KIALOA III* follows. The nuances of currents and counter currents related to the Bass Straits and to the flow of the Tasman Sea were all considered to the best of our ability and our judgment, with the help of the fisherman along the Australia and Tasmanian coast. We thank them for their help.

Before departing Hobart, we carefully analyzed our course sailed and speeds over the bottom. Since we did not sail a straight-line course, the distance sailed was longer than course distance and the actual speed of *KIALOA III* would be higher than the following speeds over course.

Calculated Speeds Over Course (knots)

TOTAL COURSE	10.06
Bass Straits – Tasman Light	10.16
Tourville-Tasman Light	11.01*
Across Storm Bay and up Derwent River	9.58

* This is an area where we had light wind conditions, while speed was higher. We consider this higher speed as a result of favorable current.

The night of the trophy presentation, we decided that we would be back in 1977 to try for an overall victory, what we jokingly referred to as the "Gordon Marshall Challenge."

In 1976, *KIALOA* returned to California and then to Florida for the start of 1977 SORC Racing. Enroute, we had two races…one major and the other an excellent race along the Baja California and Mexican coasts. The first race, the Tasman Sea Race, started a few days after the Sydney-Hobart Race (a race for the yachts sailing east to New Zealand), and the second race, the Los Angeles-Mazatlan Race was a race of 1032 miles, enroute to Florida.

1,511-MILE TRANS TASMAN RACE

The 1,511-mile Tasman Sea Race from Hobart to Auckland, New Zealand, commenced a few days after our victory celebration for the record-setting Hobart run.

In 1972, *KIALOA III*'s "little sister"—*KIALOA II*—had won the race in record fashion, establishing an elapsed time record of just over eight days. For the 1976 race, we wanted to win and again set a new record while doing so. It was a tough, self-imposed challenge.

But conditions were ideal and we had some great early sailing early on, mostly close-hauled and close-reaching. Once the wind freed a bit, we were able to hoist a kite and we rattled off a 265-mile

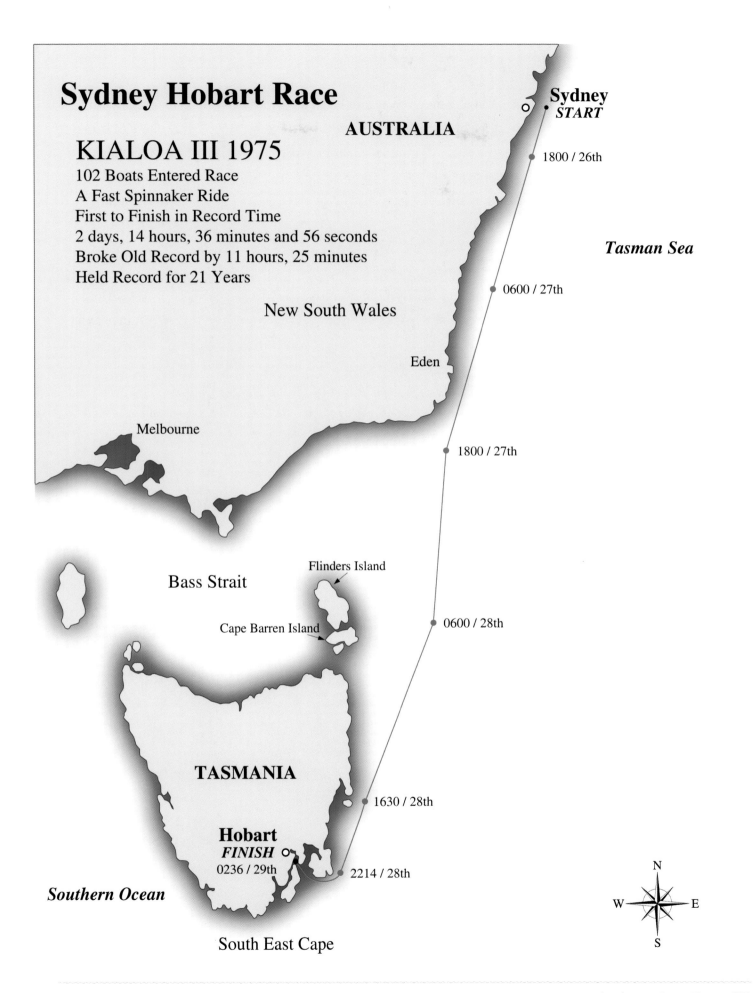

Sydney Hobart Race

KIALOA III 1975
102 Boats Entered Race
A Fast Spinnaker Ride
First to Finish in Record Time
2 days, 14 hours, 36 minutes and 56 seconds
Broke Old Record by 11 hours, 25 minutes
Held Record for 21 Years

AUSTRALIA

New South Wales

Tasman Sea

Sydney
START

1800 / 26th

0600 / 27th

Eden

1800 / 27th

Melbourne

Flinders Island

Bass Strait

Cape Barren Island

0600 / 28th

TASMANIA

1630 / 28th

Hobart
FINISH

0236 / 29th

2214 / 28th

Southern Ocean

South East Cape

N
W   E
S

day. But on January 10th, as we approached Cape May and North Cape at the top of New Zealand's North Island, the wind went on hiatus. Still, we'd put a lot of miles into the bank in the first few days, so we thought we might still be on record pace.

The "let down" came over the next 26 hours, in which we recorded only 164 miles—an average of just 6.3 knots—in light conditions. It was challenging sailing, with our crew trying to eke out every possible mile in numerous jibes.

Until that point, the most interesting moment of the voyage came in the Tasman Sea, while sailing on port tack in about 30-knots of breeze. A huge blue whale decided to say hello and put on a great show, jumping clear of the water with his huge tail high in the air. He was amazingly graceful and very big (by our rough estimates over 60 feet long.) He was also, it appeared, on a collision course with KIALOA III.

As he closed within a few "whale lengths" of our port beam, I was at the wheel wondering what avoidance tactics to employ. Suddenly, the blue whale turned aft and cut behind our stern before appearing again off our starboard beam. Then he disappeared. We were all in awe of his agility and his command of his vast territory, the wide Tasman Sea.

The whale was a distant memory as we closed on the finish line and crossed it at a little after 7:00 am, reasonably early, but not so much to dissuade a big gathering of friends and family from greeting us. Our corrected-time placement wasn't great as we were ninth. But despite the light airs down the stretch, we'd managed our second-straight record-setting performance with a time of 7 days, 19 hours, 13 minutes.

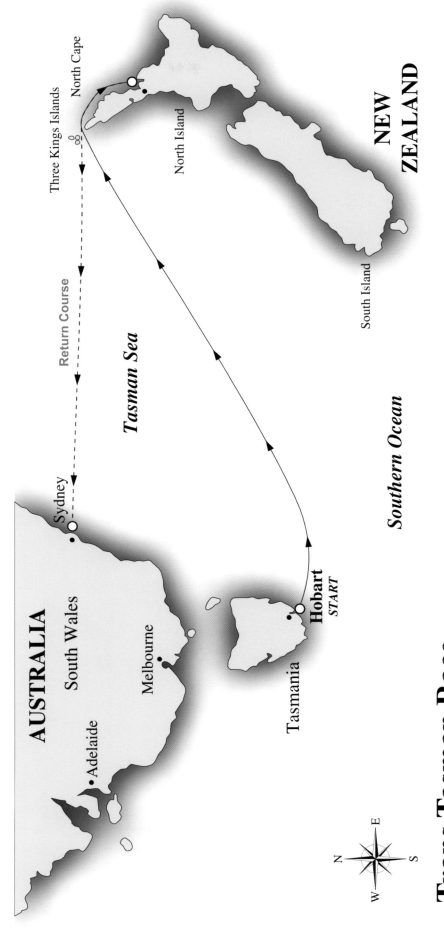

Trans Tasman Race
Hobart to Auckland

Los Angeles - Mazatlan Race

⎯⎯● 1032 Nautical Miles

San Diego - Acapulco Race

⎯⎯● 1430 Nautical Miles

1976 MAZATLAN RACE, 1032 miles

We had one more major event scheduled for 1976, all the way back across the Pacific—the 1,032-mile Mazatlan Race. Over the years, the Ensenada Race and the Acapulco Race were favorites of the *KIALOA* crews. Both races impacted the local communities substantially, in terms of both growth and economics.

Across the Gulf of California from Cabo San Lucas, Mazatlan was also expanding, with new golf courses and hotels to go along with their impressive history in sport fishing. The leaders there believed that hosting an international yacht race from Southern California would enhance the region's appeal to tourists and investors.

In '76, it had been ten years since our first race to Mazatlan. But we believed we knew the waters well. In many other races and cruises, we'd sailed the length of Baja and had a good understanding of how to round the southern tip of the peninsula, which is always a crucial and difficult area to negotiate. We'd done our homework, reviewing the currents and winds, and talking to the locals. As it turned out, our research wasn't as good or thorough as it should've been. We didn't test the local conditions closely enough at night, specifically the waters close to the south shore. It had proved to be our undoing in 1966…and '76. We took the locals at their word, and only later discovered they'd never been off the southeast corner of Baja after midnight either!

We lost big in both races when our competitors sailed wide of the southeast tip, well offshore, while we chose an inshore option. In 1966, in one night alone, we lost over forty miles of a lead position to our competitors. In 1976, we stood off and sailed a wider angle, but not far enough. We finished second in a race we probably should have won.

Still, the voyage was worthwhile for one of the added thrills it provided. We were sailing downwind along the coast of Baja, having a fine ride with great surfing conditions. Spray was flying, the droplets saturated with phosphorous. And suddenly the sky above just exploded into light; it looked like meteors crashing into other meteors. In fact, what we were witnessing was the Leonidis meteor shower. At first we didn't comprehend what we were watching until one of the crew identified the phenomenon. It was scary on one hand, beautiful on the other; we wondered what the locals made of it. That fast ride soon slowed down as the wind lightened while crossing the gulf to Mazatlan. We corrected out to second and had a lovely time ashore.

From there, it was once again through the Panama Canal and back up the east coast of Costa Rica, Central America and Mexico, en route to Florida. We had another date with destiny: the 1977 SORC.

21

1977 was a remarkable year for *KIALOA III* and its racing crew.

Four overall fleet victories in the world's most challenging races:

- The record setting SORC St. Petersburg–Fort Lauderdale Race:
  374 miles around the Florida Keys and the southern tip of Florida.

- The Miami-Montego Bay, Jamaica Race: 811 miles around the
  Bahamas and Cuba to Montego Bay.

- The 2225 mile Transpac Race: surfing to Honolulu

- The 635 mile Sydney-Hobart Race in a "Southerly Buster"
  in the Tasman Sea and Australia (Refer to Chapter 22) and

- The 3 year Yachting World Ocean Racing Championship
  and 3rd overall fleet in the 6 race SORC

We salute *KIALOA III*, "The Ordinary White Boat"
and its amateur crew and ask "Has any other yacht
equaled or bettered *KIALOA's* results in such
world famous ocean races?"

KIALOA III
An Unbelievable Success for KIALOA III and Crew in Our 21st Year

I t was 1977, our 21st year of International Sailboat Racing in major races of our World. It has been said that the 21st year is the year of Maturity...

If this applies to sailing, the *KIALOAs* and crew had matured exceedingly well. Its victory records and race results set forth in earlier chapters have made all crew aboard outstandingly capable and confident, always coming up with new ideas and techniques, sailing together as a closely integrated team.

The results of the World Ocean Racing Championship for 1975-76 and '77, appeared to be confirmed by our overall corrected time victory in the 1977 Transpacific Yacht Race, 2225 miles from Los Angeles to Honolulu, Hawaii, which followed our two earlier victories in the 374 mile 1977 SORC St. Petersburg-Fort Lauderdale Race and the 811-mile island hopping race from Miami to Montego Bay, Jamaica, described elsewhere in this book. Three major challenging international race victories in one year, and we still had the 635 mile Sydney Hobart Race to sail, starting on Boxing Day, a race of serious challenges which we knew very well and *KIALOA* had set the elapsed time record, in 1975, held for 21 years.

Our *KIALOA* crew accepted the challenge of a 4th major overall race victory in the 1977 Sydney-Hobart Race, 635 miles, pounding to weather in a 35-40 knot "Southerly Buster," finishing well ahead of our major competitor *Windward Passage*.

Four major international races in one year, upwind sailing, downwind sailing, rigorous competition—overall corrected time victories for our 21st year. As well as the overwhelming victor in the 1975-1976-1977 World Ocean Racing Championship.

We compliment our outstanding *KIALOA* crew, our teamwork, our friendship and the great sailing capabilities of each and every member of the *KIALOA* crew.

The following question has been asked...Has any yacht in major international yachting history exceeded the challenging victories of *KIALOA III*?

My thanks, my compliments to our great *KIALOA* crew, each and everyone, a winner.

~~~~~~~~

Transpac Memoirs by Terry Lalonde and Andy Rose

Terry Lalonde and Andy Rose, two of our great KIALOA *crew, have written their individual memoirs about the 1977 Transpacific Yacht Race, which follow.*

Another Record-breaking Victory by T.E. Lalonde

It was a gray, overcast day, not atypical to late June and early July along the coast in Southern California. What is known locally as a coastal eddy had set up and brought in a damp marine layer. The color of the day did not reflect the attitude of the crew. The bunks had been assigned, the new t-shirts and hats had been distributed, personal gear put away and the watches established.

Racing from the mainland in California to the Hawaiian Islands is a grand and old tradition, and it is certainly the preeminent race on the West Coast. The first Transpac race took place in 1906. It had originally been planned to start in San Francisco, but an untimely and infamous April earthquake got in the way. It was moved to start in Los Angeles and has started there ever since. This race would be its 29th running. There would be sixty-seven yachts of varying size and shape charging across 2,225 nautical miles of ocean from Point Fermin buoy to Diamond Head Light, near Honolulu. This might take nine to twelve days depending upon the speed of the yachts. In general, size determines speed, and to make for competition amongst all the yachts, a complicated handicap rating system had been devised and refined over decades of racing. The result was that there would be thirty-five foot to seventy-nine foot yachts divided into Division I, with Classes A through D, and Division II.

After our respectable start, we were first around the west end of Catalina. By degrees, and as expected, the wind began to "clock" or rotate and we were able to free up the sails. Ultimately, we went to our jib topsails. What fun. The power of a strong reach can be sensed in several ways, just letting the 3/8" plow-steel cable ease out on the headsail drum lets anyone within earshot know "she's charging," and that this will not be a cocktail cruise. The sound from the stainless steel portion of the drum as it objects to the sawing friction of the cable is somewhere between a moaning resonance and a screeching cry. A deep vibration is felt and heard in the farthest reaches of the boat. For the uninitiated, this wake up call is enough to let them know that the tremendous forces involved in a Maxi racer, if unleashed unexpectedly, by a breakage for example, can cause the greatest of harm. After a couple days of this power reaching, we established a respectable lead in the fleet. The breeze continued to freshen, while the sea displayed more of the set swell of the open ocean and the overcast dissipated. The motion of the boat in these conditions was very rhythmical.

* * *

KIALOA was perfection in her conception, design and execution of the construction, with well-coordinated efforts and input from the entire spectrum of yacht racing. All opinions were listened to and given consideration…very typical of Jim Kilroy's experienced methodology. She campaigned at what could have been the zenith of ocean racing, where races would start in one location and culminate at some distant place, and where the rules dictated welcome requirements to include interiors and some creature comforts. As such, getting off watch in the late afternoon on such a blustery reach, one could maneuver below using the well positioned overhead hand rail, walking as though in a mystery house at an angle to the horizon. Then, slipping into a comfortable settee along the varnished wood, gimbaled table, join the crew and have an excellent cooked meal with perhaps a glass of wine in the soft glow of the cabin lights.

And the camaraderie, oh yes the camaraderie…the random nature of life and it's peregrinations, the one-of-a-kind crossing of paths almost seemed to defy probability when it came to the assemblage of *KIALOA*'s crew. They came from various boats and various experiences and backgrounds as well as parts of the world. The unique quality of some of the characters is what is amazing, all well defined and confident in their personage. The sobriquets are telltale: Fang, Pig, Tink, Goose, and Bolt, to name but a few…names that are not easy to wear by the faint of heart. Intelligent and quick-witted all, the conversations and humor/repartee was something to behold and enjoy, all expressed and enhanced by the colors of accents and colloquialisms. The humor might have been self-deprecating or at someone's expense, no matter, as all were confident and balanced in their beings enough to absorb any jests. Without the psychological testing of the Navy's submarine program, this well-vetted group of individuals had been culled not only from the world at large, but more importantly from the sailing fraternity. At the time, this crew was the envy of the sailing world, but was not one to flaunt that fact. The crew was perhaps most reflective of Jim's approach to business, i.e. attempt to select the best, cultivate their strengths, create a culture of contributions from all by listening, and reward them well. The latter point in the case of sailing was winning.

* * *

The Pacific Ocean, between the mainland and Hawaii, is dominated by a large high-pressure system. This bulge in the atmosphere causes the air to descend back to earth, generally outward and away from the center. The winds generated by this falling air mass are light and variable. A good sailing strategy is to skirt this high-pressure center until reaching the stronger and more consistent northeast trade winds. Get too close to the high and you

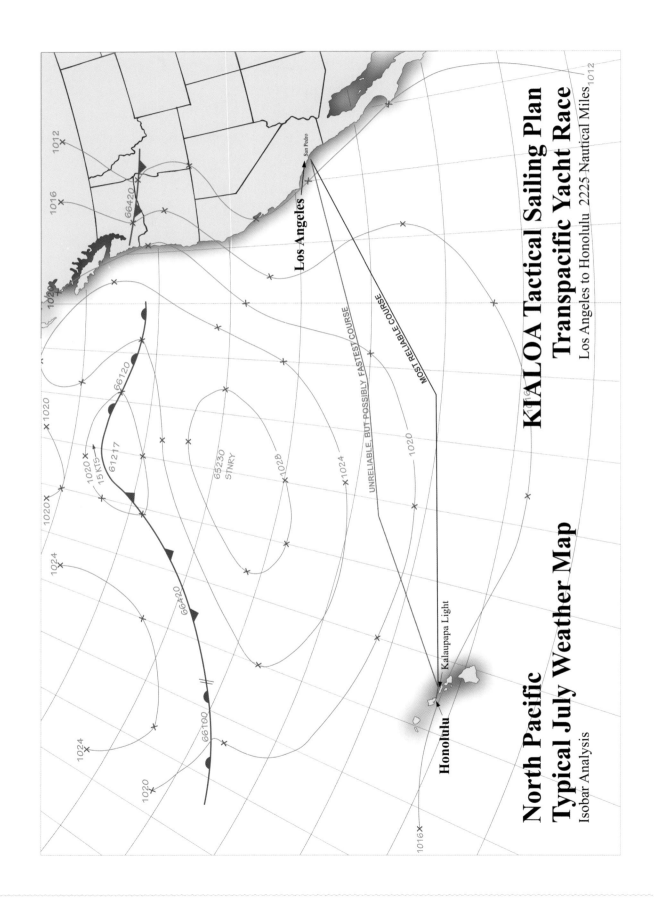

KIALOA Tactical Sailing Plan
Transpacific Yacht Race
Los Angeles to Honolulu 2225 Nautical Miles

North Pacific
Typical July Weather Map
Isobar Analysis

run out of wind; get too far away and you are sailing a much greater distance to the finish. It is a balancing act of keeping good boat speed against the shortest course.

The ULDBs in Division II were called sleds. As with all things in life, there were trade-offs. We had the advantage going to weather and on the power reaches, but now it was their medium. One learns through these experiences that no other has all the advantages and that it is best to play to your own strengths.

We were alone on this great emptiness, astride a grand contrivance catapulted along by nature's forces and managed by the will and energy of a most cohesive crew. Gradually, we entered the domain of the stronger trade winds and the heavier surfing. This is accompanied by great and serious strains on the yacht, with a motion that was not as predictably rhythmical as we had been experiencing. It was surrounded by this great loneliness, pulled by the oscillating forces of the main spinnaker, mainsail, shooter, mizzen and mizzen spinnaker staysail, a colorful display of several thousand square feet of sail area, when we spotted *Windward Passage*.

The differences in the design of the yachts in this era was perhaps more divergent than at other times. *KIALOA* was a more traditional aluminum displacement hull driven by a broad spread of canvas distributed more evenly fore and aft by her sizable main- and mizzen-masts. In contrast, *Windward Passage*, a much lighter yacht, had a larger spinnaker and smaller mizzen. But more importantly, her wooden hull was more like a giant dinghy with a broad beam carried aft to her transom. She loved to surf.

Once we got into the downwind running typical to the trade winds, *Windward Passage* caught up with us and we vied for the lead over several days in sight of one another. This became a grand chess game where the pawns were the scattered squalls amassed in vertical splendor. This game was spread out on a large liquid chessboard, except we were but little creatures forced to play out at their feet. The object of this sport was to chase these waltzing squalls and position the yacht for the favorable winds that inhabit certain portions of the surface under them. Depending upon how you played, you would receive a "lift" or "header," wind shifts pointing the boat up into the wind or down, which is combined with an increase or decrease in wind speed. These jousts in and around these pylons of nature were accomplished with a sequence of jibes. This theater is made more important by the fact that *Windward Passage* was the perpetual and venerable competition. The crews knew each other well and were of a similar ilk, not to mention friends.

Because of these cloud splendors parading across our paths, the wind had become shifty and varied in intensity and direction. After several days of weaving in and around under this great array, jockeying with *Windward Passage*, the wind disappeared into the billowing mass of clouds above.

⋆ ⋆ ⋆

Yacht racing on the grand scale of Maxi racers is expensive. For most, it includes all the adventure and rewards of witnessing nature in her unfiltered greatness, the competition, the camaraderie of a team sport; these motivations are typical to all involved in sailing. But for others, including me and (in my opinion) Jim Kilroy, it was regeneration and an intentional reality check or adjustment to one's perspective that was both necessary to keep a competitive edge in other aspects of life. In the enforced isolation of ocean racing, undisturbed by intrusions, one becomes so immersed in a completely different endeavor from the day-to-day life that select, over-worked areas of the brain get to regenerate. Although the same principals of achievement may apply, the fact that you are forced to exercise them in a completely different, intense and perhaps purer medium allows for the honing of technique and appreciation of the fine points of the mechanics involved in the pursuit of success.

Those successful enough to underwrite these great racing yachts have generally evolved by self-efforts to positions of influence and power. A driving and necessary force is always a significant conception of self, an ego. It is easy from the perspective of a constant series of successes in life to begin to believe that one's own doing has solely brought about every accomplishment. This "rich-pocket arrogance" will often cause one to attempt to duplicate his successes in a completely different medium and expect similar and equal results. This tendency can have significant and negative consequences. Yacht racing can cure this inclination and/or bring a needed focus on the numerous elements necessary for success. It is a noble adjuster, the "reality check." It can be a humbling and frustrating experience. I have seen this frustration in others as well as experienced it myself. It reminds one of a human's scale, and/or their insignificance in the grand picture. To be successful in life, one must learn to control as many of the variables as possible in any situation, stacking them in one's own favor, minimizing the risks, adjusting where finite resources shall be applied.

In the business world, for example, the successful learn to "get their hands around" most or all of the variables of an undertaking, apply talent and efforts accordingly, and make decisions based upon detailed analysis and some "gut reaction." The positive results or success can generally be estimated within small margins. Unknowns can all but be eliminated or at least minimized. Ah…but in yacht racing, you can employ, buy or attract the best architects, constructors, tacticians, crew, sails and, in general, expertise, but you cannot control the infinite number of variables that nature or luck can throw your way. An unexpected wind-shift, squall, current or that one unknown condition will put you back, appropriately, into the herd of humanity. This is not to say the rules or tricks of life's other successes do not apply to yacht racing. They do.

Assembling a talented team, respecting all opinions, open discussions of tactics and detailed analysis of the information available, weighing results, and finally making a decision: all these factors apply. The operative phrase here is simple: "Make a decision." Yacht racing, in particular, teaches that you have to make a decision and take chances, and once a decision is made, it is to be stuck with, as equivocation, the fault of so many lives, will not be tolerated. Along with recognizing that you never have all the answers, this experience also taught me, and others, to remain optimistic and never let up on the hard work necessary to win. If you are thrown an unfavorable wind shift, do not reduce your enthusiasm or efforts, for the next shift may be to your favor, and the key is to be well-positioned to take advantage of it. Further, in the great picture of life, success is comprised of numerous facets, not the least of which is luck, which is probably somewhat evenly distributed. One must strive to recognize luck for what it is, such as recognizing opportunities—often a form of luck—and take advantage of them or it. Lastly, it teaches that with hard work, and a realistic, analytical and rational approach, you are able to compete at any level, and as such should set goals and aspirations that are always well ahead of any current position. Life can be much larger and rewarding if you strive to make it so.

* * *

It was during the heavier downwind surfing conditions that I remember coming up on deck in the middle of the night and hearing the roar of the boat going fast under two spinnakers, shooter, main and mizzen. I was just getting my bearings in the blackness when Jim said, "Here, take this." Puffy eyed and still thinking of the fantasies of sleep, I was on the helm…blinking. Next thing I knew, we were on a sizable wave a little crooked. She rolled with a tremendous force and the main boom began to drag in the water, the roar deafening. I had to lay hard into the helm, and wide eyes abounded. She came back up on her feet but not before, with a burst, the boom vang, a block and tackle device that holds the boom down, broke. Even the reefed mizzen boom had been dragged in the water.

I was wide awake by then and I did get a heap of sarcastic abuse for having broken the boom vang. The lesson? Make sure you are awake before you wander near the helm. Though surfing in the blackness of night is exhilarating, it can be risky with the boat rolling from side to side, just waiting for you to not pay complete attention. One listened over their shoulder to try and determine the size and attitude of the next wave, which will pick the stern up and initially try to yaw the boat to weather. You countervailed with helm down to leeward but not too much as she wanted to enter the danger zone of the wind getting behind the mainsail—the "dreaded broach"—and at night this would be disastrous. But kept in the middle of these tendencies and nudged just so, she grabbed a hold and took off on the wave with noticeable acceleration. This act was accompanied by a tumultuous roar, the white water marching back from the bow finally reaching the area of the main shrouds, and clearly visible in the dark above deck level. It is a sign of *KIALOA*'s strength and operations that we only broke a boom vang. The same cannot be said of others in the fleet. While we were charging along with relatively insignificant failures, there were squalls running elsewhere through the fleet and five boats were ultimately dismasted, and many sails blown out, along with much other damage.

Having stood the late watch at night, breakfast and the bunk were welcome occurrences. As typical with the two watches on *KIALOA*, we had divided the 24 hours into what's known as a Swedish system. This called for three four-hour watches from 6 p.m. to 6 a.m. that would alternate; during one night your watch would stand two four-hour watches and the next night one four-hour watch. The day was split into two 6-hour watches.

Once we had gotten into the area of strong breeze and heavy surfing under a 2.2 ounce full main spinnaker and comparable mizzen spinnaker, we were concerned about chafe on the spinnaker halyards. In the rolling of the seas and the constant swaying of the boat, the spinnaker would oscillate from side to side, which caused the head (top) to move back and forth. This constant motion, and the pulsing of the spinnaker with the gusty nature of the breeze, caused the halyard to work both laterally and in and out. By necessity of design, the top block turns the halyard 90 degrees. It is at this point of greatest load that the halyard cable suffers constant chaffing friction against the block sheave. It is the habit of an experienced crew to adjust this halyard in or out a little bit to allow such wear to be spread over a larger area. This was done periodically; ultimately, however, the entire end of the halyard becomes stressed and frayed. The consequence: a parting of the cable.

Now a 5/16-inch plow steel cable does not "go into the night" peacefully. The rated strength is about 10,000 pounds. When it parts, it makes a hell of a noise that resonates down the aluminum mast into the aluminum hull like the sound of a small car having been dropped on deck. This has a lot in common with the base instrument in a marimba steel drum band, only much larger. The entire boat lets you know something is dreadfully wrong.

It was a nice sunny day with gusty breeze. I was down below in the off watch peacefully asleep in my bunk when what I thought was a cannon went off. It is amazing what adrenaline can do to a sleeping person. I was on deck in my underwear, through the open sail hatch before the kite was halfway down! I hollered for Jim, who was on the helm, to head up so as not to run over the chute which was billowing out in front of the boat. Putting the spinnaker under the boat would have caused major problems. I also yelled to let the after guy forward to facilitate the spinnaker coming down on the lee side of the boat. By the time the water drove it back against the starboard/lee rail to be gathered by both the on and the entire off watch, we were two to three minutes into the event. Turning forward, packed in stops, a new spinnaker was coming on deck, unsolicited. The alternate halyard was lead around, the spinnaker pole was dropped and the after guy hooked to the new kite; the sheet was taken off the old and now wet one and brought forward as the new one was being raised. The total time was probably in the four- to five-minute range. A new spinnaker was flying and the new halyard was being uncoiled on deck ready for someone to go aloft and re-lead it.

No one had been called. Everyone knew precisely what to do. This was *KIALOA*'s way, a team that knew each other's reaction instinctively. There was no need for protocol, instructions or oversight, just an innate ability to get the job done with an economy of words and confusion.

Big-boat ocean racing, by its very nature, requires a selective sieve through which the participants must pass. To have entered this realm is to have left the greatest majority of the populace behind. One is required to have a unique blend of strengths, traits and abilities. It is not enough to be just a sailor. You are often required to act like a high-wire exhibitionist, one who is not concerned with performing on a moving, violent platform without a net. In addition, one must have the skills of a heavy equipment operator, able to recognize the difference in scale of the tremendous loads associated with a Maxi boat versus a dingy, yet also possess the nuance of a dinghy racer. Although the crew had general positions and roles to play, all could fill any of the required positions in an all-hands situation like this. The crew had acted as one and with tremendous alacrity; they had simply done their jobs. This was an example of the discipline, coordination and confidence that had been developed through thousands of miles of racing together, and learning from one another and from knowing that we would never stop learning, or at least should not allow ourselves to stop.

These same forces that result from pulling an 80,000 pound yacht through the water by a large spinnaker, connected in only three corners by cables, were to cause another gear failure. The halyard that holds the top of the spinnaker is required to make two 90 degree turns, around sheaves, in its course from the deck level to the top of the mast. As mentioned, this puts great pressure on the halyard and gear. From the deck winch to the mast, there is a threatening-looking sheave that takes this tremendous load. At one point, the tang securing the sheave to the deck let go on the starboard halyard, with a bang, of course. This required some creative engineering to pull the halyard back to the mast in a manner that it could still be used and would not destroy itself. The crew also did this in a coordinated, efficient manner.

Having such strongly defined and fascinatingly unique characters act in such a singular manner is a tribute to the organization and management of *KIALOA*. Somehow, when I dissect the crew as a unit and look at the individuals who made it up, I am amazed at the dissimilarity of the parts…but how could they have been so unique were it not so?

Perhaps one of the most unparalleled members in this regard was Dave Kilponen, aka "Fang." Dave had the market cornered on the name "Fang" long before other, more professional comedians, had taken to using it. This appellation was earned at an early age by taking a tumble down a flight of stairs, which temporarily left his front tooth at an angle of 90 degrees to the rest. He was a bespectacled, mustachioed, often seemingly disheveled looking individual who had prioritized his life. First, there was humor, then everything else. Visually, he could be described as jolly, which was no doubt the inner man showing through. He enjoyed life and it enjoyed him, and as such he was therefore very likable. Although he had tried other forms of existence, he always came back to the sea, at which he was very good. Men who are drawn to the sea, having once committed themselves to its hazards and adventures, are compelled to go back again and again. Fang ultimately went on to becoming a much-respected international judge of yacht races and consultant to various America's Cup racing teams.

Fang was a navigator and "popped" up on deck on a sunny afternoon and said "Right!" Now "Right" in Australian is a catch-all phrase meaning such things as "here goes," "We're going to do such and such," "Just what I expected," "Now listen," and so on. In this instance, it was the "now listen" variant. There was a long pause after which he said, "This is it, we're going straight to the Molokai Channel…this will be the last jibe!"

Well, this in itself, out of context, would not seem that unusual; however, there was one troubling factor. We were well over 600 miles out from Molokai. "Right!" This was about to be the world's longest call on a racing layline. As such Fang, was required to suffer the abuse of numerous taunts…

"Ah…stay out of the rum would you!"

"Fang, you're hallucinating, get out of the sun!"

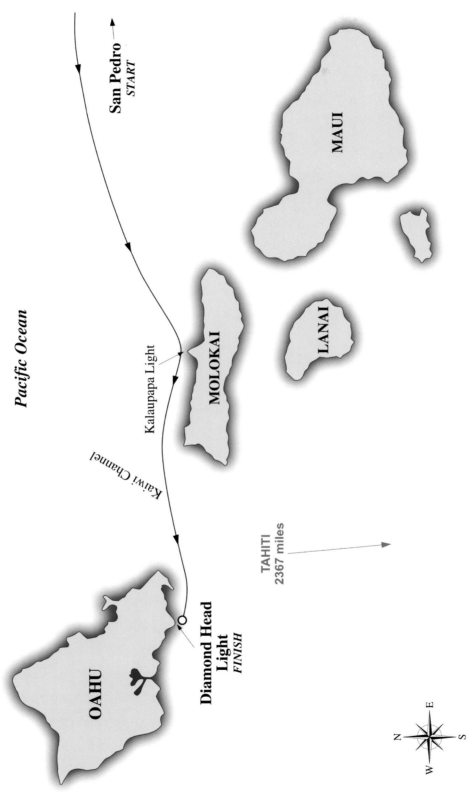

Transpacific Yacht Race (Jibe Off Molokai)

San Pedro - Diamond Head Light
2225 Nautical Miles

However, he called it, and after about two and one half days we were at the entrance to the Molokai Channel and on the same board, never having jibed again since Fang's statement. It should be pointed out that the call on this jibe was the culmination of a great debate by several experienced tacticians and navigators on board. This was typical of the business approach to decisions onboard *KIALOA*. One learns that no one has the market cornered on knowledge or ability (or lack thereof). And from these types of interactions and similar experiences, we all learned to always deal from a level perspective in personal interactions, never up nor down to anyone, and to contribute where we could.

In sailor's lore, the Molokai Channel ranks high on the list of daunting places, along with the likes of Bass Strait, which separates mainland Australia from Tasmania. The winds and seas are forced to go through a venturi and are thus required to demonstrate Bernoulli's Principle: "When an incompressible fluid moves into a region having a different and reduced cross-sectional area, it undergoes a change in speed effect which accelerates and magnifies its nature."

Put another way, the Molokai Channel is not meant for Sunday sailors, especially when carrying a full press of canvas. There is a deservedly famous picture of the 1969 dismasting of the 78-foot yacht *Mir* in Molokai. In this photograph, she is straining beyond belief, having been pushed sideways on her beam ends by the mighty seas, all sails pulling hard and the spinnaker pole determined to act like an arrow…right through the mast…which is precisely what happened!

This picture and concept was flickering in each of the crew's minds that bright, sunny day when we charged into the channel with "a bone in her teeth." There was a small repeater gauge amidships for the ship's log reading in knots. At times, the crew resembled a group of stock brokers looking "at the board" as their favorite stock left the charts. The log would peg at something just over twenty knots, and it was pegging in the large rushing swells.

The spinnaker, when running relatively square to the wind, has a tendency to want to drive the ship erratically, to turn and pull the boat to the side. The "shooter," pulling from the opposite side of the yacht, counteracts these bad characteristics of the spinnaker. When jibing, it is necessary to drop the shooter, so the spinnaker can carry on its wayward ways. It was necessary to jibe. At this point, Bruce Kendell was on the helm, the shooter was dropped, and the boat became…erratic. Bruce was not one to easily get excited, but when approaching such a point his voice had a tendency to get shrill, and this it did.

"Get the shooter back up…get the shooter back up!" he yelled as he tried to keep control of the rolling yacht. None of us wanted to become the next *Mir* picture. We were able to get the shooter back up and the yacht regained a modicum of control.

After we were about three-quarters of the way through the channel, with Jim on the helm, we caught the longest surfing ride imaginable. The entire crew was hooting and hollering. The bow wave was back at the main shrouds and fully five feet above deck level. There was a kind of eerie, harmonic singing coming from the components of the hull and rudder, which seemed a dissonant mix with the more violent and tumultuous roar of the water. We were carried along in the outstretched hands of this mighty wave for a most unbelievable length of time, all the while the log was pegged at 20 plus knots. From this grand swell, the run to the finish line at Diamond Head was truly anti-climatic, where one had time to look at the scattered signs of civilization along the shore. Finally, with a bright Hawaiian day, we paraded into the Ala Wai Yacht harbor to the expectant wives, girlfriends and leis, so to speak.

* * *

A kind of intimacy develops based on a long series of shared experiences, adventures, and dangers. There is plenty of time in the confines of a yacht to decipher the true mettle of a person. And it can be said that the mettle of each of the *KIALOA* crew was of a high standard and each shared a mutual acceptance and respect of one another as such. All were brought together seeking adventure on the sea, and perhaps this is the fundamental building block that was common in the make-up of their various, if truly unique, personalities. There was a degree of "nomadism" that was part of their nature, requiring its satisfaction to become whole. Also, the desire to act together is driven by means of some factor of selectivity, this need to perform as a team is probably more primal or inherent in mankind's fundamental structure. It dates back, no doubt, to some prehistoric requirements of troglodytes having to work together to bring down some massive mastodon for dinner. Yacht racing and the sea provides satisfaction to these needs.

The components of these various, collected personalities can convert the same energy and teamwork required in dangerous and violent situations to become rather ribald ashore, especially after a long and hard race culminating in some distant land. This phenomenon in those past days of the great sailing ships was known as "Jack Ashore;" it is a form of great release necessary in the transition of leaving the solitude of the sea and rejoining society. This activity provided some bawdy events and memories, all on the proper side of moral correctness, if sometimes marginally so.

We had finished the race and done very well. Our actual time was about nine days, two and one-half hours. *KIALOA*'s corrected time was about eight days, eleven and one half hours, approximately seven hours off the prior record and six hours lower than any other corrected time. Our corrected time put us first in Class A, and first overall. And we were fifth to finish behind archrival *Windward Passage* and the two new sleds, *Merlin* and *Drifter,* with an earlier New Zealand built sled, *Ragtime*, squeezing in for third to finish.

This Transpac win added to an already noteworthy record for *KIALOA* in 1977, e.g. first to finish in the Saint Petersburg to Fort Lauderdale (including a new elapsed time record, and first overall); wins in the Ocean Triangle, Miami-Nassau and Nassau Cup races; and a first overall in the Miami to Montego Bay Race.

These wins, along with the Transpac victory, were to be followed by a first in the world-famous Sydney-Hobart race, all of which rounded out a spectacular year for 1977. In fact, the record of wins from 1975 through 1977 allowed *KIALOA III* to win the coveted World Ocean Racing Championship, which is determined by the best-combined record over a predetermined group of races. *KIALOA*'s worst placing in this series was second, arguably winning her the reputation as being the best racing yacht ever.

Another Transpac Perspective by Andy Rose

I have memories of four things from the 1977 Transpac. First, I believe it was my first race on *KIALOA III* and I was excited and nervous even though I had been on three previous Transpacs. Anyway, on one of the first days that we were able to use a spinnaker, I remember one incident that made me think that everything I had heard about *KIALOA* and her crew was true. We had a full size chute up in about 18-20 knots or so of wind and suddenly, either the shackle at the head of the sail blew up or the head itself came off, but in any event, there was a "boom" and the top of the sail started slowly falling.

I think Jim was steering, and he merely steered up a bit, allowing the sail to fall to leeward rather than right in front of the boat. Then the crew immediately began gathering the sail in while other members prepared a new spinnaker to go up. While I don't know how long that took, it couldn't have been more than a couple of minutes until we were again sailing along with a full spinnaker at speed. I don't know that I had ever seen a sail change, especially an unexpected one, performed at that pace and with that calmness. No worries, mate!

My second memory is that Jim treated me as a person rather than a kid or, even worse, a *KIALOA* rookie kid. He attempted to teach me to use his HP 65 which was then a state of the art computer/calculator on which he was doing the navigational programs. While I admire his patience, I'm not sure I ever quite "got it" (Don't worry, Jim, I've greatly improved my computer skills since then), but the time he spent with me was wonderful.

During down times when we were off watch, we talked politics a bit. My politics were and are somewhat different than Jim's, but we always had fascinating discussions and I learned a lot. He actually asked for my thoughts on some strategic decisions during the race, the most important being allowed into the discussion of when to do the last jibe onto port tack to approach the islands. I had learned a bit about that from Danny Elliott in previous races and like to think that Jim and his brain trust listened to my input. In any event, we caught the jibe point perfectly about 600 miles out and shortened *Windward Passage*'s lead on us by about 75 miles in the next couple of days. That end-of-the-race surge allowed us to cross the finish line on a beautiful morning knowing, due to the position reports, that we had likely won the Transpac overall on corrected time, a fact later confirmed. A great feeling!

Third, I remember the laughter that was the hallmark of the *KIALOA* crew. I have never had so much fun sailing in serious races. Everyone had a personality and something to add to the mix. Specifically, one practical joke stands out. Jim had invited a friend who was also one of his bankers to sail with us to Honolulu. Richard was his name, I think. He was a good guy, but had no real sailing experience, a fact that gave the crew some evil thoughts. Since he couldn't do much as far as crew work, he was often assigned KP duty in the galley after dinner. Right above the galley was a "Dorade" vent that allowed fresh air to flow down from the deck. The boys decided to give him a thrill and got a bucket of water that they proceeded to put down the Dorade while yelling "rogue wave!" Obviously, Richard was drenched and it took him until about the third time until he finally figured out that somehow, "rogue waves" only seemed to hit after dinner when he was in the galley. He was a good sport about it and was thereafter a full-fledged member of the crew.

My final memory is from the days after the race. As usual after every major race, Jim would throw caution to the wind and host a crew party. That's where I learned about one of the many rules that I have now imposed on the racing boat I own—the 24-hour rule. That is, in order to bring a date to the crew party, you had to have known her for at least 24 hours. It was also a plus—but not required—if you actually knew her name. (I know that's sexist, but those were different times!)

In any event, this party was held at the Waikikian Hotel, which was an old style two-story bungalow hotel with a pool and a beach fronting the Hilton lagoon. The party started pretty normally but as was typical, quickly got pretty hilarious. At one point, some of the boys began "float testing" (throwing) a few people in the pool. This and the general level of boisterousness caused the management to eventually come over and sternly ask to speak to Jim. We were not privy to the conversation but in his inimitable way, Jim both defended the honor (and antics) of his crew and also reached an acceptable compromise. That is, we would not be allowed to throw anyone else in the pool, but throwing someone in the lagoon was perfectly acceptable.

Next thing we knew, two of the boys had picked up an unsuspecting couple from somewhere in the Midwest (you know, the types with matching muumuus, shorts and shirt) and slowly walked them down to the lagoon (the "long march to the sea") where they were suitably "float tested." Happily, they passed. Rather than being offended, after joining us for a rum or two, the couple later allowed as how it was the most exciting thing that had happened to them on their trip and they could hardly wait to tell the folks back home. It's amazing that we didn't make the guidebooks as a recommended excursion.

My thanks, my compliments to our great *KIALOA* crew, each and everyone, a winner.

22

KIALOA III
"The Race They Said We Couldn't Win"

The Tattersail Trophy
Sydney Hobart 1977
First to Finish – First Overall

The 1977 Sydney Hobart Race
A Clean Sweep for KIALOA III

It was December 26, 1977, Boxing Day, and a noon start for the 630-mile race from Sydney to Hobart, Tasmania, one of the most challenging races in our world of yachting. One hundred and thirty one yachts had entered the race, with only 72 crossing the finish line.

The Sydney Harbor was awash with spectators—all kinds, surfboats, ski boats, small sailboats, big sailboats, and motorboats of all sizes. Many were calling out good wishes to their favorite—and *KIALOA's* calls were some of the loudest.

"Go *KIALOA!*"

"Beat your record!"

"Win the race!"

We could not help but share in their enthusiasm. The starting gun was fired and *KIALOA* boldly crossed the starting line leading the fleet and its key competitor *Windward Passage* to the South Head, at the entry of Sydney Harbor, and steering more southerly towards Hobart, Tasmania, in moderate sea conditions. We soon set a spinnaker in what appeared to be easy race conditions.

Windward Passage and *KIALOA III* had accelerated their rivalry in a serious collision in the last race of the local Sydney Southern Cross Cup a few days before the start. Fortunately, no crew was hurt, however serious damage was done to each boat, which required overnight repairs to be able to start the Sydney Hobart Race. The following photograph shows the damage to *KIALOA III*.

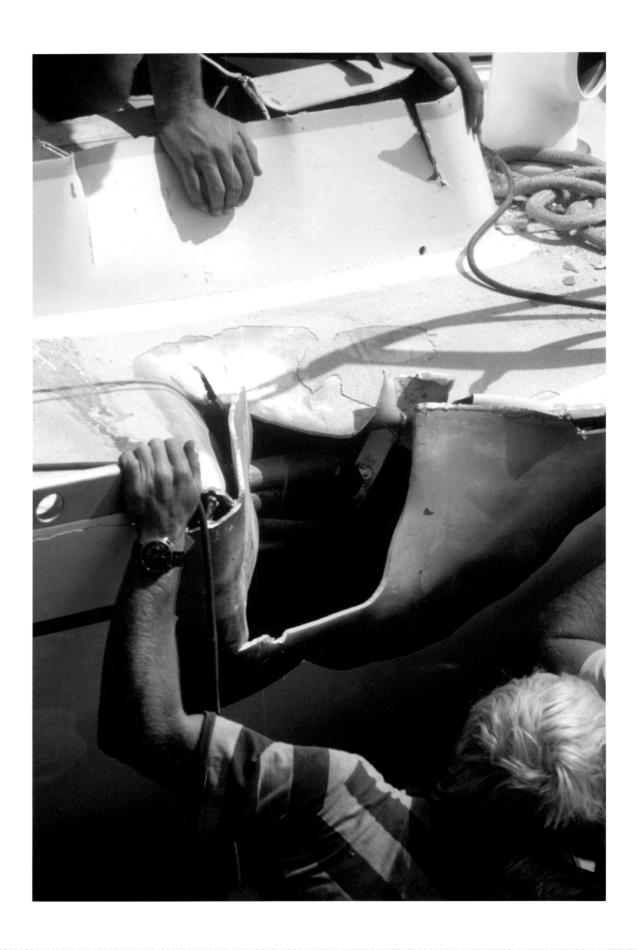

After a most thorough hearing and review by the protest committee judges, *Windward Passage* was held solely responsible for the collision and all damages to *KIALOA*, and after further debate, was still qualified to race in the Sydney Hobart Race.

Although we were seriously aggravated by the collision and damage to *KIALOA*, we supported *Windward Passage's* right to sail in the following 630-mile Sydney Hobart Race and we also wanted the intensity of our mutual competition to continue.

We had two "must" challenges embedded into our major racing plans. One was to win the 630-mile race, the Sydney Hobart Race in the Southern Ocean, and the other was to win the 605-mile, almost identical race in the Irish Sea of the North Atlantic Ocean, the Fastnet Rock Race. We had come near in the Fastnet Rock Race, but near doesn't count.

Before the start of the 1977 Sydney Hobart Race, we had reviewed our prior race planning, the wind and weather in the 1971 race aboard *KIALOA II* and the 1975 elapsed time record setting race aboard *KIALOA III*, the record we held for 21 years. We again reviewed variables of the Sydney Hobart Race with our good friends and fellow sailors, Magnus Halvorsen and Jock Sturrock.

We decided to stay as close as possible to our 1975 record setting course subject to wind, sea and current variables, with particular concern about the fan type and reverse current approaching Bass Straits.

The attached images are two sailing charts, the first one showing the actual courses sailed in the 1977 race and the second chart showing the actual courses sailed in all three races by the *KIALOA's*. Interesting comparisons, particularly when further analyzed with the log books, which offer information on speeds over the bottom and effect of currents.

Particular reference should be taken to the effect of the strong Southerly Buster, 35-45 knots, tacking upwind for over 23 hours, in the 1977 victorious race, which we will now discuss in more detail with separate observations of our outstanding crew.

The first "waypoint" we wanted to hit was off the small fishing village of Eden on the mainland coast of New South Wales. Our second was off Tourville Light, just inside the 200-meter depth line along the coast of Tasmania. From there, we'd seek smoother water and favorable current working down the coast to the Tasman Isle Light. Finally, we hoped to "speed sail" across Storm Bay to the Iron Pot, and then it was up the Derwent River to the finish.

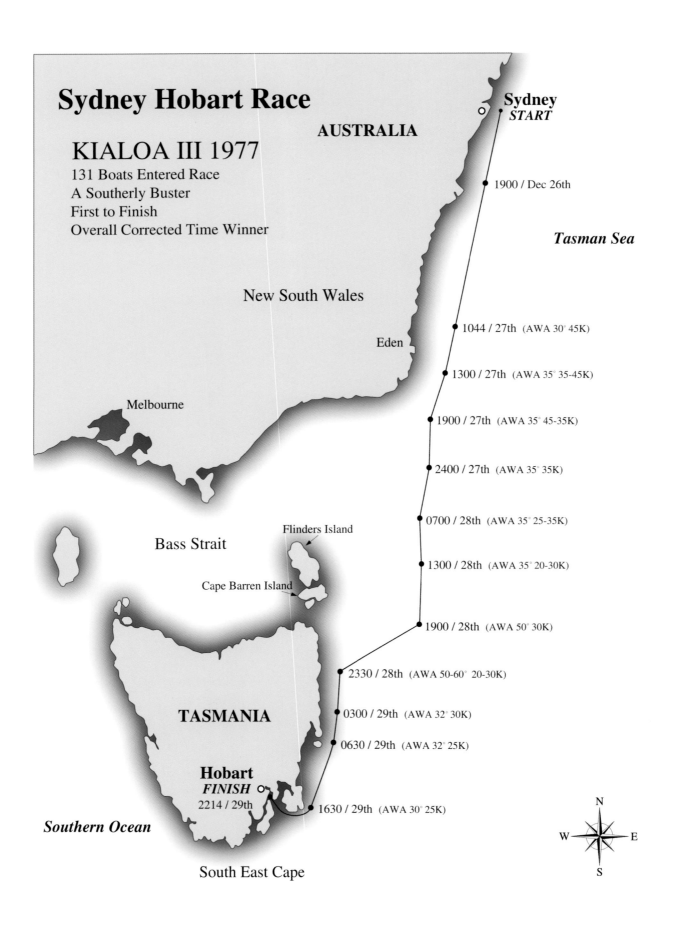

Sydney Hobart Race

KIALOA III 1977
131 Boats Entered Race
A Southerly Buster
First to Finish
Overall Corrected Time Winner

AUSTRALIA

Sydney
START

1900 / Dec 26th

Tasman Sea

New South Wales

Eden

1044 / 27th (AWA 30° 45K)

1300 / 27th (AWA 35° 35-45K)

Melbourne

1900 / 27th (AWA 35° 45-35K)

2400 / 27th (AWA 35° 35K)

0700 / 28th (AWA 35° 25-35K)

Flinders Island

Bass Strait

1300 / 28th (AWA 35° 20-30K)

Cape Barren Island

1900 / 28th (AWA 50° 30K)

2330 / 28th (AWA 50-60° 20-30K)

TASMANIA

0300 / 29th (AWA 32° 30K)

0630 / 29th (AWA 32° 25K)

Hobart
FINISH
2214 / 29th

1630 / 29th (AWA 30° 25K)

Southern Ocean

South East Cape

N
W E
S

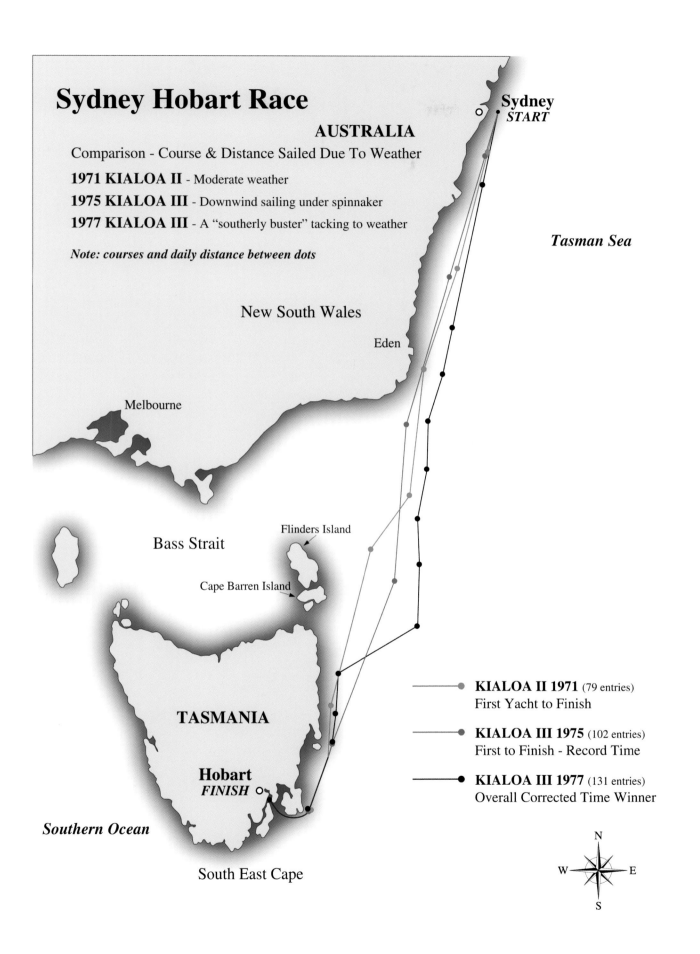

Sydney Hobart Race

AUSTRALIA

Comparison - Course & Distance Sailed Due To Weather

1971 KIALOA II - Moderate weather

1975 KIALOA III - Downwind sailing under spinnaker

1977 KIALOA III - A "southerly buster" tacking to weather

Note: courses and daily distance between dots

New South Wales

Eden

Melbourne

Tasman Sea

Sydney
START

Flinders Island

Bass Strait

Cape Barren Island

TASMANIA

Hobart
FINISH

Southern Ocean

South East Cape

● **KIALOA II 1971** (79 entries)
First Yacht to Finish

● **KIALOA III 1975** (102 entries)
First to Finish - Record Time

● **KIALOA III 1977** (131 entries)
Overall Corrected Time Winner

N
W   E
S

Once outside the Sydney Heads, we latched onto a nice northerly breeze for the next 23 hours, dueling with *Windward Passage* downwind and surfing on medium-sized waves. As we closed in on Eden, I was at the helm when the crew noticed a photo helicopter engaged in rather strange maneuvers a mile south down the course. Bruce Kendell, the other watch captain, and I agreed that it looked like a dreaded Southerly Buster was on the horizon. It was time for quick action.

We called to the crew to quickly douse the spinnaker and the mizzen staysail, triple reef the mainsail, and hoist a small, No. 5 headsail. I steered *KIALOA III* away from the storm to give the crew time to quickly make the absolutely necessary sail changes. Once everything was shipshape, the 35-45 knot southerly was upon us, and it stayed there all the way to Tourville Light, which we had abeam at 0635 on the 29th after 43 hours of hard, upwind sailing. It was tough on the crew, but at that stage, we had 70% of the course distance behind us.

For this Hobart race, we had a crew of fifteen onboard, which we split in two for the port and starboard watches, with the cook on standby. Once again we employed our heavy-weather watch system: three watches of four hours each during the day, and four watches of three hours each at night. Our challenge was to keep *KIALOA III* moving as fast as possible along with immediate repairs to any damaged sails or gear.

Consider the sleeping and dressing conditions below. The seas were rough. The boat would fly off waves while heeled with the mast and deck at a 28 degree angle to the sea, and *KIALOA III* would either slow down or accelerate depending on the wave action. On average, the crew would take 15-20 minutes to get the necessary foul weather gear on for a full watch: oilskin pants with long shoulder straps, boots and socks, a warm jacket, perhaps a vest, and an oilskin jacket. It was quite a balancing act, pulling on all this gear and sea boots with the boat heeled over, leaping from wave to wave. It was cold outside, but due to the exertion it took to get dressed, you'd come on deck hot and sweaty. But that would change almost instantly.

As we sailed down the coast of Tasmania, *KIALOA III* was still hard on the wind in heavy weather. We rounded the Tasman Isle Light at 1730 on the 29th and at long last, were able to bear off and set a spinnaker and mizzen staysails for the downwind blast across Storm Bay to the Iron Pot, the entrance buoy to the Derwent River. It took just over three hours to cover the distance.

We were an excited and highly focused crew. We knew the heavy upwind sailing had played to our strengths—we'd received reports via radio that only 72 of the original 131-strong fleet were still racing—and that we had a chance to win the race, and not just on elapsed time, but on handicap as well. Once again, the Derwent River was lined with motorists flashing their lights on and off. The Aussies knew what a challenge their race was, and they were clearly appreciative of our efforts.

KIALOA III crossed the finish line a little before midnight. It was a waiting game to see if we would save our time on handicap in relation to the rest of our fleet. Our hopes were very high. We were a tight, experienced team and close, protective friends. We'd left everything we had on the racecourse. And we were all wondering: Could we add the Hobart Race to our other three major victories in 1977?

Soon, we had our answer. Yes, we could.

All the discomfort we'd experienced was immediately forgotten. We'd faced and met a mutual challenge, and the rewards—the hugs from family and friends, the cheers from the knowledgeable spectators—were wonderful. Our amateur crew—Tasmanians, Australians, Kiwis and Americans—had once again bonded together towards a common goal. Not only were we a team, we were friends.

Our elapsed time for the race was 3 days, 10 hours, 14 minutes and 9 seconds…approximately two hours ahead of *Windward Passage. KIALOA III* had a handicap coefficient of 1.0454 which, when multiplied by the actual elapsed time, produced a corrected time of 3 days, 13 hours and 58 minutes. *Windward Passage's* corrected time was about three hours behind ours, which gave her a third place overall. *Ragamuffin* slipped between us for second.

Corrected Times
Elapsed Times
1977 Sydney Hobart

NAME	Elapsed Time	Corrected Time
KIALOA III	3.10.14.09	3.13.58
Ragamuffin	4.06.29.42	3.16.06.17
Windward Passage	3.12.39.00	3.16.19.56

It was a satisfying, clean sweep: first to finish, first in class, first overall, and it meant that *KIALOA III's* name would be engraved on the race's perpetual trophy, the Tattersall Cup. The Floating Opera House had won Australia's biggest race, and in so doing claimed two other victories: our in-house, tongue-in-cheek Gordon Marshall Challenge, and the private "race-within-a-race" with *Windward Passage*, which finished 2 hours and 25 minutes behind us on elapsed time.

Sydney-Hobart Facts
In the three Sydney Hobart races sailed by *KIALOA II* and *KIALOA III,* the following number of boats started and the following finished:
1971 – 79 started, 76 finished
1975 – 102 started, 99 finished
1977 – 131 started, 72 finished

KIALOA III's 1977 Australian Adventures by Andy Rose

Andy Rose, an outstanding young crew and tactician, has written the following article about the Southern Cross Cup Series, the tune-up for the 1977 Sydney Hobart Race, and the winning 1977 Sydney-Hobart Race. It is more detailed than my writings and also discusses the unfortunate collision with Windward Passage, which could have been disastrous. I believe the readers will find Andy's comments of great interest. Thank you, Andy, for your observations.

1977 Southern Cross Series: The Big Bang!

We all were looking forward to the Southern Cross series in Sydney before the Sydney-Hobart Race, especially because our archrival, *Windward Passage*, was also competing. The first race was a triangle, windward/leeward course and it was blowing! As I remember, it was probably about 18-20 knots at the start and increased from there. I was tactician and Jim was steering. We got the start and had an intense weather leg with *Passage* but led her to the weather mark. She was a bit faster on the reaches but we held her off to the next mark and then sailed down the second of the reaching legs on the triangle with a large chute, and full mizzen (we were still a ketch in those days).

As we approached the leeward mark, *Passage* was threatening to get an "inside overlap" on us which would have required us to give them room to round the mark and would have resulted in them passing us. My crewmate from the America's Cup on *Australia*, Michael Summerton, was on the bow of *Passage* and both boats were going about 13-14 knots. As we approached the "two boat length circle" by which time the overlap would have had to be established, they did not get quite close enough to us to establish it. I stood on the back of the boat and yelled to Mike that there was no overlap and he agreed. (They were about a half boat to a boat length or so behind us at the time).

The crew did a great job of hoisting a storm jib, dousing the chute and preparing the boat to go upwind. I then turned back to Jim and asked that he not get too close to the mark at first, and instead to turn slowly so that when the bow reached the mark, the boat would already be established on its "close hauled" course going upwind. That makes it a certainty that the boat behind will have to sail in disturbed air and then will have to tack away at a relatively slow speed. It would allow us to gain back part of what we lost on the reaches right away. But, if you didn't expect us to do a good rounding, it would seem to open up a space between the mark and us…even though when our turn was complete, there would be no such space. As Jim turned up into the wind, I happened to look back and saw that Mike was waving his helmsman to come "up" to a course that would put them between us and the mark. Or, as it turned out, a course that would put them right through our cockpit!

David "Fang" Kilponen was our navigator and he told me later than when I saw that

Passage intended to go in between us, I said something like, "I'm getting the heck out of here!" (My words may have been more vivid.) In any event, as it was clear that they were headed right at us, Fang had seen enough and jumped overboard, reckoning as he said later that I had "saved his life" (it would take more than an 80,000 pound boat hitting us to kill Fang). Evidently, I ran forward to get out of the way (Sorry, Jim!). A couple of seconds after that, they "T-boned" us, that is, hit us on a perpendicular course almost right at the steering station.

Passage had a bowsprit with a large steel bobstay that fastened the sprit to the hull and allowed the headstay to be attached at the front of the bowsprit. The solid bobstay had a diameter of an inch and a half or so, and acted like a can opener on our strong aluminum hull, punching a hole a couple of feet down from the rail and about the same distance into the deck and cockpit. They were far enough in that the bowsprit tore our mizzen.

One of our grinders was a doctor, and when he looked back and saw their bow in our cockpit, our wheel bent, and no sign of Jim. His first thought was that Jim was dead. Meanwhile, on the bow, Jim's son, John Kilroy, Jr., was thrown overboard by the force of the collision, which pivoted the boat about ten to fifteen feet into the wind and literally took the bow out from under him. He was so busy with getting the chute down and tidying up that he didn't even know that we had been hit and instead thought he had just clumsily fallen overboard. Far from it!

A couple of us tried and eventually succeeded in pushing *Passage* out of our cockpit and freed the boats, which allowed Jim to struggle up from where he was huddled under the badly bent wheel to leeward. Not only was he not dead, he wasn't even hurt. His first words to me were something like, "Well, Andy, I told you I'd do anything you told me to do." At that moment, as I have told many people over the years, I decided that I would sail around the world backward with a blindfold on if Jim asked me to. Talk about grace under pressure!

Once we got everyone back on board and returned to the dock under power, we protested *Windward Passage* and the race committee agreed with what was pretty obvious to us, that *Passage* had no overlap and therefore had no right to go inside of us. While it didn't help us much, she was disqualified from the race and would have had to pay for the cost of our repair although I don't know if Jim ever charged them. We obviously couldn't sail in the rest of the Southern Cross Series but Bruce "Goose" Kendell quickly assembled his welding equipment and some new aluminum plates and patched the holes in plenty of time for the Hobart Race. Now, we had even more reason to want to beat *Passage* in that one.

1977 Sydney Hobart Race: Winning the Double

With our unpainted but fully repaired new deck and hull, we were more than ready to take on the famous Hobart Race. *KIALOA III* had set an elapsed time record two years before and we were hoping not only to beat *Windward Passage* but to try again for a new record. While the latter was not to be, we put *KIALOA* back in the books with an even bigger honor.

The race started on a typical Sydney summer day, hot with beautiful weather and wind from the northeast. The start—where we figured that there must be a prize for the spectator boat that can get closest to a racing yacht—was crowded as usual but we managed to get out the Sydney Heads without incident.

The first boat out was a 30-foot "half tonner" steered by my great Irish friend, Harold Cudmore (later, the tactician aboard *KIALOA IV*). As Harry put it, it was just another Irish joke: "Cudmore attempts to sail a half tonner in the Hobart Race!" In any event, we began the race with a nice broad reach down the coast of New South Wales with all sails set: main, staysail, spinnaker, mizzen and mizzen spinnaker. We established a nice lead over *Passage* and all the other boats in the fleet and kept it the next day as we approached the Bass Straits, which separate mainland Australia from the island of Tasmania.

I had been on *Ballyhoo*, the first-to-finish boat the previous year, and we had experienced the infamous "Southerly Buster" a cold breeze from the south that comes up quickly and can, in a matter of minutes, turn an 80 degree day with gentle breezes from astern into a 40-50 degree day with a strong wind on the nose. As I learned the year before, you can actually see it coming.

I was not terribly pleased to see it again but in the late afternoon, there it was, approaching fast from the south. I shouted a warning and we immediately got our running sails down as soon as possible and went right to the No. 5 headsail. Somewhat unbelievably for a tactician who tries to stay back aft in "Fantasyland" (the other two aptly named parts of the boat are "Adventureland" for mid-deck crew, and "Frontierland" for the bowmen), I actually found myself on the bow helping to get the big sails down and the new, much smaller sails up. I soon realized where I was and returned to safer climes. The crew did their usual fantastic job, so when the first breeze hit, we were prepared and kept on our course to Hobart with a reefed main and a small headsail.

Passage, a couple of miles behind us, wasn't so lucky or prepared. I don't know to this day whether they realized what was about to happen and just couldn't get the sails down, or whether despite the early warning, they just blew it. There was an Australian television light plane above us as all this was going on and it provided one of my favorite yachting sequences captured on film.

The video clearly shows us getting our sails down quickly (that's how I know I was on the bow), and then shows us hitting the edge of the "Buster" and continuing on to weather into it, on towards Hobart. Then it slowly pans back those couple of miles and shows *Passage* in considerable disarray with her spinnakers flying like flags from the top of the rigs, no jib up and her course quickly heading back towards Sydney. I don't know how long it took her to get squared away but as it turned out, that was the turning point in the race. She never recovered and we beat her into Hobart by almost two and a half hours.

The next 48 hours were not very pleasant, however. I don't think the Buster was quite as strong as the year before, but we had plenty of 45-50 knot stuff and as is typical of the condition, the seas quickly built up to an amazing state. By the next day, the seas were so big that *KIALOA* would disappear between wave troughs and the sea state was confused, to say the least. Steering was quite an experience and each helmsman had to be strapped in because the seas would throw even a boat as large as *KIALOA* around as if it were in a washing machine. Happily, we had a lot of great helmsmen so no one had to steer beyond the point where exhaustion would impair their abilities.

Three things kept me from worrying about the extreme conditions. First, I had been in similar or even worse conditions the year before. Second, I knew *KIALOA* was in great shape and maintained by Jim and Bruce "Goose" in perfect condition. Finally, I have never had so much faith in a crew as I had in that crew. I have often said in the years since that if I ever had to be on a boat that was in danger of sinking and could only pick one person who could potentially save it, along with me, I would pick Bruce "Goose." The rest of the crew was also exceptional. Jim, Bruce and the team exuded confidence that made a twenty-six-year old not only comfortable, but thinking the whole thing was fun! The greatest thing was that we never stopped racing. That is, we kept the boat moving as fast as we could the whole time.

Whatever we did worked, because as we rounded Tasman Island and headed for the finish in the Derwent River, we knew that as long as we kept the boat together, we had the first to finish trophy locked up. Subsequently, as the trailing boats sailed in hours and even days later, we realized that we had won the "double"—first to finish and first overall on handicap/corrected time. Not many boats have pulled that off in the storied history of the Sydney Hobart and we were proud to have done so.

It made the "quiet little drink"—a Hobart tradition where boat owners and skippers buy or "shout" rounds of beer for the assembled crew members from all the boats—especially fun and I believe Jim must have set another record in his contribution to the effort. At any event, a happy crew (most with "Cascade Throat," resulting from a few too many of the local Tasmanian beers) headed for Sydney for New Year's Eve and the traditional food and champagne fight at the old Argyle Tavern in the Rocks area.

Tactical Sailing, and Afterthoughts, on the Sydney-Hobart Race

We sailed three Sydney Hobart Races three times with great results. The 1971 Race was sailed in *KIALOA II*, our 73-foot aluminum yawl, which was the first yacht to cross the finish line with 79 yachts competing in the race.

The 1975 race was sailed in *KIALOA III*, our new, 79-foot aluminum ketch, and was the first yacht to cross the finish line with 102 yachts competing in the race. *KIALOA III* also set a new elapsed time record of 2 days, 14 hour, 36 minutes and 56 seconds, beating the old record by 11 hours and 25 minutes. The *KIALOA III* elapsed time record was held for 21 years and then eclipsed by only 28 minutes by the latest technology and a bigger carbon fiber yacht sailed by Russell Coutts and crew. A $300,000 bonus was awarded to the winning crew.

The 1977 race was sailed in *KIALOA III*. She was the first yacht to cross the finish line and after all of the yachts finished, *KIALOA III* named the overall corrected time winner of the 1977 Sydney Hobart Race.

Each race had different wind conditions and our tactical course was modified accordingly. The 1971 race had more variable wind conditions, primarily reaching conditions. The 1975 record-setting race was an excellent downwind surfing race that allowed *KIALOA III* to set and hold the elapsed time record for 21 years. The 1977 race started as a moderate race and then became a heavy, upwind race, causing *KIALOA III* to modify its tactical plan for the shifting southerly buster.

Our tactical plans were based upon our personal study with the help of leading Australian sailors and fishermen as to the probable benefit of local currents, counter currents and the shifting southerly breeze. The Hobart Race always brought great sailing, a great challenge and a great victory.

When we designed and built *KIALOA III*, our rationale was a little different than simply building the biggest yacht in the fleet. We wanted a Maxi with a slightly lower rating that could still sail competitively against the biggest and best yachts around. Simply put, we were egotistical enough to believe that we could sail a *KIALOA* faster than its rating and have more leverage against smaller yachts. The idea was that *KIALOA* should be on the offense, not the defense.

In 1971, when we first sailed the Sydney Hobart Race in *KIALOA II*, we tried to set up a plan as to the most favorable course to sail maximizing counter current benefits, which would be around the eastern entry to Bass Straits and along the Coast of Tasmania. We asked Magnus Halvorsen and Jock Sturrock, noted Australian sailors, to sail with us as well as share their experience from previous Sydney-Hobart Races. We developed our course plan and sailed this plan as closely as possible while tactically covering our competition and seeking the most favorable sailing angles. This strategy was quite different than that of many of our competitors.

When we set the Sydney-Hobart Race elapsed time record in 1975, beating *Windward Passage* in the process, it was a great accomplishment. *Windward Passage* was an outstanding downwind yacht and the 1975 Race was a downwind race.

The *KIALOA* crew was continuously challenged by the 1971 remarks of Gordon Marshall in our discussion about the race. The IOR rule had just been adopted and the Sydney Hobart handicap formula was based upon the RORC time on time handicap system. Gordon Marshall clearly stated that a maxi could not win the Sydney Hobart on corrected time under this handicap system. I could not disagree as the Fastnet Race, the Northern Hemisphere counterpart to the Sydney-Hobart Race, used the same handicap system. *KIALOA*s had challenged this race and placed in the top few places on several occasions, but were never the winner…it was a case of "almost, almost, almost."

We accepted Gordon Marshall's comments as a challenge and believed that the Sydney Hobart Race had more tactical elements providing more options without the huge tides of the English Coast, which could be helpful or terribly adverse. I should spell adverse with a big, capital "A."

In 1977, *KIALOA III* met Gordon's challenge, and we won the Sydney Hobart Race on corrected time. Unlike the 1975 record-setting race, the 1977 race was a heavy weather upwind race. Being the overall corrected time winner of the 1977 Sydney Hobart Race was the cap of a fantastic year of first overall corrected time victories in several major, world-famous races:

The 1977 St. Petersburg – Fort Lauderdale Race in the SORC - 374 miles.
A new elapsed time record. A first overall corrected time victory.

The 1977 Miami – Montego Bay, Jamaica Race – 811 miles.
A second overall corrected time victory.

The 1977 Transpacific-Honolulu Hawaii Race – 2,225 miles.
A first overall corrected time victory.

The 1977 Sydney-Hobart Race – 635 miles.
A first overall corrected time victory.

The three year 1975 – 1977 Yachting World's Ocean Racing
Championship with lowest score in history –9 points.

The 1975-1976-1977 World Ocean Racing Championship with the most favorable score in its history. Which was?

I offer my congratulations and thanks to all *KIALOA* crew who participated in our 1977 victories and in the World Ocean Racing Championship.

There have always been questions and bragging rights in the world of Grand Prix yachting over which boat and crew is the best in the world. There are many ways to define "the best," but in handicap racing it's actually very simple: "First overall on corrected time." Old-age allowances, course distances, different rating rules: these are concepts we've mentioned in several chapters.

Aboard *KIALOA II* and *KIALOA III,* our all-amateur crew strongly believed that our boat and team should be in the forefront of the discussion about who really was "the best" in the world. Before 1975, there was no quantitative way of actually determining the top yacht and crew. But that changed in 1975-1977 with the formation of a three-year series that would ultimately crown yachting's World Ocean Racing Champions.

The series constituted twenty separate races all over the world, most of which we had raced with excellent prior results. The race instructions categorized six races as Group A events and fourteen races as Group B events. The final results would be based on seven races—three from Group A and four from Group B.

The scoring would be tallied in the following manner: The overall corrected time race results for each yacht would be added together; the winning yacht would earn a "1," second place would receive a "2," third would receive a "3," and so on. In addition, the results from Group A events would be multiplied by a factor of 1.3. A yacht could sail in all the possible races and select its top seven results (three from Group A and four from Group B), or simply sail the minimum of seven races in the respective groups. The yacht with the lowest score would win.

All aboard *KIALOA III* were pleased with the selection of races that would be used to determine the world champion, which broke down into the following groups:

GROUP A

The Bermuda Race

St. Petersburg-Ft. Lauderdale

The Channel Race

The Fastnet Race

The Sydney – Hobart

The Transpac

GROUP B

Annapolis-Newport

The Transatlantic

Auckland-Suva

Chicago-Mackinac

La Rochelle

San Diego – Acapulco

Marblehead – Halifax

Miami-Montego Bay

The Middle Sea

China Sea

Hobart – Auckland

The Swiftsure

The Skaw

Buenos Aires – Rio Race

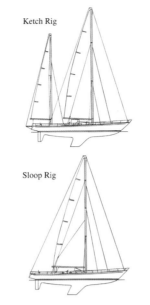

Ketch Rig

Sloop Rig

Mast Moved Back 3' with Longer Boom and Bigger Mainsail

23

Becoming a Sloop

I have wondered over the years as to how sailboat designers and racing officials ponder over the success of winning yachts using the results to penalize yachts because the yachts, and excellent crews sail faster than other yachts. We knew that yachts with a mizzen, ketches and yawls, could provide more versatility in longer races when crews were on watches, and that they could be slower in closed course racing when all of the crew were available on deck. *Windward Passage* and *KIALOA* were winning sailing ketches.

As a result of our mutual success, we believe that ketches were penalized with higher rating and it would be better to be sloops with a more favorable rating. As usual, *KIALOA III* played "wait and see" and we did see! We changed to a sloop with taller, more sail area mast. The following chapter is amusing and technical. It was also properly timed as our sails needed replacing after our successful 1977 racing year.

Ketch or Sloop?

The '78 China Sea Race, Pan Am Clipper Cup and St. Francis Big Boat Series

The year 1978 brought an interesting, eclectic racing schedule, and an important question regarding the future of *KIALOA III*: Should we change the rig from a ketch to a sloop?

In prior years, following the Sydney Hobart Race, several yachts sailed north to Hong Kong for the 565-mile China Sea Race to the Philippines, which had an unusual appeal. I had been in Hong Kong on business matters and the idea of racing there was intriguing, so we elected to make the event a "must do" for 1978. After doing the race and enjoying a bit of cruising, we would still have time to sail back across the Pacific to Honolulu in time for the Pan Am Clipper Cup series, a great event, and thereafter to San Francisco for the St. Frances Big Boat series. *Windward Passage* decided to join us so we could continue our match boat racing between the two yachts.

We had heard that *Windward Passage* would convert from a ketch to a sloop after the China Sea Race, and we would sail against the boat in its new, sloop-rigged incarnation later in the year in San Francisco. Another competitive maxi, *Ondine*, had already converted from a ketch to a sloop, and we would race against her in the Pan Am Clipper Cup regatta in mid-summer on our way to San Francisco.

The timing of all this was good, from our perspective. If, after racing against the new sloops, we discovered the rig change had improved their performance, we, too, would convert *KIALOA* to a sloop following the St. Francis Big Boat Series. This, of course, would require a new sail inventory. In the meantime, we decided to sail the 1978 schedule with our well-used, existing sails, even though they were not in the most competitive condition.

The China Sea Race was another long distance match race between the two great maxis, *Windward Passage* and *KIALOA III*. Fortunately, *KIALOA III* took the lead soon after the start and stayed ahead until crossing the finish line. The finish line was off the point of Fort Corregidor, on the island of the same name at the entrance to Manila Bay, where many American soldiers lost their lives in the defense of the fort in World War II. As we crossed the finish line, all aboard said a short prayer in their memory.

As far as weather conditions were concerned, the race was uneventful. It was mostly straight-line sailing on a close reach with very little tacking until we closed on the Philippines, when we finally got in a little spinnaker work. Along the way, we saw and became interested in the traditional Chinese Junks that were used for inter-island trading and commerce. They looked very cumbersome, but were exceedingly fast.

The '78 race from Hong Kong to Manila was definitely not a Maxi-boat race, but the competition with *Windward Passage* was, as always, vigilant. *Passage* finished about two hours behind us. Our elapsed time was 83 hours, 45 minutes, 21 seconds, which corrected out to 113 hours, 19 minutes, 48 seconds—an unusually wide discrepancy, good enough only for 14th in class and fleet. We were unaware of their handicapping system but we had a good sail, and the sponsoring yacht clubs in Hong Kong and Manila were fine hosts and put on excellent receptions.

We'd visited Hong Kong before, but Manila was an entirely new destination for the crew. It was a humorous city and the rivalry between the taxi drivers, always blaring their horns, was something to remember. There was good and constant energy among the Philippine people. We had the pleasure of staying at the same hotel used by General MacArthur, in an identical suite immediately below the MacArthur Suite. The history, and the memories of this outstanding general, and his service to our country and the Philippines, was the other reason why we enjoyed this event.

We had hoped to cruise to the Southern Islands, but the Philippine Navy would not grant us permission on the grounds that the island's revolutionaries consistently damaged visiting cruising yachts. We did manage to do some exploring and scuba diving along the country's south and southeast coastlines, and also anchored one night off the north coast of Mindoro Island, where the sea literally glowed at night from the lights of hundreds of fishing boats.

On two remarkable occasions, things happened on our sail up the west coast of Luzon from Mindoro to Manila. The Philippine Navy told us to watch out for unmarked grey P.T. boats: they were the rebels. Suddenly, to our surprise, we were sailing directly toward an unmarked P.T. boat about two miles ahead of us on a virtual collision course. What to do? Why would they want a sailboat? I called Bruce to bring up our shotgun and a rapid fire Carbine, and we would have target practice, throwing cans in the air. Of course, it was no match for their 20 millimeter "bow cannon." But at least it proved that someone might get hurt. We also identified ourselves on the radio; they looked at us with indifference as they passed by and continued heading south. Later, when we were diving, we were shocked to discover that the locals had fished with explosives, destroying the coral reefs as a quick, easy way to get food. The Philippine government was now harshly addressing this problem to save their beautiful shores.

After our visit, while *Windward Passage* sailed home to California for the conversion from ketch to sloop, we sailed on to Hawaii for the 1978 Pan Am Clipper Cup. At this juncture, we'll turn the narrative over to Ken Morrison, the staff commodore of the sponsoring Waikiki Yacht Club, and *KIALOA* crewman Andy Rose, to tell the story of the Pan Am Clipper Cup.

First, Ken Morrison's account:

Forty-one yachts, representing Australia, France (Tahiti), New Zealand, Japan, Taiwan and the United States, competed in the August 5 –12, 1978 series which featured summer winds and a balmy climate, the perfect condition for offshore racing. Adding prestige to the already blue-ribbon fleet were two of the world's fastest maxi yachts—Jim Kilroy's 79-foot ketch KIALOA and Huey Long's 79-foot sloop Ondine. *The new series would consist of a 100-mile race around the Island of Oahu, three offshore Olympic Triangle courses and the Around the State Race.*

Ondine *completed the Around Oahu Race in a record 13 hours and 18 minutes, edging KIALOA by a scant six seconds in one of the closest boat-for-boat finishes in yacht racing history. The Around the States Race presented the fleet with every sailing condition known to sailors. The fleet started in a light but steady breeze hoping to best the four-day, three hours and twenty minutes record set by Phantom in 1977. However, a record was not to be. Unfortunately, the trade winds tapered off making the lees of Kauai, Niihau and the Big Island much more difficult to get through. The race became a contest of tactics, navigation and luck in locating the elusive breeze. Finally,* Ondine, *after battling KIALOA for nearly five days, breezed past the Waikiki finish line to win line honors. KIALOA finished second, three hours later.*

And here's Andy Rose's report:

I remember this series not because we won (we didn't), but instead because of two classic races between KIALOA and Ondine. *At that time, we had been dominating a lot of races and, shall we say,* Ondine *was not. To his credit, however,* Ondine *owner Huey Long decided to do something about that and performed some radical surgery on his boat—he cut off the mizzen on this big ketch and bought a new and much taller main mast. The new sloop looked a lot better and was soon to prove that it was a lot better.*

The first race of the series was a triangle, windward/leeward course set offshore from Waikiki in typical trade wind conditions of 20-30 knots. We managed to get the start from Ondine *although my longtime friend and their tactician, David Vietor, did a good job. Soon after the start, it became pretty clear that this was indeed a new* Ondine *as for the first time, she was actually a bit faster than we were. We led them to the weather mark mainly by match racing her and kept our lead through the two reaching legs where Jim let me steer (Thanks a lot, Jim! It was like doing an hour of isometric exercises on your arms).*

Anyway, on the last weather leg, through furious effort and great crew work, we were still ahead, but only by about a boat length or two. By this time we had "lapped" some of the smaller boats and happily, one of them appeared just when we needed her. We were able to use the right of way rules and the intervening boat in such a way that we were able to "brush off" Ondine and tack for the finish line before she could do so. It won us the race, but only by about a boat length after about 25 miles of sailing.

A couple of days later, we had a similar race with her, only it was the much longer round Oahu race. I don't remember the details but we did the whole race, which I think was around 100 miles, virtually overlapped. Near Kaneohe, I think we made an ill-advised sail change and Ondine got a mile or so ahead. However, as we rounded Diamond Head to approach the finish that night, we were able to use our additional sail area and crew work to quickly close on her. We just ran out of course as she beat us across the line again by just a couple of boat lengths.

The handwriting was on the wall, however, and after the St. Francis Yacht Club Big Boat Series that September, KIALOA also had surgery and was reborn as a sloop. Ondine never seriously challenged us again.

What a magnificent sailing area Hawaii is. There is the huge variation in conditions; sailing in the lee of huge mountain peaks; heavy downwind sailing and surfing; and the constant challenge of keeping the boat moving in light winds and strong ones, with every legal sail onboard. It was powerful and dangerous, punctuated by whoops of joy from the crew. When all was said and done, we'd won a race and finished second overall in the series.

One other thing we'll remember about the '78 Clipper Cup was an accident that occurred during one race while tacking along the south shore of Oahu. Of course, unusual and unanticipated events can happen when racing competitively in tight quarters. The precursor to the Clipper Cup incident happened years earlier, on the Solent off the Isle of Wight. It just goes to show that history can repeat itself.

We were racing in Cowes Week and the Admiral's Cup aboard *KIALOA II*, sailing to weather with frequent tacks when one of our crew, Arnie Schmeling, lost the tip of a finger in a deck sheave, and we needed to put him on shore as quickly as possible. A 20-foot spectator powerboat was nearby and we asked them to come abeam and we would transfer Arnie to their boat. What a mess, with *KIALOA II* hard on the wind on a starboard tack. Transfer from the weather rail was impossible; it was too high from the leeward quarter rail, with the hull bouncing vertically in the short chop of the sea. We finally made the transfer by slowing *KIALOA II* down, but it was still too dangerous. The night after the race, I thought about a new technique for the future.

Ten years later, off Oahu, the future was now. Once again, a crewmember lost a fingertip in a mainsheet sheave; remarkably, it appeared to be in "attachable" condition. But we had to get him ashore, and this time, a fair swell was running that would make a transfer even harder than the one in Cowes.

A photo boat was nearby. We told them to station their boat about 20-feet from our starboard quarter as we continued racing upwind. To those watching, the new technique was a shocker. The finger tip was placed in a small baggie with ice, sealed with grey tape, and placed in a zipper pocket of the crew's oilskin jacket. The injured hand was placed in another baggie with ice and rubber bands right around his wrist to stop bleeding. The baggie was then sealed and weatherproofed with grey tape above the crew's wrist. A life jacket was secured for good flotation.

The crew was then "thrown" overboard, the pickup was successfully (and carefully) made by the photo boat, and the crew was rushed to the hospital. There, the fingertip was stitched back on the finger. It was an apparent success, verified by the fact that our crew returned to his home in Australia…and later became a barber and promoted an international discount haircut operation that was also quite a success. (He knew a lot about close cuts.) Sailing is full of unintended consequences. We all wondered what our crew was thinking about as he floated in the water.

From Hawaii, it was on to San Francisco for the Big Boat Series, an event that yachting writer Jay Broze captured with flair and humor:

"The Year *Passage* took *KIALOA* to the Men's Room" by Jay Broze

None-of-a-Kinders are yacht owners who sacrifice millions of dollars employing small armies of full-time New Zealanders and part-time sailors in order to save sailing from a numbing sameness. Their boats are simple craft ranging around 80 feet in length, the biggest vessels racing and among the most long-lived. They are the racers who hire the designers, sail-makers, truck drivers, instrument analysts, airfreight forwarders, boatyards, cooks, and camp followers of the world in order to pursue their own rather ill-defined unicorn—None-of-a-Kind world dominance. Their maxi-boats follow racing schedules all around the world, and in the last few years they have started gathering at fairly regular intervals to show everyone else just what's going on at the head of A Fleet.

A vintage year for None-of-a-Kinders was 1978, when five of the biggest and the best gathered on San Francisco Bay for the annual St. Francis Perpetual Trophy—the "Big-Boat Series." This September, as the tenth identical Two-Tonner whistles past the St. Francis YC in pursuit of the trophy, there will be a few of yester-year's foredeckmen, halftide in the old Men's Grill, reminiscing about the year the really big boats gathered on the bay. It doesn't take giant boats to make exciting racing, but the bay has a way of magnifying events, and out in front of the St. Francis YC, Maxis do look larger than life.

Today, nearly all of the 1978 participants are for sale, and some have given way to newer edi-

tions of their famous names. But what a fleet they were—the Johnsons' venerable 73-footer Windward Passage; *Fred Preiss's immense 85-foot* Christine; *Bill Lee's light 67-footer,* Merlin; *Huey Long's* Ondine, *the aluminum 80-footer; and Jim Kilroy's 79-foot Sparkman & Stephens-designed aluminum* KIALOA, *making her last appearance as a ketch. They seemed to have little in common except astronomical handicap ratings and white mainsails. This field put Kilroy in the unlikely position of being the lowest-rated boat in the class. It may not seem reasonable that a 79-footer could be the corrected-time favorite on any race course, but the field that year was not at all reasonable either.*

The queen of the flotilla and the unquestioned dream-realization-therapy project of the seventies was Christine. *For years her owner, Fred Preiss, had sailed a very old 12-Meter and had longed for a boat capable of getting to the finish line first. The result of these reveries and two years of hands-on effort was the immense brightwork sloop that towered over the rest of the fleet in the same way a Boeing 747 dominates a DC8. Viewed with bar-tortured optic nerves or a simple squint, she resembled a meter boat in profile—perhaps a 24-Meter-with her knuckle bow. Reverse transom, and perfectly flush decks. From the ends, however, she was obviously a very big ocean racer.*

Her spar, over 100 feet in the air, reached slightly higher than the highest spot in the state of Delaware, and when her blooper, chute, and main were all dragged up to the masthead, she displayed about 8,000 square feet of sail—not bad for a homemade boat. Preiss also designed and built the four-speed grinders himself, and their only real problem was a nasty habit of twisting the one-inch stainless steel driveshafts when four heavyweight crew shifted down to second.

Long's Ondine *caused quite a stir on the bay. Originally a ketch that looked like two big sloops in close prestart maneuvers, the "new"* Ondine *(not to be confused with one currently under construction) sported a new bow, a new stern, and a new rig to match the new underbody. By 1978, all that remained of the original design concept for* Ondine *was the color scheme, light blue on light blue, and there was great faith in her new format. As a monster sloop with 13-foot draft, the revamped* Ondine *was the stiffest and most powerful of the maxis and the only one with a separate radar mast. Around it the after-guard, grinders, messenger boys, trimmers, and powder-monkeys clustered like the last of the standers at Little Big Horn.*

The least powerful boat, but fastest of all in her design conditions, was Merlin. *As Santa Cruz's answer to speed,* Merlin *still holds the mainland-to-Hawaii record, no matter which race you choose. Bill Lee brought her to the bay to see if she could cloud the minds of men and beat the heavy iron at their own game. But with her short rig and skimpy displacement (*Merlin *was once described as a very thin joint floating on a pool of mercury), she just couldn't keep up with the leaders on a beat. She did have enough speed to grab a safe berth to weather of KIALOA on a number of weather legs, and that in itself was worth the trip.*

The oldest of the big boats on the bay that year was the veteran Windward Passage. *She, too, began her career as a ketch, and her epic started way back in 1968 as an Alan Gurney-designed Cruising Club of America (CCA) Maxi. From the beginning,* Passage *was a record-setter, and ten years after her keel was laid, she set the course mark for the Swiftsure Classic from Victoria, British Columbia. Now in semiretirement,* Passage *has been a good example of what keeps really big-boat racing going— money. Money spent on rerigging, reequipping, refitting, refinishing, redesigning, rebuilding, and simply returning year after year to see if you are still the quickest.*

By 1978, Passage *had had her rig stretched in order to make up the small, but perceptible, speed deficit against KIALOA, and then the Johnsons decided that they could do with less mizzen rather than more. The lumberjacks in Seattle removed the back stick, along with 6,000 ancillary pounds. Doug Peterson gave her a new keel, and the sum of the changes gave the old campaigner a new lease on the weather legs.*

At the bottom of the fleet, KIALOA was delivering her swan song as a ketch. The mizzen has fallen on hard times in recent years, even in the passage-making Maxi league. According to owners and designers, the nature of ocean racing is changing, with fewer "real" ocean races and more sleigh-rides and round-the-buoys events.

KIALOA suffered in 1978 as the lowest-rating boat in a field of very big rigs. Any good Men's Grill stalwart can tell you that the hardest thing to do on the bay is keep your air clear. The prevailing tide conditions force racers into rather narrow tacking lanes, so KIALOA, as the last Maxi, faced a combined total of 400 feet of mast stacked to weather of her. For all the world's sailors who have been blanketed by KIALOA, this may seem like a humorous just retribution, but for Kilroy it was very serious.

In this league, "serious" was an understatement. The owners and hands on the Maxis had been campaigning them since the day they were launched, and crews like the ones on Passage *or KIALOA were about as "pick-up" as the Pittsburgh Steelers. In fact, since the gear is a little large on an 80-footer ("The No. 1?, Oh it's about 268 pounds, dry."), it helped to look like a former all-pro tight end. Of course, the years and personal habits being what they are, you could look like a retired all-conference tackle with a beery mid-girth measurement and still get by, but then you had to be very suntanned.*

It does not take long to realize that the only things that happen really quickly on boats this big are the catastrophes. The very fast chute sets on Ondine *were the results of many minutes of preparation as the light-blue boat carved up a weather leg. Half-a-dozen foredeck hands sorted out the shambles of the spinnaker gear that was so carefully led at the dock and which then was worked over during the sail changes and tacks on the way uphill. While the bow-boys were muscling pole, guys, sheets, and sails into position, the afterguard (on* Ondine *that group included Gary Jobson of* Courageous, *Dave Vietor of Ratsey & Lapthorn, Commodore Tompkins of San Francisco and the world, and Huey Long), decided whether they could lay the mark, clear* Passage, *and avoid the whole fleet of Two-Tonners approaching on starboard. (The Big Boat Series also includes several divisions of "smaller" big boats.)*

If the answer to any of these questions was no, then the foredeck would retrofit everything and get started again after the proper evasive maneuvers had been carried out. Nonetheless, the sets on Ondine looked dinghy-quick.

The instant jibes on Passage really took close to a minute, from beginning to end, and although they were often faultless, they were certainly not instant. In fact, even at these "sedate" racing speeds, the outboard end of the pole often looked as though it had pierced Rex Banks, rather than having passed smoothly through his hands. If it had skewered him, it would have taken several minutes for the word to filter aft. In some ways it is surprising that these boats functioned at all, even glacially.

In prestart maneuvering, the boats generated their own automatic echoes as the bow man called observations that were relayed aft to the trimmers and then to the cockpit. "Come up a little," the bow-man. "Come up," the mastman. "Come Up" the trimmer. "Come UP!" the cook. "COME UP!" all the grinders in unison.

The helm was instantly put down, and despite the best efforts of everyone forward of the main companionway, a horrible collision was averted, and the Maxi and the B-Fleet boat slid by at a closing speed of 15 knots. The size of the boats also generated real echoes in light air, as the voices of one crew bounced off the sail of the other boat, which gave hails and greetings a transmitted quality, as though these were spaceships passing rather than racing yachts.

Underway, each boat created its own particular personality. On KIALOA, for instance, a Gorgon-like arrangement prevailed, with Andy Rose (ex of Australia) doing tactics, Bruce Kendell (of, by, and for KIALOA) calling trim and handling, and Jim Kilroy taking care of vetoes and the steering wheel. The exchanges went like this:

"Can we harden up a little; you're a little broad, Jim?"

"Trim the Genny… just a tweak, Stu."

"Feels good, feels good there."

And the three men, none of whom had a handle on all the information or controls available, coordinated the passage of the boat through air and water. When they disagreed, an equally formal, ordered, and polite negotiation took place.

Aboard KIALOA, the student body always had something to do. The top mark and off-wind legs of the courses were the sorts of events that many sailors have bad dreams about, a lazy man's purgatory. The helm would be put down, and all the Dacron would go out. Two men would push out the boom as the boat bore away from the mark. The pole would be hauled up on the stick, followed by the spinnaker, snaking up quickly. With luck, it would pop out like a giant flower blossoming. When the tip of the pole was up, the after guy would be hauled in, the outhaul loosened, the preventer made, the chute trimmed to course, and the genoa hauled back out of the water. That sequence would take 10 or 15 hands.

Meanwhile, another section of the crew rapidly rigged the blooper, hauling and feeding and trim-

ming, while the tribe around the mizzen fetched, rigged, and hoisted the mizzen spinnaker. Everything stayed in this configuration for about six minutes. Then "Stand by to jibe!" Down came the blooper (remember it was about 100 feet on the luff) and the mizzen spinnaker. If the course was a little shy, then the blooper would go up again, with the mizzen staysail replacing the little back chute. As the speed increased and the apparent wind hauled forward, the blooper would come down, and the biggest staysail would go up, while the next smaller mizzen staysail replaced the original. The crew on the back stick may have taken a reef by then, and the reacher perhaps had replaced the big running chute. It all sounds like standard stuff, except that the mizzen on KIALOA was about the same size as the main on a 55-footer, and not more than ten square feet of deck abaft the mainmast was free of turning blocks, winches, stays, shrouds, cleats, turnbuckles, tracks, and pad eyes. Racing around the buoys, 24 intelligent and very experienced sailors did a very complicated dance across KIALOA's deck. The stiffer the breeze, the more manic the dance. No wonder the racing ketch has died.

Windward Passage, the sloop, was hot disco to KIALOA's danse macabre. With her grinders aft, and the 70 feet of deck devoted to one tall stick, Passage handled like a giant Two-Tonner, with lots of room to work.

The hull form of Windward Passage could be described as late CCA flying disk or early IOR fat canoe. Either way, it means very speedy if you can keep her level, but once she put a shoulder in the water, she could spin like a dervish. Once during the 1978 series Christine, Ondine, and Passage arrived simultaneously at the jibe mark, with Passage on the inside and the breeze freshening. Ondine's blue destroyer-escort hull heeled momentarily as the chute changed sides, and Christine on the outside took the escape road. Passage was almost through the jibe when the hull changed modes from form-stability to merry-go-round. As a single body, the crew forward of the wheel made themselves very small, taking care not to straddle sheets and guys, while all the crew aft formed a human pyramid on the weather quarter, trying to get the ship flat again. She swooped up, chute flogging, rudder flopping in the air just above the waves; then she fell over and bounced upright again. No one moved. She swooped up, over, and back, and then she was on course again. Fortunately for Passage, 1978 was a mild year on the bay, and the reaching legs for the series were generally light and fading.

Every St. Francis Perpetual Trophy brings out the cream of the local spectator population, and when the Maxis were in town, the crowd was at its best. At the club, the late afternoon sun refracting in the wine glasses shot tiny rainbows across the faces of the golden-skinned I. Magnin blondes, while vested barristers poised alertly, their Guccis resting on the bottom rung of the seawall rail. Brokers whose markets had closed hours before led elegant ladies through the intricacies of the handicap sheet, and their audiences, who were much more familiar with hemlines than bowlines, stared back in rapt attention. The chef sliced slabs of rare beef off the skewered roast, and waitresses moved through the crowd, delivering drinks as the sound of the waves lapping on the rocks blended with the tinkle of ice cubes. That is how the select watch a yacht race.

But that year, the jolly murmur of hot tips, proposed liaisons, and delicious gossip evaporated as Windward Passage *and* KIALOA *knifed towards the club on starboard tack. Johnson was in the driver's seat and showed no sign of concern as he forced Kilroy farther and farther inshore. The shadows of their rigs raced along the breakwater, and the crowd edged back from the rail. The two Maxis continued to plow straight for the number-two blender at the service bar. The bartender stuck to his post, mixing Rhemos fizzes like a trooper. Finally, showing mercy upon their insurance brokers, the two monsters tacked just short of the lime wedges and cocktail onions. A roar rose from the crowd as the boats clocked through the same air space, and* KIALOA *salvaged her last ten yards of sea room.*

This is part of the magic of the Big-Boat Series. For the price of any two Genoas and a sailed-over blooper on KIALOA, *you could get a nice old Ferrari, a pair of Guccis, one of those knockout redheads, and then watch the races in comfort from the St. Francis YC veranda. But therein lies the difference between spectators and spectacle, and year after year the crews and owners return to provide the latter for the former. If they didn't, then the old chute trimmers in the Men's Grill wouldn't be able to lift a shaky Rhemos and relive the moments when "that Johnson boy took* KIALOA *right into the men's room on starboard tack."*

Thank you, Jay, for the use of your humorous article. Jay's triggered deep thinking—immediate modification from a ketch to a sloop and the need to consider a new *KIALOA IV*. We had made several modifications to *KIALOA III*, designed in 1972-1973 and launched in 1974 under the IOR MKIII 1971 measurement rule, which had also several modifications through 1978. All of these modifications had an effect upon *KIALOA III*'s performance—some good and some bad. In early 1979, we decided that we should consider a new *KIALOA IV* and asked our good friend and naval architect, Ron Holland, to proceed with preliminary design.

24

Sailing the *KIALOA II* ten years ago, we had won the
Transatlantic Race to Cork, Ireland. It was time to try *KIALOA III*,
now a sloop, in the identical Transatlantic Race. We had won
the major races in the Pacific Ocean and the Sydney-Hobart Race,
an almost identical race to the Fastnet Rock Race,
and we again would challenge the Fastnet Race.

We would add as crew the naval architect, Ron Holland,
whose office was in Cork. Ron would design our new *KIALOA IV*
and many design discussions would be held en route.
Many surprises would follow which would alter design criteria.

Trying for a Repeat
KIALOA III *and the 1979 Transatlantic Race*

Ten years after *KIALOA II's* victorious race in 1969 from Newport, Rhode Island to Cork, Ireland, to commemorate the 250th anniversary of the Royal Cork Yacht Club, we would again challenge the Atlantic Ocean in an almost identical 2638-mile race in *KIALOA III* starting from Marblehead, Massachusetts.

All races across the Atlantic can be very different and this would be our fourth Transatlantic Race and our second race to County Cork, Ireland, the foundational home of the Kilroy clan.

KIALOA III had raced the Atlantic from Newport, Rhode Island to Cowes, England in 1975, its first year racing, facing many challenges, a minor hurricane or violent tropical storm, had days sailing to weather, a fantastic spinnaker run averaging 14 knots over the bottom to the finish, followed by a serious protest as to the actual handicap distance, all as set forth in a prior chapter of this book.

The preparations for the 1979 race to County Cork were excellent, and we looked forward to another successful and challenging race with a great send off by the sailing enthusiasts of the Marblehead/Boston sailing community.

After modifications following the Big Boat Series in San Francisco, *KIALOA III* was now a masthead sloop, with a taller mast, a bigger mainsail, and increased sail area in the foretriangle (for the headsails) and the spinnakers. It seemed appropriate that we were again sailing to Cork, because Kiwi naval architect Ron Holland was based there, and we were considering a new *KIALOA IV* to be designed by Ron. The Transatlantic Race would provide the crew plenty of "sea time" to discuss the concepts we'd desire in a new boat.

Our primary competitors were two Maxis, our longtime rival, Huey Long's *Ondine* and Bob Bell's *Condor.* Both yachts rated slightly higher than *KIALOA III*, which is how we liked it. It gave us a psychological edge to be the "smallest" of the three boats.

Over the first three days of the race, with some fog and scattered clouds, we had excellent sailing conditions and knocked off 207-, 231.6- and 227.9-miles on reaching under headsails. On Day 4, as the wind strengthened and went aft, we hoisted a spinnaker and logged 276-miles, an 11.3-knot average. We executed many sail changes and as we passed Point Alpha—the iceberg mark—we held a favored position on *Ondine* and *Condor* and could now steer a more northerly course.

On Day 5, the wind continued to come from astern and we had another good day—272.8 miles—flying a full main, a 2.2 ounce spinnaker blooper and a forestaysail, all of which performed beautifully. So did the crew, continuously trimming the sails to maximize our performance.

In our "race within the race" with *Ondine* and *Condor*, we maintained our strong tactical position. The crew was sleeping and eating well, and delighted to be making good time right along our desired track. It was a happy, noisy ship, particularly as we accelerated on the waves with the phosphorescent spray flying. Our one-drink "Happy Hour" was a highlight of each day.

We continued our string of 200-mile-plus runs on Day 6 with a 259.1-mile effort; the skies remained overcast with minor, occasional fog. On Day 7, the wind started to move forward but we were still able to carry our medium spinnaker and notched another 220.8 miles toward the finish line, which was only 962.5-miles away.

Unfortunately, as the day progressed the wind velocity continued to move forward and drop, as did our boat speed. We began to be concerned about the wind conditions and our position in relation to the smaller yachts in the fleet.

On Day 8, with the wind still easing, we found ourselves sailing above and below our course for better wind angles to reach under spinnaker, and made just 214.8-miles.

On the ninth day, things got better: the wind moved slightly aft and increased in velocity, allowing *KIALOA III* to again steer close to the optimal course. With her full set of running sails (main, spinnaker and spinnaker staysail) up and drawing, *Ondine* was visible to the South and continued to be a threat. As we jibed to port, gaining a little distance to the north, we recorded another good day with 253.3-miles.

The navigator gave our position as 456-miles from Fastnet Rock. At the time, we had no way of knowing what tragic events would unfold later that summer off that small landmark off the southwest corner of Ireland.

In the early morning of the 10th day, *Ondine* and *KIALOA III* were within a mile of each other with about 350 miles remaining in the 2,638 mile race—reaching on spinnakers with the wind beginning to lighten along the shore.

KIALOA III began to get separation from *Ondine* as the wind lightened over the next several hours. The log entry stated "wind & lightning—only 5.25 miles to the finish line, jibing back and forth for speed."

Four hours and ten minutes later, *KIALOA III* crossed the finish line at a low average speed of 1.26 knots, finishing well ahead of *Ondine* with a total race elapsed time of 11 days 17 hours 39 minutes and 21 seconds, an average speed over the 2,638 mile course of 9.33 knots.

We calculated our assist from the Gulf Stream to be 105.47 miles. Of course, the smaller yachts would have ridden the Stream longer and enjoyed a much higher mileage boost. But our excess distance due to tacking and jibing, we figured, was a surprisingly low 24.8 miles (we anticipated it could be as much as 14% of the course distance). From the start to Fastnet Rock, we averaged 9.67 knots. But the last five miles did take forever, sailing against an ebb tide. Though we averaged only 1.25 knots, our crew made the most of the challenging conditions.

And their will, not to mention their skill, paid off. *KIALOA III* was first to finish, about six hours ahead of *Ondine* and *Condor*. Our corrected time, once our 16-hour handicap was applied, was 11 days, 1 hour, and the results were satisfying: First to finish, first in class and fifth overall. The overall winner was *Alliance*, crewed by cadets from the U.S. Naval Academy (their elapsed time was 13 days, 17 hours, which corrected out to 10 days, 12 hours after their 3 day, 5 hour time allowance was applied.) The *KIALOA* crew offered their congratulations to *Alliance* and the second-place overall yacht, *Sleuth*.

Upon finishing, we were again escorted to the Cork Yacht Club Race Committee Yacht for our arrival celebration; it was a great happy hour with good friends. Needless to say, we enjoyed the beautiful country of Ireland—the home of my father—and the courtesy, humor, self-reliance and success of the Irish people.

We have been away too long. We must return.

25

KIALOA III

1979
The Tragic Fastnet Race in the Irish Sea

Force 11 Winds – 32' High Waves

15 Sailors Lost

24 Yachts Abandoned at Sea

303 Yachts Started Race

86 Yachts Finished

Rescue Vessels Saved 125 Sailors

KIALOA III crew, saving mast after wire running back stay
and swivel block exploded, losing first place position
and about two hours due to mast repairs

A Tragic Storm
The Deadly 1979 Fastnet Race
Aboard KIALOA III

One of the most challenging yacht races on the planet is the 605-mile Fastnet Rock Race, which starts off the flagpole of the Royal Yacht Squadron in Cowes on the Isle of Wight. We've described this course before but it bears repeating: first west along the south coast of England; then at a course of about 305 degrees for 166 miles to Fastnet Rock; around the rocky outcropping and then back southeast to Bishop Rock south of the Isles of Scilly; then east to the finish line right inside the entry to Plymouth.

In terms of sailing, you can get a little of everything, from light and variable winds bucking against a current to pounding upwind in heavy seas and tides. It's a very challenging contest, a real test of seamanship, navigation, tactics and experience. In '79, it was also a very traditional affair: the racing rules stated that electronic navigation aids were prohibited and only limited use of the radio was allowed.

Each navigator practiced their craft by dead reckoning—plotting their course, speed and anticipated drift on standard navigational charts, on which they could also take bearings on fixed objects if in proximity to land—and if the skies were clear, by celestial navigation. In a big fleet, of course, enough yachts are close enough that you can indulge in "community" navigation. But in poor visibility and big seas, each crew was on their own.

That would certainly prove to be the case in this infamous 1979 Fastnet Race, the deadliest yacht race ever.

At the outset, *KIALOA III* stayed close inshore along the coast of England, frequently tacking deep into bays searching for more breeze or favorable currents. After almost twenty-eight hours of this, we entered the Irish Sea; Fastnet Rock was about 166 miles to the northeast. We thought we'd find reaching conditions, and we did for a while, but then we were headed and found ourselves once again close-hauled, steering a course of about 305°N.

Especially after our record-setting performance in the Sydney-Hobart Race, everyone aboard really wanted to win the Fastnet, one of the few important international victories that had eluded us. We'd been exasperatingly close in 1969, but we ran out of breeze in a foul tide off the finish line in Plymouth. A Fastnet win would be a second, tough ocean-racing jewel.

We charged toward Fastnet Rock with two things in mind, tactically speaking. We wanted to position ourselves for the best final approach to the rock, and we wanted to round it as cleanly and efficiently as possible.

Prior to the start, we'd learned at the race briefing that there was the probability of heavy weather. It was possible we'd see a Force 8 storm (30-46 knots). The wind was shifty, necessitating several sail changes. We weren't surprised when the barometer fell from 30.9 to 30.1. Otherwise, it was a bright, sunny day. The customary northwest swell was strong. And a new, southerly swell was building.

Forty-six hours and twenty-seven minutes after starting (including 18 hours, 43 minutes in the Irish Sea, from Land's End), *KIALOA III* rounded Fastnet Rock and set a course under proper sails of about 145 degrees magnetic for a close reach to Bishop Rock. But the fast reach didn't last long and soon we were sailing close-hauled in a southerly breeze with the seas building and the barometer continuing to fall. But, as the old northwesterly swell began to meet the new southerly wave, the cross-seas were making it a tough ride. Whoever was driving had to compensate for the moment when the northwest swell met our stern and rolled the leeward bow down.

At this juncture, our competition was well behind us, and *KIALOA III* was in serious contention to win. However, in the middle of such a wild race, we knew anything could happen. *Condor,* the second boat to round Fastnet Rock, owed us handicap time and was over an hour-and-a-half behind on elapsed time. Another strong contender, *Mistress Quickly,* was two-and-a-half hours behind. *Il Moro di Venezia,* sailed by Paul Cayard, was over three-and-one-half hours behind, and *Tenacious,* sailed by Ted Turner and crew, was about eight hours behind *KIALOA III.* Our navigator, Christy Steinman, reported only 227 miles to the finish with much of the distance off the wind, and we only had to average 7.44 knots for the remaining distance to set a new elapsed time record.

Yes, we were in good shape. But we also knew from previous Fastnet races that the last miles were the hardest.

At about 4:30 p.m. on the 13th of August, as we continued on toward Bishop Rock, the British Meteorological Office (BMO) forecast a Force 8 blow, with wind of nearly 50 knots, 18-25 foot seas and a barometer falling to about 29 inches.

Simply put, we were already there.

Thirty minutes later, they upgraded the storm to a Force 10, with winds of 47-54 knots and waves up to 32-feet high, though slightly rougher seas over the Labadie Bank…exactly where we were.

Aboard *KIALOA,* the crew was making constant adjustments and sail changes to provide the most balanced and suitable power for the wave and wind conditions. We doused the No. 4 storm

1979 KIALOA III
Approaching Fastnet Rock before the Storm.

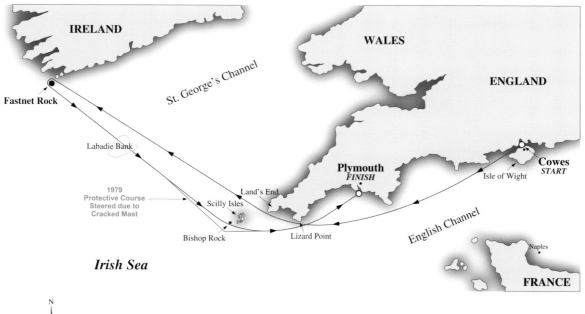

IRELAND

Fastnet Rock

St. George's Channel

Labadie Bank

WALES

ENGLAND

1979
Protective Course
Steered due to
Cracked Mast

Scilly Isles

Land's End

Plymouth
FINISH

Cowes
START

Isle of Wight

Bishop Rock

Lizard Point

English Channel

Irish Sea

Naples

FRANCE

N
W   E
S

Fastnet Rock Race
605 Nautical Miles

Genoa and set a forestaysail on the inner forestay, reducing sail while better balancing our fore and aft trim to help the driver in the confused and heavy seas. The mainsail traveler was secured well to weather for the wind conditions and sailing angle, with ample twist in the upper leach of the mainsail. *KIALOA* felt good and powerful.

At 2100 on the 13th, the BMO reported 50-60 knot winds over our area, continuing on another sixty miles to the east of our position. This wind forecast covered the waters where the smaller yachts in the fleet would still be sailing toward Fastnet Rock. This is important because later reports indicated that the bigger yachts, at the front of the fleet, did not experience the same heavy winds as the smaller yachts. In fact, we did; we were just heading in the opposite direction.

As the race progressed, the winds and seas both became higher and stronger.

At 0245 the next morning, the 14th of August, the BMO continued to classify the storm as a Force 10, with the barometer now bottomed out at 28.94 inches. At 0600, they downgraded the storm to Force 9.

Through it all, we kept the boat moving well. The *KIALOA* technique for heavy weather sailing was to always have strong sail power in the rougher water of the trough between the tops of high waves. The power was necessary to steer through or around the "pot holes" or "diamonds" of conflicting waves. You'd then roll into the big wave with power, feathering the sail angle, and sailing a bit higher, with "twist," if there was too much wind at the top of the wave. Sailboats need power for control in heavy, confused seas.

And there's no question we had big seas at the intersection of the three big waves descending upon us. We could not let the northwest wave get under our weather quarter (stern area) because it would roll our port bow down into the southerly wave, and we could have trouble steering into the big primary wave from the southwest. The system was working very well. One crew was assigned to call out the position of the quarter wave from the northwest. Three of us, all well experienced—captain and starboard watch captain Bruce Kendell; Syd Brown, a great sailor and fisherman from New Zealand; and myself, the port watch captain and racing skipper—did the steering.

Considering the wind and sea conditions, all was going well for *KIALOA III*. Our navigator, who was below at the navigation station, was listening for the BMO reports and also hearing that some yachts behind us were quitting the race and that other yachts were calling for help. We were advised that no yachts near us had called for help and that we could focus on the race.

Later that morning, I was at the helm when I heard a big bang, and the mast near the gooseneck, where the mainsail boom is attached, vibrated violently. At that instant, the starboard running back stay and the check stay attached to the deck—which stabilized the middle of the mast—blew off to leeward, almost horizontal to the sea.

The accompanying sketch shows the failed items and the complications of the repair.

The swivel block that secured this rigging in place, about 7' above the deck, had exploded, and a new block had to be installed, reconnected and properly tensioned to save the 100-foot mast. Some of the crew found a replacement swivel block, made some helpful sail trim adjustments, and centered the traveler, while the rest of the crew tried to retrieve the running back stay and check stay, which were being blown away from the boat by the force of the breeze, and the roll of the heavy seas.

Catching the wire pennants was not an easy task for the crew, who were "fastened" to the deck by safety harnesses. To help them, I was carefully but sharply rolling the boat so the pennants would swing over the deck and be easier to snag. It may sound silly now, but I was singing, "Roll, Roll, Roll Your Boat" to rhythmically control the swing of the pennants. It worked! With one sailor sitting securely on top of the boom, others were able to hook and hold onto the swinging pennants with boat hooks while they were reconnected to a new swivel block and deck lines. Our mast was still standing. The accompanying sketch by Gary Miltimore depicts *KIALOA III* in the wild seas while the crew recovers the check stay and running backstay pennants. It was a wild, dangerous and successful maneuver.

But now came the big question. Had we damaged the mast? I felt strongly that it had. The mast had inverted violently, forward and back several times, when the swivel block was broken. As it moved, there was no support in the mid-section of the spar, and, in my mind, I could even foresee a failure point—the upper weld area just above the inner fore stay sheave box. Depending on how severely it was damaged, the mast might or might not fail. Bruce agreed with me that the mast had been weakened in the incident.

We were, as they say, between a rock and a hard place...just to

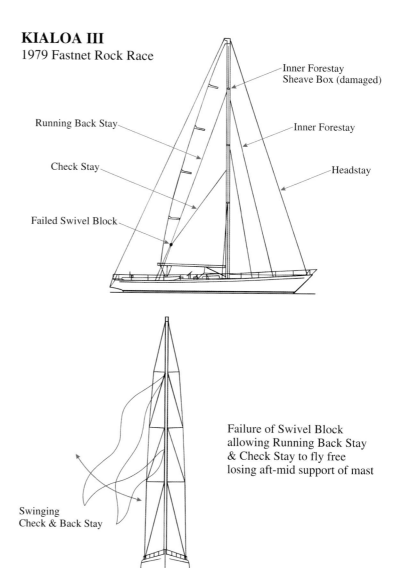

KIALOA III
1979 Fastnet Rock Race

Inner Forestay
Sheave Box (damaged)

Running Back Stay

Inner Forestay

Check Stay

Headstay

Failed Swivel Block

Failure of Swivel Block
allowing Running Back Stay
& Check Stay to fly free
losing aft-mid support of mast

Swinging
Check & Back Stay

weather of Bishop Rock and the Scilly Islands. If the mast did fail, we could be blown towards and even upon the dangerous lee shores. Should we risk it? We could still win the actual race…or lose a much bigger one. The answer was simple. We could steer a further 10-degrees to the south to clear both Bishop Rock and the Scillys under greatly reduced sail. We would then be off the wind and could safely set proper sails for the course to Plymouth. This was our plan. We would sail on a triple reefed mainsail with no headsail until we jibed at a much slower speed, losing time and distance to other boats.

Bruce and Syd went below to rest. I stayed on deck and drove for a while, and then decided to have one of our crew take the wheel as the helm was substantially unloaded.

We had not learned of the tragic events happening behind us with the smaller fleet. We did see a nearby steamer showing lights that would indicate they were in trouble. I was looking off to starboard, leaning on the cockpit coaming next to the running backstay winch, when our helmsman "lost it." He stubbed the port bow into an extremely large wave, and green water cascaded down on *KIALOA III*, throwing my right chest into the running backstay winch. Another three harnessed crew, seated forward of me on the deck, were also washed aft and directly on top of me, driving me even further and harder into the winch.

Bruce and Syd were immediately on deck and they pulled me away from the winch with great pain. I could not move my arms and felt some funny bulges in my right chest. I was placed in my bunk below, and given codeine and some other pills. Tied into my bunk, where I'd stay for most of the remainder of the race, I could hear the emergency calls over the ship's radio from other racing yachts:

"We're sinking…"

"Crew in the water…"

"Have abandoned yacht…"

And then we'd hear the response from the rescue vessel: "We can't find you…"

What an unnecessary tragedy. Without electronic navigation aids, and in high seas and stormy skies that obscured celestial observations, it was impossible to relay exact or even approximate positions.

In my bunk, I kept thinking, "How can this happen in 1979 when so many security and navigational devices are available at so little cost?" I also said to myself, "What are you doing tied in your bunk while so many others are in such pain and tragic difficulties?" It was frustrating and terrible.

Bruce and Syd and the rest of the *KIALOA* crew executed our plan, sailing cautiously and underpowered to the southeast before jibing and hoisting the proper sails. Down below, while partially asleep, I continued listening to the horror story unfolding off Fastnet Rock.

Finally, I couldn't take it anymore, listening to such heartbreaking calls for help. Very slowly,

Bishop Rock

Bishop Rock
Turbulent Sea

noticing the bumps and bruises but with the pain partially subdued by the codeine, I got out of the bunk and realized I could tentatively use my arms to get dressed and move cautiously on deck. My crew offered wonderful greetings and support as we approached the finish line at Plymouth.

On crossing the finish line, we learned that *Condor* had finished 28 minutes ahead of *KIALOA*, gaining about 2 hours since our mast rigging failure, which placed her 6 minutes ahead of *KIALOA* on corrected time. We later learned that Ted Turner's *Tenacious* had received favorable wind shifts as the wind moved more to the west, providing easier seas and faster sailing, beating *KIALOA III* on corrected time by 4 hours and 19 minutes, and ultimately, placing first in fleet overall corrected time. While *Condor* placed eighth, *KIALOA* placed ninth overall corrected time.

I have often wondered how much time *KIALOA III* lost in making repairs and our protective sailing, on a mainsail only, sailing a wider, easier course at a slower speed until we could jibe to a wider, easier sailing angle on which we could set larger downwind sails.

One never knows. We never second guessed our decision. We must protect our crew and our rig—a failure could be significantly serious and was not a worthwhile gamble.

When *KIALOA III* docked, the race sponsors greeted us. They carried magnums of champagne to celebrate our arrival and our record-breaking elapsed-time finish. (Both *KIALOA* and *Condor* beat the previous race record by over seven hours.) Our crew immediately offered a toast to all of the sailors at sea and a prayer to those injured or lost in this tragic 1979 Fastnet Rock Race.

I was escorted across the floating dock to a ladder that extended 20-25 feet vertically to the top of the pier. Someone offered me help climbing the ladder. I said to myself, "My problem is minor, just a discomfort, and it's repairable. There are many who won't make it back to the dock to their wives, their children, their families." I said, "I can make it if Bruce climbs behind me," and was driven to the hospital.

After X-rays, they told me that I had cracked ribs and torn cartilage, which was protruding outward from the ribs with some lung damage. They said they would operate in the morning. I asked them to delay any operation as I needed to talk to my doctor and would like him to talk to their lead doctor. I called Dr. Toby Friedman, my doctor and a noted sports doctor, former Air Force surgeon and a physician.

After his conversation with the hospital doctors, he asked, "Can you make it home as is?" My response was, "If Toby would okay it, I would immediately fly home." I caught my flight a day later, after talking with race officials about the need to modify the racing rules in the future to better protect all who may sail this powerful and challenging race.

On the way home, I couldn't forget those antiquated race instructions, and the trouble that rescue helicopters and Coast Guard personnel had locating people due to faulty dead reckoning positions. I'd heard the conversations and despair in the voices of the racers. I'd heard helicopter pilots radio, "We can't find you," as a sailor drifted away.

Here's the official record: Three hundred and three yachts entered in the 1979 Fastnet Race. Only eighty-six yachts finished the race; one hundred and ninety-four retired. Twenty-four yachts were abandoned. But the biggest disaster? Fifteen sailors were lost, drowned at sea.

Once back in Los Angeles, I was met by my wife, Kathy, and taken to the sports-medicine clinic. Looking back, it was kind of a humorous occasion. It seems my injury was almost identical to that suffered by an NFL quarterback the doctors had treated a day or two before. All three doctors had the same question, one that almost made me laugh…uncomfortably: "How could two sports so different create the same injuries?"

Though we once again had lost the racing "star" we'd hoped to gain, it didn't seem very important as I pondered over the issues and tragedies of the 1979 Fastnet Race.

After the Fastnet Tragedy:
Comments to the New England Sailing Symposium

I was asked to speak before the New England Sailing Symposium about the 1979 Fastnet Race and Safety at Sea, and consolidated my thoughts in an article as follows, dated March 22, 1980:

I have read many articles about the 1979 Fastnet Race. A few were written by seasoned sailors and writers who participated in the race. Many were written by designers, sailors or writers who gained their observations through the after-the-race landside commentary of crew members of participating yachts.

I have since read many comments about safety at sea indirectly related to the problems of the Fastnet Race criticizing certain types of yachts, certain types of sail plans and rigging, safety gear and almost anything else that might be criticized; yet, I have heard little commentary on techniques of boat handling so absolutely essential in such adverse sea state conditions. We had a serious and tragic storm with exceedingly adverse sea conditions that were the root cause of many deaths. As a result, the 1979 Fastnet Race and tragedy were highly publicized in this world of instant communication.

Comments made by dockside crew, such as, "This is the worst storm I have ever been in," can give false assurances of the probability of future storms. I feel such comments were made, in some instances, by enthusiastic young crewmembers who very likely were never in a serious storm before.

The Royal Ocean Racing Club (RORC) conducted an inquest and their results were published. Skippers of all participating yachts were asked to respond to set questions by selecting and checking a box for one of several alternate answers suggested. Some supplemental comments could be provided where appropriate.

For *KIALOA*, I not only put my check in the box for most appropriate response but provided supplemental comments on the questionnaire. I also sent letters to the RORC with further comment.

It is not my intent to criticize the RORC format of having a popular vote inquest; however, I am somewhat concerned that it might perpetuate the basic problems that provided the inherently weak safety foundation of the 1979 Fastnet Race. The published results of the inquest furthered my concern in this regard. My comments, which I have forwarded to the RORC, are as follows:

Experience of skipper and crew.

The use the Category 1 Safety Rules and Regulations instead of Category 2.

Rigorous pre-race yacht inspection.

Limit minimum size of yacht to ¾-ton or one-ton rating.

Mandatory use of two-way radios.

Permit the use of electronic navigation except for radar.

Do away with sail limitations under rule 892.

There is no need to provide a detailed recounting of the tragic statistics of the race and how they support some of the foregoing concerns.

Suffice it to say that deaths came from hypothermia, resulting from abandonment of yachts that did not sink, poor safety gear, including rafts, and yachts that were apparently too small for the wave form. I further presume that failure to have a disciplined and mandatory plan for the use of radios limited not only the security aboard, or feel thereof, but also made problems of rescue much more complicated.

The need for accurate electronics navigation during such conditions speaks for itself. Knowing where you are in relation to marks, obstructions, or a safe port is essential to safety. It is further essential in identifying a yacht's position to a rescue vessel or helicopter in case of emergency. The cost of good electronics navigation gear is minimal and is essential safety gear. Let me ask all of you two questions: How much leeway do each of you think a yacht makes in such storm conditions? How accurate of a course do you think can be steered? The order of magnitude of the variance to both questions can be startling.

These answers and the variance will obviously depend upon the yacht's sailing angle and speed in relation to the wind, the primary wave, the storm wave and any secondary waves coupled with the inherent current or tidal flow. These, of course, will further vary for different kinds of hulls, different kinds of rigs and sail plans used along with the helmsman's ability to handle the sea and wind conditions.

We now go to the major issue of the disaster—experience—versus storm conditions.

Would a highly experienced, knowledgeable and competitive yachtsman compete in the 1981 Fastnet race without again reviewing the root cause of the 1979 disaster? Would he not consider the variables existent in the Irish Sea as compared to the Bermuda Race, the Transatlantic Race, the Sydney Hobart Race, the Trans Tasman Race and other races for which data is available or of which he may have sailed in at another time?

Each race has unique characteristics of potential weather and sea state resulting from the variations in wind direction, bottom depth, tidal and current conditions, and bounce back characteristics resulting from the bottom and land form obstructions, including the primary wave effect.

The Australian Admiral's Cup Team did exceedingly well in the 1979 Fastnet Race. As a group, their sailing experience in heavy, confused waveforms is probably greater than the other Admiral's Cup Teams; they handled the wind and wave conditions in the Fastnet Race admirably well. This results from experience with the wave conditions of the East Australian Coast and on down to Hobart, Tasmania and across Bass Strait.

In the 1977 Sydney Hobart Race, in which *KIALOA* participated as well as won on corrected time, the fleet encountered a "Southerly Buster" with wind velocities up to 50 to 60 knots for over 36 hours. This storm had stalled in Bass Strait and to the south for some time before moving north, and as a result, developed a severe sea state when coupled with the heavy currents and tides around Bass Strait.

About half of the fleet dropped out of the race, no yachts were sunk and no sailors were lost. The Cruising Yacht Club of Australia advised all yachts, at the skipper's meeting, to make their own determination of whether to proceed or drop out of the race as they approached Bass Strait dependent upon the weather conditions. Needless to say, weather conditions were such that some yachts dropped out voluntarily and others involuntarily. Radio reporting in the morning and evening was mandatory and weather data was provided at each broadcast, as well as by commercial radio stations.

I cite this race as an example of skippers knowing their capabilities personally, and of the yacht and crew acting in a responsible fashion, plus having the obligation of safe radio communication.

The Transatlantic Yacht Race of 1975 was another vigorous race as we encountered the first hurricane of the year, with full-blown hurricane conditions and some yachts in the northwest quadrant of the hurricane. Although no yachts were lost and there were no fatalities, some yachts were damaged and retired from the race. The sea state in this hurricane, although confused, was much different than in the Sydney Hobart Race. The sea state of the Transatlantic Race and the Sydney Hobart Race were much different than the sea state of the Fastnet Race.

Although the "sea states" were different, the Transatlantic Race and the Sydney Hobart Race had one thing in common – the sailing angle in each was hard on the wind. This permitted the essential steering of sailing "fuller" with more drive in the troughs and "feathering" the yacht as it approached the crest of the wave to both unload the rig as the wave blanketing was reduced, and also to be able to come off the wave "flat," keeping options open, and thereby reduce falling off the wave sideways as you would do if the yacht were sailed full over the top of the wave. Less helm, better control, safety of the yacht by rig and rudder imbalance problems is eliminated when this technique is used.

A bit more power (sail) can also be used with this technique working to keep a balanced rig, unloading where appropriate by feathering and using maximum power when appropriate to dodge or work around the most unfriendly waves.

Helm balance with a little weather helm is most appropriate for driving in these conditions. A leeward helm can be most disadvantageous and tends to load or trip the leeward bow.

Let us now discuss some of the helm and driving conditions from the perspective of *KIALOA* in the 1979 Fastnet Race. Let me say again that confusion reigns as to where the center of the storm was in relation to the fleet and where the large and small yachts were in relation to each other.

Perhaps, I should first verbalize the course. After departing the Solent, the course goes westerly along the south coast of England to Land's End, and then on a course of about 300 degrees to the Fastnet Rock off the southwest coast of Ireland, then a course of about 135 degrees to Bishop Rock (which lies a little south of west from Land's End) thence, around the Scilly's and north of east back to Plymouth, England.

The course from Land's End to Fastnet and Fastnet to Bishop Rock are only 15 degrees to 20 degrees out of reciprocal. All yachts on course, either up or down, were in reaching conditions.

The larger yachts had rounded Fastnet and were on their way to Bishop, the smaller yachts were on their way up, and so all yachts were in the same general area.

When you picture this area of the Irish Sea, you have the southern coast of Ireland to the north, the continuation by the Irish Sea to the northeast, between the west coast of England and the east coast of Ireland, the west coast of England to the east and Scilly's to the south.

The primary ground wave from the Atlantic is from the west-northwest and is shifted somewhat by bounce back waves from the 50-60 fathom bottom and the land obstructions.

In the morning, the wind had been from the west, counter-clocking early midday to the southwest, and then moving more to the south and increasing in velocity. *KIALOA* had rounded Fastnet around noon, about an hour ahead of the second yacht *Condor*, and we were hard on the wind with a No. 1 heavy Genoa. In the later afternoon, the velocity began to increase and after several sail changes, we finally ended up with a No. 4 Genoa and a triple-reefed main sailing at about a 75 degree apparent wind angle with velocities substantially above 60 knots.

The wave conditions were as follows: a remainder primary wave from about 280 degrees, a left over southerly wave, and the storm wave from about 225 degrees. In the shoal water (50-60 fathoms), all intercept wave conditions were magnified and the storm waves were very close and irregular in form. When the primary wave would intercept the storm wave, it would lift the stern and tend to roll the port bow down, loading the bow and requiring some weather helm to hold the bow up. The southerly wave could also roll the bow down creating the same problem.

Due to the height of the wave, there was some blanketing effect of the wind in the trough, and as KIALOA was lifted by the storm wave or the other wave, the rig was raised over the storm wave and the wind velocity increased again, loading the bow and causing the addition of weather helm.

Our technique of compensating for this rig helm balance condition was to roll the bow into the storm wave and feather the rig then accelerate off the backside of the wave by footing off on the backside of the wave then again unloading the rig into the following wave.

We carried a short-hoist No. 4 Genoa changing to a forestaysail instead of the No. 4 Genoa with a triple-reefed main at the height of the storm. It was our intention to change from the forestaysail to a No. 5 Genoa with the forestaysail only as a changing sail; however, the running back stay blew up, and we had an interesting period of time saving the mast and rebuilding the running backstay. This was a great surprise to us as the block was purportedly a 24,000-pound test block only carrying about 9,000-10,000 pounds of load at the time it blew up.

Due to mast damage, we were reduced to a triple-reefed main with no headsail until we rounded the Scilly's and began running for Plymouth, at which time we were able to set a jib topsail on a spinnaker pole, increasing area as appropriate.

As you can deduce from my commentary, I feel it essential to keep maximum power on during a storm, feathering as appropriate over the waves to unload the rig and helm and keep the hull flat. Too little power, as well as too much power, can create a serious problem. You must be able to accelerate and decelerate as appropriate to steer around waves and protect the hull or rig from taking charge.

I personally feel that the storm trysail is a sail of last resort used when the main can no longer be used due to damage to the main sail or boom. The process of change from the main to the trysail is quite dangerous, leaving the hull and crew vulnerable during the changing process. I give no credibility to the value of a track and slides over a luff groove as some sailors or designers have made an issue about. I have had problems with slides jamming, sails blowing off the slides and other problems with trysails and sail slides. I have had no problems with a luff groove and personally favor the luff groove. Incidentally, I cannot recommend a reel winch as a main halyard winch for any reefing operation; I consider them quite dangerous.

In my opinion, the use of a storm trysail limits your options in maneuvering a yacht, which, when coupled with the dangerous changing process, makes it a "reserve" sail more than a "use" sail.

The use of a forestaysail or headsail without a main creates serious problems of rig and helm balance, limiting maneuvering problems and tending to trip the bow in combination with the sea when coming up out of a trough, making the yacht highly vulnerable to serious knockdown in heavy reaching conditions such as the Fastnet Race.

The use of head stay hydraulics for rig trim and helm balance could be a definite safety advantage in heavy sea conditions. Unfortunately, the present rules restrict the use of head stay hydraulics.

While we are speaking of sails, I wish excess legislation of sail inventories would go away. I have reason to believe that many inappropriate sails were aboard the Fastnet yachts due to the limits of Rule 892.

Let's face facts. All highly competitive yachts will have a full inventory of sails, and will select from that inventory suitable sails to fit what they believe to be the weather conditions for a given race. No yacht desires to carry more sails than appropriate, as added weight reduces available horsepower. Therefore, the amount of sails actually carried becomes self-limiting. It is the slightly less competitive yachts that get hurt and become more vulnerable to weather conditions as they will limit their inventory and sometimes take inappropriate sails within the restrictions of the limitation. The ITC, USYRU and RORC know my position in this regard.

The foregoing are a few of my personal reflections on the 1979 Fastnet Race. In summary, the personal preparation of skipper and crew and their understanding of the pressure interrelationship between wind, wave, hull and rig are the keys to handling a sailing yacht in adverse sea conditions. This preparation, coupled with sensible security and safety conditions for open sea races and sailing can go a long way toward limiting future tragedies at sea.

26

Transitional Thoughts –
KIALOA III to *KIALOA IV*

The help of Jack Sutphen, Dennis Conner,
testing sailing helmsman and occasional *KIALOA* crew

KIALOA III's future and *KIALOA III*'s past

Wonderful worldwide cruising to be set forth
in another book and on the website

A Goodbye to Bruce Kendell

Retirement of *KIALOA III*
A Wonderful Record,
But Could She Have Done Better?

K IALOA III's last year of competition was 1980. After a few wins in the 1980 SORC, *KIALOA III* became the aggressive sparring partner for our new *KIALOA IV* and, through 2006, our outstanding World Ocean Cruiser.

Jack Sutphen, who has notably been Dennis Conner's sparring partner in the America's Cup Campaigns and an occasional *KIALOA* crew, became the challenging skipper sailing *KIALOA III* against *KIALOA IV* in our friendly but serious testing in St. Petersburg, Florida.

We received the following article from Jack, an outstanding sailor and friend, regarding our mutual cooperation. We have had wonderful times sailing with each other and against each other. I thought the reader might be interested in Jack's comments.

KIALOA the Famous Maxi
Two Boat Testing

by Jack Sutphen

In the late 1980s, I not only got to sail on the famous *KIALOA* but spent some time at the helm of both *KIALOA III* and *KIALOA IV*. It all started when Jim Kilroy asked Dennis Conner if he could come to St. Petersburg, Florida, to drive *KIALOA III* for a week of testing to tune the new *KIALOA IV*. Dennis couldn't do it, but he told Jim that I had been sailing the trial horse for Team Dennis Conner and knew the routine and felt I could do the job, so I was invited.

Skipper Kilroy had divided up his experienced crew, so I had good sail trimmers and a well-tuned boat in *KIALOA III*. We put in a full week of testing sails and rig and they learned a lot about the new boat and the new large feathering propeller, which was being tried for the first time.

The testing was quite successful and great fun for me as I got to drive upwind and down for a lot of hours just as we did with *Stars & Stripes*. As they made changes on *KIALOA IV*, she began beating us. All this led to my sailing on *IV* in the SORC (Southern Ocean Racing Circuit). Our main competition was *Windward Passage*, which made for exciting racing. I had brought our statometer that we used to judge the downwind testing of the Cup boats and it was helpful when we were using the fine downwind angles that Jim had developed. (Today, a laser gun does the job of the statometer.)

I felt sorry for one of the crew – the young lady who did the cooking and served two sittings of ten crew each for breakfast, lunch, and dinner. That's 60 meals a day! It sure made for a happy crew.

Many in our sailing world have said that *KIALOA III's* racing record will show unequalled success in major races of the world, sailing in all weather conditions and that *KIALOA III* had the potential to win even more victories.

One of the foundations for this positive response was the error in the calculation of the actual displacement of *KIALOA III* as set forth in the following sketch.

KIALOA III's actual displacement was about 82,000 pounds. The IOR MKIII measurement calculation was 20,000 pounds lighter at about 62,000 pounds. This incorrect calculation reduced our handicap time allowance credit from other yachts. We discussed this incorrect calculation under the IOR MKIII displacement formula with appropriate measurement authorities on many occasions during *KIALOA III's* racing career, to no avail. The IOR MKIII displacement measurement formula was not revised until after the retirement of *KIALOA III*.

KIALOA III
Hull Shapes
Measurement Line "Waterline"

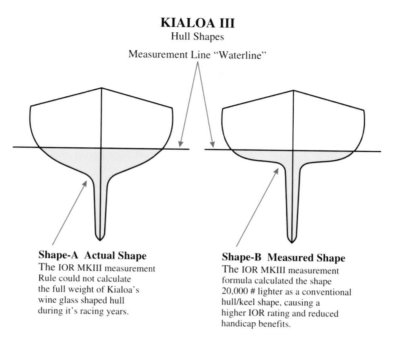

Shape-A Actual Shape
The IOR MKIII measurement
Rule could not calculate
the full weight of Kialoa's
wine glass shaped hull
during it's racing years.

Shape-B Measured Shape
The IOR MKIII measurement
formula calculated the shape
20,000 # lighter as a conventional
hull/keel shape, causing a
higher IOR rating and reduced
handicap benefits.

1973 - 1981
Measurement Penalty

In retirement, after her racing days were over, *KIALOA III* cruised extensively from 1981 through 2006 with family and guests aboard. Many areas of the world were visited: the Caribbean, England and Ireland, the Mediterranean, the Aegean, the Indian Ocean, Thailand, the South Pacific, Central America, Patagonia and many offshore islands. All aboard were forever amazed at how many large photographs and drawings of *KIALOA III* were on display in so many of these areas, surfing on a beautiful sea with her complement of red, white and blue downwind sails set.

We were constantly asked about *KIALOA III*—where she had sailed, what races she had won, and why she quit racing. It was hard to believe that such an extensive distribution of *KIALOA III's* photographs had been printed and displayed. Interestingly, many of the photographs we saw were in bars, restaurants and small seaside stores run by merchants from India and Greece.

Maybe that wasn't entirely surprising. We remembered the first time we cruised in Greece, when we were greeted by Greek nationals who'd immigrated to Australia but had returned home for a visit, who remembered *KIALOA III's* record-setting victory in the Sydney-Hobart Race. We were always flattered by the attention. I was always amazed how news and matters relating to the sea traveled so quickly from one port to another. It goes to show what a tight-knit community yacht racing is.

As a yacht travels through the South Pacific, it seems the islanders always know that you're coming. The Savusavu ritual is another example of how mariners respect one another, narrowing cultural divides. As a whole, throughout so much of the world, *KIALOA* and all aboard were courteously accepted and frequently honored by unexpected gifts to which we would always respond gratefully.

After cruising Patagonia, we anchored *KIALOA III* at the Punta del Este Yacht Club in Uruguay, where we have a summer home, and cruised the local area. Sadly, but appropriately, we decided to gift *KIALOA III* so that many others could enjoy her sailing and cruising. *KIALOA III* returned to Newport Beach, California under her new flag, in the sailing program of Orange Coast College.

Bruce Kendell—A Key Member of the *KIALOA* Team

Bruce Kendell joined the *KIALOA II* crew in 1969 after our victorious race to Ireland. We met in Cowes Week and Bruce was aboard a kiwi boat from New Zealand, his home country. A robust, enthusiastic sailor with a good engineering education, a good communicator and the strength to be a leader, Bruce joined *KIALOA II* as a crew and demonstrated his capability on the sail back to California. To be a leader and a skipper, he became a member of the *KIALOA* team and skipper of *KIALOA II*.

It was a good time. We had a newly launched rival, an unusually designed Maxi, launched in time for the 1969 SORC. *Windward Passage,* a yacht more like a big dinghy—very beamy—to provide beam stability, and very light to provide good reaching and running, off the wind speed.

W.P. as *Windward Passage* was called, and another key competitor, Ted Turner's *American Eagle*, strongly told us that we should consider a new *KIALOA*, which was emphasized by another engineering challenge. A new measurement rule was to become effective in 1971, the IOR MKIII rule which had been in process for some time. Concepts for the new rule were tested by modifications of the existing CCA rule over the past three of four years.

Another serious issue raised (it's perhaps righteous, but with an ugly head) is the old age allowance for boats designed under the then existing CCA rule, such as the newer *Windward Passage*, which would receive up to an 11% benefit under the new IOR MKIIIA version.

KIALOA II was launched in 1962, so this meant serious problems and time for a new boat, as the latest technology and the new IOR MKIII rule would "pass her by."

Bruce would become the skipper of *KIALOA II* and the coordinator with Sparkman and Stephens for the construction of *KIALOA III*, working closely with me and our aerospace friends that I called our design consultant team, offering many contributions of successful ideas to *KIALOA III*'s future performance. The design and construction of the great and versatile *KIALOA III* was a challenging and successful experience for all concerned. The combination of experiences, sailing, design, construction and project management were all a great foundation for the excellent capabilities of Bruce Kendell. Every day was a learning day to all of us; the exchange of ideas, the rational and different concepts and the practical testing for a final decision. Bruce became a full and contributing member of our team and the skipper of *KIALOA III*.

We worked well together on the shore and at sea and could easily communicate verbally or in writing. Bruce was the skipper, in charge, subject to my approval or direction, in non-race activities. I was the captain during race activities. I was the port watch captain and

Bruce was the starboard watch captain when racing. We blended our talents in a successful and open manner. Neither of us were what one could call shy or indecisive, which was one of the *KIALOA's* strengths. Two Irishmen aboard a boat—in many ways a great key to success—always ready for a challenge.

We continued to become involved in *KIALOA III* success, and then came the time for *KIALOA IV*. Bruce was the coordinator with Ron Holland, the naval architect, for *KIALOA IV's* construction, as well as *KIALOA III's* racing in Florida and the east coast.

Bruce and his wife, Patti, had children and fortunately lived in Florida close to where *KIALOA IV* was built and where *KIALOA III* was being raced. This became too challenging and we had to bring in another skipper to help because of the two boats. It was time for Bruce to make a change and he became the construction coordinator for a development project that we had in Florida, working for our company and sailing aboard *KIALOA IV* when he could. The design, development and construction experience was a wonderful fit for the talents of Bruce Kendell.

When we sold our interests in the Florida project, Bruce Kendell decided to continue living in Florida and became a successful consultant in development planning, and construction for hi tech projects. He and Patti had two children, a pleasant home in Clearwater, Florida and Bruce would sail with us when convenient to do so.

His successful activities were local and beyond the Tampa and Clearwater area and Bruce Kendell learned to fly airplanes, acquired his license, and would use the airplane for business travel. On a return flight from Northern Florida, with another pilot and his son Brad aboard, they encountered intensive cross wind puffs, nasty puffs as they approached contact with the runway. A very severe puff caused a crash and Bruce was killed and his son Brad was seriously injured. A tragedy for the Kendell family and regrets from all the *KIALOA* crew.

Patti with her courage and strengths, gained in part from her experience at sea as the *KIALOA* cook on deliveries across the oceans, took charge of the family. With the joint courage of her sons, Sean and Brad, they have lived challenging and successful lives.

Brad entered into the challenge of business as well as paraplegic sports, sailing, fishing, and other sports successfully shown in the following photograph.

Bruce and Pattie's other son, Sean, has been successful in his own activities. Patti continues her friendship with the *KIALOA* crew. A photograph follows of Bruce, Patti, and their sons taken before the terrible accident.

Bruce and Patti, we thank you for your joint participation in the success of the *KIALOAs*.

above: Brad Kendell
below: The Kendell family: (L to R) Sean, Patti, Brad, Bruce

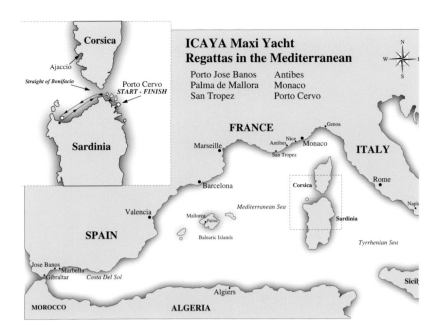

27

KIALOA IV crew and skipper

A big fat stern—a new tacking technique

A career extending rule change—elimination of interiors
in *KIALOA IV*—extending *KIALOA III's* life as a cruising yacht
for another 25 years

Test sailing—*KIALOA IV* vs. *KIALOA III*

Jack Sutphen and so many *KIALOA* crew—good results—
learning to sail with speed

Our last Fastnet Rock Race and the entry to
Plymouth Sound—ebb tide and offshore light breeze
early in the morning a true frustration is further interpreted
by the chart within this chapter

Sailing in the Mediterranean—a big maxi playground
for the ICAYA Maxis

KIALOA III's 1980 Turnover to KIALOA IV
Testing the New Concepts of Design

K IALOA IV, designed by Ron Holland at his office in Cork, Ireland, along with much help from KIALOA crew and our aerospace supporters, would be our new racing machine, under construction in Clearwater, Florida. KIALOA IV's design was strongly influenced by the midsize *Imp*, which won the 1979 SORC with tremendous victories over all of the SORC competition

Carbon fibre hulls were the new thing and we decided to join the concept, except there was no example of stress loading on a powerful Maxi. We were conservative, probably too conservative. We saved a little weight but not much at a higher cost.

We mimicked some of the design of *Imp* with a big fat stern that seemed to help in some circumstances, but was slow accelerating in the tacks. I found it necessary when tacking in a moderate breeze to stay a bit wider than usual to gain acceleration before completing the tack and when at proper speed to finish the tack at a higher sailing angle, an excellent angle after the slight delay.

We ultimately cut off about 8' of the stern and replaced it with a less bulbous section, improving its tacking and improving acceleration. We continued to improve all speed characteristics of the great winning yacht. The construction process proceeded and other design ideas were also modified. Ron and our builder were very cooperative.

One measurement rule modified about a year later was a real shocker. Over all of my racing in *KIALOA I, KIALOA II,* and *KIALOA III,* the rules required that the yachts have a cruising interior. KIALOA IV had a lightweight beautiful interior, similar to *KIALOA III's,* installed for pleasure when cruising.

The new rule said clearly no cruising interior required. And so, we removed the interior and lost the potential of cruising on *KIALOA IV,* a cost in and a COST OUT!!! Fortunately, we still had *KIALOA III,* our favorite. So we kept *KIALOA III* in motion, cruising throughout much of the world for an additional 25 years.

In the early winter of 1980, *KIALOA IV* was ready to test sail off the St. Petersburg, Florida coast and was challenged by *KIALOA III.* We began a rigorous test sailing program between *KIALOA IV* and *KIALOA III.* The noted sailor and helmsman, Jack Sutphen, would drive *KIALOA III* and I would sail *KIALOA IV*; both boats were crewed by key *KIALOA* sailors so we could see which boat was the fastest. At times, Jack and I—and the crews—would switch boats. In everything but extremely light conditions, *KIALOA IV* did prove to be the faster boat. *KIALOA III* was still a very quick boat and an excellent sparring partner that helped improve *KIALOA IV's* performance. *KIALOA IV* rated a little higher than *KIALOA III,* and we still adopted the proven concept of having a handicap rating slightly below our key competitors. We always want to be the aggressor, to sail against slightly "faster rated" boats. It was a great psychological position.

Arvil Gentry, a leading aerodynamicist and Boeing engineer, was a great help in our trials. He installed special testing gear that gave us computer printouts of speed, tacking angles and other performance information that could be used to make comparisons against *KIALOA III.* In many ways, our two-boat speed trials were well ahead of their time. All yachts have strengths and weaknesses, and we always hoped to leverage our strengths against our competitor's weaknesses. To do so, we needed a full, unbiased look at our true capabilities. With more sailing and testing, we were able to make small speed revisions as we conducted our evaluations.

Of course, you only learn so much on trials. Competing in the 1981 SORC against a fleet of 89 yachts would tell us a great deal about our new yacht, which came in rating at 69.5. Despite the familiar obstacles—the Gulf Stream and old-age allowances—*KIALOA IV* passed her first tests.

In the first race, the 183-mile contest from St. Petersburg to Boca Grande, we were first to finish, second in class and fifth overall. In the sixth race in the Bahamas, the 24-mile Nassau Cup (no Gulf Stream!), we scored a clean sweep: first to finish, first in class and first overall. When all was said and done, *KIALOA IV* was first to finish on elapsed time in all six events, setting new course records for the 135-mile Ocean Triangle and the 174-mile Miami-Nassau Race. In the two races in which the Gulf Stream did not come into play, we did quite well.

The '81 SORC also included an ICAYA Maxi series that ran concurrently but was scored separately. In this regatta, *KIALOA IV* dominated the field—first to finish, first in class and first overall, a clean sweep. When our European results were added later that year, *KIALOA IV* was crowned as the 1981 World Champion.

From Florida, *KIALOA IV* was delivered to England for Cowes Week and the '81 Fastnet Race. Cowes Week was an interesting regatta. We were sailing against the new *Condor* with Dennis Conner their skipper, a virtual sister ship of *KIALOA III* in the Queen's Cup Race around the Isle of Wight. *Condor* was about a boat length and a half ahead of us on a port tack on the west side of the island, where there are "fingers" of sand bars extending from the shore into the Solent. *Condor* was squarely on our wind, calling for unusual tactics by *KIALOA*.

Aboard *KIALOA*, we thought there was a small bay between the next sand bar and us. We wondered if we could trick Dennis into heading closer to shore, where there just might be a sand bar in his way. So we steered more towards shore. Dennis took the bait and did the same, focusing on us. He hit the sand bar. *KIALOA IV* quickly tacked to starboard and sailed past *Condor*, which was hard aground. It took them a while to break free, and they finished a few hours after us. The ploy worked, and we won the race.

Next up was the Fastnet Race, two years after the tragic 1979 event. We still hadn't won it and were as eager and motivated as ever. We had a good start and a reasonably fast race, up until about 18 miles from the finish. At that point, time and distance were both in our favor. But then the light offshore wind slowly dropped and kept dropping, as did our boat speed. Against the ebbing tide, tacking and tacking, trying to make forward speed into Plymouth Sound and the finish line, we were first to finish, but our corrected time put us in 69th place, a terrible result and nowhere near first overall. Once again, the British time-on-time handicap system favored the small boats, which were at the front of the fleet. It was our last shot at the Fastnet Race, but a victory remained a blank page in our winning resume.

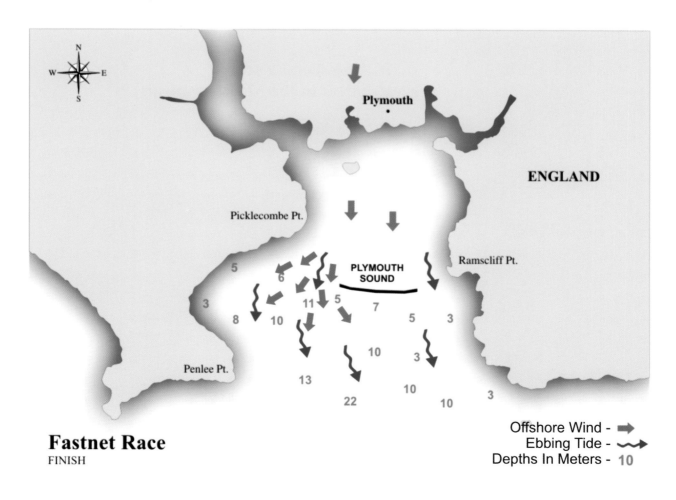

Fastnet Race
FINISH

Offshore Wind - ➡
Ebbing Tide - ⤳
Depths In Meters - 10

But we didn't linger over the results, and instead sailed on to Costa Smeralda, Sardinia, the headquarters for the ICAYA Maxi fleet and *KIALOA IV's* first racing visit to this beautiful island.

The ICAYA regatta that followed, conducted under the auspices of the Yacht Club Costa Smeralda, was sailed in the Straits of Bonifacio between the beautiful islands and coastlines of Sardina and Corsica, overlooked by the high hills of Corsica and the ancient city of Bonifacio—the birthplace of Napoleon—a lovely area to spend a few days and take in the views. The north end of Sardinia was the location of both the yacht club and Porto Cervo, a lavish port developed by the Aga Khan, a yachting enthusiast. This was our base for the regatta. Future regattas in the Mediterranean would be held at the locations set forth on the following chart.

The 1981 ICAYA event was comprised of a series of races. The distance race started in Porto Cervo, took the fleet to Asinara on the northwest coast of Sardinia and returned to Porto Cervo. The middle-distance course was set through the islands in the Straits of Bonifacio. Finally, there were three round-the-buoys triangles off Porto Cervo.

The Asinara Race was won by *Helisara*, a yacht owned by Maestro Herbert von Karajan, the world-renowned conductor of the Berlin Symphony and the leader of the wonderful Salzberg Festival for over 25 years,. *KIALOA IV*, busy covering *Condor II* for most of the race, was a minute behind. But it was a pleasure to see the Maestro—not only a fine sailor, but a speed enthusiast who owned and drove

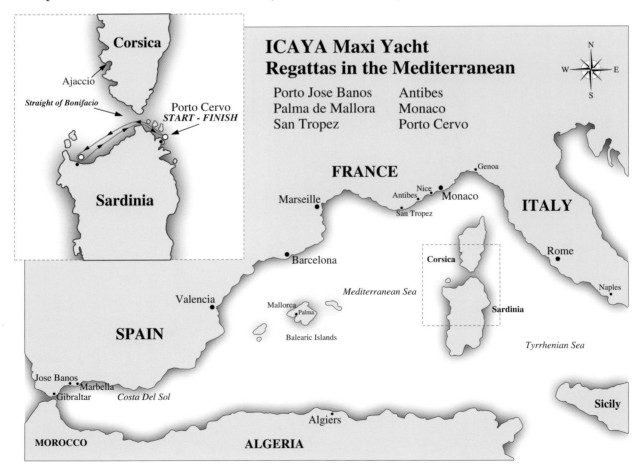

fast cars and piloted his own Learjet—earn the victory. We'd become personal friends. Unfortunately, he suffered from terrible arthritis and other ailments, and died a few years later.

Von Karajan wasn't the only member of ICAYA with interesting careers, which made for serious post-race discussions about the competition and other matters. Most of the Maxi competitors employed internationally-known sailors to drive their boats, which prompted me, as the helmsman/skipper/owner, to sail that much harder. One such helmsman was Paul Cayard, the skipper of Raul Gardini's *Il Moro de Venezia*. Along with *Condor, Boomerang* and *Matador*, *Il Moro* became one of our closet competitors.

Our final results were good: second in the Asinara Race and three firsts in the triangles. Combined with our earlier results from England and the SORC, we were the ICAYA's World Champions, and by hosting the first World Championships at Yacht Club Costa Smeralda, the Aga Khan also considered the event a personal victory. The awards party and presentation were magnificent, with many of Italy's political and financial leaders in attendance. The *KIALOA IV* crew had an excellent time.

Afterwards, we enjoyed a few days of cruising Sardinia and Corsica before *KIALOA IV* sailed back to Florida, with a short delay and cruise in the Virgin Islands. The following 1982 season was going to be most challenging.

Presentation of Trophy to KIALOA IV by the Aga Khan.

28

Our *KIALOA* Crew

I can only say that chapter 28 is
The ultimate display of
The Will
The Skill
The Mutual Protection
and
The Mutual Respect
of
The *KIALOA* crew

I thank all my crew for their comments and support.

The KIALOA IV Chronicles
SORC—Antigua—Pan Am Clipper/Kenwood Cup
(1982–1984)

Following the ICAYA annual meeting at Porto Cervo in 1981, the three-regatta series that was laid out for 1982 comprised of sixteen races: six in the SORC, five in the Pan Am Clipper Cup in Waikiki, Hawaii, and five in the St. Francis Perpetual Series in San Francisco Bay. It was an exceedingly challenging year that included long, transoceanic deliveries.

In the 1982 SORC, oddly, the Gulf Stream was almost at rest, flowing north at slower speeds and positioned farther away from the coast of Florida. This played to the strengths of the big boats and *KIALOA IV* scored well in the overall 78-boat fleet SORC (second overall in one race, and third overall in two races) and also winning the ICAYA series.

Though it wasn't part of the ICAYA championships, we had ample time before sailing to Hawaii, so we made a quick sail to the north for the famous Antigua Sailing Week festivities, which included an excellent four-race series of races. Racing off Antigua, with its beautiful shores, excellent beaches and resort hotels, was a treat. Our favorite resort was the Curtain Bluff Hotel, with rooms on the top of a hill and dining right on the beach. We'd invited a few non-sailor friends and business guests to join us to experience the excitement of sailboat racing in the Carribean.

Looking back, we can laugh at something that happened in the longest, most important race in the series, which ended up in a protest…that we lost. We were tacking upwind along the beach, leading the fleet, and the second mark on the course was about three-quarters of a mile off the shore. Well, it was supposed to be, but it wasn't there. We decided we'd "dead reckon" where we believed the mark should've been set, and round that imaginary buoy, allowing for a bit of extra distance just to be sure.

We had no idea how the race committee would react. We guessed they'd either assume that the yachts had "rounded" the missing mark at its correct location and count the race, or just cancel it altogether. Well, they chose the former option and gave everyone else the benefit of the doubt. However, we were protested by a yacht about a half mile behind us stating that we'd tacked too early and didn't round the precise spot where the mark should've been.

The "logic" behind this was funny. There was no mark to round, nobody rounded it, and we were tossed out of the race for not rounding the mark that wasn't there…but the lack of the mark was perfectly acceptable for everyone else.

We didn't complain when we were disqualified. It was their race, but our fun, and we still enjoyed the regatta. However, we couldn't help teasing the race committee, and sent them over a round of drinks to help straighten out their decision. Later that evening, the mark was found drifting at sea. Good sailing for all.

After Antigua, *KIALOA IV* sailed back to Miami so all the racing gear could be shipped by container to Honolulu, and all the cruising gear could be loaded on board for the long trip. It was a logistical enterprise. We actually had two containers: a 40-footer for heavy storage like big sails and other large items, and a 20-footer that we used as a virtual machine shop for repair work.

The next time we saw the boat was at Marina del Rey in Los Angeles, where we hosted friends, clients and associates so they too could experience and understand the technical aspects of sailing. The boat was then delivered to Honolulu, more or less on the same route in which *KIALOA III* had triumphed in the 1977 Transpac.

The five-race, 1982 Clipper Cup series, provided a strong, world-class, 80-boat fleet including four Class A ICAYA Maxis: *KIALOA IV*, *Windward Passage*, *Condor III* and *Ondine*. After our strong showing at the SORC, we were committed to winning our second ICAYA World Championship.

It was now 25 years after our first race to Hawaii in 1957, and we knew the waters well. For the 1982 Clipper Cup, the racing schedule, with point scores for first-place, were as follows:

Race 1	Ocean Triangle off Waikiki	100 Points	30+ miles
Race 2	Ocean Triangle off Waikiki	100 Points	30+ miles
Race 3	Molokai Race	200 Points	148 miles
Race 4	Ocean Triangle Offshore	100 Points	30+ miles
Race 5	Around the State Race	300 Points	775 miles

THE MOLOKAI RACE

We referred to the first two races as warm up races, usually an excellent breeze out of the northeast, with some shiftiness due to the southwest corner of Oahu, Makapu Point and Diamond Head.

Instead, there was a hurricane to the south of the Isle of Hawaii, providing shifting and sometimes virtually no wind and *KIALOA IV* did poorly – a 4th overall and a terrible 32nd overall. The hurricane had departed as we started the middle distance race, the 148-mile Molokai Race.

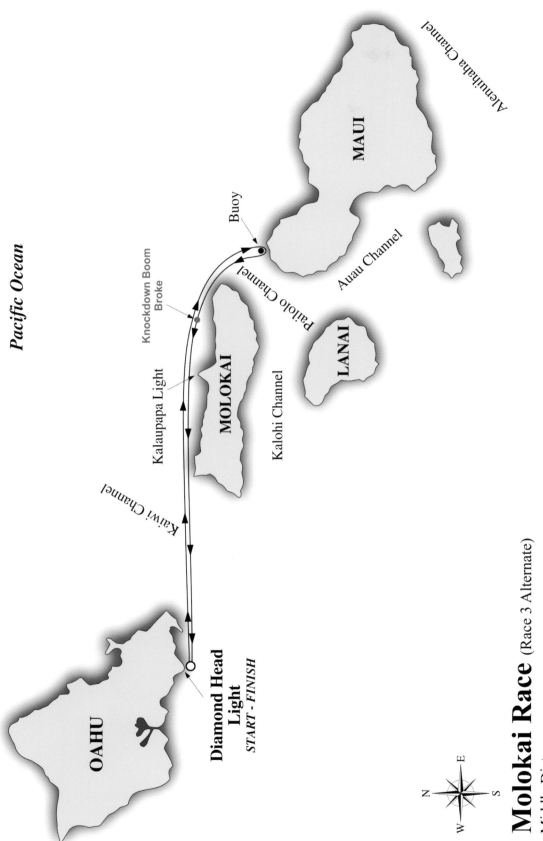

Pacific Ocean

OAHU

MOLOKAI

MAUI

LANAI

Diamond Head Light
START - FINISH

Kaiwi Channel

Kalaupapa Light

Knockdown Boom Broke

Buoy

Pailolo Channel

Auau Channel

Alenuihaha Channel

Kalohi Channel

N
E
S
W

Molokai Race (Race 3 Alternate)
Middle Distance
140 Nautical Miles

The start was off Diamond Head followed by a beat, tacking to weather up the Oahu Coast, and slightly east of Makapu Point looking across to the Island of Molokai, and then a continuing beat to windward up the rugged Molokai Coast with a short slightly offwind sail to the windward mark along the Maui Coast.

After rounding the mark, a short reaction headsails to Cape Hawala where we would set a spinnaker for a high speed run to the finish line. At least, this was our plan. We were ahead of our primary competition, perhaps 20-25 minutes ahead of *Windward Passage* as we set our spinnaker at Cape Hawala with *Condor* 10 or 15 minutes behind *Windward Passage.*

I had been driving much of the windward sail up the coast of Molokai and my son John, an excellent downwind helmsman, would be at the helm as we set a spinnaker and made our fast run towards the finish line. We were in an excellent position for a possible overall victory.

John called for a replacement helmsman as he went below for a new pair of glasses, as his original pair had broken. A crew close to John took over the helm and lost control and *KIALOA* sharply took charge and rounded up to weather as the new helmsman provided maximum leeward helm and lost control. *KIALOA IV* went into what we call "a flying jibe" from which the helmsman could not recover.

As the starboard deck rolled into the sea, the spinnaker pole was broken and the spinnaker was torn to small pieces, with the spinnaker halyard removing the electronic wind guide equipment from the top of *KIALOA's* mast and the main boom trying to change sides, was broken in two pieces, with a big tear in the mainsail.

John rushed up from below deck and gained control so we could count heads and make jury rig repairs to continue the race. I was below in my bunk, asleep, when I found myself in the air and then slammed against the hull and bulkhead, rigorously dashing onto the deck.

We quickly organized a plan to keep *KIALOA* moving towards the finish line, losing much time, with less than 50% of normal sail over the last 35 miles of the race. *Windward Passage* and *Condor* quickly passed us by. *Windward Passage* gained about an hour finishing 32 minutes ahead of *KIALOA* and *Condor II* finished 20 minutes ahead.

It amazed me how quickly the *KIALOA* crew recovered, to maximize our capabilities to continue the race. *Windward Passage*, the first boat to finish, placed third overall corrected time and *Condor II* placed 8th overall.

KIALOA IV placed 14th overall. We were obviously disappointed as we thought we could be the overall corrected time winner, while I was also proud of our quick ability to stay in the race and gain at least 14th place, with 80 yachts in the fleet.

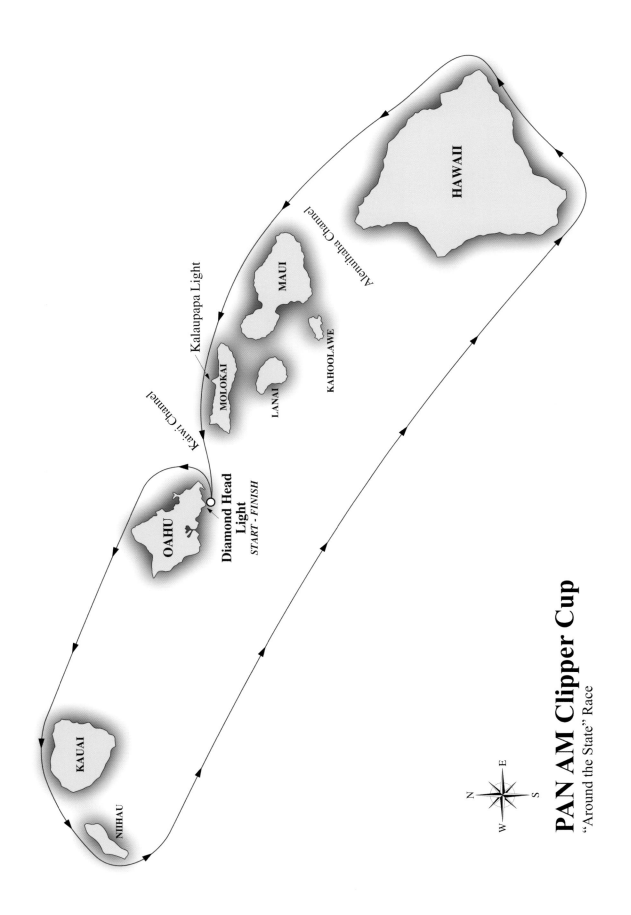

PAN AM Clipper Cup
"Around the State" Race

KAUAI

NIIHAU

OAHU

Diamond Head
Light
START - FINISH

Kaiwi Channel

Kalaupapa Light

MOLOKAI

LANAI

MAUI

KAHOOLAWE

Alenuihaha Channel

HAWAII

N
E
W
S

AROUND THE STATE RACE

We made quick repairs before the final two races, the third short triangle, which was worth 100 points, and the big climax, the 775-mile "Around the State" race, which was worth a whopping 300 points to the winner.

When the pressure was on, the *KIALOA IV* crew really responded, and we maintained our aggressive attitude toward fixing the boat and preparing for the final races. And it paid off. We won the 30-mile triangle and earned the hundred points. Now the real challenge was ahead of us. The race around the tricky Big Island could have a bit of everything: some windward work, hopefully some spinnaker reaching and running after the Alenuihaha Channel, and negotiating the large wind shadow along the southeast coastline cast by large, volcanic island.

We hit it right and it was *KIALOA* sailing at its best, with outstanding crew work among wonderful friends, all amateurs sailing for fun, satisfaction and fellowship. At the finish line, we were four hours ahead of our closest competitor, winning a clean sweep, First to Finish, First in Class and First Overall, setting a new course record. In spite of our poor races earlier in the series, we'd earned a third overall for the entire regatta in intense international competition.

KIALOA IV was a representative of the USA team, which also included *Great Fun* and *Bullfrog*, against other teams from New Zealand, Australia and other nations. And, we were also the big overall team winners. After the victory, the parties and visits with many international racing friends, Kathy and I flew home and *KIALOA IV* sailed to San Francisco.

It wasn't the last time we'd race *KIALOA IV* in Hawaii, a wonderful and challenging place to sail. We were back in 1984 for the renamed Kenwood Cup, an excellent series without the drama of 1982. We didn't win any individual races but we didn't break any glasses, either. We did sail a consistent series in lighter winds and scored a second place overall on corrected time. We'd now earned a second and third overall in the Kenwood/Pan Am Cup Series. We'd return in 1988 aboard *KIALOA V*…a different—and dramatic—experience altogether.

Unusual Events Following the 1982 Around-the-State Race

KIALOA IV finished the 1982 "Around the State Race" over four hours ahead of the next competitor, the yacht *Condor II*. A new elapsed time record was set, and it was obvious that we were the overall corrected time winner against the entire fleet. As we sailed into the docks of the Waikiki Yacht Club, it was time for a victory celebration.

Actually, we were a little late; the party had already begun. Crowds were gathered on the docks and the outside terrace. The bars were jammed and everyone was obviously in an enthusiastic, partying mood. The *KIALOA* crew was jubilant and, as always at major events, we had a lot of friends and supporters on hand.

It was a fine affair and perhaps we stayed a bit longer than we should have. Eventually, we bid everyone farewell for some quiet time at our Hawaiian rental home on the beach just east of Diamond Head, where we could see and hear the surf and the yachts pass by the finish line off Diamond Head Light.

The next morning I received a call from the club's commodore, and first he offered congratulations. But then he said that we had a problem to discuss. I was concerned, and became more so when he said the club's attorney was with him. Had we done something incorrectly in connection with the race? The answer was a very formal "No." But I agreed to join them for a "cup of coffee."

I arrived at the club and an interesting discussion followed. The yacht club was advised that they were going to be sued by an attractive young lady over a "material incident." They'd captured my attention. What could this be?

As one might anticipate, after Kathy and I left, the victory party became more, shall we say, "enthusiastic." The refreshment bar was next to the terrace that joined the navigable water of the canal, and a few celebrants apparently found themselves in the drink.

The attractive young lady in question had an interesting story. She was on her way to pick up her boyfriend from California at the airport and realized that she was much too early. She decided to pass the extra hour or so while watching the excitement at the yacht club. She was not a member, and not an invited guest. She said that she was just sitting, and watching, when a huge sailor in a red shirt boldly picked her up out of her chair, took her to the edge of the terrace deck, and while holding her tightly, jumped into the water of the navigable channel.

The sailor helped her out, and as everyone could clearly see, she wore a thin lace dress that left nothing to the imagination. At this juncture, the sailor allegedly lifted her up again and jumped back into the water. Following the second dunking, there was even less left to the imagination. She said she was very embarrassed, and a photograph taken of her might affect her job as an insurance adjuster.

While I was reading her letter to the club, quite fortuitously, Allan Prior, who was in charge of *KIALOA IV* and the starboard watch captain while racing, happened to walk by. We had a discussion. He said he knew little about it and continued on to *KIALOA IV*.

He returned shortly and summed everything up with three short words: "It was me."

Not surprisingly, as far as the young lady's participation in the incident was concerned, he had a slightly different story. But he did agree that there was nothing left to the imagination. He emphasized that she had nothing to be embarrassed about; in fact, she should be complimented.

The commodore and the attorney, both sailors, were attentive and amused by all of this. They also made it clear that it wasn't a club problem. It was a *KIALOA* problem.

I had no choice but to call the girl and invite her to have lunch with me at the club to discuss the matter. I immediately arranged for the most visible table from all four sides.

When she arrived, she told me her story. Apparently, she had never been to the yacht club before and had heard about the *KIALOA IV* victory over the radio. It seemed a good time to stop and see the private club and perhaps meet more people before driving to the airport.

I asked her if she understood the enthusiasm of sailors after a challenging offshore yachting victory and her response was that she had no idea, no concept, and that she was overwhelmed. We then discussed her being thrown in the water and I asked if she was comfortable coming back to the club. She responded, "Yes, it's a lovely club."

Our conversation was very civil and I asked if she'd been embarrassed about being tossed in the water in her very light dress, and her emergence from the water in that very light dress afterwards.

"Yes," she said.

I then told her that everyone I'd talked to who'd witnessed the incident said she had no reason to be embarrassed and had every right to be proud.

"Do you really think so?" she wondered.

"Absolutely," I said. Surprisingly, she immediately agreed to drop the potential lawsuit. She then asked if she thought the club would allow her to ever come back again.

My response was that I could not make such a statement for the club; however, I believed that the membership would be very pleased. Once she agreed to drop her proposed case, I asked her to sign off on a copy of her letter. Did she ever come back? I have no idea.

Sailboat racing provides many interesting duties for the yacht, skipper and owner.

Another almost illegal, laughable incident happened soon after, on a lay day following one of our races. We noticed that our spinnaker after guys—⅜" braided wire and rope about 160 feet long—became kinked in the steel wire section. It was necessary to straighten them out by stretching out their length and whipping them up and down, some 10 to 12 feet in the air.

The site for this strange activity was a narrow park along the beach with a paved road in the center running parallel to the shore. The two sailors stretched the after guys across the roadway and stationed themselves on either side. They brought along a radio to keep rhythm during their up and down whips. It must have been rhythmical music because they were not concentrating.

A car drove down the road and the driver must have been looking at the waves along the beach. Suddenly, the sound of heavy noise similar to the beat of a Caribbean steel drum occurred, along with screams to stop. The crew looked up to find they were destroying a rental car with two terrified occupants—a man and his girlfriend.

I was at the yacht club with one of our crew, the cook, and by coincidence, our insurance agent. The only thing we could say was, "Unbelievable." Everyone ended up with a laugh, including the driver and his friend. The last I heard they were at the yacht club bar having a drink and smiling. No wonder they were happy. They would be driving a nicer, bigger rental car.

Racing Aboard KIALOA: An Inside Perspective

Justin was a young man who sailed with us as a bowman in charge of the foredeck and became one of our three permanent paid crew, maintaining and delivering *KIALOA IV*. Justin was also one of our two crew who supervised the construction of *KIALOA IV*. Because of his technical capabilities, we asked Justin to become involved in our companies, and he is now head of our construction division.

I can remember Justin for his many capabilities; however, a most unusual event always flashes through my mind. Justin was about 20-30 feet in the air above the bow, suspended by his handhold on a wire spinnaker after guy. I was at the helm, focused on a single question: Could I steer *KIALOA IV* in the rough surfing conditions so that he would fall on the bow and not in the water? I could, it worked. But how did we get in this mess in the first place?

It was during the 1982 SORC, in the 1982 St. Petersburg-Ft. Lauderdale Race. We were surfing downwind towards a buoy off Rebecca Shoals, slightly inside the lay line. At the buoy, we'd need to jibe around the mark. Everyone was in position, the chart showed ample water depth, and I called "jibe." Justin was on the bow holding the lazy wire after guy to insert in the spinnaker pole on the other side of the boat after the jibe.

Our navigator, Allen Puckett, having carefully reviewed our navigational chart, was behind me on the short afterdeck. Boat speed suddenly stopped from about 11-12 knots to zero; *KIALOA IV* had hit the sandy bottom. Allen Puckett flew over my head and Justin was 20 – 30 feet in the air above KIALOA's bow.

My job was to keep the bow under Justin. (Don't worry about Allen. He had already landed on the deck.) Well, we did, and Justin made a soft landing. A potential disaster was now a funny, humorous event—a good sea story that was told many times after. I can still remember the look in Justin's eyes! Unusual to say the least!

In the latter stages of writing this book, I received the following note from Justin about his days racing aboard *KIALOA*. It provides some interesting insight about our crew's experiences in our program:

by Justin Smart

Dear Jim,

I have been pondering the following for some time. I have many things to be thankful for, and as time goes by, I realize just how fortunate I was to be part of KIALOA *as a young man. Thank you for all the lessons, both those learned the hard way and those that were there for learning, should we take the initiative to do so.*

For me, it was a rich tapestry of enduring memories from an era of IOR Maxi boat sailing aboard the KIALOAs, woven around the characters that campaigned aboard through the heyday of offshore racing in big IOR boats.

Sailing aboard KIALOA was a great proving ground for us as youngsters. We were executing the operational side of a multi-million dollar organization and were responsible for a large part of the sailing operations. We never seemed to have any time off; we seemed to work at it every day and occasionally not on Sunday. The short-handed safe delivery across the great open oceans of the world between regattas was left to us, and was always an adventure. With each trip came a fair measure of drama, as you might expect, with equal measure of recreational adventures on landfall. Some of the stories are the stuff of legend. The preparation for racing, the constant implementation of design upgrades and physical improvements to large sections of the boat at a time fell to us as members of the permanent crew to organize, manage and complete between small openings in a packed schedule of ocean crossings and regattas. Frequently, the planned workload to ready the boat for each regatta seemed daunting and usually required a supreme effort to pull off.

This endless pursuit of getting the boat to the next venue in a ready-to-race condition was nothing new to those that had campaigned KIALOA's past. Jim had been doing it for years, with a long record of ringing up victories and setting new records around the world. There was a clear and distinct culture on the boat, a culture that was established at the top and started with Jim. It was a hard-driving, winning culture that required of each person a consistent high level of performance no matter the task, along with a sporting attitude and willingness to get it done under all conditions. This culture was evident to those that campaigned against us; it permeated the whole KIALOA organization and was admired by many. It was different than any boat large or small that I had sailed on before; we expected to win and were prepared to do whatever was required in terms of sailing the boats intelligently and hard to do so.

The palpable aura surrounding KIALOA was so strong in my view, that no matter who the competition, deep down they knew that when we showed up on the start line, they were going to be competing for second place—beating KIALOA was a long shot for any boat.

The KIALOA approach to offshore racing was well-established long before my time on the boat; it was burned into the DNA of the organization through a line of successful yachts that had been circling the globe for many years prior, crewed by a cast of characters who had seen it all. Many of those same guys were there for racing on successive KIALOAs. They brought with them the experience and expertise gleaned through past battles; they knew how to handle an over-pressed IOR boat in full anger, and under Jim's command we were a formidable force. There was great camaraderie on the boat and we weren't shy about carrying a swagger when ashore, where we knew how to have fun, too! Some of the crew dinners were raucous memorable affairs, and of course some of the antics of a night out with the KIALOA crew are best left untold.

The crew pool that Jim called upon at race time was deep with countless great sailors from all over the globe and with tremendous resumes all, characters of all kinds. There was never a shortage of skill or humor, strength or determination aboard and the mix would change from regatta to regatta. On occasion, we were accompanied by a guest or a guest sailor or two for a race. Sometimes they were both guest and sailors; regardless they were always thrown into the thick of things. Often, you would find yourself sharing a task in the dead of night on an offshore race with one of these guys and you would find out that your right hand man of the moment was in fact the current US Ambassador to some foreign land when he wasn't out sailing with us, or he was responsible for a major national defense initiative. We sailed with Kings and aerospace pioneers, captains of industry and geniuses of all descriptions. There was no fanfare or standing on ceremony, we were about the business of winning and they were expected to be part of the crew just the same as we were, and if they were unfamiliar with the workings of a beast of an IOR Maxi boat, then we would get them acquainted and make sure they joined in, ducked at the right times and made sure they kept one hand for themselves when things got tough.

It's true, not all guests were gifted sailors, but if they showed the willingness, they were shown the way. They fought along side us and sometimes celebrated along side us too! KIALOA was the great equalizer in that way. When racing the boat, we as crew were level pegging with some very accomplished individuals. Racing a Maxi boat well was our field, our expertise, and as such we had to engage and work with some extraordinary people we otherwise would only have read about.

Jim always expressed a genuine interest in the well-being of his crew. He frequently asked about how we were doing, dispensing sage advice, providing an opinion and suggesting ideas and thoughts for consideration. You had to be on your toes when sailing; Jim could solicit you for an opinion at any given moment about any given point related to how the boat was trimmed or what we might do to go faster, or whether you thought we were doing the right thing at that point in the race. You were encouraged to participate and offer different views if you had them. Jim didn't want yes men in his crew, he wanted people that could follow, but those people had to think while they were working as a team. We were expected to think about better ways to do things and sail with our heads. Jim fostered this aspect in the crew, and it was central to the culture of the boat. KIALOA guys are always confident, they have been through *thick and thin, seen and experienced things from angles that few others have. We experienced big boat sailing in a way that few have experienced.*

I remember seeing a small picture of KIALOA III *for the first time in a* Seahorse *magazine when I was about thirteen or so; it must have been taken shortly after she had been launched, as she was in her ketch configuration. The scale of the boat was incredible to me. I could not believe that her pure grace, power, sleek lines and towering rigs were really just one boat. Surely what looked like a super tall mizzen was in fact the mast of another boat in the background of the photo? Little did I know just how lucky I would be to sail on the next succeeding two* KIALOAs *as well as the great* KIALOA III.

The lessons learned aboard, the friendships gained through sharing of sometimes outlandish experiences at sea, and the range and breadth of the exposure we had to all sorts of situations from challenging through hilarious, to sometimes dangerous and sometimes down right impossible, are irreplaceable, and have proven to be a solid grounding for the challenges and opportunities that have come later in life. I often find myself—when faced with difficult or tricky situations—analyzing things in racing terms, the parallels in business are there. The tactical and strategic options, the planning to avoid adverse events, the decisions necessary to optimize positive outcomes can all be related to sailing situations where you face similar choices or parallel situations. This habit frames things in familiar terms, allows you to draw on experience and add depth to your thinking.

I don't think a week has gone by since, without a thought or a conversation with someone about some aspect of KIALOA *surfacing to the forefront.* KIALOA *has a soul and always will. The* KIALOAs *were man-powered boats, sailed by men who could sail through anything, do anything, fix and figure out a way around anything; they sailed for each other and loved the man they sailed for.*

My strong feelings,

Justin

29

The Start

Absolute Concentration
Absolute Teamsmanship
Amazing Enthusiasm

KIALOA V
New Techniques and Ideas

Keeping in or on top of the ICAYA (MaxiYachts) Winner's Circle was a rigorous challenge. The IOR measurement rule that determined our ratings, (speed numbers) was forever adjusting measurement techniques and rating numbers. It was 1985, *KIALOA IV* was an outstanding winner of the ICAYA World Championships, and we wanted to continue with a new *KIALOA V.*

The new world championship series of races could be up to five regattas a year in challenging waters and different weather conditions. The planned locations could be: St. Thomas, in the Carribbean; Newport, Rhode Island; Palma, Mallorca; Porto Cervo, Sardinia; St. Tropez, France; A regatta would customarily have :

Three 25-30-mile triangles

One middle distance race about 150 miles

One longer distance—over 200 miles.

There was also an alternate plan, which would reduce the championship series to three regattas: St. Thomas, Hawaii, San Francisco.

With the different racing areas and wind conditions, the world championship sailing would be greatly enhanced.

When racing so many regattas with two to three short races in each regatta, as well as the longer races, winning the start with the most favored position was essential. We decided to have two steering wheels in the cockpit for better visibility, primarily in close contact on the starting line.

The picture on the starting line shows the challenge, and the need for instant response. Tom Whidden is on one wheel while I am on the other, and we talk our way through the fast moving competition.

Having raced a *KIALOA* in most of these areas, we had definite ideas of what we wanted for our *KIALOA V* racing machine. Our general specifications were subject to performance in substantial tank testing of models, about 30% in size, at the outstanding tank in Holland. Maxi Yachts must have an IOR measurement of 70.05 or less, a specific requirement.

We believed that a slightly different approach in design of our new *KIALOA* as compared to *KIALOA IV* or the other key challengers would be an ongoing winner. We wanted a tradeoff—a slightly shorter waterline length, a slightly bigger sail plan, and just a bit less in displacement (weight). The architect agreed, and several hull models were tested with successful results. The most successful model, hopefully exceeding our expectations, was selected and the architect was told to proceed with the construction and design plans, including the sails and sailing rig specifications.

Two of our racing crew, Allan Prior, skipper of *KIALOA IV*, and Alex Wadson, our mainsail trimmer and sail coordinator on *KIALOA IV*, supervised construction. I intentionally did not walk them through the conceptual design criteria and the tank testing criteria as I wanted them to concentrate on all phases of construction to expedite completion of a sound, high-performance yacht.

We decided to construct *KIALOA V* at the small shipyard of the Sitges family in Aviles, Spain, located along the Bay of Biscay. The Sitges family had their shipyard as an adjunct to their other large commercial manufacturing facilities, which had an excellent computerized machining facility with aluminum plate roll forming capacity, ideal for building aluminum hull sailboats.

They were also knowledgeable Maxi boat sailors, competing with their successful Maxi Yacht *XARGO*. They had also been the shipyard for the Admiral's Cup Yachts raced by Juan Carlos, the King of Spain, who was a frequent *KIALOA* crew when we were racing in Europe, an outstanding sailor and a close personal friend.

Juan Carlos, King of Spain, and Jim Kilroy

We now considered revised sailing techniques while Allan and Alex were coordinating the rapid and quality construction of *KIALOA V*. Launch time was arriving with no big issues having occurred during construction; a smooth, well-coordinated project by all concerned.

A launching schedule was agreed upon and I arrived a few days early to review documents and to make a preliminary inspection. I was shockingly surprised as I reviewed the mast, rig, and sail plans and specifications. They were for a smaller sized mast and rig than initially agreed upon after the tank testing in Holland. How could this be? Allan, Alex and I reviewed the documents provided to them for construction and they were for a smaller IOR measurement sail plan than had been agreed upon in Holland.

I immediately asked Alex and Allan how this could be and they advised they had never been provided with the tank testing information nor the preliminary and accepted tank test criteria. They were right; I intentionally did not do so.

The only information that they had was the new smaller rig and sail plan based upon a newly calculated rating certificate which showed that the constructed sail plan, to be placed in *KIALOA*, was the maximum sail plan that could be placed in *KIALOA V* to meet the maximum IOR rating of 70.05.

In essence, this meant that the tank test results were not accurate because a bigger sail plan was improperly used, instead of a rating compliant sail plan—an obvious miscalculation by the architect, and an arbitrary and inconsiderate matter of not advising me of such a serious issue. My immediate thought was to make a big issue with the architect—and if I did—could we race in the following regattas—how should we proceed?

My decision was to advise, but not to make a big issue until after the first regatta in Newport, Rhode Island as well as the knowledge gained from the delivery trip from Spain across the Atlantic to the Newport, Rhode Island regatta. We would know much more about the problems at that time.

Allan, Alex and other *KIALOA* crew had numerous comments, made after the delivery across the Atlantic, with a lot of close hauled sailing. Corrective issues were immediately addressed as best possible and we now had the issue of obtaining the required IOR measurement number for handicap racing, "the speed number," which had to be under 70.05. US Sailing asked for hull plans and keel plans and came up with an immediate comment, "The winglets below the trim tab must be removed." US Sailing had coordinated with European sailing authorities who also agreed. This removal caused a further loss of stability.

Amidst growing aggravation and only a short time before the start of our first race series, we knew that we had to face reality, sailing the best possible race against our competitors, to see how *KIALOA V* performed and what we should do to improve our performance.

As we sailed *KIALOA V* in our first ICAYA series, we solicited opinions from our crew and other outstanding sailors as to what we might do to increase performance. We needed more sail, we needed more stability. We were fortunate to have Bill Tripp, a bright young naval architect as part of our crew.

We knew that we needed more sail area, we knew that we needed more stability, which meant a new deeper keel, and we would remove the trim tab, as we would not have the "heavy helm" initially anticipated. We also increased the mainsail area and other minor adjustments made in the Fall of 1986 so that we could make the 1987 SORC as the first part of our 1986 series, which would be our first real testing of *KIALOA V*'s performance capabilities.

With our collective ideas and the substantial help of Bill Tripp, we designed a new deeper keel, removing the concept of a trim tab and related lead wings, increased the mainsail area, carefully worked out what we believed should be the proper flotation and had what we called a "newer new boat," and hopefully, we could be prepared for the 1987 SORC and a fleet of highly competitive yachts including our key Maxi competition. The ICAYA (Maxi) fleet would effectively be racing in two regattas—the SORC regatta of about 40 yachts and the separately scored Maxi Regatta.

In the SORC, the revised *KIALOA V* was 1st to finish in two of the races, 2nd to finish in two of the races and a 3rd and 4th in two of the races, with a 1st place overall fleet, a 2nd place overall and a 5th place overall in the SORC series, with a 7th overall SORC fleet position. In consideration of the advantage given to smaller yachts by the Gulf Stream and double old age allowances, we considered these excellent results.

In our ICAYA results, *KIALOA V* placed 1st overall and we still had much to learn about the new and revised *KIALOA V*. The next ICAYA series would be the 1987 Newport, Rhode Island regatta which *KIALOA V* handily won with three 1st places, a 3rd place and a 6th place.

The SORC races counted towards the 1987 ICAYA championship, which we eventually won. And during the series, we learned much about sailing the updated *KIALOA V*, how to sail to our strengths and protect our weakness, close reaching.

For instance, on the starting line, we could not start at the pin as we desired in a hard on the wind start. When sailing slightly off the wind in maneuvers, we lost accelerating speed to our competition with longer waterline yachts. Instead, we would start about 20% up the line from the pin, have clear air and then, an excellent surprise… we could sail a higher upwind angle with speed than our competition, and sail lower and faster under spinnaker than our competition—a tremendous benefit at each end of the sailing spectrum.

As it turned out, 1987 was an outstanding year for *KIALOA V*, another ICAYA World Championship. Along with the SORC, there were events in Newport, R.I.; Palma de Mallorca; Porto Cervo, Sardinia; St. Tropez; and a two-day series in Monaco. Prince Albert of Monaco had become a sailing enthusiast and occasional crew aboard *KIALOA*, and we were pleased to put on a victorious show in his "hometown." Monaco magnificently saluted our victory.

In 1988, following another ICAYA overall victory in the excellent, five-race St. Thomas Regatta in the Caribbean, it was *KIALOA V*'s turn to race in Hawaii's Kenwood Cup. Once again, Paul Cayard would be helming *Il Moro del Venezia,* owned by my good friend, Raul Gardini. Before the first race, as was our custom, we agreed to a test sail with a key rival, in this case Paul and *Il Moro di Venezia.*

We had a mid-morning start, and our performance was very good. In medium breeze, we started to leeward behind *Il Moro,* and were able to move ahead and "over the top." Afterwards, we had lunch and waited for the customary trade winds to fill in. Then we started another leg a bit farther out to sea. And, as we started, *Il Moro* was again ahead of us.

I was at *KIALOA*'s helm when a series of peculiar, flat-sided seas appeared. I was careful as to where I placed the bow. Two more waves rolled past, which were fine. On the fourth wave, *KIALOA V* lost all helm and the 100-foot mast toppled to leeward. My first thought was, "There goes the series and perhaps another World Championship." The regatta was over before it began. Our score for the Kenwood Cup was last place!

We immediately organized a repair program. Our mast was flown to Los Angeles for a quick and hopefully good repair. *KIALOA V* and all other gear were put on a barge to Los Angeles, with hope that everything would be fixed in time for the St. Francis Perpetual Series in San Francisco.

Once again, everything came together. *KIALOA I, II, III* and *IV* had all sailed in the St. Francis Perpetual Series with reasonable success. It was now *KIALOA V*'s turn, and we wanted to do well in the regatta, the last series in the 1988 ICAYA World Championship. Because of the broken mast in Hawaii, we weren't in contention for the overall 1988 title, but could still have a say in the results of the St. Francis Perpetual Series.

One thing that hadn't changed over the years was San Francisco Bay itself. The shape of the harbor, the islands, and the tides and variable currents made it a challenging venue for sailboat racing. To race successfully, one must realize that there are few legs of the course that may be sailed in a straight line. Tidal and current planning are essential ingredients to success.

The south shoreline, in close, near the yacht club, may provide refuge from the tidal flow and even favorable counter current. But staying inshore requires quick tacking and jibing, providing a racing spectacle for those on shore. Currents in the narrow passage between the city front and Alcatraz can be especially wicked. Local knowledge is essential to successful sailing on the Bay. The changing skyline also influenced the breeze. Starting with *KIALOA I* in the 1950s, we'd learned all of this the hard way.

Getting *KIALOA V* ready for the regatta had been a rush, we were still not satisfied with the tuning of the repaired mast, and we didn't have the ability to bend or control it to optimize our sail

shapes. We'd need a new mast for 1989.

Going into the regatta, the favorite was *Il Moro*, whose skipper, Paul Cayard, lived in San Francisco and knew the waters like the back of his hand. *KIALOA V* sailed reasonably well, despite the limitations of our repaired mast and placed third in the St. Francis Series. To our surprise, as *KIALOA V* only sailed two of the three events, missing Hawaii because of the broken mast, *KIALOA V* still placed fourth in the 1988 ICAYA World Championship.

A short match boat race followed the St. Francis Series, usually the first and second place yachts. However, *Il Moro* asked us to fill their place. We agreed and felt that we needed some redemption, and that we needed to win the match race by winning the start. With Tom Whidden calling tactics, we did win the start, and went on to win the match race…our final race in San Francisco. Jim DeWitt, a San Francisco yachtsman-painter, provided a painting so that we could remember our last match boat race in San Francisco Bay. *KIALOA* with Jaime Marina, mid-air, tending the spinnaker.

KIALOA V *ahead and covering*
Match Boat Racing in St. Tropez

For 1989, the ICAYA schedule called for events in St. Thomas; Newport, R.I.; Palma de Mallorca; Porto Cervo, Sardinia; and finally, St. Tropez. We earned a third, fourth and sixth, respectively, in the first three races. In Palma, we installed our new mast and had another fourth, followed by a third in St. Tropez.

The overall scores for St. Tropez were not great: two 3rd , two 4th, and a 6th . The overall winner was Gianni Varasis' new *Longobarda*. It was a new breed of boat, a light carbon-fiber rocket with a longer waterline and easily-driven hull…a game-changer. It was faster on every point of sail than *KIALOA V*. It was time for the *KIALOA* crew to make decisions; however, we could not do so until ICAYA determined if they would race under the IOR Rule or the IMS Rule. We believed that the new IMS rule was the only way to go.

The *KIALOA* crew had much to discuss about future ICAYA competition.

30

Victorious Sailing

ICAYA WORLD CHAMPIONSHIPS
1981	KIALOA IV
1982	KIALOA IV
1983	KIALOA IV
1984	KIALOA IV
1985*	BOOMERANG
1986	no series
1987	KIALOA V
1988**	IL MORO DI VENEZIA
1989***	LONGOBARDA

Other high placement
*	KIALOA IV 2nd place
**	KIALOA V 3rd place
***	KIALOA V 4th place

The Big Question
A New KIALOA...*or Retirement?*
A Rethink on SORC

We knew that the day would come. Carbon-fiber hulls, fractional rigs, lighter and faster yachts and longer waterlines all signaled a new era in yacht design and racing.

The days of *KIALOA V* were past. The question was simple: Should we build a *KIALOA VI*? A related question was almost equally important: Would the IOR MKIII measurement rule continue or would the new IMS rule take over?

I believed that the new, "less compromised" designs of the IMS would be selected. What were our thoughts on this development? I commissioned Bill Tripp to work on a concept that incorporated our mutual ideas. He provided a wonderful platform on which we might build.

But that led to another, crucial question: Should we risk being the first new design, in effect becoming the foundation for many new ideas by other naval architects, or should we wait a year or two?

The *KIALOA* crew all talked. We would come to a decision through a collaborative process. We reviewed our remarkable record of success. Could we duplicate it or do better? Should we stay in the game? Or should we retire, letting our achievements speak for themselves? I thought I had made up my mind but wasn't sure.

In a peculiar way, the decision was already made. We were all amazed at what we had done—the victories, the records, the mutual satisfaction that we'd achieved as a crew. Let other yachts, newer designs, and the latest technology challenge our results, our records, our satisfaction. It was late 1989, and the *KIALOA* era of worldwide, world-class yacht racing was over.

Has any other yacht ever met and exceeded the challenges faced by the five *KIALOA*'s and their crews? As with all sports and competitive endeavors, it's open to discussion and argument, which is one of the reasons we compete. But in my opinion, no yachting team ever matched the friendship amongst us, or the collective identity we enjoyed from being a member of the *KIALOA* crew.

SORC: The Series We Loved to Hate, While Too Good to Miss!

The old-age handicaps, the Gulf Stream, the advantages to the smaller boats…we've discussed all these matters in detail in earlier chapters. Not withstanding these issues, sailing in the SORC was just too good to miss. From 1969-1987, we raced our various *KIALOAs* in 71 SORC races. We had some good years, and some not-so-good years. Our greatest SORC victory was the 1977 St. Petersburg-Fort Lauderdale Race, in which we also set an elapsed time record as well as being the overall fleet winner. The 374-mile St. Petersburg-Fort Lauderdale race was always the most challenging race in the SORC.

Windward Passage, American Eagle, Il Moro di Venezia, Boomerang, Matador and *Condor* were always our key challengers; with those spirited competitors, we were always sailing a race within a race.

I suggest that the following article written by Coles Phinizy for the February 23, 1981 issue of *Sports Illustrated* provides a reasonable perspective of racing in the SORC:

To predict an overall winner of the Southern Ocean circuit is foolish, if not impossible, but this much can be safely said: this year, as so often before, the honor will probably go to a craft between 36 and 48 feet overall. It might be an old boat with a famous name like Robin, *so blessed with age allowance on her handicap rating that, short of swamping, she cannot help but do well.*

Big boats don't win. In 1971, Running Tide, *a 60-foot sloop built somewhat along the deep, narrow lines of an America's Cup contender, did take the overall title in a series marked by heavy seas and windward work that were to her liking. The nine years since have been bad for all the biggies except one: a 79-footer called* KIALOA, *the third ocean racer so named and owned by John B. (Jim) Kilroy, a California real-estate developer who has always operated slightly in defiance of the pregame odds. From her debut in 1975 until her retirement last year,* KIALOA *(a Hawaiian word for "long, beautiful canoe") took part in 24 SORC races. Time and again, she was first across the line only to have some little 42-foot creep bring the wind from behind and beat her on corrected time. Still,* KIALOA *won four of her 24 SORC tests on corrected time—a remarkable showing, considering that in the same period only three other biggies out of a total of 19 won so much as one race without benefit of age allowance.*

To handicap boats that are far different in size, under the International Offshore Rule, just about everything is carefully measured except the diameter of the owner's bankroll, the navigator's IQ and the length of the crew's fingernails. For all the exactitude, though, there are inequities. In the case of Kilroy's third KIALOA, *it was her displacement. According to IOR measurement, she was rated at 66,000 pounds, while she truly weighed closer to 89,000. To put it simply, in all her trials and triumphs on seas near and far—in the Sydney-Hobart Race and the Jamaica Race, in the Trans-Atlantic, the Transpac, the Edlu, the Fastnet, the Channel and the St. Petersburg-Fort Lauderdale—she was lugging more than 11 tons, for which she got no credit.*

For this year's SORC series, Kilroy has a new, bigger, lighter and faster KIALOA. Although it is safe to say the new girl will whomp the rest when it comes to crossing the finish line—she has done so twice already—how she fares on corrected time depends on how the wind blows and the Gulf Stream flows.

Two weeks ago, the current SORC began for the big boats as so often before, only worse. In the course of the first race, a 138-miler from St. Petersburg to Boca Grande and back, which 79 boats started, fine weather deteriorated into a soggy mess of fitful squalls, leaving some craft stalled while others forged ahead. Despite a bad stall, the new KIALOA finished first and took seventh in fleet on corrected time. The 48-foot Williwaw won.

Two days later, a dark, filthy cold front was sweeping across the U.S., so for the last week's second and most important race of the series, 370 miles from St. Petersburg to Fort Lauderdale, there was promise of still conditions—through which big boats could plow while lesser rivals would likely stagger up one side of a deep sea and fall off the other. But the nasty weather front tarried to the north, flooding roads and blowing off roofs, as the SORC fleet headed south to round the Keys under 25 knots of southeast wind. By nightfall the leader, KIALOA, had only two rivals in sight, both well behind.

If the front had come through in normal fashion, with only modest slackening as the wind clocked around to the north quadrant, KIALOA and the other biggies would have had it all their way, but, alas, it was not to be. The dying southerly left a big windless hole between itself and the approaching front. Early on the second afternoon, as KIALOA ghosted along, struggling to keep under way, her crew could see the dark cloud line of the belated weather front climbing in the north sky, and under it the bright spinnakers of smaller boats that had no business being in sight. "It was like suddenly seeing a cavalry troop charging over the horizon," an on-board photographer, Dick Enerson, said. "They were headed for our water hole, and there was no way of stopping them."

The big wind that the little boats brought with them—steady over 30 knots and gusting to 50—not only dashed the chances of the big boats, but was also sufficient to do in 14 craft. Two boats went aground southwest of Key West; five abandoned the race with minor failures; seven were dismasted, among them the new 45-foot Scaramouche, which had as good a chance as any of winning the whole series.

By the time everyone had limped into Fort Lauderdale and the computers had finished their work, KIALOA was 50th in fleet, well behind the race winner, the 36-foot Robin. *But once again,* KIALOA *was first across the line.*

Regrettably, as the Ft. Lauderdale race amply proved, despite the talent of all her deck animals, in a dead calm KIALOA *does no better than Noah's Ark.*

We have tried to analyze the performance of *KIALOA II, III, IV* and *V* in the SORC and must say that we are proud of the results in spite of the Gulf Stream issues. *KIALOAs* had their "pet races", such as the Governor's Cup off Nassau (out of the Gulf Stream) and the St. Petersburg-Ft. Lauderdale Race.

Each SORC drew an average of 60-80 yachts per series, so simple math suggests that over the years, we sailed against about 5,000 contenders.

KIALOA's All-Amateur Crews

In the racing of *KIALOA's I, II* and *III*, we had more longer distance races than with *KIALOA IV* and *KIALOA V*. The International Class A Yachting Association, ICAYA, committed to more regatta racing with four to five shorter races, one medium distance race and one overnight race. As a result, crew lists for *KIALOA IV* and *KIALOA V* were not as rigidly maintained. Instead of trying to list crews aboard for each major race, they are listed on the website, kialoa-us1.com.

I should qualify this expression. We raced as an all-amateur crew; however, we did have to maintain the *KIALOAs*, and enlist paid crew to make changes or modifications and to "set up" the boats for a specific race or area.

Bruce Kendell had this responsibility for the last few years of *KIALOA II*, for *KIALOA III* and for the initial period of *KIALOA IV*. Bruce was my paid coordinator for design, construction, maintenance and delivery, with two hired assistants. In yachting language, Bruce was called the "skipper" and was deck boss and starboard watch captain when racing. I was the "captain," the port watch captain and in overall command; however, we worked as a team, which also included the navigator and key crewmembers.

Sailboat racing requires intense cooperation and communication between all members of the racing crew. When racing *KIALOA III*, we sailed with a total crew of 15 to 17 dependent on the length of the race and the probable sea conditions. For closed-course racing or inshore events, *KIALOA V* would sail with a crew of 26 people. We had special rules for certain part-time crew who were professional sailors in other programs, primarily Dennis Conner, who sailed with us over the years. If Dennis did not have a paid contract, he would frequently sail with us; however, he would have to bring the beer, drive one or two legs, and even be a grinder!

My son John is an outstanding sailor, trained aboard the *KIALOAs* since he was a little boy. The *KIALOA* crew structure provided that I would be captain of the boat during all racing—captain of the port watch—and the yacht skipper, Bruce Kendell, Allan Prior, or similar skipper-crew, would be the starboard watch captain. My son John would be on the starboard watch with the regular yacht skipper.

KIALOAs, in my opinion, needed balance between owner-skipper and non owner-skipper to provide full participation and opportunity for the crew. I had a similar structure in our company. I required my son to be fully capable, forever learning, totally qualified, with expertise, in both sailing and in business, competition, verified capability—learning from challenge and competition.

John has raced his own boats for many years and has been successful in World Wide Competition. Perhaps we have an unusual result—a father-son overall corrected time victory in the same major race, 32 years apart, the 2225-mile Transpacific Yacht Race to Honolulu and maybe others.

On occasions, one of my four daughters, all sailors, would also join us.

To deliver a KIALOA across the Atlantic, Pacific or Southern Oceans, it usually took about seven to nine crewmen. Most came aboard for the love of sailing and the opportunity to sail offshore aboard a KIALOA. For cook/sailors, we occasionally paid a salary or a specific fee. Most of our racing cooks were volunteers.

Sometimes, "in lieu of shipyard work," we'd pay one or two of our racing crew to perform specific tasks we'd otherwise pay a boatyard to complete. They would not be paid for deliveries or racing, and we provided crew housing for events.

Each crewmember felt that they were an integral part of the KIALOA program and all worked together as a closely-knit team; many remain in close touch with each other, either directly or through the KIALOA "network." I retired from serious racing in 1990 and now, in 2012, I find KIALOA crew continuing to keep in touch through the Internet, sending photos of family back and forth, and holding meetings of smaller groups across the country.

In previous chapters, I've limited the reference to specific crewmembers because there were so many. Each and every one was a skillful sailor devoted to the success of the KIALOA team. I continuously encouraged the crew to critique our performance and offer new ideas.

Eventually, Allan Prior succeeded Bruce Kendell. We had fun delegating different responsibilities to the skippers. As an example, during yacht races there were always crowds along the docks watching the crew prepare for a race or return to the dock. It was certainly a good place for our crew to become acquainted with other young people, particularly young ladies.

For many of the yachts, the owner would become the center of attention as he pulled his slick, aggressive-looking boat away from the docks. Aboard KIALOA, Bruce, Allan or one of the other crew did the honors, which I considered a bonus. Everybody focused on them, particularly the attractive girls watching from shore, as they issued smooth commands. I would not resume control command until we were ready to set the sails and do a little tune up sailing prior to the start of the race. The docking honor was significant even when cruising.

The crew coveted our blazing red KIALOA T-shirts; it was easy to spot our team by their winning colors. We did have to ration the red T-shirts because we would always see "locals" wearing them after a few days ashore. The world of yachting forged many friendships.

With much satisfaction, recognition and respect, we've published on our website the crew lists for many of *KIALOA*'s races. As some records have been lost or damaged, there may be omissions, for which we offer our apologies.

Thought from KIALOA's Final Racing Skipper by Allan Prior

I was invited to sail aboard *KIALOA III* after sailing with the noted Peter Blake as first mate on *Condor* of Bermuda in the Whitbread 1977-1978 Around the World Race and other major international races.

I met Jim Kilroy in a fortunate but unfortunate way. I was a witness in a protest hearing—*KIALOA III* had protested *Condor* of Bermuda in a starting line maneuver, which could have been a nasty protest. Instead, Jim was calm and cool, clearly winning the protest. I liked his style.

I was surprised when later that year I was asked to sail as crew aboard *KIALOA III* in the 1979 Transatlantic and following 1979 Fastnet Rock Race. I was given my long sleeved red "*KIALOA*" t-shirt and became a "Red Shirted King of the Oceans," and sailed with Jim for more than 12 years. I was with the best crew and had the greatest time of my life.

Jim's nickname was JBK. He always pushed people to do more than we thought we could, not aggressively, simply taking it for granted that we could perform—and we did. With each challenge, we became an even more confident and capable crew. I was third in crew command. Bruce Kendell, Tink Chambers, and then me. Of course, Jim was overall Captain, a great delegator and primary helmsman.

We sailed a great Transatlantic Race, first to finish, first in class and second overall—and would have handily won the race if the handicap distance had been properly measured.

The course handicap distance was 229 miles too long, giving over a free day's handicap credit to the corrected time winning yacht, the smallest boat in the race. I understand that details of the issue are in other chapters.

This race was followed by the tragedy of the 1979 Fastnet Race, with many lives lost on other yachts—and unfortunate gear failure on *KIALOA III*, losing hours of time. However, with great crew work—and Jim hurt—we still placed eighth and were the second yacht to finish.

I was pleased to face Jim's challenge: 3rd in crew position, 2nd and then 1st in crew position. I became skipper of *KIALOA III,* and was involved in the new *KIALOA IV* building program. In January 1982, I made it to the top—skipper of *KIALOA IV* and also responsible for *KIALOA III*, which was now the "Cruising Boat."

As skipper of *KIALOA IV*, we sailed about 95,000 miles, racing and cruising with 22 Maxi boat victories. Time rapidly passed as handicap formulas also rapidly changed, and we made a new *KIALOA V*.

I was the project manager living in Spain, supervising construction of *KIALOA V* and racing when I could. *KIALOA V* was another winning yacht requiring many updates and changes to keep up with the new handicap rules and constant challenges against rigorous competition, always with an outstanding amateur crew.

Sailing on a *KIALOA,* all crew contributed ideas, motivation and modifications as necessary. We were all challenged and the results confirmed our desires. All crew were motivated to higher achievements, and I was a full and willing participant. We all had many laughs—a happy and successful crew. I compliment the "Can Do" attitude of all of our crew, all active participants. We learned from each other, and as Jim says, we improved by our mistakes—quickly correcting them.

Upon the retirement of *KIALOA's* racing, I was asked to become the construction manager of a new 156-foot sailing yacht for Jim Clark, to be built by Huisman Shipyard, Walter Huisman. The yacht for Jim Clark was a very successful accomplishment, and I have supervised construction and design concepts for many other owners.

Walter Huisman passed away in 2005, and I wrote the following tribute:

"In my 50 years, I have worked and sailed with many of the greats in the sailing world. Of these, there have been three men I have looked up to as a father figure and teacher. It has been a privilege to have known and to learn greatly from them. They are my dad, Maurice Prior, gentleman Jim Kilroy, who was the owner of the *KIALOAs* and Walter Huisman. I have indeed been lucky in that they chose to teach me all that I know about life, sailing, racing and building boats."

Challenge and motivation with respect were gifted to me. I thank you, those who helped me so much.

Sincerely,

Allan Prior

January 24, 2011

31

Remembrance and Involvement

Dennis Conner and I have been strong competitive
sailing friends since the early 1960s, sailing with each other
and sailing against each other.

We have been honored by being one of his America's Cup
supporters and *KIALOA* crew have frequently sailed with Dennis
in his America's Cup victories.

We call the readers attention to personal letters from Dennis,
one letter written in 1965 in the years of *KIALOA II*,
refer to chapter 7, and a more recent letter in 2011 in chapter 32.

Remembrance and Involvement
Pride of Performance

W e initially planned to list the names of all crew aboard for each *KIALOA* race specifically discussed in this book. We knew that we could not discuss all races and hence could not discuss the names of all of the crew. Instead, we are placing the crew lists on our website KIALOA-US1.com. We know that some of the crew lists have been lost or misplaced, which we sincerely regret. We also have hundreds of photographs that will be displayed on the website. If you have information to provide, please do so through our website. Come join us. We trust that you will be satisfied with the outstanding *KIALOA* race results and accomplishments.

We know of no other successful world-wide racing yachts that have equaled or bested the *KIALOA's* success. If you have records or information on any, please let me know. I am, of course, talking about conventional sailing yachts; fixed keel, or center board keel, no use of power, sailing under the customary yacht racing and handicap rules such as CCA, IOR, RORC, IMS or basic racing formulas. Competing today with power-driven swing keels, hydraulic winches, water pumped ballasts and power source sailing, is much like racing a jet engine airplane against a propeller airplane.

I must ask how many yachts have raced and been successful, with versatility, in upwind, downwind, heavy conditions and light weather conditions similar to *KIALOA III's* performance of winning four major Ocean Races in 1977, all discussed within this book, as well as winning the 1975-1977 World Ocean Racing Championship, over 3 years, with the most favorable score in history.

I am proud—proud of the boats, and so proud of the *KIALOA* amateur crew, of our coordination and skill. And I think of our continuing friendships, our rules of performance, and the crew's after-racing successes in business and life.

We should remember our focus, the humor and jokes aboard, and Bob Harris—dear friend, business executive, and gourmet cook. Bob Harris had been ill—seriously ill—when Nelly and I last visited Bob and his wife Sherry at their home. He was in bed much of the time. However, at our dinner, he was exceedingly well-dressed, tasting the best wines and telling the best jokes, and we all knew he could tell stories for hours. There were many laughs, an exquisite dinner, a delightful evening. We said good night and left for home. Bob did not arise the next morning. The theme of his memorial was a reaffirmation of his love and respect for the *KIALOAs* and the *KIALOA* crew.

I think of how *KIALOA* friendships do travel the world of yachting. In 1966, we sailed *KIALOA II* to the east coast to challenge the champions of the east coast. *KIALOA II* performed exceedingly well, winning major races. An immediate admirer was a young engineer from South America, studying at the Massachusetts Institute of Technology (MIT). His name was Horacio Garcia Pastori.

It was almost forty years later and my wife Nelly was introducing me to Buenos Aires and her summer home at Punta del Este, Uruguay, on the southeastern tip of the Uruguayan Peninsula, surrounded by beaches and the waters of the South Atlantic Ocean, recognized by many as the "Riviera of South America."

The Yacht Club Punta del Este was also recognized as the major Yacht Club for all North-South traffic between Buenos Aires, Argentina and Rio de Janeiro, Brazil and the host for many international regattas.

It was there that we again met Horacio Garcia Pastori, the MIT student, now Commodore of the Yacht Club, as well as the principal of a major engineering and construction company, and continued our yachting identities with a more personal relationship, particularly since the Commodore and Nelly were friends in their school years and Nelly had a summer home in Punta del Este.

We became members of the Yacht Club Punta del Este and I was personally surprised of their knowledge of the *KIALOA's* outstanding victories in the world of international sailboat racing. This became another victory for Nelly, who continued telling me—strongly—that I should write a book of my lifetime story with particular reference to International Sailboat racing. We know that *KIALOAs* had a strong identity in many areas of the world.

This reaction prompted us to have *KIALOA III*, our current cruising yacht, sail from New Zealand to Puerto Montt, Argentina, along the Patagonian west coast of Argentina and Chile, with magnificent cruising along the many glacier filled bays and coves and thence in the Straits of Magellan to the east coast of Argentina towards Punta del Este.

I was again reminded of the many pictures of the *KIALOAs*, particularly *KIALOA III*, in so many ports, restaurants, and yacht clubs around the world—and Nelly finally emphasized her challenge to me, "you must write your book about life and the *KIALOAs*."

We had now become part of the sailing community of South America and sailed *KIALOA III* to Yacht Club Punta del Este, her new home for about three years, with much sailing and cruising with Uruguayan, Argentinean, Chilean, Brazilian and South America's outstanding sailors.

We then decided to gift *KIALOA III* to Orange Coast College in Southern California. Our U.S./South American/New Zealander crew sailed *KIALOA III* back to California. Yachting makes it such a small world.

Our book, *KIALOA US-1: Dare to Win*, will be published in the Summer of 2012, the beautiful start of the sailing season. Nelly and I are personally pleased with our results—and of course we pray that our readers will join us. We have also established a website KIALOA-US1.com. Come join us. It will have many more race results, photographs, correspondence and history.

I had written a chapter for this book about my emulating the movie "Mr. Smith Goes to Washington" in the middle of the 1970-1980-1990 Real Estate Credit Crisis. I took many papers and relative documents with me outlining the foundational issues of this major credit crisis, its origin and its expansion. Much of my presentation was coordinated with John E. Robson, Deputy Secretary of Treasury, as well as other personal contact.

I have had the pleasure of thorough and private discussions about the credit crisis and other subjects with President George H.W. Bush and his close associates, the OMB, OCC, and have testified before the appropriate Senate Committee, speaking before the Bank Regulators and other

pertinent groups. I am told that the information I provided was helpful in solving this crisis. It was my original intention to provide a separate chapter with appropriate documentation regarding the 1970-1980-1990 Real Estate Credit Crisis as well as information on the following credit crisis of the 2000s, now underway.

My final decisions were that I should not mix the negativity of the two serious credit crises with the positive issues contained within the body of my book *KIALOA-US1: Dare to Win*, which emphasizes facing reality. Instead, all of the information which I have written about will be placed on our website KIALOA-US1.com.

I will add the gracious letter dated December 4, 1997 from John E. Robson, Deputy Secretary of the Treasury, which states "Your analysis of the current credit crisis is right on target, and the chronology of recent events that you provided, once again, demonstrates that there is no relationship between wisdom and politics." A copy of the letter follows.

I thank you John Robson and we have become thoughtful and respectful friends.

THE DEPUTY SECRETARY OF THE TREASURY
WASHINGTON

December 4, 1992

Mr. John B. Kilroy
Chairman of the Board
Kilroy Industries
2250 East Imperial Highway
El Segundo, California 90245

Dear Jim:

Your analysis of the current credit crisis is right on target, and the chronology of recent events that you provided once again demonstrates that there is no relationship between wisdom and politics.

Everyone agrees that small and medium-size businesses are the creator of jobs and the engines of a healthy economy. In light of this fact, the challenge is for the government to insure an adequate availability of bank credit for such entities, which include most real estate operations.

Simply stated, banks must take risks . . . that is why they exist, and that is the basis for the government guarantees provided to them. Having made that statement, the task for the next Administration is to find a way to promote the extensions of credit to small and medium-size businesses without jeopardizing the safety and soundness of the banking system.

There are fundamentally two potential tracks to follow. The first would be some system of mandating the extension of credit either by some affirmative action or by prohibiting certain activities. This approach, in our opinion, is not the way to go because it is counter-productive to a free economic system.

We would prefer to see a plan that removes barriers to extending bank loans to all creditworthy borrowers, including small business. This would involve elimination of the micro-management of lending by the Congress, the bank regulators changing their apparent motto of "when in doubt criticize," and FASB, GAO and the SEC pursuing avenues that lead to a healthy economy rather than accounting purity.

When all the parties work together to create a strong economy, this credit crisis will be history.

Sincerely,

John E. Robson

32

The following chapter contains a few letters
written by sailing friends
and intense competitors over many years.

They have all been successful in all phases of their lives
and I salute them for our friendly competition
as well as their outstanding success.

Competition and Friendship
The Strength of a Letter

The writing of this book is much more than the recount of what happens after the starting gun of a race. It includes the skill and mutual challenges of the participants, quick decisions based upon the sailing team, and above all, mutual respect. All aboard *KIALOAs* are pleased with the friendships that have been made over the many years of sailing, the crews, the afterguards, and the skippers. The challenges are on the sea, not on the shore.

I have received much help from our *KIALOA* crew in writing this book, ideas, favorable comments and even written subchapters. Terry Lalonde and Andy Rose have expressed their overview of certain races without my guidance; Allan Prior and Justin Smart have written about the impact of *KIALOAs* upon their life. Their writings are set forth in this book and we have received many other letters which we have placed on our website.

We have also received letters from great competitors, not just those who have challenged the *KIALOAs* but truly those who have challenged the world, in sailing and in many other ways. I thank them for their success and fulfillment of our great American spirit.

I have written about the friendship and challenging competition between the *KIALOAs* and Ted Turner's *American Eagle* and *Tenacious*. Ted Turner has written about the challenge and friendship between the two of us and I have received the unsolicited letter from Jim Mattingly, Ted's crew boss and starboard watch captain. Jim Mattingly is a key factor in the success of Ted's many victories.

I share the following letters with our readers.

TED TURNER: Winner of 1977 America's Cup. Owner-Skipper of *American Eagle* and *Tenacious*, both key competitors to *KIALOAs*, writes:

T E D   T U R N E R

August 30, 2011

Mr. Jim Kilroy
Kialoa III US1
Unit 504
13600 Marina Pointe Drive
Marina del Rey, California 90292

Dear Jim:

I offer the following comments to be used in your book <u>KIALOA – US1: Dare to Win.</u>

"Some of my greatest days of international sailboat racing competition were the challenge of you and your KIALOAs in major races of our yachting world.

The Sydney-Hobart races and other racing in Australia and Tasmania, the Transatlantic Race to Ireland and the Fastnet Rock Race in the Irish Sea, and other racing in Europe, the many southern ocean racing circuits in Florida and the Caribbean and other races in our competitive world of ocean racing are memorable.

We mutually enjoyed successful years as you have set forth in your book <u>KIALOA – US1: Dare to Win.</u> The bond of friendship between two racing skippers and their synergistic talented crews is undeniable."

Sincerely,

[signature]

TO: Jim Kilroy, a true gentleman and great yachtsmen.

FROM: Jim Mattingly, Ted Turner's crew boss and watch captain.

At age 18, my first introduction to Jim Kilroy and his magnificent yacht *KIALOA II* was after a grueling St. Petersburg to Ft. Lauderdale race. *KIALOA* was docked and was perfectly "shipshape" with her owner about to depart for home. The yacht was the most "proper" yacht I had seen at that time and I told the owner so, "What a beautiful yacht you have, Sir," I said.

"Thanks, Son," He replied and off he dashed. At the time *KIALOA* was the envy of the yachting world.

That encounter with *KIALOA* gave me the dream and inspiration to someday become part of the elite yachting scene that Jim Kilroy was already part of.

Fortunately, a short time later I was able to team up with Ted Turner and compete in many yacht races around the coasts of the United States and abroad. Our greatest nemesis on that circuit was Jim Kilroy and his series of yachts named *KIALOA*.

It didn't matter if it was the Sydney-Hobart (*KIALOA* broke the Sydney to Hobart elapsed time record and held it for 21 years), the Transatlantic, the Southern Ocean Racing Series, the World Ocean Racing Championship or the Fastnet race off England's southwest coast, It became "Ted versus Jim", or "Jim versus Ted."

"Sure there's a fleet we're competing against, but remember, the one boat we must beat is *KIALOA*." We as crew of the many Ted Turner yachts heard that time and again from the owner. On the 1979 Fastnet race, the 79-foot *KIALOA* was the first to round the "rock" on which the lighthouse stood. In the 64-foot *Tenacious,* we rounded fifth. As the gale built *KIALOA* ran before it atrocious seas, seeing gusts that exceeded 70 knots only to finish just behind the 77-foot *Condor of Bermuda* who dared to fly a spinnaker in gale force winds. Behind her *Tenacious* saw as much wind and was knocked flat several times. *Tenacious* finished the race on Tuesday night to win the race on corrected time. But without *KIALOA* to aim for, we might never have pushed so hard.

Being able to compete against *KIALOA* was the standard by which many boat owners judged and were judged by their peers. Jim Kilroy set a standard aboard *KIALOA* that even today stands out as a example of superb sportsmanship, hard competition and enjoyable racing.

Sincerely, Jim Mattingly

I am particularly pleased to hear of Jim Mattingly's success in business, a frequent product of the skill of sailing and the success of sailing: the attention to detail, the focus on both major and minor items, understanding the variables of the winds, the seas in both light and stormy conditions, and the absolute need to be honest with oneself and all members of your fellow crew; a great part which develops strong friendships. As Jim indicates, Ted Turner's *Tenacious* won the exceedingly stormy, compound heavy seas race, the Fastnet Rock Race in the Irish Sea, the race in which 17 sailors were tragically lost, definitely a most challenging race. They skillfully managed a victory by both yacht and crew performance and keeping *American Eagle* in one piece.

We thought we had them, well ahead in handicap time as we rounded Fastnet Rock, and sailed our return course towards Bishop Rock, the Scilly Islands, and Plymouth Harbor in the South Coast of England. We almost congratulated our performance but knew that there were many dangers ahead, huge seas with winds that puffed up to 70+ knots according to our wind instruments.

I was driving when an explosion occurred, a swivel block failure, as set forth in chapter 26. Our weather running back stay and check stay were flying in the air with little support to our mast in the 70 knot puffs. We closed all sails and made repairs, losing much valuable time, saving the mast and able to complete the race, slow sailing for safety as we were off Bishop Rock and the Scilly Islands, not a place to go against; to an 8th place corrected time.

We were happy for Ted Turner and Jim Mattingly's overall victory. We were also happy that we were able to stay in the race without additional serious mast failures, slowly safely sailing to the finish line and almost surprised that we were able to finish 8th overall with our big victory being the ability to finish the race without a further mast failure or crew injury.

We fully congratulated Ted, Jim and their outstanding crew on their victory and we all passed our regrets in our private prayers to those who could never return again to the finish line.

Thank you, Jim, I appreciate your letter and our continuing friendship.

DENNIS CONNER: America's Cup winner in 1974, 1980, 1987, and 1988, as well as a frequent *KIALOA* crew since the 1960s. Dennis writes:

May 22, 2011
Dear Jim,

Congratulations on your new book "*KIALOA*." From the late 50's, your racing programs were always amongst the best. Having an opportunity to be part of your crew was one of the highlights of my sailing. I remember how excited I was making the drive north from San Diego to be part of your crew. You always had the boat perfectly prepared and had a wonderful group of experienced crew which also knew how to enjoy life and each other. I learned a lot from how you managed and organized us before and during the races. Your vision of the "big picture" allowed the program to be on the leading edge of sailing and made it possible for *KIALOA* to go from a Southern California program to a world wide effort known by all in the sailing world. The lessons I learned from you about organization, leadership, and will to win have been a big part of all my racing. Thanks again for letting me be part of your life!!

Respectfully yours,
Dennis

And I must state, Dennis failed to insert a few other victories:

28 World Championships, 4 America's Cup victories, and an Olympic medal, "All got started on *KIALOA*."

The above letter from Dennis reminds us of an earlier letter written in the 1960s, displayed in chapter 7, which we will also display again on the following page.

DEAR MR KILROY

I AM WRITING YOU THIS
NOTE TO THANK YOU FOR THE
WONDERFUL THINGS I HAVE ENJOYED
ABOARD KIALOA IN THE LAST 4
MONTHS. IT WAS AN EXPERIENCE
WHICH WILL BE INVALUEABLE TO
ME IN LATER LIFE.

I WANT YOU TO KNOW THAT
I HAVE REALLY APPRECIATED THE
OPPORTUNITY TO BE ABOARD YOOR
BOAT AND IT WAS A REAL HONOR TO
SAIL WITH SUCH A TALANTED
SKIPPER AND CREW.

I KNOW I SHALL NEVER
FORGET THE FANTASTIC TRIP
TO AONALULU OR THE RIDE HOME
FROM SAN NICHLOS ISLAND.

IF EVER YOU OR JOHN
WOULD LIKE TO SAIL IN SAN

DIEGO AND ARE IN NEED OF
A BOAT IT WOULD BE MY
PLEASURE TO ACCOMADATE YOU.
IN ANY CASE, PLEASE CALL IF YOU
HAVE THE CHANCE.

I WANT TO WISH YOU
ALL THE LUCK IN THE WORLD IN
YOUR FUTURE SAILING AND I
AM LOOKING FORWARD TO SEEING
YOUR NAME APPEAR WHERE IT
BELONGS ..... IN FIRST PLACE.
THANK YOU AGAIN FOR EVERY-
THING.

YOUR FRIEND,

Dennis Conner

TOM WHIDDEN: Tactician *KIALOA IV and KIALOA V*, and tactitian for Dennis Conner in the America's Cup writes:

June 16, 2011

Dear Jim,

The first time that I saw *KIALOA* was in the SORC during the early 1970's. Immediately, I was impressed by its power, beauty, size and speed, which at that point in my life, motivated me, no end, to someday be in the crew.

KIALOA was always the establishment of the Maxi Class. I began sailing on *KIALOA IV* in the early '80s. I was able to help a bit with the sails and tuning, but frankly, I still had a lot to learn about how to get the most out of a Maxi boat and to be a decent crew. The crew on K4 was fantastic. They had lots of fun, but when they were racing, they were serious with lots of respect for how big the boat was and what could go wrong if they didn't work well together as a team. As a result, we had very few breakages and really good crew maneuvers. In fact at that point, the crew work was as good as smaller boats that I sailed on and darn close to the America's Cup teams that I sailed with. Jim was a great leader and his middle management team was just as great at working with the guys in the middle and front of the boat to form an amazingly quiet and competent crew, through almost any wind strength.

When I joined *North Sails*, the number one boat that I wanted our sails to be on was *KIALOA*. If Jim, and the *KIALOA* crew, liked North Sails the rest of the fleet would take notice. *North* needed to work hard to accomplish the level that was expected but we went on to win the World Maxi Championship that first year and many more regattas and match races to follow. I was Jim's tactician for many years as we continued to race *KIALOA V* successfully. We had a great relationship, and just like any good CEO, he left the tactics to me and he steered the boat brilliantly. We also became great friends.

The *KIALOA* model for success has been copied often since. But the red *KIALOAs*, with the distinctive "Kilroy was here logo" on the stern, will always be remembered for their sailing excellence because they had great leadership, a superior technical approach, a no stone unturned attitude, fantastic organization and a motivated and highly experienced loyal winning crew who all had lots of mutual respect for each other.

KIALOA VI……..I'm ready, Jim!

Best to all……Tom

GEORGE COUMANTAROS: Owner-Skipper of *Boomerang,* 1985 winner of ICAYA World Ocean Racing Championship and many other international races writes:

George S. Coumantaros

712 Fifth Avenue, New York, N.Y. 10019-4102

September 15, 2011

Dear Jim,

I am pleased to offer these comments which I hope you will include in your upcoming book dealing with Ocean Maxi racing and competition:

The presence of KIALOA III in the seventies set the stage for big water line competition. The intensity of KIALOA's crew raised the level of ocean racing. Your personal involvement as a founding member of the International Class A Yacht Association (ICAYA) which subsequently became the Maxi Boat Association marked the beginning of level racing with big boats.

KIALOA IV and KIOLOA V continued the tradition which must have spanned more than three decades. The big boats required intense preparation and organization with world-wide racing and crews of 30 members. The talented sailors that were trained in these events on the Maxi boats fanned out across many yacht racing forums and, in a way, the individual Maxi boats became small universities. Through it all there was great competition, excellent socializing and maturing of many friendships in fantastic racing venues.

Thank you for your contribution and that of the KIALOA program.

Sincerely,

George

Mr. John B. Kilroy
13600 Marina Pointe Drive, Unit #504
Marina Del Rey, CA 90292

KIALOA III: Cruising Areas of Our World
Wayne Avery and Jim Keefe

In 1981, *KIALOA III* was replaced by our new racing machine *KIALOA IV*, the latest of rapidly changing technology. *KIALOA III* would be the sparring partner for *KIALOA IV*, racing and testing sailing angles and how we could improve the performance of *KIALOA IV*, a very helpful and challenging activity.

The initial question for the new *KIALOA III* cruising life was who would become *KIALOA III's* crew and skipper. In the first two or three years, we relied upon former *KIALOA III* racing crew as much of our cruising would be in the New England area of our East Coast, in the Caribbean and the Gulf of Mexico. We then broadened our base to have permanent skippers who were not committed to their business, with which we did not want to interfere and conflict with their ongoing success. Wayne Avery from New Zealand and Jim Keefe from England and Mallorca became the two longer term skippers of *KIALOA III*.

There were always compromises to adjust: Wayne had more racing experience, while Jim had more mechanical and electronics experience, and we provided the necessary balance of needed capabilities by our selection of the "mate," the second in command. *KIALOA III* as our cruising boat had a crew of three, the captain, the mate, and the third crew being the cook and deck assistant. Additional crew, as needed would be provided, an easy challenge, as *KIALOA III* was so well recognized in the world of sailing.

Jim Keefe and Wayne Avery were well recognized in the sailing world, and fully met our challenging capabilities, in sailing skill, in yacht maintenance, and in personal value and integrity.

After a few years of world cruising, Wayne retired and returned to New Zealand and Jim Keefe became the new skipper. It has been interesting to follow them in their future successful life, their marriage and families. Nelly and I are proud of their success.

Jim Keefe replaced Wayne for several years until we gifted *KIALOA III* to Orange Coast College in Southern California. The gifting was a tough decision. Nelly and I had a very tight psychological bond with the success and memories of this outstanding racing machine, its world famous racing success, its safe and comfortable cruising, and instant recognition by others in so many areas of our wonderful world.

Jim Keefe's letter, along with hundreds of other letters from other *KIALOA* crew, is on file at the KIALOA-US1 website, and all of our crew have the capability of communicating with each other.

The reader of this book is invited to join our website to read a more detailed record of the five *KIALOAs*, their crews, and other historic race results.

We attach a recent letter from Jim Keefe about experiences aboard *KIALOA III*. We sincerely appreciate his comments, our continuing friendship, a lifetime member of our *KIALOA* crew.

Dear Nelly and Jim:

I first joined *KIALOA III* during her stopover in Palma de Mallorca, October 1995. I had lost a very dear friend to a motorcycle accident and was looking to escape, starting with a trip to the Caribbean. The skipper at the time, Wayne Avery, took me on for a trial after a recommendation from Billy Porter who regularly raced with the crew of *KIALOA V* and was the Skipper of my last boat. It was also evident that KIII, on the final leg of her circumnavigation, was in need of a good engineer to nurse her suffering engine back to the US.

My experience up to then had been in dinghy racing, classic yachts and push button super yachts, so *KIALOA's* raw sailing power, and the need for precise sail trim and balance, was a big learning curve for me. I felt that I had gone back to school or rather an advance school for sailing skills. After my year as engineer in Perini Navi my love of sailing had been fully renewed. There is nothing to compare to the pleasure of powering along and finding yourself totally attuned to your surroundings. It's a feeling that has been lost on many larger yachts today.

On my first meeting with the towering figure of Jim Kilroy, my life changed. Effectively, I had been saved from a life of drifting. KIII was more than a job; I had joined the *KIALOA* family and like many crew before and after me, Big Jim became my mentor. I could spend many pages describing the lessons that were learned at the school of *KIALOA* but in essence, for me they boiled down to this: In life everyone needs a purpose because without it, well you're just not living. *KIALOA III* and Jim Kilroy gave me that purpose. I was sorry to have missed the era of racing and the lessons that it brought but cruising KIII presented many new challenges of logistics, organization, research and seamanship.

In 1997, I left KIII to spend a few years working on several other notable yachts before returning in 1999 to take over as skipper. The future for her was uncertain at the time, but soon developed into yet another adventure. Plans were laid to once again circumnavigate after a summer in the Mediterranean. Our goal was to arrive in New Zealand at the end of 2001, refit her, continue into the Indian Ocean in 2002 and return home via The Cape and South Atlantic.

We crossed from Antigua in May and spent the rest of 2000 in the Mediterranean sailing as far as Sardegna. Early in 2001, we returned to the lower Caribbean transiting the Canal in April. We made stopovers in the Galapagos, The Marquesas, The Tuamotus, Tahiti, Tonga and Fiji. Jim and his family joined us for many of the stops to enjoy the adventure.

It was 12th September 2001, we were in Fiji when in the small hours of one morning a friend called from Mallorca with devastating news: the Twin Towers on Wall Street in New York, had been bombed and destroyed. The news was confirmed on the TV screen at Suva Yacht Club that morning. Our plans changed and for the two years after the refit in New Zealand, we remained and cruised the islands of the Pacific. After watching the Americas Cup event at the beginning of 2003, we laid the plans for yet another adventure, to sail back to the USA via South America.

At the end of 2003, we set sail for the long trip to Chile, 5000 NM across the Southern Ocean. In Porto Montt, we were joined by Jim and his family, who shared the rugged trip down through the many inland passages to the Magellan Straits, a desolate and harshly beautiful part of the world.

The experiences of *KIALOA* will live with her crews forever. The lessons we took away form a big part of what we've done and what we do in our futures. Through the challenges of organization, research, passage making, maintenance programs and cruising itineraries, I gained a huge amount of experience. The lessons I learned are innumerable, one of which is that to make a success of any challenge you need to have the right team around you.

I feel lucky in that KIII and Jim Kilroy seemed to attract the right kind of person to them. After a shaky start I was lucky to always have an excellent crew to support me. The crew of the *KIALOA* family all had something, a dedication, an under-standing and a passion that is sadly lacking in most of the crew of the commercial yacht scene where I now work. Skills earned through experience have been replaced by certifications from land-based courses and an inbuilt work ethic and dedication by contracts and lists of duties.

In 2006, KIII was gifted to Orange Coast College Sailing School. At the same time, I met my future wife Eli and thus began a new adventure, and like the adventures of KIII, this is a shared one.

David (Jim) Keefe
Captain S/Y ZIGZAG

Wayne is married with children and involved in the ranching world in New Zealand.

Jim is married, and has one child, with a home along the south coast of France and is captain of the sailing yacht *ZIGZAG*.

33

Kathy and Nelly

All net funds received from this book go to our charitable foundation
The John B. and Nelly Llanos Kilroy Foundation

At a fundraising party in earlier years.
Helping and Thinking of Others.

Where Life Takes Us

I have been challenged for many years by two beautiful ladies, the dearest of friends with overwhelming good fortune, interphased with the vagaries of life. The two beautiful players, the harmony between them, and the magnificence of their friendship, was a remarkable experience.

Kathy Kilroy and Nelly Llanos first met at a French language school, beginning a lasting friendship and mutual respect. Kathy was from our country's heartland during its economic drought of the 1930s, struggling and successfully obtaining an education for her successful future in the real estate world.

Nelly's family was from Germany, moving to the "grain port" Rosario in Argentina during the late 1870s. Recognized as the oldest family owned business in Argentina, the Schellhas family established a successful optical business, with 137 years of success in spite of the many political problems over the years. Nelly, educated in the "German school" of Rosario, married an outstanding young medical doctor, Miguel Llanos, the winner of a Rockefeller scholarship to the United States, which became their new home.

As Dr. Miguel Llanos developed a major medical practice in Los Angeles, Nelly became a mother of five children and an active participant in the St. Vincent's Hospital Meals on Wheels Program; the Los Angeles County Museum of Art, leading their renowned Costume Council acquiring and displaying the styles and fabrics of clothing worn by leaders of nations over the centuries; and other philanthropic projects.

Upon their meeting in the Beverly Hills French Language School, both ladies discovered their common interest in familiar museums and philanthropic campaigns. They became joint players, along with Sister Alice Marie Quinn, in expanding the St. Vincent's Meals on Wheels Program which prepares and delivers over 1,300,000 meals a year to needy senior citizens. Kathy also assumed the responsibility of being stepmother of my five children and Nelly had her own five children.

As their participation in the French Language School continued, we became better acquainted, and the two ladies spoke better French. They would tour France while we were racing *KIALOA* in Europe, or Nelly would join us when cruising in the South Pacific. Kathy and I were amazed at the energy and enthusiasm Nelly had in climbing an island mountain to be first to see the ocean on the other side of the island or a beautiful sunset.

Kathy had trouble with her breathing. First we thought the issue was allergies and then slowly learned that it was the effect of a terrible disease named scleroderma which caused hardening and tightening of the skin, muscles, lungs and other body parts—a horrible tragedy. We consulted with the leading doctors of our world to see how we might relieve this horrible problem. Kathy and I were avid scuba divers and would dive whenever we were anchored at a reasonable diving area. After a dive, she would comment about how much better she would feel, how much easier it was to breathe the air from her tank and regulator than the surface with no pressured air.

We concluded that the added pressure of air through the tank and regulator made it easier for the lungs to intake the necessary oxygen. As Kathy's scleroderma worsened, Nelly's husband Miguel (who had serious medical problems of his own) was also hospitalized, operated upon and over a short period of time, passed away. I participated in his highly attended memorial service and was extremely sad for Nelly and her five children. Kathy passed one month later, a victim of the horrors of scleroderma. A large memorial service was held along the beach of Malibu which she so dearly loved.

Out of the tragedy of these two passings, Nelly and I found a mutuality of interests that led to our already 15 years of marriage, which also prompted the writing of this book. In chosen words, Nelly said, "You must write your book and I will continue to remind you of your commitment until it is completed. It's hopefully now completed."

A complicated story about the many issues and joys in which I have participated, challenges as a boy, building a business, participating in the wonders, dangers, challenges and success of World Wide sailboat racing and being an active participant in marriage and life.

Nelly, my loving wife, your stimulating thoughts and expressions have now caused the completion of this book. I thank you. I dedicate the book KIALOA-US1: Dare to Win *to you and then debate whether I should write a little more.*

With love, your husband,
Jim

A LAST WORD: Nelly and I had completed our last cruise of New Zealand several years ago. Before leaving, we attended mass at St. John the Evangelist Chapel and were handed the following card, which we read carefully. On our return to our home, I placed the card in a remote drawer of my antique desk. Years later, as I was finishing the draft of this last chapter, without thinking, I opened this remote drawer and again read this card.

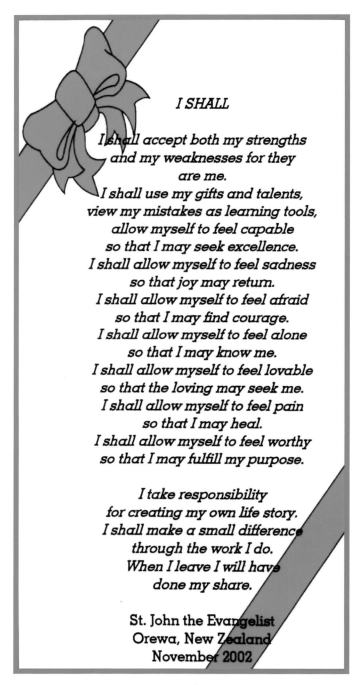

I SHALL

I shall accept both my strengths
and my weaknesses for they
are me.
I shall use my gifts and talents,
view my mistakes as learning tools,
allow myself to feel capable
so that I may seek excellence.
I shall allow myself to feel sadness
so that joy may return.
I shall allow myself to feel afraid
so that I may find courage.
I shall allow myself to feel alone
so that I may know me.
I shall allow myself to feel lovable
so that the loving may seek me.
I shall allow myself to feel pain
so that I may heal.
I shall allow myself to feel worthy
so that I may fulfill my purpose.

I take responsibility
for creating my own life story.
I shall make a small difference
through the work I do.
When I leave I will have
done my share.

St. John the Evangelist
Orewa, New Zealand
November 2002

"89 Years of Trying"
I pray that you find my forthright and factual story of interest.

It's The Reader's Turn
Come Sail with Me and the KIALOA *Crew*

Explore a photographic perspective of Maxi Boat racing in the Oceans of the World, the North and South Atlantic, North and South Pacific, China Sea, Tasman Sea, Mediterranean, Caribbean, and other beautiful sailing waters.

Enjoy the thrill of the race, the challenge of the sea, and the taste of victory! Share in lasting memories, lasting friendships and witness mutual respect.

JIM KILROY and the KIALOA Crew

KIALOA House Flag

"We will not retire!
Memories live forever."

KIALOA's
Dare to Win—Dare to Write

So many years, so many challenges, so much documentation, photographs, geography and competitive challenges required a great, thoughtful, and investigative research team. After boxes of data, log books in hiding, between charts, photos, and other racing records, we are now enthusiastic as we finish and review.

OUTSTANDING PERFORMANCE,

PATIENT AND UNDERSTANDING,

BIG SMILES, OUR TEAM BELOW.

Alexis (Brown) Alvarado

Parris Bauer

Johanna Fontanilla

Cece Llanos

Gary Miltimore

Trice Kilroy

Mike Llanos

1st LT. Mariano Alvarado, USMC

To the KIALOA Crew

Y ou, the *KIALOA* CREW, are the foundation for the World Wide Victories and success of the *KIALOAS*. Your mental and physical strengths, your attention to detail, working as a team, provided the engine for our victories.

We have written about the *KIALOAS* and other important issues, however, it became impossible to write all of the crew names, their duties and individual strengths and successes within the pages of the book. Instead, they will be noted on the *KIALOA* Web Site so that they may be recognized for their contribution to the the *KIALOA* success.

We have been told that the challenge of being a *KIALOA* crew has brightened their potential of future success. I know that being the racing Skipper of the *KIALOAS* has certainly helped mine and that it has been further enhanced by the good humor and successful efforts of our crew.

I thank all of the *KIALOA* crew for their participation and friendship. The *KIALOA* website KIALOA-US1.com also welcomes contributions about their sailing days aboard *KIALOA*.

Respect and sincere regards to all,

Jim Kilroy
(JBK)

Index